Specimens of Prose Composition

The Athenæum Press
GINN & COMPANY · PRO-
PRIETORS · BOSTON · U.S.A.

PREFACE

The editors of this book have compiled these specimens of prose composition because they have not found an entirely satisfactory volume of a similar nature. They have tested this book by actual use in their own class-room practice. The book has several special features. In one volume it illustrates all the kinds of writing. It includes good compositions by students themselves. Its classification is more explicit and suggestive than can be found elsewhere. Its introduction points out, with special reference to these particular selections, that the principles of composition, usually studied as if they applied inflexibly to all kinds of writing, really undergo important modifications according as the writer's purpose is to analyze or to depict.

In choosing these selections careful attention has been paid to length and to quality. Most of the specimens are so short that the student is able to get a total impression of structure and of style, and to make a careful analysis of entire selections, in a single recitation. Many others, of greater length and of greater complexity, permit the study of problems of material and of structure, — notably in the case of Argument and of Narration, — which the shorter selections do not afford. As regards quality, these models have been drawn from the writings of the best authors, but neither in style nor in material are they so far beyond the student's reach as to be discouraging. Believing that English Composition should not be based exclusively upon subject-matter of a literary nature, but that, particularly for elementary students, it should be based upon familiar and interesting material, the editors have chosen extracts from books on widely varied subjects. For example, in Exposition the selections deal with government, history, biography, science, war, literature, pioneer life, farming, economics, etc.; in Narration they deal with such simple topics as fishing and hunting, as well as with more complicated subjects. Nor are the models chosen entirely from masters of style: students' themes have been added which will be not only interesting but encouraging to young writers.

The editors take pleasure in returning thanks to the following authors and publishers, who have kindly permitted the reproduction of portions of their books: to Professor G. L. Kittredge, Professor G. H. Palmer, Captain A. T. Mahan, President Roosevelt, the Right Honorable James Bryce, President C. W. Eliot, Mr. C. T. Copeland, President A. T. Hadley, the Reverend Lyman Abbott, Mr. Joseph Conrad, Professor Brander Matthews, Mr. G. W. Cable, Mr. John Burroughs, Mr. W. D. Howells, Mr. Rudyard Kipling, Mr. H. M. Rideout, Miss S. O. Jewett, Mr. W. A. White, and Mr. Thomas Hardy; and to Messrs. Houghton, Mifflin & Co., Little, Brown & Co., T. Y. Crowell & Co., G. P. Putnam's Sons, D. Appleton & Co.,

Charles Scribner's Sons, the American Unitarian Association, the Century Co., Dodd, Mead & Co., *The Outlook*, Henry Holt & Co., Harper & Bros., Doubleday, Page & Co., and McClure, Phillips & Co.; to Mr. E. R. Lewis for the use of his brief and argument on the question "Should the United States Collect the Debts of San Domingo?", and to Mr. W. H. Bishop for the use of his brief and argument on the question "Should a National Forest Reserve be Established in the White Mountains?", as well as to the other students who, in permitting the reproduction of their themes, have furnished an indispensable part of these specimens of composition.

Particular thanks are due to Mr. C. T. Copeland, of Harvard College, for suggestions, and to Mr. W. S. Booth, of Houghton, Mifflin & Co., for invaluable counsel.

THE EDITORS

CONTENTS

ARGUMENT

DESCRIPTION

ARGUMENT

DESCRIPTION

CONTENTS

INTRODUCTION

The specimens of prose composition in this book have two purposes: first, to illustrate the special elements and qualities in Exposition, Argument, Description, and Narration; and, second, to show the relations of the principles of structure to the various kinds of composition.

All writing is divided into these four classes, according to the purpose of the writer. If his purpose is to explain a term or a set of facts, the result is called Exposition; if his purpose is to convince or to persuade another person of the truth of a particular set of facts, it is called Argument; if his purpose is to represent objects which appeal to the senses, it is called Description; if his purpose is to recount events in sequence of time, it is called Narration. Clearly, the first two classes appeal to the intellect, and the last two appeal to the emotions and to the imagination. De Quincey calls these two divisions "the literature of *knowledge* and the literature of *power*. The function of the first is to *teach;* the function of the second is to *move*." Inasmuch, then, as Exposition and Argument appeal primarily to the intellect, they are in mood *analytic;* and inasmuch as Description and Narration appeal primarily to the senses and to the imagination, they are in mood *pictorial*.

In actual practice, however, all kinds of writing are so closely inter-related that a novel, for instance, may be both analytical and pictorial. Biography, again, may include analytic, narrative, and descriptive passages, but, since it aims to explain facts about a man's character and life, the union of these elements will be Exposition. It should be remembered, then, that although such selections have been chosen for this book as for the purposes of rhetorical study may be considered wholes, these specimens originally appeared as parts of larger wholes of possibly a different kind of writing.

We come now to investigate the relations of the principles of structure — Unity, Coherence, and Mass or Emphasis — to analytic and to pictorial composition. These principles of structure are usually studied as if they applied to all kinds of writing inflexibly. The truth of the matter is, however, that they hold with equal firmness, but vary in application according as the writer's purpose is to analyze or to depict. When the mood changes, methods of structure and of style change. The logical way of treating this subject would be to study the application of Unity, Coherence, and Emphasis to whole compositions, paragraphs, and sentences in analytic and in pictorial writing. But such a study, essential as it is to the full understanding of style, is far too extensive and too exhaustive for treatment in this Introduction. It is sufficient here to explain how the fundamental principle of Unity in whole compositions applies to Exposition, the most common form of analytic writing, and to Description and to Narration, the most common forms of pictorial writing.

Analytic writing, which, by its very nature, is intellectual, must be planned with great precision. When a student chooses a subject for composition, he faces an entire panorama of possible material. An interest in American Indians may lead him to choose Indian life for a subject, and immediately Indian life is unrolled before him in all its variety of warfare, costume, implements, and camps, from the capture of Hannah Duston to Custer's Last Fight. All these facts possess unity, but a colossal unity which is beyond the scope of any one but the historian of the North American Indian. The student, then, can choose only a small field in this huge panorama, — " Indian War Councils," or " Methods of Fighting," or " The Building of an Indian House." Suppose he chooses the last (see Parkman, *An Indian House*, p. 19). Many details connected with the subject at once occur to him, — saplings, poles, sheets of oak and spruce bark, split poles for the roof, cords of linden bark, an opening in the roof for the smoke to escape, a place for storing food, scaffolds, mats and skins, fireplaces, one large room where several families live. Not one of these details has to do with " Indian War Councils," or " Methods of Fighting." Since this rough list of details, then, will tell him what he is to write about and what he is not to write about, it is the simplest means of obtaining Unity. When, later, the student reduces these rough notes to a well-constructed plan, he has before him a guide which will prevent him from introducing extraneous material.

AN INDIAN HOUSE

I. INTRODUCTION.
    A. Location of the house.
II. BODY.
    A. Construction of the house.
        1. Size.
        2. Shape.
        3. Method of building.
           a. The frame.
           b. The sides.
           c. The roof.
           d. The porches.

B. Arrangement of the interior.
  1. Scaffolds for beds.
  2. Fireplace in the middle.
  3. Poles for hanging weapons and corn.

III. CONCLUSION.

When subject-matter can be reduced to an outline like this, in which each heading is clearly included under the title, the whole composition will possess Unity. A subject as simple as " An Indian House " yields itself easily to such an outline ; when the matter is complicated the many subdivisions necessitate a more detailed plan.

A plan, then, expresses the limits of a writer's subject-matter ; it gives no hint of his attitude toward this subject-matter. Before a student can write his exposition, he must decide who his readers are to be. In analytic writing the matter of an audience is of vital importance. An exposition of corals and coral reefs may be written for an audience of oceanographers, or of workingmen, or of children. Although the facts remain true in any one of the explanations, the treatment will invariably change. For the chief purpose of an explanation is to be understood, and consequently clearness must be its distinguishing quality. To achieve this clearness, a writer must assume a definite attitude, or, technically speaking, adopt a mental point of view, toward his subject and toward his audience, and hold this point of view consistently. The problem, therefore, of explaining his subject, no matter how well it is planned, to a particular audience is the severest task of the writer of Exposition. An admirable example of skill in adopting a point of view is *The Popular Ballad* (p. 10). This explanation is effective because the author has conceived — as the writer of Exposition always

should conceive — the precise state of his reader's information. He approaches the matter of impersonal composition, a matter familiar and comprehensible to him as a
scholar, by the easy stages along which the mind of a
layman would inevitably proceed.

Though the writer may be sure of his attitude toward
his subject, he is liable, in the course of his work, to commit two errors : false beginnings and digressions. False
beginnings are due to the fact that an untrained writer is
uncertain how much to assume his reader knows. This
desire to tell all the preliminary facts is comically illustrated by Miss Bates in Jane Austen's *Emma*. The trained
mind, however, ignoring all encumbering preliminaries,
seizes the right moment for beginning. " I purpose," says
Macaulay, in opening his *History of England*, " I purpose
to write the history of England from the accession of King
James the Second down to a time which is within the
memory of men still living." The loquacious Miss Bates
serves again as an example of digression.

"My dear Miss Woodhouse, I am just run across to entreat the
favour of you to come and sit down with us a little while, and give
us your opinion of our new instrument — you and Miss Smith. How
do you do, Miss Smith? — Very well, I thank you. — And I begged
Mrs. Weston to come with me, that I might be sure of succeeding."

" I hope Mrs. Bates and Miss Fairfax are — "

" Very well, I am much obliged to you. My mother is delightfully
well; and Jane caught no cold last night. How is Mr. Woodhouse?
I am so glad to hear such a good account. Mrs. Weston told me you
were here. — ' Oh, then,' said I, ' I must run across; I am sure Miss
Woodhouse will allow me just to run across and entreat her to come
in : my mother will be so very happy to see her; and now we are
such a nice party, she cannot refuse.' ' Ay, pray do,' said Mr. Frank
Churchill, ' Miss Woodhouse's opinion of the instrument will be worth
having.' — ' But,' said I, ' I shall be more sure of succeeding if one of

you will go with me.' — 'Oh,' said he, 'wait half a minute, till I have
finished my job : ' for, would you believe it, Miss Woodhouse, there
he is, in the most obliging manner in the world, fastening in the
rivet of my mother's spectacles. The rivet came out, you know, this
morning ; so very obliging ! — For my mother had no use of her
spectacles — could not put them on. And, by the by, every body
ought to have two pair of spectacles ; they should indeed. Jane
said so. I meant to take them over to John Saunders the first thing
I did, but something or other hindered me all the morning ; first one
thing, then another, there is no saying what, you know. At one time,
Patty came to say she thought the kitchen chimney wanted sweeping.
'Oh,' said I, 'Patty, do not come with your bad news to me. Here is
the rivet of your mistress's spectacles out.' Then the baked apples
came home ; Mrs. Wallis sent them by her boy ; they are extremely
civil and obliging to us, the Wallises, always. I have heard some
people say that Mrs. Wallis can be uncivil and give a very rude answer ; but we have never known anything but the greatest attention
from them. And it cannot be for the value of our custom now, for
what is our consumption of bread, you know ? only three of us. Besides, dear Jane, at present, — and she really eats nothing, — makes
such a shocking breakfast, you would be quite frightened if you saw
it. I dare not let my mother know how little she eats ; so I say one
thing, and then I say another, and it passes off. But about the middle of the day she gets hungry, and there is nothing she likes so well
as these baked apples, and they are extremely wholesome ; for I took
the opportunity the other day of asking Mr. Perry ; I happened to
meet him in the street. Not that I had any doubt before. I have so
often heard Mr. Woodhouse recommend a baked apple. I believe it
is the only way that Mr. Woodhouse thinks the fruit thoroughly
wholesome. We have apple-dumplings, however, very often. Patty
makes an excellent apple-dumpling. Well, Mrs. Preston, you have
prevailed, I hope, and these ladies will oblige us."

The inability of Miss Bates to resist the allurements of
a bewildering number of associated facts is common in the
inexperienced writer, — indeed, it is common in every
human being. But, though it may enhance the charm of

the garrulous yarn of a sea captain, it is fatal to the success of the writer of Exposition. If, at the mention of the word " torpedoes," Captain Mahan had been led away from his main purpose — which was to explain the two "factors " in preparation for naval war — to an account of the varieties of torpedoes, and of the methods of manufacturing, laying, and exploding them, he would have scattered his fire.

For avoiding these dangers of false beginnings and digressions there are various mechanical devices. Most effective are short announcements of procedure, either in the beginning of an article or just before the treatment of a subdivision. An example of the first is in Professor Palmer's *Self-Cultivation in English.*

> Watch your speech, then. That is all which is needed. Only it is desirable to know what qualities of speech to watch for. I find three, — accuracy, audacity, and range, — and I will say a few words about each (p. 24).

Captain Mahan's *Preparation for War* furnishes several examples of the second.

> In kind, preparation is twofold, — defensive and offensive (p. 33).
> Coast defence implies coast attack. To what attacks are coasts liable? Two, principally, — blockade and bombardment (p. 34).

Another valuable device is the use of summaries, which may be either intermediary or final. The former may come in the course of an article after the treatment of one or more divisions, as in the following example from John Fiske's *Taxation and Government:*

> Government, then, is the directing or managing of such affairs as concern all the people alike, — as, for example, the punishment of criminals, the enforcement of contracts, the defence against foreign

enemies, the maintenance of roads and bridges, and so on. To the directing or managing of such affairs all the people are expected to contribute, each according to his ability, in the shape of taxes. Government is something which is supported by the people and kept alive by taxation. There is no other way of keeping it alive (p. 6).

The simplest form of the latter is a brief enumeration of the chief points which have been made:

Such, then, are the excellences of speech. If we would cultivate ourselves in the use of English, we must make our daily talk accurate, daring, and full. I have insisted on these points the more because in my judgment all literary power, especially that of busy men, is rooted in sound speech (*Self-Cultivation in English*, p. 32).

This crisp and enumerative summary may easily become, in the hands of a less skilful writer, wooden and mechanical. That final summaries may possess variety and flexibility is shown by the longer enumerative summary of Captain Mahan (pp. 37, 38); the illustrative summary of John Fiske (pp. 8, 9); the epigrammatic summary of Professor Kittredge (p. 15); and the ethical summary of President Eliot (p. 78).

When we turn from the application of Unity to analytic writing to its application to pictorial writing, the fact that this application is more subtle does not mean good-bye to structure. Too often the careless or inexperienced writer thinks that vividness of phrase is the chief virtue of Description, and that order, though it may be the first law of Heaven, is not a statute of pictorial writing. It is true that vividness of phrase does arouse the imagination, but, if the structure is unorganized, the effect is comparable to that of the performance of a Symphony Orchestra, if each member plays an independent melody. Unity of effect is as necessary in pictorial writing as in the orchestra. Since, however, one division of pictorial writing has to do with sensations, and the other with action, the application of the principle of Unity to Description and to Narration is influenced by the nature of the material.

Inasmuch as Description is a representation of nature as it appeals simultaneously to various senses, the task of re-, cording such representation is very difficult. In order that, amid the possible confusion of sensations, we may understand the principle of Unity in its simplest form, we will deal first with the sensation of seeing. The vision of the eye is limited to what is within range; and the faithful record of what we see in front of us at any one time is the simplest form of Unity in Description, and serves the same function in Description that the rough plan of *An Indian House* serves in Éxposition. This method of securing Unity by excluding extraneous material is called "the point of view."

There are two varieties of the point of view: the physical, which may be stationary or moving; and the mental. An amusing instance of the violation of the stationary. point of view is that of the boy, who, describing the pit of an abandoned quarry from a brink high above, gave an idea of the depth of the pit by comparing an over-turned gravel-car at the bottom to a child's cart, and then added "beside it lay an old shovel with the initials 'J. W.' carved on the handle." How carefully the skilful writer holds his point of view is shown by Irving's *A Stable-Yard on a Rainy Day* (p. 314). Irving so faithfully follows the maxim "Write with your eye on the object," that he pictures not only the objects which are visible from his window, but the appearance of those objects under a certain condition of weather. A writer has not made an accurate transcript of a scene if he has failed to catch the temporal characteristics of light and shade, sun, or rain. The moving point of view differs from the stationary only in that it is a connected series of stationary points of view. Instead of a single photograph we have the biograph. In this case the blurred image resulting from the confusion of several points of view may be avoided by a careful indication of the transition from one point of view to another. In *The Domain of Arnheim*, Poe is always careful to tell the reader of the change in the point of view by such hints as, —

> Having threaded the mazes of this channel for some hours, the gloom deepening every moment, a sharp and unexpected turn of the vessel brought it suddenly, as if dropped from heaven, into a circular basin of very considerable extent when compared with the width of the gorge (p. 322).
>
> The visitor, shooting suddenly into this bay from out the gloom of the ravine, is delighted but astounded by the full orb of the declining sun . . . (p. 323).

In the preceding cases the writer looks at his object from a physical position in time and in place. The term "point of view" is also figuratively applied to a mental attitude. The relation of the two is well illustrated by Stevenson's conscious study (p. 320) of the choice of a point of view from which he is to describe the Water of Leith. The first twelve lines deal with the place as seen from the physical point of view; the rest of the article is a sympathetic treatment of the mental point of view. Stevenson realizes that to see the Water of Leith as he saw it when a boy, he must put himself into the boy's frame of mind, when "the trees on the steep opposite side" seemed "to climb to heaven," and "the sand by the water-door" seemed "as low as Styx." This matter of the attitude toward the subject, so important in analytic writing, is a valuable method of securing Unity in pictorial writing. For it means that the subject-matter is constantly but subtly infused with the writer's personality. In fact, because of this infusion, pictorial writing is a fine art. Art is not a photograph, but nature seen through a temperament.

Thus far we have considered only a limited field of vision, as viewed by one personality. Here are two elements of unity : the exclusion of irrelevant material and the constant personal attitude. Is there another method inherent in the subject-matter itself? Whenever we consider a scene, we are impressed with the presence of some predominant trait or characteristic which makes itself felt through all the subordinate details which appeal to all our senses. Treasure Island, by virtue of its sad coloring, its spires of rock, strangely shaped, its surf "foaming and thundering on the steep beach," impresses us with an indefinable sense of gloom. Heat radiating "in an oily quivering shimmer," shade "dwindled to the breadth of a mere line," "a pale, scorched sky," the prolonged drone of insects, a cat dozing complacently in the sun, hens wallowing "in the baking hot dust," impress us with the sense of intense heat. A summer day may be prevailingly cheerful; Mulberry Bend may be prevailingly squalid. This chief trait, inherent in the material itself, which suffuses its quality throughout the subject is technically called "dominant tone." The selection of details which produce this dominant tone is a vital means of impressing upon a reader the unity of a scene. Through this technical element of dominant tone a writer may make his descriptive writing as firm in structure as ever the analytical writer may make his.

In cases where the chief interest is in the shape or form
of our object, or in its geographical position, a shrewd
observer will often see the latent figure which will most
effectively suggest its topography or shape. Such a "fundamental image," if it is natural, will aid in producing
Unity. The force of comparison depends, of course, upon
the familiarity of the image. Cardinal Newman compares
Attica to a triangle; Ruskin compares Santa Croce to the
letter T; Victor Hugo compares the field of Waterloo to
the letter A; Stevenson compares the Bay of Monterey to
a bent fish hook; Drake compares the five corps of Hooker's
army, marching north to meet Lee at Gettysburg, to the
outstretched fingers of a hand. If the fundamental image
can be held consistently, the fact that all the details are
related to one chief figure will produce on the reader
singleness of impression. Wordsworth, in his *Guide to the
Lakes*, successfully employs for this purpose the figure of
a wheel.

To begin, then, with the main outlines of the country; — I know
not how to give the reader a distinct image of these more readily,
than by requesting him to place himself with me, in imagination,
upon some given point; let it be the top of either of the mountains,
Great Gavel, or Scawfell ; or, rather, let us suppose our station to be
a cloud hanging midway between those two mountains, at not more
than half a mile's distance from the summit of each, and not many
yards above their highest elevation ; we shall then see stretched at
our feet a number of valleys, not fewer than eight, diverging from
the point, on which we are supposed to stand, like spokes from the
nave of a wheel. First, we note, lying to the south-east, the vale of
Langdale, which will conduct the eye to the long lake of Winandermere, stretched nearly to the sea; or rather to the sands of the vast
bay of Morcamb, serving here for the rim of this imaginary wheel;
— let us trace it in a direction from the south-east towards the south,
and we shall next fix our eyes upon the vale of Coniston, running up

likewise from the sea, but not (as all the other valleys do) to the nave of the wheel, and therefore it may be not inaptly represented as a broken spoke sticking in the rim . . . and lastly, the vale of Grasmere, Rydal, and Ambleside, brings you back to Winandermere, thus completing, though on the eastern side in a somewhat irregular manner, the representative figure of the wheel.

Whether we rely chiefly upon the point of view or upon dominant tone or upon fundamental image to give unity of effect, we must so end our description that the salient details shall be well summarized. The summary need not be so formal as in analytic writing, but it may be light and flexible, analogous to the all-embracing glance which we take before leaving the hilltop. An example of this is the concluding sentence in *Autumn on Cape Cod*.

Hereafter when I look on a richer rug than usual, and study its figures, I shall think, there are the huckleberry hills, and there the denser swamps of boxberry and blueberry; there the shrub-oak patches and the bayberries, there the maples and the birches and the pines (p. 328).

Narration, which deals with events in sequence of time, seems at first to resist the effort to limit the field of material. To know where to begin and where to end a narrative so that the result may leave upon his reader unity of impression, a writer must decide whether his material will yield a simple story of adventure or the more complicated series of events which form a plot. If his material reduces itself to the simple act of catching a fish, he can then very easily limit his field by avoiding a false beginning which might include the arrival in camp, the first night in the woods, the trip to the pond, etc., and by opening with the event itself. And he should end with the natural close of the event. A writer who thus cuts away superfluities in action at the beginning and the ending, as Mr. Kipling does in *How I Caught Salmon in the Clackamas* (p. 374), will achieve singleness of impression in time no less than the descriptive writer, by limiting his range of vision, achieves it in space. An account of an incident or an adventure which thus has this one main action may be represented by a straight line, which graphically expresses the fact that the event proceeds, logically and without deviation, from beginning to end.

If, on the other hand, the material yields two or more lines of action which intersect, the result is called "plot." Plot in this case does not mean, as many students suppose, conspiracy; but it means the complication or weaving together of events. This complication may not necessarily be intricate. It may be the fusion of two lines of action, as in *A Winter Courtship* (p. 410). Jefferson Briley, armed with a pistol to prevent capture by a highwayman, is driving from Sanscrit Pond to North Kilby. Mrs. Fanny Tobin, a widow, is going from Sanscrit Pond to North Kilby in the same vehicle. On the way Mr. Briley is led to propose, and thus he is "taken on the road in spite of his pistol." But plot typically means the intersection of three or more lines of action. A convict has escaped from a jail. The hangman is travelling to that jail to execute the convict. The convict's brother is also going to the jail to bid him farewell. The three meet in a shepherd's house. In this meeting, which is the basis of Mr. Hardy's *The Three Strangers* (p. 421), our attention is concentrated, not upon any one of these three lines of action, but upon their peculiar weaving together to form a new situation. When we achieve a situation which thus produces on the reader a unified effect, — in this case, the effect of irony, — we have achieved unity of plot. How we may secure "the immense force derivable from totality" Poe explains in his criticism on *Hawthorne's Tales*.

A skilful literary artist has constructed a tale. If wise, he has not fashioned his thoughts to accommodate his incidents; but having conceived, with deliberate care, a certain unique or single *effect* to be wrought out, he then invents such incidents — he then combines such events as may best aid him in establishing this preconceived effect. If his very initial sentence tend not to the out-bringing of this effect, then he has failed in his first step. In the whole composition there should be no word written of which the tendency, direct or indirect, is not to the one pre-established design.

The same principle is re-inforced by Stevenson in *A Humble Remonstrance*.

Let him [the writer] choose a motive, whether of character or passion ; carefully construct his plot so that every incident is an illustration of the motive, and every property employed shall bear to it a near relation of congruity or contrast; avoid sub-plot, unless, as sometimes in Shakespeare, the sub-plot be a reversion or complement of the main intrigue ; suffer not his style to flag below the level of the argument; pitch the key of conversation, not with any thought of how men talk in parlors, but with a single eye to the degree of passion he may be called on to express ; and allow neither himself in the narrative nor any character in the course of the dialogue, to utter one sentence that is not part and parcel of the business of the story or the discussion of the problem involved.

This totality of effect is the form which "dominant tone" takes in Narration. In producing this dominant tone, not only action, but characters and background play important parts.

Those characters should be chosen who will help to bring out the particular tone the writer wishes the story to possess. This is true in all narratives. In the novel,

however, where there is great opportunity for a character
to develop, he not only must contribute his share to the
dominant tone of the story, but he must have the many-
sidedness of a human being. In short stories, though the
character must seem a natural human being and not a
mere type, his chief purpose is to contribute to the dominant tone. This does not mean that he is to be the per-
sonification of an abstract quality, but that his presence
in the story should exhale a peculiar quality necessary for
the preconceived effect. Take, for example, the second
stranger in *The Three Strangers* (p. 421). The mere reiteration of the phrase "the stranger in cinder-gray" becomes an
ominous note. The " obscure revelations " in his remarks, —

'I do work, and I must work. And even if I only get to Casterbridge by midnight I must begin work there at eight to-morrow
morning. Yes, het or wet, blow or snow, famine or sword, my day's
work to-morrow must be done.'

'The oddity of my trade is that, instead of setting a mark upon
me, it sets a mark upon my customers,'

and, finally, the song to the glory of his gruesome trade, —

> 'My tools are but common ones,
> Simple shepherds all —
> My tools are no sight to see:
> A little hempen string, and a post whereon to swing,
> Are implements enough for me!'

fill the reader with the same sense of repulsion which caused
the peasants at Shepherd Fennel's party to shrink away.

This illustration serves also to show the relation of dialogue to the whole. The purpose of dialogue is to reveal
character, to expound the situations, and to propel the
narrative. At the same time it must give the illusion of
real life by seeming to be the natural talk of human beings.

To make dialogue conduce to the "pre-established design" and at the same time reveal no artificiality of invention is so delicate a method of obtaining Unity, that it demands the keenest observation and the nicest adjustment of the means to the end. So perfect an example of the function of dialogue in Narration are the first two chapters of *Pride and Prejudice* (p. 393) that if the lines were spoken by actors on a stage the story would be completely told.

Characters, moreover, should be more than figures which we watch the author manipulate. A character may be the medium through which a writer makes various events significant. An author often lets a character tell his own story, as Defoe let Robinson Crusoe tell his. Or, still limiting the narrative to the point of view of a single character, he may tell the story in the third person, as Mr. White views events through Piggy Pennington's eyes (*The King of Boyville*, p. 400). Whether the phrasing is that of direct or of indirect discourse, the consequent gain in unity of conception and in vividness of treatment is worth the continual care to make the narrative a faithful account of only those facts which this one character knows. This constant factor of one personality through whom all incidents and emotions reach the reader is a subtle means of enforcing dominant tone.

A writer will not obtain final Unity until his background, or setting, harmonizes with his motive. This harmony may be one of concord or of discord. Stevenson analyzes the harmony of scene and action in a poignant way.

One thing in life calls for another; there is a fitness in events and places. The sight of a pleasant arbor puts it in our mind to sit there. One place suggests work, another idleness, a third early rising and long rambles in the dew. The effect of night, of any flowing water, of lighted cities, of the peep of day, of ships, of the open ocean, call up in the mind an army of anonymous desires and pleasures. Something, we feel, should happen; we know not what, yet we proceed in quest of it. And many of the happiest hours of life fleet by us in this vain attendance on the genius of the place and moment. It is thus that tracts of young fir and low rocks that reach into deep soundings, particularly torture and delight me. Something must have happened in such places, and perhaps ages back, to members of my race; and when I was a child I tried in vain to invent appropriate games for them, as I still try, just as vainly, to fit them with the proper story. Some places speak distinctly. Certain dank gardens cry aloud for a murder; certain old houses demand to be haunted; certain coasts are set apart for ship-wreck (*A Gossip on Romance*).

But it may be the writer's intention to produce the effect of incongruity, and in that case an apparent discord, perhaps of gay action and grim scenery, may be a subtler kind of harmony.

It has been the purpose of this Introduction to show the relations of the principles of structure to the kinds of composition by means of one signal example, — Unity. Whether a writer appeals to our intellect or to our imagination, the principle of Unity itself suffers no change. It always controls the selection of material and always demands that the selected material shall gratify our sense of completeness. The nature of the material, however, influences the way in which the principle of Unity is applied to produce this effect of completeness. How easily and by what methods Unity may be applied to the subject-matter of Exposition, Description, and Narration has been shown in the case of whole compositions only. An exposition of the entire subject, which would mean the application of Unity, Coherence, and Emphasis to whole compositions, paragraphs, and sentences, in all kinds of writing, the editors can treat adequately only in a later book. In the present book their aim has been to suggest how these specimens of prose composition may be studied to illustrate the various problems of technique.

SPECIMENS OF PROSE COMPOSITION

MODELS OF EXPOSITION

TAXATION AND GOVERNMENT[1]

JOHN FISKE

What, then, are taxes? The question is one which is
apt to come up, sooner or later, to puzzle children. They
find no difficulty in understanding the butcher's bill for
so many pounds of meat, or the tailor's bill for so many
suits of clothes, where the value received is something 5
that can be seen and handled. But the tax bill, though
it comes as inevitably as the autumnal frosts, bears no
such obvious relation to the incidents of domestic life;
it is not quite so clear what the money goes for; and
hence it is apt to be paid by the head of the household 10
with more or less grumbling, while for the younger
members of the family it requires some explanation.

It only needs to be pointed out, however, that in every
town some things are done for the benefit of all the inhabitants of the town, things which concern one person just 15
as much as another. Thus roads are made and kept in
repair, school-houses are built and salaries paid to school-
teachers, there are constables who take criminals to jail,
there are engines for putting out fires, there are public
libraries, town cemeteries, and poor-houses. Money raised 20

[1] From *Civil Government in the United States*, pp. 3–8. Houghton,
Mifflin & Co., Boston, 1896.

3

for these purposes, which are supposed to concern all the inhabitants, is supposed to be paid by all the inhabitants, each one furnishing his share; and the share which each one pays is his town tax.

5 From this illustration it would appear that taxes are private property taken for public purposes; and in making this statement we come very near the truth. Taxes are portions of private property which a government takes for its public purposes. Before going farther, let us pause to
10 observe that there is one other way, besides taxation, in which government sometimes takes private property for public purposes. Roads and streets are of great importance to the general public; and the government of the town or city in which you live may see fit, in opening a
15 new street, to run it across your garden, or to make you move your house or shop out of the way for it. In so doing, the government either takes away or damages some of your property. It exercises rights over your property without asking your permission. This power of govern-
20 ment over private property is called "the right of eminent domain." It means that a man's private interests must not be allowed to obstruct the interests of the whole community in which he lives. But in two ways the exercise of eminent domain is unlike taxation. In the first place,
25 it is only occasional, and affects only certain persons here or there, whereas taxation goes on perpetually and affects all persons who own property. In the second place, when the government takes away a piece of your land to make a road, it pays you money in return for it; perhaps not
30 quite so much as you believe the piece of land was worth in the market; the average human nature is doubtless such that men seldom give fair measure for measure unless

they feel compelled to, and it is not easy to put a government under compulsion. Still it gives you something; it
does not ask you to part with your property for nothing.
Now in the case of taxation, the government takes your
money and seems to make no return to you individually; 5
but it is supposed to return to you the value of it in the
shape of well-paved streets, good schools, efficient protection against criminals, and so forth.

In giving this brief preliminary definition of taxes and
taxation, we have already begun to speak of " the govern- 10
ment" of the town or city in which you live. We shall
presently have to speak of other "governments," — as
the government of your state and the government of the
United States; and we shall now and then have occasion
to allude to the governments of other countries in which 15
the people are free, as, for example, England; and of some
countries in which the people are not free, as, for example,
Russia. It is desirable, therefore, that we should here at
the start make sure what we mean by "government," in
order that we may have a clear idea of what we are talking 20
about.

Our verb "to govern" is an old French word, one of
the great host of French words which became a part of
the English language between the eleventh and fourteenth
centuries, when so much French was spoken in England. 25
The French word was *gouverner*, and its oldest form was
the Latin *gubernare*, a word which the Romans borrowed
from the Greek, and meant originally " to steer the ship."
Hence it very naturally came to mean "to guide," "to
direct," "to command." The comparison between govern- 30
ing and steering was a happy one. To govern is not to
command as a master commands a slave, but it is to issue

orders and give directions for the common good; for the
interests of the man at the helm are the same as those of
the people in the ship. All must float or sink together.
Hence we sometimes speak of the "ship of state," and we
5 often call the state a "commonwealth," or something in the
weal or welfare of which all the people are alike interested.

Government, then, is the directing or managing of such
affairs as concern all the people alike, — as, for example,
the punishment of criminals, the enforcement of contracts,
10 the defence against foreign enemies, the maintenance of
roads and bridges, and so on. To the directing or managing of such affairs all the people are expected to contribute, each according to his ability, in the shape of taxes.
Government is something which is supported by the people
15 and kept alive by taxation. There is no other way of
keeping it alive.

The business of carrying on government — of steering
the ship of state — either requires some special training,
or absorbs all the time and attention of those who carry
20 it on; and accordingly, in all countries, certain persons
or groups of persons are selected or in some way set apart,
for longer or shorter periods of time, to perform the work
of government. Such persons may be a king with his
council, as in the England of the twelfth century; or a
25 parliament led by a responsible ministry, as in the England of to-day; or a president and two houses of congress,
as in the United States; or a board of selectmen, as in a
New England town. When we speak of "a government"
or "the government," we often mean the group of persons
30 thus set apart for carrying on the work of government.
Thus, by "the Gladstone government" we mean Mr. Gladstone, with his colleagues in the cabinet and his Liberal

majority in the House of Commons; and by "the Lincoln government," properly speaking, was meant President Lincoln, with the Republican majorities in the Senate and House of Representatives.

"The government" has always many things to do, and there are many different lights in which we might regard it. But for the present there is one thing which we need especially to keep in mind. "The government" is the power which can rightfully take away a part of your property, in the shape of taxes, to be used for public purposes. A government is not worthy of the name, and cannot long be kept in existence, unless it can raise money by taxation, and use force, if necessary, in collecting its taxes. The only general government of the United States during the Revolutionary War, and for six years after its close, was the Continental Congress, which had no authority to raise money by taxation. In order to feed and clothe the army and pay its officers and soldiers, it was obliged to *ask* for money from the several states, and hardly ever got as much as was needed. It was obliged to borrow millions of dollars from France and Holland, and to issue promissory notes which soon became worthless. After the war was over it became clear that this so-called government could neither preserve order nor pay its debts, and accordingly it ceased to be respected either at home or abroad, and it became necessary for the American people to adopt a new form of government. Between the old Continental Congress and the government under which we have lived since 1789, the differences were many; but by far the most essential difference was that the new government could raise money by taxation, and was thus enabled properly to carry on the work of governing.

If we are in any doubt as to what is really the government of some particular country, we cannot do better than observe what person or persons in that country are clothed with authority to tax the people. Mere names, as
5 customarily applied to governments, are apt to be deceptive. Thus in the middle of the eighteenth century France and England were both called "kingdoms"; but so far as kingly power was concerned, Louis XV. was a very different sort of a king from George II. The French king
10 could impose taxes on his people, and it might therefore be truly said that the government of France was in the king. Indeed, it was Louis XV.'s immediate predecessor[1] who made the famous remark, "The state is myself." But the English king could not impose taxes; the only power
15 in England that could do that was the House of Commons, and accordingly it is correct to say that in England, at the time of which we are speaking, the government was (as it still is) in the House of Commons.

I say, then, the most essential feature of a government —
20 or at any rate the feature with which it is most important for us to become familiar at the start — is its power of taxation. The government is that which taxes. If individuals take away some of your property for purposes of their own, it is robbery; you lose your money and get
25 nothing in return. But if the government takes away some of your property in the shape of taxes, it is supposed to render to you an equivalent in the shape of good government, something without which our lives and property

---

[1] Louis XIV., the Grand Monarch, who personally ruled France from 1661 until his death in 1715. That he addressed the words "L'État c'est moi" to the President of the Parliament of Paris is a fairly well established tradition; that the famous dictum represents his belief and practice is a matter of history.

would not be safe. Herein seems to lie the difference between taxation and robbery. When the highwayman points his pistol at me and I hand him my purse and watch, I am robbed. But when I pay the tax-collector, who can seize my watch or sell my house over my head 5 if I refuse, I am simply paying what is fairly due from me toward supporting the government.

THE POPULAR BALLAD[1]

GEORGE LYMAN KITTREDGE

A ballad is a song that tells a story, or — to take the other point of view — a story told in song. More formally, it may be defined as a short narrative poem, adapted for singing, simple in plot and metrical structure, divided into stanzas, and characterized by complete impersonality so far as the author or singer is concerned. This last trait is of the very first consequence in determining the quality or qualities which give the ballad its peculiar place in literature. A ballad has no author. At all events, it appears to have none. The teller of the story for the time being is as much the author as the unknown (and for our purposes unimportant) person who first put it into shape. In most forms of artistic literature the personality of the writer is a matter of deep concern to the reader. The style, we say, is the man. The individuality of one poet distinguishes his works, however they may vary among themselves, from the works of all other poets. Chaucer, for instance, has his way, or his ways, of telling a tale that are not the way, or the ways, of William Morris. If a would-be creative literary artist has no individuality that we can detect, we set him down as conventional, and that

---

[1] From the Introduction to *English and Scottish Popular Ballads,* edited from the collection of Francis James Child by Helen Child Sargent and George Lyman Kittredge, pp. xi–xiii. Houghton, Mifflin & Co., Boston, 1904.

10

is an end of him and of his works. In the ballad it is not
so. There the author is of no account. He is not even
present. We do not feel sure that he ever existed. At
most, we merely infer his existence, at some indefinite
time in the past, from the fact of his product: a poem, we 5
think, implies a poet; therefore somebody must have composed this ballad. Until we begin to reason, we have no
thought of the author of any ballad, because, so far as we
can see, he had no thought of himself.

We may go a step farther in this matter of impersonality. 10
Not only is the author of a ballad invisible, and, so far as
the effect which the poem produces on the hearer is concerned, practically non-existent, but the teller of the tale
has no rôle in it. Unlike other songs, it does not purport
to give utterance to the feelings or the mood of the 15
singer. The first person does not occur at all, except in
the speeches of the several characters. Finally, there are
no comments or reflections by the narrator. He does not
dissect or psychologize. He does not take sides for or
against any of the *dramatis personæ*. He merely tells 20
what happened and what people said, and he confines the
dialogue to its simplest and most inevitable elements.
The story exists for its own sake. If it were possible to
conceive a tale as *telling itself* without the instrumentality
of a conscious speaker, the ballad would be such a tale. 25

So far we have dealt in generalities and impressions.
What has been said is obvious enough, and it is admitted
by everybody. There is, as we shall see presently, no
agreement among scholars as to the origin and history of
what are called popular ballads, but as to the fact of 30
their impersonal quality there is no dispute. Nor will
it be denied that this quality puts them in a class by

themselves. Whatever the cause or causes, the bare fact
is clear and undeniable. No one can read 'The Hunting of
the Cheviot,' or 'Mary Hamilton,' or 'Johnie Armstrong,'
or 'Robyn and Gandeleyn,' or 'The Wife of Usher's
5 Well,' and fail to recognize that, different as they are
from each other in theme and in effect, they belong
together. Yet no two of them are the works of the same
author. Their common element is not the personality of
the writer but his impersonality; and this distinguishes
10 the ballad, as a class, from the productions of the conscious
literary artist. In studying ballads, then, we are studying
the "poetry of the folk," and the "poetry of the folk" is
different from the "poetry of art."

Poetry of the folk is, perhaps, a dangerous phrase; but
15 it is too convenient to be lightly rejected, and, if we proceed
with caution, we may employ it without disaster. Let us
hasten to acknowledge that in introducing the term at this
stage of our discussion we have gone somewhat farther
than the logic of the situation warrants. We have seen, to
20 be sure, that all poetry is divisible into two great classes, —
that which is manifestly the work of the conscious artist,
and that which is not. We have recognized a characteristic
difference between 'The Prioress's Tale' and 'Julian and
Maddalo' on the one hand, and 'Johnie Armstrong' and
25 'The Wife of Usher's Well' on the other. But we have
not yet discovered anything that justifies us in calling the
ballads *folk*-poetry, and we have not defined the folk, though
that is a term which assuredly requires explanation.

The alphabet was no doubt a great invention, and every-
30 body should be happy to know that he can write. But now
and then it would be convenient if one's thoughts could
dissociate literature for a moment from the written or

printed page. In theory this is easy enough to do. Practically, however, it is difficult for even a professed student of linguistics to remember that a word is properly a sign made with the vocal organs, and that the written word is merely a conventional symbol standing for the word that 5 is spoken. We are in the habit of thinking that a word should be pronounced as it is spelled, rather than that it should be spelled as it is pronounced. *Author* means to us a man with a pen in his hand, — a *writer*, as we call him. It requires a combined effort of the reason and the imagina- 10 tion to conceive a poet as a person who cannot write, singing or reciting his verses to an audience that cannot read. History, as we understand it, is the written record or even the printed volume; it is no longer the accumulated fund of tribal memories, handed down from father to son by oral 15 tradition. Yet everybody knows that, quite apart from what we usually call literature, there is a great mass of song and story and miscellaneous lore which circulates among those who have neither books nor newspapers. To this oral literature, as the French call it, education is no 20 friend. Culture destroys it, sometimes with amazing rapidity. When a nation learns to read, it begins to disregard its traditional tales; it feels a little ashamed of them; and finally it loses both the will and the power to remember and transmit them. What was once the possession of the 25 folk as a whole, becomes the heritage of the illiterate only, and soon, unless it is gathered up by the antiquary, vanishes altogether.

To this oral literature belong the popular ballads, and we are justified, therefore, in calling them "folk-poetry." 30 They are not, like written literature, the exclusive possession of the cultivated classes in any community. They

belonged, in the first instance, to the whole people, at a
time when there were no formal divisions of literate and
illiterate ; when the intellectual interests of all were substantially identical, from the king to the peasant. As civi-
5 lization advanced, they were banished from polite society,
but they lived on among the humble, among shepherds
and ploughboys and "the spinsters and the knitters in the
sun," until even these became too sophisticated to care for
them and they were heard no more.

10 . The process just sketched is not imaginary or merely
inferential. It is, to be sure, impossible, from the nature
of the case, to cite documentary evidence for every step in
the history of the ballads of a given people. But we are
not confined to the limits of a single nationality. Every
15 country of Europe may be laid under contribution for evidence, and not a little testimony has come in from other
continents. All stages of civilization are represented in
the material that scholars have brought together, so that
we are enabled to speak with entire confidence. Positive
20 chronology may be out of the question, but relative chronology is all that one can require in such matters. The
hostility between education and balladry is not con-
jectural ; its history is known in Great Britain for at least
two hundred years. The homogeneous folk — that is, the
25 community whose intellectual interests are the same from
the top of the social structure to the bottom — is no fiction ;
examples in abundance have been observed and recorded.
The ability of oral tradition to transmit great masses of
verse for hundreds of years is proved and admitted. Ballads
30 themselves exist in plenty, fortunately preserved in old
manuscripts or broadsides or taken down from singing
or recitation in recent years. It is possible to be ignorant

of the evidence, no doubt, but it is not possible to doubt when once the evidence is known. *The popular ballads are really popular, that is, they belong to the folk.*

A GENTLEMAN[1]

JOHN HENRY CARDINAL NEWMAN

Hence it is that it is almost a definition of a gentleman to say he is one who never inflicts pain. This description is both refined and, as far as it goes, accurate. He is mainly occupied in merely removing the obstacles which hinder
5 the free and unembarrassed action of those about him; and he concurs with their movements rather than takes the initiative himself. His benefits may be considered as parallel to what are called comforts or conveniences in arrangements of a personal nature: like an easy-chair or
10 a good fire, which do their part in dispelling cold and fatigue, though nature provides both means of rest and animal heat without them. The true gentleman in like manner carefully avoids whatever may cause a jar or a jolt in the minds of those with whom he is cast; — all
15 clashing of opinion, or collision of feeling, all restraint, or suspicion, or gloom, or resentment; his great concern being to make every one at their ease and at home. He has his eyes on all his company; he is tender towards the bashful, gentle towards the distant, and merciful towards
20 the absurd; he can recollect to whom he is speaking; he guards against unseasonable allusions, or topics which may irritate; he is seldom prominent in conversation, and never wearisome. He makes light of favours while he does them,

[1] From *The Idea of a University*, pp. 208–211. Longmans, Green & Co., London, 1886.

and seems to be receiving when he is conferring. He never
speaks of himself except when compelled, never defends
himself by a mere retort, he has no ears for slander or
gossip, is scrupulous in imputing motives to those who
interfere with him, and interprets everything for the best. 5
He is never mean or little in his disputes, never takes
unfair advantage, never mistakes personalities or sharp
sayings for arguments, or insinuates evil which he dare
not say out. From a long-sighted prudence, he observes
the maxim of the ancient sage, that we should ever con- 10
duct ourselves towards our enemy as if he were one day
to be our friend. He has too much good sense to be affronted
at insults, he is too well employed to remember injuries,
and too indolent to bear malice. He is patient, forbearing,
and resigned, on philosophical principles; he submits to 15
pain, because it is inevitable, to bereavement, because it is
irreparable, and to death, because it is his destiny. If he
engages in controversy of any kind, his disciplined intellect
preserves him from the blundering discourtesy of better,
perhaps, but less educated minds; who, like blunt weapons, 20
tear and hack instead of cutting clean, who mistake the
point in argument, waste their strength on trifles, miscon-
ceive their adversary, and leave the question more involved
than they find it. He may be right or wrong in his opinion, but he is too clear-headed to be unjust; he is as simple 25
as he is forcible, and as brief as he is decisive. Nowhere
shall we find greater candour, consideration, indulgence: he
throws himself into the minds of his opponents, he accounts
for their mistakes. He knows the weakness of human
reason as well as its strength, its province and its limits. 30
If he be an unbeliever, he will be too profound and large-
minded to ridicule religion or to act against it ; he is too

wise to be a dogmatist or fanatic in his infidelity. He respects piety and devotion ; he even supports institutions as venerable, beautiful, or useful, to which he does not assent ; he honours the ministers of religion, and it con-
5 tents him to decline its mysteries without assailing or denouncing them. He is a friend of religious toleration, and that, not only because his philosophy has taught him to look on all forms of faith with an impartial eye, but also from the gentleness and effeminacy of feeling, which
10 is the attendant on civilization.

Not that he may not hold a religion too, in his own way, even when he is not a Christian. In that case his religion is one of imagination and sentiment ; it is the embodi-ment of those ideas of the sublime, majestic, and beautiful,
15 without which there can be no large philosophy. Some-times he acknowledges the being of God, sometimes he in-vests an unknown principle or quality with the attributes of perfection. And this deduction of his reason, or crea-tion of his fancy, he makes the occasion of such excellent
20 thoughts, and the starting-point of so varied and systematic a teaching, that he even seems like a disciple of Chris-tianity itself. From the very accuracy and steadiness of his logical powers, he is able to see what sentiments are con-sistent in those who hold any religious doctrine at all, and
25 he appears to others to feel and to hold a whole circle of theological truths, which exist in his mind no otherwise than as a number of deductions.

AN INDIAN HOUSE[1]

FRANCIS PARKMAN

The region whose boundaries we have given was an alternation of meadows and deep forests, interlaced with footpaths leading from town to town. Of these towns, some were fortified, but the greater number were open and defenceless. They were of a construction common to all [5] tribes of Iroquois lineage, and peculiar to them. Nothing similar exists at the present day.[2] They covered a space of from one to ten acres, the dwellings clustering together with little or no pretension to order. In general, these singular structures were about thirty or thirty-five feet in [10] length, breadth, and height; but many were much larger, and a few were of prodigious length. In some of the villages there were dwellings two hundred and forty feet long, though in breadth and height they did not much exceed the others.[3] In shape they were much like an arbor overarching [15]

---

[1] From *The Jesuits in North America*, Introduction, pp. 11–14. (Parkman's Works, New Library Edition, II.) Copyrighted by Little, Brown & Co., Boston, 1905.

[2] The permanent bark villages of the Dahcotah of the St. Peter's are the nearest modern approach to the Huron towns. The whole Huron country abounds with evidences of having been occupied by a numerous population. "On a close inspection of the forest," Dr. Taché writes to me, "the greatest part of it seems to have been cleared at former periods, and almost the only places bearing the character of the primitive forest are the low grounds."

[3] Brébeuf, *Relation des Hurons*, 1635, p. 31. Champlain says that he saw them, in 1615, more than thirty fathoms long; while Vanderdonck reports the length, from actual measurement, of an Iroquois house, at a hundred and eighty yards, or five hundred and forty feet!

19

a garden-walk. Their frame was of tall and strong saplings, planted in a double row to form the two sides of
the house, bent till they met, and lashed together at the
top. To these other poles were bound transversely, and
5 the whole was covered with large sheets of the bark of
the oak, elm, spruce, or white cedar, overlapping like the
shingles of a roof, upon which, for their better security,
split poles were made fast with cords of linden bark. At
the crown of the arch, along the entire length of the house,
10 an opening a foot wide was left for the admission of light
and the escape of smoke. At each end was a close porch
of similar construction ; and here were stowed casks of
bark, filled with smoked fish, Indian corn, and other stores
not liable to injury from frost. Within, on both sides,
15 were wide scaffolds, four feet from the floor, and extending the entire length of the house, like the seats of a
colossal omnibus.[1] These were formed of thick sheets of
bark, supported by posts and transverse poles, and covered
with mats and skins. Here, in summer, was the sleeping-
20 place of the inmates, and the space beneath served for
storage of their firewood. The fires were on the ground,
in a line down the middle of the house. Each sufficed for
two families, who, in winter, slept closely packed around
them. Above, just under the vaulted roof, were a great
25 number of poles, like the perches of a hen-roost; and here

---

[1] Often, especially among the Iroquois, the internal arrangement was
different. The scaffolds or platforms were raised only a foot from the
earthen floor, and were only twelve or thirteen feet long, with intervening spaces, where the occupants stored their family provisions and other
articles. Five or six feet above was another platform, often occupied
by children. One pair of platforms sufficed for a family, and here during
summer they slept pellmell, in the clothes they wore by day, and without pillows.

were suspended weapons, clothing, skins, and ornaments. Here, too, in harvest time, the squaws hung the ears of un-shelled corn, till the rude abode, through all its length, seemed decked with a golden tapestry. In general, how-ever, its only lining was a thick coating of soot from the [5] smoke of fires with neither draught, chimney, nor window. So pungent was the smoke that it produced inflammation of the eyes, attended in old age with frequent blindness. Another annoyance was the fleas; and the third, the un-bridled and unruly children. Privacy there was none. [10] The house was one chamber, sometimes lodging more than twenty families.[1]

[1] One of the best descriptions of the Huron and Iroquois houses is that of Sagard, *Voyage des Hurons*, 118. See also Champlain (1627), p. 78; Brébeuf, *Relation des Hurons*, 1635, p. 31; Vanderdonck, *New Netherlands*, in N. Y. *Hist. Coll.*, Second Ser., I. 196; Lafitau, *Mœurs des Sauvages*, II. 10. The account given by Cartier of the houses he saw at Montreal corresponds with the above. He describes them as about fifty yards long. In this case, there were partial partitions for the several families, and a sort of loft above. Many of the Iroquois and Huron houses were of similar construction, the partitions being at the sides only, leaving a wide passage down the middle of the house. Bartram, *Observations on a Journey from Pennsylvania to Canada*, gives a description and plan of the Iroquois Council-House in 1751, which was of this construction. Indeed, the Iro-quois preserved this mode of building, in all essential points, down to a recent period. They usually framed the sides of their houses on rows of upright posts, arched with separate poles for the roof. The Hurons, no doubt, did the same in their larger structures. For a door, there was a sheet of bark, hung on wooden hinges, or suspended by cords from above.

On the site of Huron towns which were destroyed by fire, the size, shape, and arrangement of the houses can still, in some instances, be traced by remains in the form of charcoal, as well as by the charred bones and fragments of pottery found among the ashes.

Dr. Taché, after a zealous and minute examination of the Huron country, extended through five years, writes to me as follows: "From the remains I have found, I can vouch for the scrupulous correctness of our ancient writers. With the aid of their indications and descriptions,

He who entered on a winter night beheld a strange
spectacle: the vista of fires lighting the smoky concave;
the bronzed groups encircling each, — cooking, eating,
gambling, or amusing themselves with idle badinage;
5 shrivelled squaws, hideous with threescore years of hardship; grisly old warriors, scarred with Iroquois war-clubs;
young aspirants, whose honors were yet to be won; dam-
sels gay with ochre and wampum; restless children pellmell with restless dogs. Now a tongue of resinous flame
10 painted each wild feature with·vivid light; now the fitful
gleam expired, and the group vanished from sight, as their
nation has vanished from history.

I have been able to detect the sites of villages in the midst of the forest,
and by the study, *in situ*, of archæological monuments, small as they
are, to understand and confirm their many interesting details of the habits,
and especially the funeral rites, of these extraordinary tribes."

SELF–CULTIVATION IN ENGLISH [1]

George Herbert Palmer

First, then, "Look well to your speech." It is commonly supposed that when a man seeks literary power he goes to his room and plans an article for the press. But this is to begin literary culture at the wrong end. We speak a hundred times for every once we write. The 5 busiest writer produces little more than a volume a year, not so much as his talk would amount to in a week. Consequently through speech it is usually decided whether a man is to have command of his language or not. If he is slovenly in his ninety-nine cases of talking, he can seldom 10 pull himself up to strength and exactitude in the hundredth case of writing. A person is made in one piece, and the same being runs through a multitude of performances. Whether words are uttered on paper or to the air, the effect on the utterer is the same. Vigor or feebleness 15 results according as energy or slackness has been in command. I know that certain adaptations to a new field are often necessary. A good speaker may find awkwardnesses in himself when he comes to write, a good writer when he speaks. And certainly cases occur where a man exhibits 20 distinct strength in one of the two, speaking or writing, and not in the other. But such cases are rare. As a rule, language once within our control can be employed for

[1] From *Self-Cultivation in English*, pp. 9 ff. T. Y. Crowell & Co., New York, 1897.

23

oral or for written purposes. And since the opportunities for oral practice enormously. outbalance those for written, it is the oral which are chiefly significant in the development of literary power. We rightly say of the accom-
5 plished writer that he shows a mastery of his own tongue.

Fortunate it is, then, that self-cultivation in the use of English must chiefly come through speech; because we are always speaking, whatever else we do. In opportunities for acquiring a mastery of language, the poorest and
10 busiest are at no large disadvantage as compared with the leisured rich. It is true the strong impulse which comes from the suggestion and approval of society may in some cases be absent, but this can be compensated by the sturdy purpose of the learner. A recognition of the beauty of
15 well-ordered words, a strong desire, patience under discouragements, and promptness in counting every occasion as of consequence, — these are the simple agencies which sweep one on to power. Watch your speech, then. That is all which is needed. Only it is desirable to know what
20 qualities of speech to watch for. I find three, — accuracy, audacity, and range, — and I will say a few words about each.

Obviously, good English is exact English. Our words should fit our thoughts like a glove, and be neither too
25 wide nor too tight. If too wide, they will include much vacuity beside the intended matter. If too tight, they will check the strong grasp. Of the two dangers, looseness is by far the greater. There are people who say what they mean with such a naked precision that nobody not familiar
30 with the subject can quickly catch the sense. George Herbert and Emerson strain the attention of many. But niggardly and angular speakers are rare. Too frequently

words signify nothing in particular. They are merely thrown out in a certain direction, to report a vague and undetermined meaning or even a general emotion. ⌊The first business of every one who would train himself in language is to articulate his thought, to know definitely 5 what he wishes to say, and then to pick those words which compel the hearer to think of this and only this. For such a purpose two words are often better than three. The fewer the words, the more pungent the impression. Brevity is the soul not simply of a jest, but of wit in its 10 finest sense where it is identical with wisdom. He who can put a great deal into a little is the master. Since firm texture is what is wanted, not embroidery or superposed ornament, beauty has been well defined as the purgation of superfluities. And certainly many a paragraph might 15 have its beauty brightened by letting quiet words take the place of its loud words, omitting its " verys," and striking out its purple patches of " fine writing." Here is Ben Jonson's description of Bacon's language: " There happened in my time one noble speaker who was full of 20 gravity in his speech. No man ever spoke more neatly, more pressly, more weightily, or suffered less emptiness, less idleness, in what he uttered. No member of his speech but consisted of his own graces. His hearers could not cough or look aside without loss. He commanded when 25 he spoke, and had his judges angry or pleased at his discretion." Such are the men who command, men who speak " neatly and pressly." But to gain such precision is toilsome business. While we are in training for it, no word must unpermittedly pass the portal of the teeth. Some- 30 thing like what we mean must never be counted equivalent to what we mean. And if we are not sure of our

meaning or of our word, we must pause until we are sure.
Accuracy does not come of itself. For persons who can
use several languages, capital practice in acquiring it can
be had by translating from one language to another and
5 seeing that the entire sense is carried over. Those who
have only their native speech will find it profitable often
to attempt definitions of the common words they use.
Inaccuracy will not stand up against the habit of definition. Dante boasted that no rhythmic exigency had ever
10 made him say what he did not mean. We heedless and
unintending speakers, under no exigency of rhyme or
reason, say what we mean but seldom and still more
seldom mean what we say. To hold our thoughts and
words in significant adjustment requires unceasing con-
15 sciousness, a perpetual determination not to tell lies; for
of course every inaccuracy is a bit of untruthfulness. We
have something in mind, yet convey something else to our
hearer. And no moral purpose will save us from this untruthfulness unless that purpose is sufficient to inspire the
20 daily drill which brings the power to be true. Again and
again we are shut up to evil because we have not acquired
the ability of goodness.

But after all, I hope that nobody who hears me will
quite agree. There is something enervating in conscious
25 care. Necessary as it is in shaping our purposes, if allowed
too direct and exclusive control consciousness breeds hesitation and feebleness. Action is not excellent, at least,
until spontaneous. In piano playing we begin by picking
out each separate note; but we do not call the result
30 music until we play our notes by the handful, heedless
how each is formed. And so it is everywhere. Con-
sciously selective conduct is elementary and inferior.

People distrust it, or rather they distrust him who exhibits it. If anybody talking to us visibly studies his words, we turn away. What he says may be well enough as school exercise, but it is not conversation. Accordingly, if we would have our speech forcible, we shall need to put into it quite as much of audacity as we do of precision, terseness, or simplicity. Accuracy alone is not a thing to be sought, but accuracy and dash. Of Patrick Henry, the orator who more than any other could craze our Revolutionary fathers, it was said that he was accustomed to throw himself headlong into the middle of a sentence, trusting to God Almighty to get him out. So must we speak. We must not, before beginning a sentence, decide what the end shall be; for if we do, nobody will care to hear that end. At the beginning, it is the beginning which claims the attention of both speaker and listener, and trepidation about going on will mar all. We must give our thought its head, and not drive it with too tight a rein, nor grow timid when it begins to prance a bit. Of course we must retain coolness in courage, applying the results of our previous discipline in accuracy; but we need not move so slowly as to become formal. Pedantry is worse than blundering. If we care for grace and flexible beauty of language, we must learn to let our thought run. Would it, then, be too much of an Irish bull to say that in acquiring English we need to cultivate spontaneity? The uncultivated kind is not worth much; it is wild and haphazard stuff, unadjusted to its uses. On the other hand, no speech is of much account, however just, which lacks the element of courage. Accuracy and dash, then, the combination of the two, must be our difficult aim; and we must not rest satisfied so long as either dwells with us alone.

But are the two so hostile as they at first appear? Or can, indeed, the first be obtained without the aid of the second? Supposing we are convinced that words possess no value in themselves, and are correct or incorrect only
5 as they truly report experience, we shall feel ourselves impelled in the mere interest of accuracy to choose them freshly, and to put them together in ways in which they never co-operated before, so as to set forth with distinctness that which just we, not other people, have seen or felt.
10 The reason why we do not naturally have this daring exactitude is probably twofold. We let our experiences be blurred, not observing sharply, nor knowing with any minuteness what we are thinking about; and so there is no individuality in our language. And then, besides, we
15 are terrorized by custom, and inclined to adjust what we would say to what others have said before. The cure for the first of these troubles is to keep our eye on our object, instead of on our listener or ourselves; and for the second, to learn to rate the expressiveness of language more highly
20 than its correctness. The opposite of this, the disposition to set correctness above expressiveness, produces that peculiarly vulgar diction known as "school-ma'am English," in which for the sake of a dull accord with usage all the picturesque, imaginative, and forceful employment of words
25 is sacrificed. Of course we must use words so that people can understand them, and understand them, too, with ease; but this once granted, let our language be our own, obedient to our special needs. "Whenever," says Thomas Jefferson, "by small grammatical negligences the energy of an idea
30 can be condensed, or a word be made to stand for a sentence, I hold grammatical rigor in contempt." "Young man," said Henry Ward Beecher to one who was pointing

out grammatical errors in a sermon of his, "when the English language gets in my way, it does n't stand a chance." No man can be convincing, writer or speaker, who is afraid to send his words wherever they may best follow his meaning, and this with but little regard to whether any other person's words have ever been there before. In assessing merit, let us not stupefy ourselves with using negative standards. What stamps a man as great is not freedom from faults, but abundance of powers.

Such audacious accuracy, however, distinguishing as it does noble speech from commonplace speech, can be practised only by him who has a wide range of words. Our ordinary range is absurdly narrow. It is important, therefore, for anybody who would cultivate himself in English to make strenuous and systematic efforts to enlarge his vocabulary. Our dictionaries contain more than a hundred thousand words. The average speaker employs about three thousand. Is this because ordinary people have only three or four thousand things to say? Not at all. It is simply due to dulness. Listen to the average school-boy. He has a dozen or two nouns, half a dozen verbs, three or four adjectives, and enough conjunctions and prepositions to stick the conglomerate together. This ordinary speech deserves the description which Hobbes gave to his *State of Nature*, that "it is solitary, poor, nasty, brutish, and short." The fact is, we fall into the way of thinking that the wealthy words are for others and that they do not belong to us. We are like those who have received a vast inheritance, but who persist in the inconveniences of hard beds, scanty food, rude clothing, who never travel, and who limit their purchases to the bleak necessities of life. Ask such people why they endure niggardly living while

wealth in plenty is lying in the bank, and they can only
answer that they have never learned how to spend. But
this is worth learning. Milton used eight thousand words,
Shakespeare fifteen thousand. We have all the subjects
5 to talk about that these early speakers had; and in addition, we have bicycles and sciences and strikes and political
combinations and all the complicated living of the modern
world.

Why, then, do we hesitate to swell our words to meet
10 our needs? It is a nonsense question. There is no reason.
We are simply lazy; too lazy to make ourselves comfortable. We let our vocabularies be limited, and get along
rawly without the refinements of human intercourse, without refinements in our own thoughts; for thoughts are
15 almost as dependent on words as words on thoughts. For
example, all exasperations we lump together as "aggravat-
ing," not considering whether they may not rather be dis-
pleasing, annoying, offensive, disgusting, irritating, or even
maddening; and without observing, too, that in our reck-
20 less usage we have burned up a word which might be convenient when we should need to mark some shading of
the word "increase." Like the bad cook, we seize the
frying-pan whenever we need to fry, broil, roast, or stew,
and then we wonder why all our dishes taste alike while
25 in the next house the food is appetizing. It is all unnecessary. Enlarge the vocabulary. Let any one who wants
to see himself grow, resolve to adopt two new words each
week. It will not be long before the endless and enchanting variety of the world will begin to reflect itself in his
30 speech, and in his mind as well. I know that when we
use a word for the first time we are startled, as if a fire-
cracker went off in our neighborhood. We look about

hastily to see if any one has noticed. But finding that no one has, we may be emboldened. A word used three times slips off the tongue with entire naturalness. Then it is ours forever, and with it some phase of life which had been lacking hitherto. For each word presents its own point of view, discloses a special aspect of things, reports some little importance not otherwise conveyed, and so contributes its small emancipation to our tied-up minds and tongues.

But a brief warning may be necessary to make my meaning clear. In urging the addition of new words to our present poverty-stricken stock, I am far from suggesting that we should seek out strange, technical, or inflated expressions, which do not appear in ordinary conversation. The very opposite is my aim. I would put every man who is now employing a diction merely local and personal in command of the approved resources of the English language. Our poverty usually comes through provinciality, through accepting without criticism the habits of our special set. My family, my immediate friends, have a diction of their own. Plenty of other words, recognized as sound, are known to be current in books, and to be employed by modest and intelligent speakers, only we do not use them. Our set has never said " diction," or " current," or "scope," or " scanty," or " hitherto," or "convey," or " lack." Far from unusual as these words are, to adopt them might seem to set me apart from those whose intellectual habits I share. From this I shrink. I do not like to wear clothes suitable enough for others, but not in the style of my own plain circle. Yet if each one of that circle does the same, the general shabbiness is increased. The talk of all is made narrow enough to fit the thinnest

there. What we should seek is to contribute to each of the little companies with which our life is bound up a gently enlarging influence, such impulses as will not startle or create detachment, but which may save from humdrum,
5 routine, and dreary usualness. We cannot be really kind without being a little venturesome. The small shocks of our increasing vocabulary will in all probability be as helpful to our friends as to ourselves.

Such, then, are the excellences of speech. If we would
10 cultivate ourselves in the use of English, we must make our daily talk accurate, daring, and full. I have insisted on these points the more because in my judgment all literary power, especially that of busy men, is rooted in sound speech.

PREPARATION FOR WAR[1]

CAPTAIN ALFRED THAYER MAHAN

In the matter of preparation for war, one clear idea should be absorbed first by every one who, recognizing that war is still a possibility, desires to see his country ready. This idea is that, however defensive in origin or in political character a war may be, the assumption of a simple defen- 5 sive in war is ruin. War, once declared, must be waged offensively, aggressively. The enemy must not be fended off, but smitten down. You may then spare him every exaction, relinquish every gain; but till down he must be struck incessantly and remorselessly. 10

Preparation, like most other things, is a question both of kind and of degree, of quality and of quantity. As regards degree, the general lines upon which it is deter- mined have been indicated broadly in the preceding part of this article. The measure of degree is the estimated 15 force which the strongest *probable* enemy can bring against you, allowance being made for clear drawbacks upon his total force, imposed by his own embarrassments and re- sponsibilities in other parts of the world. The calculation is partly military, partly political, the latter, however, 20 being the dominant factor in the premises.

In kind, preparation is twofold, — defensive and offen- sive. The former exists chiefly for the sake of the latter,

---

[1] From "Preparedness for Naval War," in *The Interest of America in Sea Power, Present and Future*, pp. 192–200. Little, Brown & Co., Boston, 1897.

in order that offence, the determining factor in war, may
put forth its full power, unhampered by concern for the
protection of the national interests or for its own resources.
In naval war, coast defence is the defensive factor, the
5 navy the offensive. Coast defence, when adequate, assures
the naval commander-in-chief that his base of operations
— the dock-yards and coal depots — is secure. It also re-
lieves him and his government, by the protection afforded
to the chief commercial centres, from the necessity of
10 considering them, and so leaves the offensive arm perfectly free.

Coast defence implies coast attack. To what attacks
are coasts liable? Two, principally, — blockade and bombardment. The latter, being the more difficult, includes
15 the former, as the greater does the lesser. A fleet that
can bombard can still more easily blockade. Against bombardment the necessary precaution is gun-fire, of such
power and range that a fleet cannot lie within bombarding distance. This condition is obtained, where surround-
20 ings permit, by advancing the line of guns so far from the
city involved that bombarding distance can be reached only
by coming under their fire. But it has been demonstrated,
and is accepted, that, owing to their rapidity of movement,
— like a flock of birds on the wing, — a fleet of ships can,
25 without disabling loss, pass by guns before which they
could not lie. Hence arises the necessity of arresting or
delaying their progress by blocking channels, which in
modern practice is done by lines of torpedoes. The mere
moral effect of the latter is a deterrent to a dash past, —
30 by which, if successful, a fleet reaches the rear of the
defences, and appears immediately before the city, which
then lies at its mercy.

Coast defence, then, implies gun-power and torpedo lines placed as described. Be it said in passing that only places of decisive importance, commercially or militarily, need such defences. Modern fleets cannot afford to waste ammunition in bombarding unimportant towns, — at least 5 when so far from their own base as they would be on our coast. It is not so much a question of money as of frittering their fighting strength. It would not pay.

Even coast defence, however, although essentially passive, should have an element of offensive force, local in 10 character, distinct from the offensive navy, of which nevertheless it forms a part. To take the offensive against a floating force it must itself be afloat — naval. This offensive element of coast defence is to be found in the torpedo-boat, in its various developments. It must be kept distinct 15 in idea from the sea-going fleet, although it is, of course, possible that the two may act in concert. The war very well may take such a turn that the sea-going navy will find its best preparation for initiating an offensive movement to be by concentrating in a principal seaport. Fail- 20 ing such a contingency, however, and in and for coast defence in its narrower sense, there should be a local flotilla of small torpedo-vessels, which by their activity should make life a burden to an outside enemy. A distinguished British admiral, now dead, has said that he believed half 25 the captains of a blockading fleet would break down — "go crazy" were the words repeated to me — under the strain of modern conditions. The expression, of course, was intended simply to convey a sense of the immensity of suspense to be endured. In such a flotilla, owing to the 30 smallness of its components, and to the simplicity of their organization and functions, is to be found the best sphere for naval volunteers; the duties could be, learned with comparative ease, and the whole system is susceptible of rapid development. Be it remembered, however, that it is essentially defensive, only incidentally offensive in character.

Such are the main elements of coast defence — guns, lines of torpedoes, torpedo-boats. Of these none can be extemporized, with the possible exception of the last, and that would be only a makeshift. To go into details would exceed the limits of an article, — require a brief treatise. . Suffice it to say, without the first two, coast cities are open to bombardment; without the last, they can be blockaded freely, unless relieved by the sea-going navy. Bombardment and blockade are recognized modes of warfare, subject only to reasonable notification, — a concession rather to humanity and equity than to strict law. Bombardment and blockade directed against great national centres, in the close and complicated network of national and commercial interests as they exist in modern times, strike not only the point affected, but every corner of the land.

The offensive in naval war, as has been said, is the function of the sea-going navy — of the battle ships, and of the cruisers of various sizes and purposes, including sea-going torpedo-vessels capable of accompanying a fleet, without impeding its movements by their loss of speed or unseaworthiness. Seaworthiness, and reasonable speed under all weather conditions, are qualities necessary to every constituent of a fleet; but, over and above these, the backbone and real power of any navy are the vessels which, by due proportion of defensive and offensive powers, are capable of taking and giving hard knocks. All others are but subservient to these, and exist only for them.

What is that strength to be? Ships answering to this description are the *kind* which make naval strength; what is to be its degree? What their number? The answer — a broad formula — is that it must be great enough to take the sea, and to fight, with reasonable chances of success, the largest force likely to be brought against it, as shown by calculations which have been indicated previously. Being, as we claim, and as our past history justifies us in claiming, a nation indisposed to aggression, unwilling to extend our possessions or our interests by war, the measure of strength we set ourselves depends, necessarily, not upon our projects of aggrandizement, but upon the disposition of others to thwart what we consider our reasonable policy, which they may not so consider. When they resist, what force can they bring against us? That force must be naval; we have no exposed point upon which land operations, decisive in character, can be directed. This is the kind of the hostile force to be apprehended. What may its size be? There is the measure of our needed strength. The calculation may be intricate, the conclusion only approximate and probable, but it is the nearest reply we can reach. So many ships of such and such sizes, so many guns, so much ammunition — in short so much naval material.

In the material provisions that have been summarized under the two chief heads of defence and offence — in coast defence under its three principal requirements, guns, lines of stationary torpedoes, and torpedo-boats, and in a navy able to keep the sea in the presence of a probable enemy — consist what may be called most accurately preparations for war. In so far as the United States is short of them, she is at the mercy of an enemy whose naval

strength is greater than that of her own available navy. If her navy cannot keep the enemy off the coast, blockade at least is possible. If, in addition, there are no harbor torpedo-boats, blockade is easy. If, further, guns and tor-
5 pedo lines are deficient, bombardment comes within the range of possibility, and may reach even the point of entire feasibility. There will be no time for preparation after war begins.

LIFE IN THE WILDERNESS[1]

Theodore Roosevelt

Long before the first Continental Congress assembled, the backwoodsmen, whatever their blood, had become Americans, one in speech, thought, and character, clutching firmly the land in which their fathers and grandfathers had lived before them. They had lost all remembrance of [5] Europe and all sympathy with things European; they had become as emphatically products native to the soil as were the tough and supple hickories out of which they fashioned the handles of their long, light axes. Their grim, harsh, narrow lives were yet strangely fascinating and full of [10] adventurous toil and danger; none but natures as strong, as freedom-loving, and as full of bold defiance as theirs could have endured existence on the terms which these men found pleasurable. Their iron surroundings made a mould which turned out all alike in the same shape. They [15] resembled one another, and they differed from the rest of the world — even the world of America, and infinitely more the world of Europe — in dress, in customs, and in mode of life.

Where their lands abutted on the more settled districts [20] to the eastward, the population was of course thickest, and their peculiarities least. Here and there at such points they built small backwoods burgs or towns, rude,'

[1] From *The Winning of the West*, Vol. I, chap. v, pp. 108–113. G. P. Putnam's Sons, New York, 1889.

straggling, unkempt villages, with a store or two, a tavern,
— sometimes good, often a "scandalous hog-sty," where
travellers were devoured by fleas, and every one slept and
ate in one room,[18] — a small log school-house, and a little
church, presided over by a hard-featured Presbyterian
preacher, gloomy, earnest, and zealous, probably bigoted
and narrow-minded, but nevertheless a great power for
good in the community.[19]

However, the backwoodsmen as a class neither built
towns nor loved to dwell therein. They were to be seen
at their best in the vast, interminable forests that formed
their chosen home. They won and kept their lands by force,
and ever lived either at war or in dread of war. Hence
they settled always in groups of several families each, all
banded together for mutual protection. Their red foes
were strong and terrible, cunning in council, dreadful in
battle, merciless beyond belief in victory. The men of the
border did not overcome and dispossess cowards and weak-
lings; they marched forth to spoil the stout-hearted and
to take for a prey the possessions of the men of might.
Every acre, every rood of ground which they claimed had
to be cleared by the axe and held with the rifle. Not only
was the chopping down of the forests the first preliminary
to cultivation, but it was also the surest means of subduing the Indians, to whom the unending stretches of choked
woodland were an impenetrable cover behind which to
move unseen, a shield in making assaults, and a strong

[18] MS. Journal of Matthew Clarkson, 1766. See also "Voyage dans les États-Unis," La Rochefoucauld-Liancourt, Paris, L'an VII, i, 104.

[19] The borderers had the true Calvinistic taste in preaching. Clarkson, in his journal of his western trip, mentions with approval a sermon he heard as being "a very judicious and alarming discourse."

tower of defence in repelling counter-attacks. In the conquest of the west the backwoods axe, shapely, well-poised,
with long haft and light head, was a servant hardly standing second even to the rifle; the two were the national
weapons of the American backwoodsman, and in their use 5
he has never been excelled.

When a group of families moved out into the wilderness they built themselves a station or stockade fort; a
square palisade of upright logs, loop-holed, with strong
block-houses as bastions at the corners. One side at least 10
was generally formed by the backs of the cabins themselves, all standing in a row; and there was a great door
or gate, that could be strongly barred in case of need.
Often no iron whatever was employed in any of the buildings. The square inside contained the provision sheds and 15
frequently a strong central blockhouse as well. These forts,
of course, could not stand against cannon, and they were
always in danger when attacked with fire; but save for
this risk of burning they were very effectual defences
against men without artillery, and were rarely taken, 20
whether by whites or Indians, except by surprise. Few
other buildings have played so important a part in our
history as the rough stockade fort of the backwoods.

The families only lived in the fort when there was
war with the Indians, and even then not in the winter. 25
At other times they all separated out to their own farms,
universally called clearings, as they were always made by
first cutting off the timber. The stumps were left to dot
the fields of grain and Indian corn. The corn in especial
was the stand-by and invariable resource of the western 30
settler; it was the crop on which he relied to feed his
family, and when hunting or on a war trail the parched

grains were carried in his leather wallet to serve often as
his only food. But he planted orchards and raised melons,
potatoes, and many other fruits and vegetables as well;
and he had usually a horse or two, cows, and perhaps hogs
5 and sheep, if the wolves and bears did not interfere. If he
was poor his cabin was made of unhewn logs, and held but
a single room; if well-to-do, the logs were neatly hewed,
and besides the large living- and eating-room with its huge
stone fireplace, there was also a small bedroom and a
10 kitchen, while a ladder led to the loft above, in which the
boys slept. The floor was made of puncheons, great slabs
of wood hewed carefully out, and the roof of clapboards.
Pegs of wood were thrust into the sides of the house, to
serve instead of a wardrobe; and buck antlers, thrust into
15 joists, held the ever ready rifles. The table was a great
clapboard set on four wooden legs; there were three-
legged stools, and in the better sort of houses old-fashioned
rocking chairs.[20] The couch or bed was warmly covered
with blankets, bear-skins, and deer-hides.[21]

20   These clearings lay far apart from one another in the
wilderness. Up to the door-sills of the log-huts stretched
the solemn and mysterious forest. There were no openings
to break its continuity; nothing but endless leagues on
leagues of shadowy, wolf-haunted woodland. The great
25 trees towered aloft till their separate heads were lost in
the mass of foliage above, and the rank underbrush choked
the spaces between the trunks. On the higher peaks and

---

[20] McAfee MSS.

[21] In the McAfee MSS. there is an amusing mention of the skin of a
huge bull elk, killed by the father, which the youngsters christened "old
ellick"; they used to quarrel for the possession of it on cold nights, as
it was very warm, though if the hairside was turned in it became slippery
and apt to slide off the bed.

ridge-crests of the mountains there were straggling birches and pines, hemlocks and balsam firs;[22] elsewhere, oaks, chestnuts, hickories, maples, beeches, walnuts, and great tulip trees grew side by side with many other kinds. The sunlight could not penetrate the roofed archway of mur- 5 muring leaves; through the gray aisles of the forest men walked always in a kind of mid-day gloaming. Those who had lived in the open plains felt when they came to the back-woods as if their heads were hooded. Save on the border of a lake, from a cliff top, or on a bald knob, — that 10 is, a bare hill-shoulder, — they could not anywhere look out for any distance.

[22] On the mountains the climate, flora, and fauna were all those of the north, not of the adjacent southern lowlands. The ruffed grouse, red squirrel, snow bird, various Canadian warblers, and a peculiar species of boreal field-mouse, the evotomys, are all found as far south as the Great Smokies.

THE UNIFORMITY OF AMERICAN LIFE[1]

JAMES BRYCE

To the pleasantness of American life there is one, and
only one, serious drawback — its uniformity. Those who
have been struck by the size of America, and by what they
have heard of its restless excitement, may be surprised
5 at the word. They would have guessed that an unquiet
changefulness and turmoil were the disagreeables to be
feared. But uniformity, which the European visitor begins
to note when he has travelled for a month or two, is the
feature of the country which Englishmen who have lived
10 long there, and Americans who are familiar with Europe,
most frequently revert to when asked to say what is the
"crook in their lot."

It is felt in many ways. I will name a few.

It is felt in the aspects of Nature. [This point Mr. Bryce
15 discusses in two paragraphs, of which the conclusion is :

"The man who lives in the section of America which
seems destined to contain the largest population, I mean
the States on the Upper Mississippi, lives in the midst of
a plain wider than the plains of Russia, and must travel
20 hundreds of miles to escape from its monotony."]

When we turn from the aspects of Nature to the cities
of men, the uniformity is even more remarkable. With
five or six exceptions to be mentioned presently, American

[1] From *The American Commonwealth*, Vol. III, chap. cxiii. Macmillan
& Co., London, 1888.

cities differ from one another only herein, that some of
them are built more with brick than with wood, and others
more with wood than with brick. In all else they are
alike, both great and small. In all the same wide streets,
crossing at right angles, ill-paved, but planted along the 5
sidewalks with maple-trees whose autumnal scarlet sur-
passes the brilliance of any European foliage. In all the
same shops, arranged on the same plan, the same Chinese
laundries, with Li Kow visible through the window, the
same ice-cream stores, the same large hotels with seedy 10
men hovering about in the dreary entrance-hall, the same
street cars passing to and fro with passengers clinging to
the door-step, the same locomotives ringing their great bells
as they clank slowly down the middle of the street. I
admit that in external aspect there is a sad monotony in 15
the larger towns of England also. Compare English cities
with Italian cities, and most of the former seem like one
another, incapable of being, so to speak, individualized as
you individualize a man with a definite character and
aspect unlike that of other men. Take the Lancashire 20
towns, for instance, large and prosperous places. You
cannot individualize Bolton or Wigan, Oldham or Bury,
except by trying to remember that Bury is slightly less
rough than Oldham, and Wigan a thought more grimy
than Bolton. But in Italy every city has its character, its 25
memories, its life and achievements wrought into the
pillars of its churches and the towers that stand along
its ramparts. Siena is not like Perugia, nor Perugia like
Orvieto ; Ravenna, Rimini, Pesaro, Fano, Ancona, Osimo,
standing along the same coast within seventy miles of one 30
another, have each of them a character, a sentiment, what
one may call an idiosyncrasy, which comes vividly back to

us at the mention of its name. Now, what English towns
are to Italian, that American towns are to English. They
are in some ways pleasanter; they are cleaner, there is less
poverty, less squalor, less darkness. But their monotony
5 haunts one like a nightmare. Even the irksomeness of
finding the streets named by numbers becomes insufferable.
It is doubtless convenient to know by the number how far
up the city the particular street is. But you cannot give
any sort of character to Twenty-ninth Street, for the name
10 refuses to lend itself to any association. There is something wearisomely hard and bare in such a system.

I return joyfully to the exceptions. Boston has a
character of her own, with her beautiful Common, her
smooth environing waters, her Beacon Hill crowned by the
15 gilded dome of the State House, and Bunker's Hill, bearing
the monument of the famous fight. New York, besides
a magnificent position, has in the grandeur of the buildings
and the tremendous rush of men and vehicles along the
streets as much the air of a great capital as London itself.
20 Chicago, with her enormous size and the splendid ware-
houses that line her endless thoroughfares, leaves a strong
though not wholly agreeable impression. Richmond has
a quaint old-world look which dwells in the memory: few
cities have a sea front equal in beauty to the lake front of
25 Cleveland. Washington, with its wide and beautifully-
graded avenues, and the glittering white of the stately
Capitol, has become within the last twenty years a singularly handsome city. And New Orleans — or rather the
. Creole quarter of New Orleans, for the rest of the city is
30 commonplace — is delicious, suggesting old France and
Spain, yet a France and Spain strangely transmuted in
this new clime. I have seen nothing in America more

picturesque than the Rue Royale, with its houses of all
heights, often built round a courtyard, where a magnolia
or an orange tree stands in the middle, and wooden
external staircases lead up to wooden galleries, the house
fronts painted of all colours, and carrying double rows of 5
balconies decorated with pretty iron work, the whole standing languid and still in the warm soft air, and touched with
the subtle fragrance of decay. Here in New Orleans the
streets and public buildings, and specially the old City
Hall, with the arms of Spain still upon it, speak of history. 10
One feels, in stepping across Canal Street from the Creole
quarter to the business parts of the town, that one steps
from an old nationality to a new one, that this city must
have had vicissitudes, that it represents something, and
that something one of the great events of history, the sur- 15
render of the northern half of the New World by the
Romano-Celtic races to the Teutonic. Quebec, and to a
less degree Montreal, fifteen hundred miles away, tell the
same tale : Santa Fé in New Mexico repeats it.

It is the absence in nearly all the American cities of 20
anything that speaks of the past that makes their external
aspect so unsuggestive. In pacing their busy streets and
admiring their handsome city halls and churches, one's
heart sinks at the feeling that nothing historically interesting ever has happened here, perhaps ever will happen. In 25
many an English town, however ugly with its smoke and
its new suburbs, one sees at least an ancient church, one
can discover some fragments of a castle or a city wall.
Even Wigan and Northampton have ancient churches,
though Northampton lately allowed the North-Western 30
Railway to destroy the last traces of the castle where Henry
II. issued his Assize. But in America hardly any public

building is associated with anything more interesting than
a big party convention; and nowadays even the big con-
ventions are held in temporary structures, whose materials
are sold when the politicians have dispersed. Nowhere,
5 perhaps, does this sense of the absolute novelty of all
things strike one so strongly as in San Francisco. Few
cities in the world can vie with her either in the beauty or
in the natural advantages of her situation; indeed, there
are only two places in Europe — Constantinople and Gibral-
10 tar — that combine an equally perfect landscape with what
may be called an equally imperial position. Before you
there is the magnificent bay, with its far-stretching arms
and rocky isles, and beyond it the faint line of the Sierra
Nevada, cutting the clear air like mother-of-pearl; behind
15 there is the roll of the ocean; to the left, the majestic
gateway between mountains through which ships bear in
commerce from the farthest shores of the Pacific; to the
right, valleys rich with corn and wine, sweeping away to
the southern horizon. The city itself is full of bold hills,
20 rising steeply from the deep water. The air is keen, dry,
and bright, like the air of Greece, and the waters not less
blue. Perhaps it is this air and light, recalling the cities
of the Mediterranean, that make one involuntarily look up
to the top of these hills for the feudal castle, or the ruins
25 of the Acropolis, which one thinks must crown them. I
found myself so looking all the time I remained in the
city. But on none of these heights is there anything more
interesting, anything more vocal to the student of the past,
than the sumptuous villas of the magnates of the Central
30 Pacific Railway, who have chosen a hill-top to display their
wealth to the city, but have erected houses like all other
houses, only larger. San Francisco has had a good deal of

history in her forty years of life ; but this history does not, like that of Greece or Italy, write itself in stone, or even in wood.

Of the uniformity of political institutions over the whole United States I have spoken already. Everywhere the same system of State governments, everywhere the same municipal governments, and almost uniformly bad or good in proportion to the greater or smaller population of the city, the same party machinery organized on the same methods, " run " by the same wire-pullers, and " workers." In rural local government there are some diversities in the names, areas, and functions of the different bodies, yet differences slight in comparison with the points of like- ness. The schools are practically identical in organization, in the subjects taught, in the methods of teaching, though the administration of them is as completely decentralized as can be imagined, even the State commissioner having no right to do more than suggest or report. So it is with the charitable institutions, with the libraries, the lecture- courses, the public amusements. All these are more abundant and better of their kind in the richer and more cultivated parts of the country, generally better in the North Atlantic than in the inland States, and in the West than in the South. But they are the same in type everywhere. It is the same with social habits and usages. There are still some differences between the South and the North ; and in the Eastern cities the upper class is more Europeanized in its code of etiquette and its ways of daily life. But even these variations tend to disappear. Eastern customs begin to permeate the West, beginning with the richer families ; the South is more like the North than it was before the war. Travel where you will, you feel that what you have

found in one place that you will find in another. The
thing which hath been, will be; you can no more escape
from it than you can quit the land to live in the sea.

Last of all we come to man himself — to man and to
5 woman, not less important than man. The ideas of men
and women, their fundamental beliefs and their superficial
tastes, their methods of thinking and their fashions of
talking, are what most concern their fellow-men; and if
there be variety and freshness in these, the uniformity of
10 nature and the monotony of cities signify but little. If I
observe that in these respects also the similarity of type
over the country is surprising, I shall be asked whether I
am not making the old mistake of the man who fancied all
Chinese were like one another, because, noticing the dress
15 and the pigtail, he did not notice minor differences of
feature. A scholar is apt to think that all business men
write the same hand, and a business man thinks the same
of all scholars. Perhaps Americans think all Englishmen
alike. And I may also be asked with whom I am compar-
20 ing the Americans. With Europe as a whole? If so, is it
not absurd to expect that the differences between different
sections in one people should be as marked as those between
different peoples? The United States are larger than
Europe, but Europe has many races and many languages,
25 among whom contrasts far broader must be expected than
between one people, even if it stretches over a continent.

It is most clearly not with Europe, but with each of the
leading European peoples that we must compare the people
of America. So comparing them with the people of Britain,
30 France, Germany, Italy, Spain, one discovers more varieties
between individuals in these European peoples than one
finds in America. Scotchmen and Irishmen are more

unlike Englishmen, the native of Normandy more unlike
the native of Provence, the Pomeranian more unlike the
Wurtemberger, the Piedmontese more unlike the Neapoli-
tan, the Basque more unlike the Andalusian, than the
American from any part of the country is to the American   5
from any other. Differences of course there are between
the human type as developed in different regions of the
country, — differences moral and intellectual as well as
physical. You can generally tell a Southerner by his look
as well as by his speech. A native of Maine will probably 10
differ from a native of Kentucky, a Georgian from an
Oregonian. But these differences strike even an American
observer much as the difference between a Yorkshireman
and a Lancastrian strikes the English, and are slighter '
than the contrast between a middle-class southern English- 15
man and a middle-class Scotchman, slighter than the differences between a peasant from Northumberland and a
peasant from Dorsetshire. Or, to take another way of
putting it: If at some great gathering of a political party
from all parts of the United Kingdom you were to go 20
round and talk to, say, one hundred, taken at random, of
the persons present, you would be struck by more diversity
between the notions and the tastes and mental habits of
the individuals comprising that one hundred than if you
tried the same experiment with a hundred Americans of 25
the same education and position, similarly gathered in
a convention from every State in the Union.

CORAL AND CORAL REEFS [1]

Thomas Henry Huxley

The progress of discovery has made us very completely acquainted with the structure and habits of all these polypes. We know that, among the sea-anemones and coral-forming animals, each polype has a mouth leading
5 to a stomach, which is open at its inner end, and thus communicates freely with the general cavity of the body ; that the tentacles placed round the mouth are hollow, and that they perform the part of arms in seizing and capturing prey. It is known that many of these creatures are
10 capable of being multiplied by artificial division, the divided halves growing, after a time, into complete and separate animals; and that many are able to perform a very similar process naturally, in such a manner that one polype may, by repeated incomplete divisions, give rise to
15 a sort of sheet, or turf, formed by innumerable connected, and yet independent, descendants. Or, what is still more common, a polype may throw out buds, which are converted into polypes, or branches bearing polypes, until a tree-like mass, sometimes of very considerable size, is formed.

20 This is what happens in the case of the red coral of commerce. A minute polype, fixed to the rocky bottom of the deep sea, grows up into a branched trunk. The end

[1] From "On Coral and Coral Reefs," in *Critiques and Addresses*, pp. 114-120. Reprinted by courtesy of the publishers, D. Appleton & Co., New York, 1873.

of every branch and twig is terminated by a polype; and all the polypes are connected together by a fleshy substance, traversed by innumerable canals which place each polype in communication with every other, and carry nourishment to the substance of the supporting stem. It is a sort of natural co-operative store, every polype helping the whole, at the same time as it helps itself. The interior of the stem, like that of the branches, is solidified by the deposition of carbonate of lime in its tissue, somewhat in the same fashion as our own bones are formed of animal matter impregnated with lime salts ; and it is this dense skeleton (usually turned deep red by a peculiar colouring matter) cleared of the soft animal investment, as the heart-wood of a tree might be stripped of its bark, which is the red coral.

In the case of the red coral, the hard skeleton belongs to the interior of the stem and branches only ; but in the commoner white corals, each polype has a complete skeleton of its own. These polypes are sometimes solitary, in which case the whole skeleton is represented by a single cup, with partitions radiating from its centre to its circumference. When the polypes formed by budding or division remain associated, the polypidom is sometimes made up of nothing but an aggregation of these cups, while at other times the cups are at once separated and held together, by an intermediate substance, which represents the branches of the red coral. The red coral polype again is a comparatively rare animal, inhabiting a limited area, the skeleton of which has but a very insignificant mass ; while the white corals are very common, occur in almost all seas, and form skeletons which are sometimes extremely massive.

With a very few exceptions, both the red and the white coral polypes are, in their adult state, firmly adherent to the sea-bottom; nor do their buds naturally become detached and locomotive. But, in addition to budding and
5 division, these creatures possess the more ordinary methods of multiplication; and, at particular seasons, they give rise to numerous eggs of minute size. Within these eggs the young are formed, and they leave the egg in a condition which has no sort of resemblance to the perfect animal.
10 It is, in fact, a minute oval body, many hundred times smaller than the full-grown creature, and it swims about with great activity by the help of multitudes of little hair-like filaments, called cilia, with which its body is covered. These cilia all lash the water in one direction, and so drive
15 the little body along as if it were propelled by thousands of extremely minute paddles. After enjoying its freedom for a longer or shorter time, and being carried either by the force of its own cilia, or by currents which bear it along, the embryo coral settles down to the bottom, loses
20 its cilia, and becomes fixed to the rock, gradually assuming the polype form and growing up to the size of its parent. As the infant polypes of the coral may retain this free and active condition for many hours, or even days, and as a tidal or other current in the sea may easily flow
25 at the speed of two or even more miles in an hour, it is clear that the embryo must often be transported to very considerable distances from the parent. And it is easily understood how a single polype, which may give rise to hundreds, or perhaps thousands, of embryos, may, by this
30 process of partly active and partly passive migration, cover an immense surface with its offspring. The masses of coral which may be formed by the assemblages of polypes which

spring by budding, or by dividing, from a single polype, occasionally attain very considerable dimensions. Such skeletons are sometimes great plates, many feet long and several feet in thickness; or they may form huge half globes, like the brainstone corals, or may reach the mag- 5 nitude of stout shrubs or even small trees. There is reason to believe that such masses as these take a long time to form, and hence that the age a polype tree, or polype turf, may attain, may be considerable. But, sooner or later, the coral polypes, like all other things, die; the 10 soft flesh decays, while the skeleton is left as a stony mass at the bottom of the sea, where it retains its integrity for a longer or a shorter time, according as its position affords more or less protection from the wear and tear of the waves.

The polypes which give rise to the white coral are found, 15 as has been said, in the seas of all parts of the world; but in the temperate and cold oceans they are scattered and comparatively small in size, so that the skeletons of those which die do not accumulate in any considerable quantity. But it is otherwise in the greater part of the ocean which 20 lies in the warmer parts of the world, comprised within a distance of about 1,800 miles on each side of the equator. Within the zone thus bounded, by far the greater part of the ocean is inhabited by coral polypes, which not only form very strong and large skeletons, but associate to- 25 gether into great masses, like the thickets and the meadow turf, or, better still, the accumulations of peat, to which plants give rise on the dry land. These masses of stony matter, heaped up beneath the waters of the ocean, become as dangerous to mariners as so much ordinary rock, and to 30 these, as to common rock ridges, the seaman gives the name of "reefs."

Such coral reefs cover many thousand square miles in the Pacific and in the Indian Oceans. There is one reef, or rather great series of reefs, called the Barrier Reef, which stretches, almost continuously, for more than 1,100 miles
5 off the east coast of Australia. Multitudes of the islands in the Pacific are either reefs themselves, or are surrounded by reefs. The Red Sea is in many parts almost a maze of such reefs, and they abound no less in the West Indies, along the coast of Florida, and even as far north as the
10 Bahama Islands. But it is a very remarkable circumstance that, within the area of what we may call the "coral zone," there are no coral reefs upon the west coast of America, nor upon the west coast of Africa; and it is a general fact that the reefs are interrupted, or absent, opposite the
15 mouths of great rivers. The causes of this apparent caprice in the distribution of coral reefs are not far to seek. The polypes which fabricate them require for their vigorous growth a temperature which must not fall below 68° Fahrenheit all the year round, and this temperature is
20 only to be found within the distance on each side of the equator which has been mentioned, or thereabouts. But even within the coral zone this degree of warmth is not everywhere to be had. On the west coast of America, and on the corresponding coast of Africa, currents of cold
25 water from the icy regions which surround the South Pole set northward, and it appears to be due to their cooling influence that the sea in these regions is free from the reef builders. Again, the coral polypes cannot live in water which is rendered brackish by floods from the land, or
30 which is perturbed by mud from the same source, and hence it is that they cease to exist opposite the mouths of rivers, which damage them in both these ways.

Such is the general distribution of the reef-building corals, but there are some very interesting and singular circumstances to be observed in the conformation of the reefs, when we consider them individually. The reefs, in fact, are of three different kinds: some of them stretch out from the shore, almost like a prolongation of the beach, covered only by shallow water, and in the case of an island, surrounding it like a fringe of no considerable breadth. These are termed "fringing reefs." Others are separated by a channel which may attain a width of many miles, and a depth of twenty or thirty fathoms or more, from the nearest land; and when this land is an island, the reef surrounds it like a low wall, and the sea between the reef and the land is, as it were, a moat inside this wall. Such reefs as these are called "encircling" when they surround an island; and "barrier" reefs, when they stretch parallel with the coast of a continent. In both these cases there is ordinary dry land inside the reef, and separated from it only by a narrower or a wider, a shallower or a deeper, space of sea, which is called a "lagoon," or "inner passage." But there is a third kind of reef, of very common occurrence in the Pacific and Indian Oceans, which goes by the name of an "Atoll." This is, to all intents and purposes, an encircling reef, without anything to encircle; or, in other words, without an island in the middle of its lagoon. The atoll has exactly the appearance of a vast, irregularly oval, or circular, breakwater, enclosing smooth water in its midst. The depth of the water in the lagoon rarely exceeds twenty or thirty fathoms, but, outside the reef, it deepens with great rapidity to 200 or 300 fathoms. The depth immediately outside the barrier, or encircling, reefs, may also be very considerable; but, at the outer edge of a fringing reef, it does not amount usually to more than twenty or twenty-five fathoms; in other words, from 120 to 150 feet.

Thus, if the water of the ocean could be suddenly
5 drained away, we should see the atolls rising from the sea-bed like vast truncated cones, and resembling so many volcanic craters, except that their sides would be steeper than those of an ordinary volcano. In the case of the encircling reefs, the cone, with the enclosed island, would
10 look like Vesuvius, with Monte Nuovo within the old crater of Somma; while, finally, the island with a fringing reef would have the appearance of an ordinary hill, or mountain, girded by a vast parapet, within which would lie a shallow moat. And the dry bed of the Pacific might
15 afford grounds for an inhabitant of the moon to speculate upon the extraordinary subterranean activity to which these vast and numerous "craters" bore witness!

ÆS TRIPLEX [1]

ROBERT LOUIS STEVENSON

The changes wrought by death are in themselves so
sharp and final, and so terrible and melancholy in their
consequences, that the thing stands alone in man's experience, and has no parallel upon earth. It outdoes all other
accidents because it is the last of them. Sometimes it leaps 5
suddenly upon its victims, like a Thug; sometimes it lays
a regular siege and creeps upon their citadel during a score
of years. And when the business is done, there is sore
havoc made in other people's lives, and a pin knocked out
by which many subsidiary friendships hung together. 10
There are empty chairs, solitary walks, and single beds at
night. Again, in taking away our friends, death does not
take them away utterly, but leaves behind a mocking,
tragical, and soon intolerable residue, which must be
hurriedly concealed. Hence a whole chapter of sights and 15
customs striking to the mind, from the pyramids of Egypt
to the gibbets and dule trees of mediæval Europe. The
poorest persons have a bit of pageant going towards the
tomb; memorial stones are set up over the least memorable; and, in order to preserve some show of respect for 20
what remains of our old loves and friendships, we must
accompany it with much grimly ludicrous ceremonial, and
the hired undertaker parades before the door. All this, and

[1] From *Virginibus Puerisque.* Charles Scribner's Sons, New York.

much more of the same sort, accompanied by the eloquence
of poets, has gone a great way to put humanity in error;
nay, in many philosophies the error has been embodied and
laid down with every circumstance of logic; although in
5 real life the bustle and swiftness, in leaving people little
time to think, have not left them time enough to go danger-
ously wrong in practice.

As a matter of fact, although few things are spoken of
with more fearful whisperings than this prospect of death,
10 few have less influence on conduct under healthy circumstances. We have all heard of cities in South America
built upon the side of fiery mountains, and how, even in
this tremendous neighbourhood, the inhabitants are not a jot
more impressed by the solemnity of mortal conditions than
15 if they were delving gardens in the greenest corner of England. There are serenades and suppers and much gallantry
among the myrtles overhead; and meanwhile the foundation shudders underfoot, the bowels of the mountain growl,
and at any moment living ruin may leap sky-high into the
20 moonlight, and tumble man and his merry-making in the
dust. In the eyes of very young people, and very dull old
ones, there is something indescribably reckless and desper-
ate in such a picture. It seems not credible that respect-
able married people, with umbrellas, should find appetite
25 for a bit of supper within quite a long distance of a fiery
mountain; ordinary life begins to smell of high-handed
debauch when it is carried on so close to a catastrophe;
and even cheese and salad, it seems, could hardly be
relished in such circumstances without something like a
30 defiance of the Creator. It should be a place for nobody
but hermits dwelling in prayer and maceration or-mere
born-devils drowning care in a perpetual carouse.

And yet, when one comes to think upon it calmly, the situation of these South American citizens forms only a very pale figure for the state of ordinary mankind. This world itself, travelling blindly and swiftly in overcrowded space, among a million other worlds travelling blindly and swiftly in contrary directions, may very well come by a knock that would set it into explosion like a penny squib. And what, pathologically looked at, is the human body with all its organs, but a mere bagful of petards? The least of these is as dangerous to the whole economy as the ship's powder-magazine to the ship; and with every breath we breathe, and every meal we eat, we are putting one or more of them in peril. If we clung as devotedly as some philosophers pretend we do to the abstract idea of life, or were half as frightened as they make out we are, for the subversive accident that ends it all, the trumpets might sound by the hour and no one would follow them into battle — the blue-peter might fly at the truck, but who would climb into a sea-going ship? Think (if these philosophers were right) with what a preparation of spirit we should affront the daily peril of the dinner-table: a deadlier spot than any battle-field in history, where the far greater proportion of our ancestors have miserably left their bones! What woman would ever be lured into marriage, so much more dangerous than the wildest sea? And what would it be to grow old? For, after a certain distance, every step we take in life we find the ice growing thinner below our feet, and all around us and behind us we see our contemporaries going through. By the time a man gets well into the seventies, his continued existence is a mere miracle; and when he lays his old bones in bed for the night, there is an overwhelming probability that he will

never see the day. Do the old men mind it, as a matter of
fact? Why, no. They were never merrier; they have their
grog at night, and tell the raciest stories; they hear of the
death of people about their own age, or even younger, not
5 as if it was a grisly warning, but with a simple childlike
pleasure at having outlived some one else; and when a
draught might puff them out like a guttering candle, or a
bit of a stumble shatter them like so much glass, their old
hearts keep sound and unaffrighted, and they go on, bub-
10 bling with laughter, through years of man's age compared
to which the valley at Balaclava was as safe and peaceful
as a village cricket-green on Sunday. It may fairly be
questioned (if we look to the peril only) whether it was a
much more daring feat for Curtius to plunge into the gulf,
15 than for any old gentleman of ninety to doff his clothes
and clamber into bed.

We live the time that a match flickers; we pop the
cork of a ginger-beer bottle, and the earthquake swallows
us on the instant. Is it not odd, is it not incongruous,
20 is it not, in the highest sense of human speech, incredible, that we should think so highly of the ginger-beer,
and regard so little the devouring earthquake? The
love of Life and the fear of Death are two famous
phrases that grow harder to understand the more we
25 think about them. It is a well-known fact that an immense proportion of boat accidents would never happen if people held the sheet in their hands instead of
making it fast; and yet, unless it be some martinet
of a professional mariner or some landsman with shat-
30 tered nerves, every one of God's creatures makes it fast.
A strange instance of man's unconcern and brazen bold-
ness in the face of death!

We confound ourselves with metaphysical phrases, which
we import into daily talk with noble inappropriateness.
We have no idea of what death is, apart from its circumstances and some of its consequences to others ; and
although we have some experience of living, there is not 5
a man on earth who has flown so high into abstraction as
to have any practical guess at the meaning of the word
life. All literature, from Job and Omar Khayyam to
Thomas Carlyle or Walt Whitman, is but an attempt to
look upon the human state with such largeness of view as 10
shall enable us to rise from the consideration of living to
the Definition of Life. And our sages give us about the
best satisfaction in their power when they say that it is a
vapour, or a show, or made out of the same stuff with dreams.
Philosophy, in its more rigid sense, has been at the same 15
work for ages ; and after a myriad bald heads have wagged
over the problem, and piles of words have been heaped
one upon another into dry and cloudy volumes without
end, philosophy has the honour of laying before us, with
modest pride, her contribution towards the subject : that 20
life is a Permanent Possibility of Sensation. Truly a fine
result ! A man may very well love beef, or hunting, or a
woman ; but surely, surely, not a Permanent Possibility
of Sensation ! He may be afraid of a precipice, or a den-
tist, or a large enemy with a club, or even an undertaker's 25
man ; but not certainly of abstract death. We may trick
with the word life in its dozen senses until we are weary
of tricking ; we may argue in terms of all the philosophies
on earth, but one fact remains true throughout — that we
do not love life, in the sense that we are greatly preoccu- 30
pied about its conservation ; that we do not, properly
speaking, love life at all, but living. Into the views of the

least careful there will enter some degree of providence ;
no man's eyes are fixed entirely on the passing hour ; but
although we have some anticipation of good health, good
weather, wine, active employment, love, and self-approval,
5 the sum of these anticipations does not amount to anything like a general view of life's possibilities and issues ;
nor are those who cherish them most vividly, at all the
most scrupulous of their personal safety. To be deeply
interested in the accidents of our existence, to enjoy keenly
10 the mixed texture of human experience, rather leads a.
man to disregard precautions, and risk his neck against a
straw. For surely the love of living is stronger in an
Alpine climber roping over a peril, or a hunter riding mer-
rily at a stiff fence, than in a creature who lives upon a
15 diet and walks a measured distance in the interest of his
constitution.

STUDENTS' THEMES: EXPOSITION

HOW TO SAIL A KNOCKABOUT

It will be necessary before describing the sailing of a
boat to give a brief description of its hull and rigging.
Let us take, for example, the small knockabout. This is
a trim little craft about twenty-five feet from stem to stern.
The rig is a small sail or jib before the mast and a main- 5
sail aft of the mast, comprising together an area of about
four hundred square feet. Ropes, called sheets, haul in or
let out the sails, and a rudder connected with a tiller in
the standing-room, controls the direction in which the boat
sails. Ballast, fastened on the keel, prevents her capsiz- 10
ing, and makes her a safe boat for a beginner.

After hoisting the sails, we must see that the halyards,
which raise and lower the sails, are carefully coiled and that
the sheets are clear. Make the tender fast to the end of
the mooring line and pull in on this rope until the boat 15
swings away from the tender. Now jump quickly aft and,
by hauling in the jib sheet, cause the jib to fill and the
boat's head to swing slowly off to leeward. Now, hauling
in the main sheet, which is the rope which controls the
mainsail, make it fast as she gathers headway. 20

Suppose that the wind is coming from the left or port
side of the boat, while both jib and mainsail are hauled in
flat. This is called sailing "close hauled on the port tack."

If the boat is well designed, the tendency of the wind pressure in the jib to force the boat's head off to leeward will
be exactly counteracted by the wind-pressure in the mainsail, which tends to make the boat's head point toward the
5 direction from which the wind is coming. In this case there
will be little occasion to use the rudder to keep her on her
course, since she will practically steer herself.

To tack, or come about on the starboard tack, push the
tiller toward the starboard side of the boat as far as it will
10 go. Quickly she will point up into the wind until the
sails flutter and spill the wind. This is the exact time to
let go the leeward jib sheet. As soon as the wind, coming
now from the other side of the boat, begins to fill the
mainsail, haul in and make fast the leeward jib sheet, —
15 that one which was on the windward side of the boat on
the other tack. This manœuvre, which takes considerable
space for explanation, will be accomplished in a few seconds, during which time the boat will lose little headway.

To run off before the wind, pull the tiller in the direc-
20 tion opposite to that which you wish to take, at the same
time slacking off the main and jib sheets until the boat is
following the direction of the wind. The mainsail will
now be at right angles to the hull and will do most of the
pulling, since the jib will not draw unless held out to
25 windward. It can be held out by a pole extending from
the mast to the lower after end of the jib.

To jibe, — to shift the mainsail from one side of the
mast to the other without coming up into the wind, —
with the sails on the port side of the boat, pull the tiller
30 slowly to starboard, at the same time hauling in the main-
sheet rapidly until the pressure of the wind comes on the
other side of the mainsail. Then let the sheet run until

the sail is at the desired angle on the starboard side. The jib must now be hauled over again to leeward as soon as possible. It is advisable to come about rather than to jibe when there is a strong wind, since the wind is apt to get behind the sail before you can get the main sheet in taut; and this will cause the boom and sail to go over with a force which may prove disastrous to the mast or boom.

When the novice has started back to the anchorage, after going through these manœuvres until he has mastered the first principles, he will have time to look about him. Then he will notice a number of red and black buoys anchored at different places in the harbor. It will be well for him to understand their signification. He will find, on inquiry, that a red buoy is to be left on the starboard hand on entering a harbor, a black buoy on the port. Striped red and black buoys, which indicate an obstruction, may be left on either hand.

As the boat nears the mooring, the question rises how best to approach it. Get directly to leeward of the mooring and luff, — that is, get the mooring directly between the boat and the point from which the wind is coming and put the tiller hard down — namely, following the direction of the wind — so that the boat points directly into the wind's eye. Steer directly for the mooring until the tender is alongside. The shaking sails will act as a brake, and, if the distance has been judged accurately, the boat will lose headway just as she reaches the mooring.

As the beginner furls the sails and makes everything "shipshape," he will consider his afternoon most delightfully spent, unless he is woefully lacking in appreciation of one of the finest sports.

HOW TO MAKE HAY

To explain how a farmer makes hay we must necessarily begin with the time when the grass is ready to be cut, and end when the cured hay is stored away in the barn. This, then, is the extent of the field we intend to
5 cover.

The time when hay should be cut cannot be definitely stated; but experience has taught that by making due allowance for climatic variations, an approximate time may be set. The condition of the grass is, of course, the
10 determining factor. Ordinarily, grass should be cut when the greatest number of valuable plants are beginning to bloom. If left much longer, the nourishment is transferred from the stem to the seeds and leaves, and these are apt to be lost in the making of the hay. To illustrate
15 this, let us take clover as an example. Clover makes excellent food for cows and is, therefore, in great demand. Hay, then, should be cut when the clover, growing up with the grass, contains most of its nourishment in its stem. Thus, all the strength is saved and the value of
20 the hay increased. If, on the contrary, the hay is left until the clover has matured and gone to seed, just so much nourishment is lost. The time when the proper condition is reached varies in different parts of the country, and depends upon the weather. Thus, in the southern states

68

of New England, the grass is usually in a condition to be cut earlier in the season than in the more northern states. As a rule, however, we find that hay-making generally begins either in July or August and continues through August and perhaps into September. Still, this time is subject to change. If a very rainy season sets in, the hay-making is delayed. On the other hand, favorable weather will hasten the time for mowing. On the whole, we may say that the time for cutting hay depends upon the condition of the grass.

When nature has prepared the grass, man is ready to cut it. This cutting should be done on a fine day, as we know from the old saying, "Make hay while the sun shines." If hay is cut while it is raining, the quality is likely to be impaired because of the fact that the grass dries more slowly when down than when standing. Therefore, a fine day should be chosen for the cutting, and the mower should stop work at once if a shower comes up. As soon as the shower has passed, it is well to turn whatever hay has been cut, if there be any, in order that the danger of having bad hay may be minimized. The actual cutting may be done in two ways : either by hand or by machine. In the good old days the farmer took down his scythe from the rafter in the woodshed, ground it a little, and then went to his task of mowing. Now all this is changed. The modern mowing machine does most of the work while man merely drives the team. So completely has the mowing machine revolutionized the method of harvesting hay that it is now used in every accessible place. Only on very hilly ground or in trimming a field is the scythe brought into play. Some men prefer it on

heavy hay, believing that the clean cut which it makes is better for the crop, but this is a point of minor importance. It is true that the working of the blade of the mowing machine necessarily tears the grass and, not in-
5 frequently, injures the aftergrowth. In spite of this injury, however, the labor saved amply rewards the use of a machine. So much for the mowing of the hay.

The real skill displayed in hay-making is shown in the handling of the grass after it is down. If it is cut in the
10 morning, it should be turned over with the fork during the afternoon, or perhaps tedded. Tedding the hay is merely turning it by machine instead of by hand, the advantages being that it does the work quicker and more evenly, and shakes the hay out so that it is better exposed
15 to the action of the wind and sun. The tedder is a light machine usually drawn by a single horse, and has, behind the driver's seat and between the wheels, six or more short forks that alternately kick up and down, three at a time, with the revolving of the wheels. As these forks go down
20 they pick up the hay on the ground and throw it over as they fly up. In this way every bit of hay is thoroughly turned. In the evening it should be raked up into wind-rows and cocked for the night. Cocking the hay consists merely in throwing it together into small piles; but in
25 the construction of these piles much skill may be shown. They should be carefully built so that, if it should rain during the night, they will shed water. Some farmers prefer to cover each haycock with a canvas cover, thus insuring dryness. This practice is to be recommended
30 because, in addition to acting as a protection against rain, the hay is given an opportunity to dry during the night

from its own heat. Like the mowing, the raking is now done almost entirely by machine instead of by hand. The raking machine, usually drawn by one horse, consists essentially of a huge rake with long, curving, iron teeth. Each tooth is so loose that it can slide easily over any 5 large obstacle like a stone. A lever near the driver's seat so controls the frame that it may be raised or lowered as desired. Thus, as soon as enough hay has been gathered, the driver trips the lever and the hay is dumped. However, it is not dumped in any haphazard way, but always 10 in regular windrows. After it has thus been raked and cocked it should be left in cock until the next morning, when, as soon as the dew is off the ground, it should be shaken out and left exposed until cured. The time required for curing depends entirely upon the day. A hot 15 sun and gentle breeze are very favorable, but under ordinary conditions it should be ready to gather up for the barn by noon. Here, then, we have the hay ready for the barn, entirely cured.

All that remains now is to gather it and stow it away 20 in the barn. The loading of the hay upon the wagon is usually done by hand, although a machine has been invented that saves this labor. This machine may well be used if there is a great deal of hay, but the ordinary farmer will pitch it on by hand. In this case an assistant 25 stands in the wagon to spread the hay evenly and trample it down firmly. At the barn the hay may be unloaded either by hand or by a big fork worked by horse-power. The latter method is most frequently used, for the exertion of pitching matted hay off the wagon by hand is very 30 great.

Many farmers nowadays succeed in putting into barns at night the grass which they cut in the morning. Generally, however, these various processes of cutting, tedding, raking and storing the hay, if the weather is fair, 5 will take three or four days.

MODELS OF BIOGRAPHY

JOHN GILLEY [1]

CHARLES WILLIAM ELIOT

John Gilley's first venture was the purchase of a part of a small coasting schooner called the *Preference*, which could carry about one hundred tons, and cost between eight and nine hundred dollars. He became responsible for one-third of her value, paying down one or two hundred dollars, 5 which his father probably lent him. For the rest of the third he obtained credit for a short time from the seller of the vessel. The other two owners were men who belonged on Great Cranberry Island. The owners proceeded to use their purchase during all the mild weather — perhaps six 10 months of each year — in carrying paving-stones to Boston. These stones, unlike the present rectangular granite blocks, were smooth cobblestones picked up on the outside beaches of the neighboring islands. They of course were not found on any inland or smooth-water beaches, but only where 15 heavy waves rolled the beach-stones up and down. The crew of the *Preference* must therefore anchor her off an exposed beach, and then, with a large dory, boat off to her the stones which they picked up by hand. This work was possible only during moderate weather. The stones 20

[1] From *John Gilley, Maine Farmer and Fisherman*, pp. 31–35, 62–72. The American Unitarian Association, Boston, 1904. Copyright owned by The Century Company, New York.

must be of tolerably uniform size, neither too large nor too small; and each one had to be selected by the eye and picked up by the hand. When the dory was loaded, it had to be lifted off the beach by the men standing in the
5 water, and rowed out to the vessel; and there every single stone had to be picked up by hand and thrown on to the vessel. A hundred tons having been thus got aboard by sheer hard work of human muscle, the old craft, which was not too seaworthy, was sailed to Boston, to be dis-
10 charged at what was then called the "Stone Wharf" in Charlestown. There the crew threw the stones out of her hold on to the wharf by hand. They therefore lifted and threw these hundred tons of stone three times at least before they were deposited on the city's wharf. The cobble-
15 stones were the main freight of the vessel; but she also carried dried fish to Boston, and fetched back goods to the island stores of the vicinity. Some of the island people bought their flour, sugar, dry-goods, and other family stores in Boston through the captain of the schooner. John Gilley
20 soon began to go as captain, being sometimes accompanied by the other owners and sometimes by men on wages. He was noted among his neighbors for the care and good judgment with which he executed their various commissions, and he knew himself to be trusted by them. This business
25 he followed for several years, paid off his debt to the seller of the schooner, and began to lay up money. It was an immense satisfaction to him to feel himself thus established in an honest business which he understood, and in which he was making his way. There are few solider satisfactions
30 to be won in this world by anybody, in any condition of life. The scale of the business — large or small — makes little difference in the measure of content.

. . . .

In 1884 the extreme western point of Sutton's Island was sold to a "Westerner," a professor in Harvard College, and shortly after a second sale in the same neighborhood was effected ; but it was not until 1886 that John Gilley made his first sale of land for summering purposes. In the next year he made another sale, and in 1894 a third. The prices he obtained, though moderate compared with the prices charged at Bar Harbor or North-East Harbor, were forty or fifty times any price which had ever been put on his farm by the acre. Being thus provided with what was for him a considerable amount of ready money, he did what all his like do when they come into possession of ready money — he first gave himself and his family the pleasure of enlarging and improving his house and other buildings, and then lent the balance on small mortgages on village real estate. Suddenly he became a prosperous man, at ease, and a leader in his world. Up to this time, since his second marriage, he had merely earned a comfortable livelihood by diversified industry ; but now he possessed a secured capital in addition to his farm and his buildings. At last, he was highly content, but nevertheless ready as ever for new undertakings. His mind was active, and his eye and hand were steady.

When three cottages had stood for several years on the eastern foreside of North-East Harbor, — the nearest point of the shore of Mount Desert to Sutton's Island, — John Gilley, at the age of seventy-one, undertook to deliver at these houses milk, eggs, and fresh vegetables every day, and chickens and fowls when they were wanted. This undertaking involved his rowing in all weathers nearly two miles from his cove to the landings of these houses, and back again, across bay waters which are protected

indeed from the heavy ocean swells, but are still able to produce what the natives call " a big chop." Every morning he arrived with the utmost punctuality, in rain or shine, calm or blow, and alone, unless it blew heavily from
5 the northwest (a head wind from Sutton's), or his little grandson — his mate, as he called the boy — wanted to accompany him on a fine, still morning. Soon he extended his trips to the western side of North-East Harbor, where he found a much larger market for his goods than he had
10 found thirty-five years before, when he first delivered milk at Squire Kimball's tavern. This business involved what was new work for John Gilley, namely, the raising of fresh vegetables in much larger variety and quantity than he was accustomed to. He entered on this new work with
15 interest and intelligence, but was of course sometimes defeated in his plans by wet weather in spring, a drought in summer, or by the worms and insects which unexpectedly attacked his crops. On the whole he was decidedly successful in this enterprise undertaken at seventy-one.
20 Those who bought of him liked to deal with him, and he found in the business fresh interest and pleasure. Not many men take up a new out-of-door business at seventy, and carry it on successfully by their own brains and muscles. It was one of the sources of his satisfaction that he thus
25 supplied the two daughters who still lived at his house with a profitable outlet for their energies. One of these — the school-teacher — was an excellent laundress, and the other was devoted to the work of the house and the farm, and was helpful in her father's new business. John Gilley
30 transported the washes from North-East Harbor and back again in his rowboat, and under the new conditions of the place washing and ironing proved to be more profitable than school-keeping.

In the fall of 1896 the family which had occupied that summer one of the houses John Gilley was in the habit of supplying with milk, eggs, and vegetables, and which had a young child dependent on the milk, lingered after the other summer households had departed. He consented to 5 continue his daily trips a few days into October that the child's milk might not be changed, although it was perfectly clear that his labor could not be adequately recompensed. On the last morning but one that he was to come across from the island to the harbor a strong northeast 10 wind was blowing, and some sea was running through the deep passage between Sutton's Island and Bear Island, which he had to cross on his way to and fro. He took with him in his boat the young man who had been working for him on the farm the few weeks past. They 15 delivered the milk, crossed to the western side of North-East Harbor, did some errands there, and started cheerfully for home, as John Gilley had done from that shore hundreds of times before. The boy rowed from a seat near the bow, and the old man sat on the thwart near the stern, 20 facing the bow, and pushing his oars from him. They had no thought of danger; but to ease the rowing they kept to windward under Bear Island, and then pushed across the deep channel, south by west, for the western point of Sutton's Island. They were more than half-way across 25 when, through some inattention or lack of skill on the part of the young man in the bow, a sea higher or swifter than the rest threw a good deal of water into the boat. John Gilley immediately began to bail, and told the rower to keep her head to the waves. The overweighted boat 30 was less manageable than before, and in a moment another roller turned her completely over. Both men clung to the boat and climbed on to her bottom. She drifted away before the wind and sea toward South-West Harbor. The oversetting of the boat had been seen from both Bear Island and Sutton's Island; but it was nearly three quarters of an hour before the rescuers could reach the floating boat, and then the young man, though unconscious, was still clinging to the boat's keel, but the old man, chilled by the cold water and stunned by the waves which beat about his head, had lost his hold and sunk into the sea. In half an hour John Gilley had passed from a hearty and successful old age in this world, full of its legitimate interests and satisfactions, into the voiceless mystery of death. No trace of his body was ever found. It disappeared into the waters on which he had played and worked as boy and man all his long and fortunate life. He left his family well provided for, and full of gratitude and praise for his honorable career and his sterling character.

This is the life of one of the forgotten millions. It contains no material for distinction, fame, or long remembrance; but it does contain the material and present the scene for a normal human development through mingled joy and sorrow, labor and rest, adversity and success, and through the tender loves of childhood, maturity, and age. We cannot but believe that it is just for countless quiet, simple lives like this that God made and upholds this earth.

SIR WILLIAM TEMPLE[1]

Thomas Babington Macaulay

To say of a man that he occupied a high position in
times of misgovernment, of corruption, of civil and religious faction, and that, nevertheless, he contracted no great
stain, and bore no part in any crime; — that he won the
esteem of a profligate court and of a turbulent people, 5
without being guilty of any great subserviency to either,
— seems to be very high praise; and all this may with
truth be said of Temple.

Yet Temple is not a man to our taste. A temper not
naturally good, but under strict command, — a constant 10
regard to decorum, — a rare caution in playing that mixed
game of skill and hazard, human life, — a disposition to be
content with small and certain winnings rather than go on
doubling the stake, — these seem to us to be the most
remarkable features of his character. This sort of modera- 15
tion, when united, as in him it was, with very considerable
abilities, is, under ordinary circumstances, scarcely to be
distinguished from the highest and purest integrity; and
yet may be perfectly compatible with laxity of principle,
with coldness of heart, and with the most intense selfish- 20
ness. Temple, we fear, had not sufficient warmth and
elevation of sentiment to deserve the name of a virtuous

[1] From *Critical and Miscellaneous Essays.*

man. He did not betray or oppress his country: nay, he rendered considerable service to her; but he risked nothing for her. No temptation which either the King or the Opposition could hold out ever induced him to come for-

5 ward as the supporter either of arbitrary or of factious measures. But he was most careful not to give offence by strenuously opposing such measures. He never put himself prominently before the public eye, except at conjunctures when he was almost certain to gain, and could not possibly

10 lose; — at conjunctures when the interest of the state, the views of the court, and the passions of the multitude all appeared for an instant to coincide. By judiciously avail-ing himself of several of these rare moments, he succeeded in establishing a high character for wisdom and patriotism.

15 When the favourable crisis was passed, he never risked the reputation which he had won. He avoided the great offices of state with a caution almost pusillanimous, and confined himself to quiet and secluded departments of public busi-ness, in which he could enjoy moderate but certain advan-

20 tage without incurring envy. If the circumstances of the country became such that it was impossible to take any part in politics without some danger, he retired to his Library and his Orchard; and, while the nation groaned under oppression, or resounded with tumult and with the

25 din of civil arms, amused himself by writing Memoirs and tying up Apricots. His political career bore some resem-blance to the military career of Louis XIV. Louis, lest his royal dignity should be compromised by failure, never repaired to a siege, till it had been reported to him by the

30 most skilful officers in his service that nothing could pre-vent the fall of the place. When this was ascertained, the monarch, in his helmet and cuirass, appeared among the

tents, held councils of war, dictated the capitulation, received the keys, and then returned to Versailles to hear his
flatterers repeat that Turenne had been beaten at Marien-
dal, that Condé had been forced to raise the siege of Arras,
and that the only warrior whose glory had never been 5
obscured by a single check was Louis the Great! Yet
Condé and Turenne will always be considered captains of
a very different order from the invincible Louis; and we
must own that many statesmen who have committed very
great faults, appear to us to be deserving of more esteem 10
than the faultless Temple. For in truth his faultlessness
is chiefly to be ascribed to his extreme dread of all responsibility; — to his determination rather to leave his country
in a scrape than to run any chance of being in a scrape
himself. He seems to have been averse from danger; and 15
it must be admitted that the dangers to which a public
man was exposed, in those days of conflicting tyranny and
sedition, were of the most serious kind. He could not bear
discomfort, bodily or mental. His lamentations when, in
the course of his diplomatic journeys, he was put a little 20
out of his way, and forced, in the vulgar phrase, to *rough* it,
are quite amusing. He talks of riding a day or two on a
bad Westphalian road, of sleeping on straw for one night,
of travelling in winter when the snow lay on the ground, as
if he had gone on an expedition to the North Pole or to the 25
source of the Nile. This kind of valetudinarian effeminacy,
this habit of coddling himself, appears in all parts of his
conduct. He loved fame, but not with the love of an
exalted and generous mind. He loved it as an end, not at
all as a means; — as a personal luxury, not at all as an 30
instrument of advantage to others. He scraped it together
and treasured it up with a timid and niggardly thrift; and

never employed the hoard in any enterprise, however virtuous and honourable, in which there was hazard of losing one
particle. No wonder if such a person did little or nothing
which deserves positive blame. But much more than this
5 may justly be demanded of a man possessed of such abilities
and placed in such a situation.

Of course a man is not bound to be a politician any
more than he is bound to be a soldier; and there are perfectly honourable ways of quitting both politics and the
10 military profession. But neither in the one way of life, nor
in the other, is any man entitled to take all the sweet and
leave all the sour. A man who belongs to the army only
in time of peace, — who appears at reviews in Hyde Park,
escorts the sovereign with the utmost valour and fidelity
15 to and from the House of-Lords, and retires as soon as he
thinks it likely that he may be ordered on an expedition, —
is justly thought to have disgraced himself. Some portion
of the censure due to such a holiday-soldier may justly fall
on the mere holiday-politician, who flinches from his duties
20 as soon as those duties become difficult and disagreeable;
— that is to say, as soon as it becomes peculiarly important
that he should resolutely perform them.

A POOR RELATION[1]

CHARLES LAMB

At my father's table (no very splendid one) was to be
found, every Saturday, the mysterious figure of an aged
gentleman, clothed in neat black, of a sad yet comely
appearance. His deportment was of the essence of gravity;
his words few or none; and I was not to make a noise in 5
his presence. I had little inclination to do so, for my cue
was to admire in silence. A particular elbow-chair was
appropriated to him, which was in no case to be violated.
A peculiar sort of sweet pudding, which appeared on no
other occasion, distinguished the days of his coming. I 10
used to think him a prodigiously rich man. All I could
make out of him was, that he and my father had been
school-fellows a world ago at Lincoln, and that he came
from the Mint. The Mint I knew to be a place where all
the money was coined — and I thought he was the owner 15
of all that money. Awful ideas of the Tower twined themselves about his presence. He seemed above human infirmities and passions. A sort of melancholy grandeur invested
him. From some inexplicable doom I fancied him obliged
to go about in an eternal suit of mourning; a captive — a 20
stately being let out of the Tower on Saturdays. Often
have I wondered at the temerity of my father, who, in
spite of an habitual general respect which we all in common

---

[1] From "Poor Relations" in *Essays of Elia.*

83

manifested toward him, would venture now and then to
stand up against him in some argument touching their
youthful days. The houses of the ancient city of Lincoln
are divided (as most of my readers know) between the
5 dwellers on the hill and in the valley. This marked distinction formed an obvious division between the boys who
lived above (however brought together in a common school)
and the boys whose paternal residence was on the plain;
a sufficient cause of hostility in the code of these young
10 Grotiuses. My father had been a leading Mountaineer;
and would still maintain the general superiority in skill
and hardihood of the *Above Boys* (his own faction) over
the *Below Boys* (so were they called), of which party his
contemporary had been a chieftain. Many and hot were
15 the skirmishes on this topic.— the only one upon which
the old gentleman was ever brought out — and bad blood
bred; even sometimes almost to the recommencement (so I
expected) of actual hostilities. But my father, who scorned
to insist upon advantages, generally contrived to turn the
20 conversation upon some adroit by-commendation of the old
Minster; in the general preference of which, before all
other cathedrals in the island, the dweller on the hill and
the plain-born could meet on a conciliating level, and lay
down their less important differences. Once only I saw the
25 old gentleman really ruffled, and I remember with anguish
the thought that came over me: " Perhaps he will never
come here again." He had been pressed to take another
plate of the viand, which I have already mentioned as the
indispensable concomitant of his visits. He had refused,
30 with a resistance amounting to rigour, when my aunt, an
old Lincolnian, but who had something of this, in common
with my cousin Bridget, that she would sometimes press

civility out of season, uttered the following memorable
application: "Do take another slice, Mr. Billet, for you
do not get pudding every day." The old gentleman said
nothing at the time, but he took occasion in the course
of the evening, when some argument had intervened 5
between them, to utter, with an emphasis which chilled
the company, and which chills me now as I write it —
"Woman, you are superannuated." John Billet did not
survive long after the digesting of this affront; but he
survived long enough to assure me that peace was actually 10
restored! and, if I remember aright, another pudding was
discreetly substituted in the place of that which had occa-
sioned the offense. He died at the Mint (anno 1781) where
he had long held what he accounted a comfortable independence; and with five pounds, fourteen shillings, and a 15
penny, which were found in his escritoir after his decease,
left the world, blessing God that he had enough to bury
him, and that he had never been obliged to any man for a
sixpence. This was — a Poor Relation.

FRANK DICKSON [1]

Thomas Carlyle

Frank was a notable kind of man, and one of the memorabilities, to Irving as well as me; a most quizzing, merry, entertaining, guileless, and unmalicious man; with very considerable logic, reading, contemptuous observation and
5 intelligence, much real tenderness too, when not obstructed, and a mournful true affection especially for the friends he had lost by death! No mean impediment *there* any more (that was it), for Frank was very sensitive, easily moved to something of envy, and as if surprised when contempt
10 was not possible; easy banter was what he habitually dwelt in; for the rest an honourable, bright, amiable man; alas, and his end was very tragic! I have hardly seen a man with more opulence of conversation, wit, fantastic bantering, ingenuity, and genial human sense of the ridic-
15 ulous in men and things. Charles Buller, perhaps, but he was of far more refined, delicately managed, and less copious tone; finer by nature, I should say, as well as by culture, and had nothing of the fine *Annandale Rabelais* turn which had grown up, partly of will and at length by
20 industry as well, in poor Frank Dickson in the valley of Dryfe amid his little stock of books and rustic phenomena. A slightly built man, nimble-looking and yet lazy-looking, our Annandale Rabelais; thin, neatly expressive aquiline

[1] From *Reminiscences*, pp. 115-117. Scribner, New York, 1881.

face, grey genially laughing eyes, something sternly serious and resolute in the squarish fine brow, nose specially aquiline, thin and rather small. I well remember the
play of point and nostrils there, while his wild home-
grown *Gargantuisms* went on. He rocked rather, and 5
negligently wriggled in walking or standing, something
slightly twisted in the spine, I think; but he made so
much small involuntary tossing and gesticulating while
he spoke or listened, you never noticed the twist. What
a childlike and yet half imp-like volume of laughter lay in 10
Frank; how he would fling back his fine head, left cheek
up, not himself laughing much or loud even, but showing
you such continents of inward gleesome mirth and victorious mockery of the dear stupid ones who had crossed
his sphere of observation. A wild roll of sombre eloquence 15
lay in him too, and I have seen in his sermons sometimes
that brow and aquiline face grow dark, sad, and thunder-
ous like the eagle of Jove. I always liked poor Frank, and
he me heartily. After having tried to banter me down
and recognized the mistake, which he loyally did for him- 20
self and never repeated, we had much pleasant talk together first and last.

STUDENT'S THEME: BIOGRAPHICAL PORTRAIT

A PURITAN OF TO–DAY

When a man has a wife and children to be provided for by the toil of his hands, he rarely bothers himself or others with speculations about the unknown. To pay his rent, rather than to solve the problem of man's relation to his
5 Maker, is his chief concern. In these days, therefore, when every one is busy getting money, it is good to meet a man who thinks as the Hebrew prophets used to think.

Such a man is Joseph Grayson. Up in his Vermont home he is known to his neighbors as a skilful gardener
10 and a good husbandman; but he is better known as a champion of orthodoxy, a cool and formidable debater, a stout defender of the faith. Woe to the unwary theologian who errs in his presence! Grayson's beard may be shaggy, but it frames a shrewd face; his hat may be torn, but it
15 covers a well-rounded and shapely head; his speech may be ungrammatical, but it goes where it is aimed. Of the lore of the Old Testament and the doctrine of the New, Grayson is an oracle; for he was born and bred in a community where the Scriptures were feared and studied.

20 This community was the North of Ireland, where, years ago, there settled certain emigrants from Scotland who had stoutly wrestled with Ritualism and the Papacy.

Their book was the Bible; their interpretation of it was Calvin's *Institutes*. Faithful to their rugged creed, they lived frugal lives and eschewed evil. Born among such conditions, in a home where every Sunday he had to commit whole chapters of the Bible to memory, listen to arguments on Predestination and the Trinity and harrowing descriptions of the final condition of the damned, Grayson not only acquired a familiarity with the Scriptures but a stern and uncompromising loyalty to their Puritan interpretation.

These principles he brought with him to a new country just at the time when "higher criticism," with its theory of evolution and its "God in Everything," was first making inroads upon the hitherto inflexible orthodoxy of the Puritans. Grayson's God was not a "God in Everything," but the Jehovah in the Burning Bush; his Eve was not an improved and evolved oyster, but a direct piece of manufacture from Adam's rib. When he arrived in this country his education was limited, his manners, although well intentioned, were crude. His quick Celtic blood occasionally flashed out; and in daily conversation he developed a pugnacity of argument which was naturally taken for bitterness and fanaticism. But as people came to know him better, as their attacks upon him grew less severe, his steel-plated intolerance softened. Thus he grew up, giving and taking. Gradually he relaxed his insistence upon certain old-fashioned theories of church conduct and church discipline; little by little he ripened and became more equable.

In politics Mr. Grayson does his duty regularly at the polls, not because he likes to vote or because he takes pleasure in the excitement of rival issues, but because it

is unpleasant : whatever is unpleasant seems to this stern
Puritan to be man's duty. With that pessimism which
tinges the view of those who cling to his faith, he beholds
the things of this world as mere idols deep dyed in the
5 depravity that lurks everywhere since man's original sin.
Never will purity and unselfishness triumph, never will
man cease to be guided in the long run by jealousy, cow-
ardice, and meanness, until an angel shall come down
and, binding the Devil with a large chain, send him into
10 solitary confinement. Then, when the Devil is below
instead of rampant in this world, will the great Millen-
nium of Good be ushered in.

As with the older Puritans, John Grayson's theology
tinges not only his politics but his entire life. His read-
15 ing is devoted to the Bible. Equally familiar with the
gentle Sermon on the Mount and the anathemas of Jere-
miah, with the dry legal lore of Leviticus and the subtle
doctrine of Paul, he has at his command a range of information which makes the Bible for him an armory for his
20 Holy War. With what effect he uses his weapons may
be seen from an anecdote. An old Methodist, a renowned
champion of his church, walked into the local grocery
store and, seeing Grayson stroking his beard meditatively,
proceeded thus to draw out the well known oracle: "Gray-
25 son, what do Baptists believe on infant responsibility for
sins?" Without hesitation Grayson answered that the
Scriptures did not show how far they were responsible, but
that since babies were born in sin they would require some
purging to enter into the abode of the sinless. At this
30 the Methodist declared that every sensible man knew that
an infant was innocent and therefore righteous. With a
wise air Grayson inquired how many righteous Lot was

compelled to find if Sodom was to be saved. Said the
Methodist, " If there be ten found righteous, the city will
not be destroyed." " Were there not ten babes in Sodom?"
asked Grayson derisively.

Yet it must not be imagined for a moment that John 5
Grayson is unpractical. Honest as the day is long, he is
nevertheless a shrewd bargainêr. He has acquired money
and he knows how to make it grow. In spite of many
mouths to feed, he has managed each year to lay by a
substantial addition to his savings. 10

So lives a sturdy man. Like the rest of us, his mind,
no doubt, is full of errors. He is opinionated; he is stub-
born. And yet one always knows where he stands. The
world needs just such men. Because in an age of laxity
and extravagance loyalty to faith and simplicity in life 15
and thinking are rarer than they used to be, so are they
the more to be appreciated. So, at least, it has seemed
in the little Vermont village where John Grayson lives.
His tall, broad figure, his dignified walk, his downcast
head are no longer hooted at by the children. There was 20
a time when clerks in the stores would look significantly
at each other and smile as he passed. They do it no
longer. Every one who knows him has learned that
beneath that rather rough exterior there abides a chival-
rous soul, and that John Grayson is truly a man of God. 25

MODELS OF CRITICISM

SIR WALTER SCOTT[1]

Gilbert Keith Chesterton

Walter Scott is a writer who should just now be re-emerging into his own high place in letters, for unquestionably the recent, though now dwindling, schools of severely technical and æsthetic criticism have been unfavourable to him.
5 He was a chaotic and unequal writer, and if there is one thing in which artists have improved since his time, it is in consistency and equality. It would perhaps be unkind to inquire whether the level of the modern man of letters, as compared with Scott, is due to the absence of valleys or
10 the absence of mountains. But in any case we have learnt in our day to arrange our literary effects carefully, and the only point in which we fall short of Scott is in the incidental misfortune that we have nothing particular to arrange.
15 It is said that Scott is neglected by modern readers; if so, the matter could be more appropriately described by saying that modern readers are neglected by Providence. The ground of this neglect, in so far as it exists, must be found, I suppose, in the general sentiment that, like the
20 beard of Polonius, he is too long. Yet it is surely a peculiar

---

[1] From *Varied Types*, Dodd, Mead & Co., New York, 1903.

thing that in literature alone a house should be despised because it is too large, or a host impugned because he is too generous. If romance be really a pleasure, it is difficult to understand the modern reader's consuming desire to get it over, and if it be not a pleasure, it is difficult to 5 understand his desire to have it at all. Mere size, it seems to me, cannot be a fault. The fault must lie in some disproportion. If some of Scott's stories are dull and dilatory, it is not because they are giants, but because they are hunchbacks or cripples. Scott was very far indeed from being 10 a perfect writer, but I do not think that it can be shown that the large and elaborate plan on which his stories are built was by any means an imperfection. He arranged his endless prefaces and his colossal introductions just as an architect plans great gates and long approaches to a really 15 large house. He did not share the latter-day desire to get quickly through a story. He enjoyed narrative as a sensation; he did not wish to swallow a story like a pill, that it should do him good afterwards. He desired to taste it like a glass of port, that it might do him good at the time. The 20 reader sits late at his banquets. His characters have that air of immortality which belongs to those of Dumas and Dickens. We should not be surprised to meet them in any number of sequels. Scott, in his heart of hearts, probably would have liked to write an endless story without either 25 beginning or close.

Walter Scott is a great, and, therefore, mysterious man. He will never be understood until Romance is understood, and that will only be when Time, Man, and Eternity are understood. To say that Scott had more than any other 30 man that ever lived a sense of the romantic seems, in these days, a slight and superficial tribute. The whole modern

theory arises from one fundamental mistake — the idea
that romance is in some way a plaything with life, a fig-
ment, a conventionality, a thing upon the outside. No
genuine criticism of romance will ever arise until we have
5 grasped the fact that romance lies not upon the outside of
life, but absolutely in the centre of it. The centre of every
man's existence is a dream. Death, disease, insanity, are
merely material accidents, like toothache or a twisted
ankle. That these brutal forces always besiege and often
10 capture the citadel does not prove that they are the citadel.
The boast of the realist (applying what the reviewers call
his scalpel) is that he cuts into the heart of life; but he
makes a very shallow incision, if he only reaches as deep as
habits and calamities and sins. Deeper than all these lies a
15 man's vision of himself, as swaggering and sentimental as
a penny novelette. The literature of candour unearths
innumerable weaknesses and elements of lawlessness which
is called romance. It perceives superficial habits like murder
and dipsomania, but it does not perceive the deepest of sins
20 — the sin of vanity — vanity which is the mother of all
day-dreams and adventures, the one sin that is not shared
with any boon companion, or whispered to any priest.

In estimating, therefore, the ground of Scott's preëmi-
nence in romance we must absolutely rid ourselves of the
25 notion that romance or adventure are merely materialistic
things involved in the tangle of a plot or the multiplicity
of drawn swords. We must remember that it is, like
tragedy or farce, a state of the soul, and that, for some
dark and elemental reason which we can never understand,
30 this state of the soul is evoked in us by the sight of certain
places or the contemplation of certain human crises, by a
stream rushing under a heavy and covered wooden bridge,

or by a man plunging a knife or a sword into tough timber.
In the selection of these situations which catch the spirit
of romance as in a net, Scott has never been equalled or
even approached. His finest scenes affect us like fragments
of a hilarious dream. They have the same quality which 5
is often possessed by those nocturnal comedies — that of
seeming more human than our waking life — even while
they are less possible. Sir Arthur Wardour, with his
daughter and the old beggar crouching in a cranny of the
cliff as night falls and the tide closes around them, are 10
actually in the coldest and bitterest of practical situations.
Yet the whole incident has a quality that can only be called
boyish. It is warmed with all the colours of an incredible
sunset. Rob Roy trapped in the Tolbooth, and confronted
with Bailie Nicol Jarvie, draws no sword, leaps from no 15
window, affects none of the dazzling external acts upon
which contemporary romance depends, yet that plain and
humorous dialogue is full of the essential philosophy of
romance which is almost equal betting upon man and
destiny. Perhaps the most profoundly thrilling of all 20
Scott's situations is that in which the family of Colonel
Mannering are waiting for the carriage which may or may
not arrive by night to bring an unknown man into a
princely possession. Yet almost the whole of that thrilling scene consists of a ridiculous conversation about food, 25
and flirtation between a frivolous old lawyer and a fashionable girl. We can say nothing about what makes these
scenes, except that the wind bloweth where it listeth, and
that here the wind blows strong.

It is in this quality of what may be called spiritual 30
adventurousness that Scott stands at so different an elevation to the whole of the contemporary crop of romancers

who have followed the leadership of Dumas. There has, indeed, been a great and inspiriting revival of romance in our time, but it is partly frustrated in almost every case by this rooted conception that romance consists in the vast
5 multiplication of incidents and the violent acceleration of narrative. The heroes of Mr. Stanley Weyman scarcely ever have their swords out of their hands ; the deeper presence of romance is far better felt when the sword is at the hip ready for innumerable adventures too terrible to be
10 pictured. The Stanley Weyman hero has scarcely time to eat his supper except in the act of leaping from a window or whilst his other hand is employed in lunging with a rapier. In Scott's heroes, on the other hand, there is no characteristic so typical or so worthy of humour as their
15 disposition to linger over their meals. The conviviality of the Clerk of Copmanhurst or of Mr. Pleydell, and the thoroughly solid things they are described as eating, is one of the most perfect of Scott's poetic touches. In short, Mr. Stanley Weyman is filled with the conviction that the
20 sole essence of romance is to move with insatiable rapidity from incident to incident. In the truer romance of Scott, there is more of the sentiment of " Oh ! still delay, thou art so fair ! " more of a certain patriarchal enjoyment of things as they are — of the sword by the side and the wine-
25 cup in the hand. Romance, indeed, does not consist by any means so much in experiencing adventures, as in being ready for them. How little the actual boy cares for inci- dents in comparison to tools and weapons may be tested by the fact that the most popular story of adventure is
30 concerned with a man who lived for years on a desert island with two guns and a sword, which he never had to use on an enemy.

ROBERT LOUIS STEVENSON [1]

CHARLES TOWNSEND COPELAND

I

The term *fin de siècle* has come to be one of unmitigated reproach. Whatsoever things are weary, whatsoever things are corrupt, whatsoever things are (or used to be) unmentionable in polite society, are all opprobriously grouped under these three hard-working words. With but four [5] more New Year's Days in the nineteenth century for robust resolutions, four happy new years for a decadent keeping of the same, the anxious question rises whether the hour that begins a hundred new years will mark a stage of progress or only an imaginary line. Will the decadents [10] stop decaying, and the symbolists devise a healthier code of signals demanded by a healthier art? Will there be all sorts of dewy beginnings in literature, and will Paris, ever equal to the occasion, produce some matutinal phrase that shall drive out this hateful vesper term of ennui and [15] disease?

Whatever the event, men may be sure that when the glass has been turned, the scythe whetted, and the joy-bells rung, they will still find time for many backward glances at the hundred years behind them. And they will note [20] the fact that although prose romance in English died with

[1] From "Robert Louis Stevenson," in *The Atlantic Monthly*, April, 1895.

Scott long before the sand was half run out, it was born again, but in less vigor, with Stevenson, another man of his race, while the century-glass yet lacked twenty years of turning. It will be recorded that while the historian of
5 Wessex celebrated the three Fates until people shuddered to see the thread both spun and cut, and a strong young Occidental in the East took pains to show that men's motives are not always better than those which stir the jungle, this northern teller of tales, who shared his empire
10 with them, took upon himself the different and truly romantic task of giving the world pleasure unmixed with pain. And it will likewise be observed, I think, with the wisdom which, I seem to hear the reader say, sits so easily upon critics, whether for prophecy or for retrospect, that
15 Stevenson not only quickened an admirable art, but also founded a school of more and less unsuccessful imitators
. of himself.

Judgment of Mr. Stevenson in his varied activity must be left to *aube de siècle* judges. He will·take the place
20 proper to him without our help; it may be, without theirs. Of obituary lament there has been already enough and to spare ; but the moment admits, perhaps, now that the multitude who mourn him have recovered somewhat from the sorrow and confusion brought by his death to all who
25 care for letters, a brief lingering over a few of those qualities which one reader, at least, has found most salient. That Stevenson was gay and resolute enough to found a school of romance in the midst of opposing tendencies is, of course, the chief quality of all. He loves the past for
30 the courageous picture of it which survives. He blows his wild war-note, unfurls his banner to the breeze of long ago, and goes forth always to the motto, "*Esperance* and set

on." This watchword, indeed, might be set above essay as well as story, travels and verse as well as essay, for in almost all the extraordinary variety of his writing Robert Louis Stevenson is the consistent preacher of courage and cheer. The writer's own brave and most pathetic life was, 5 as the world knows, a consistent practicing of what he preached. In most of his published words, optimism is at the height of the Selkirk grace, or of Happy Thought in a Child's Garden of Verses : —

> " The world is so full of a number of things, 10
> I 'm sure we should all be as happy as kings."

And never, even in A Christmas Sermon or Pulvis et Umbra, does he decline farther into the vale of pessimism than the stage once dubbed meliorism by a great novelist whom he did not love. It is indubitably a help to this 15 philosophy that arrival and success are not among its dreams. The beckoning road and the roadside inn are ever better with Stevenson than the end of the passage. Pleasure lies in running, not in reaching the goal ; and hunger is an infinitely sweeter thing than satiety. "A man's 20 reach " — I have wondered that he nowhere quotes a line with which he everywhere agrees—"a man's reach should exceed his grasp, or what's a heaven for ? "

II

Next in importance, perhaps, to the cardinal trait of Mr. Stevenson's career, that he was a romantic in an age 25 of realism, come the facts that he was a Scotchman, born within the frown of Edinburgh Castle, and that his father and grandfather were engineers to the Board of Northern Lights. This sounds like a business connection with the

Aurora Borealis, but it means merely that the lives of the Stevensons had the relish both of salvation and of adventure, because they were the builders of Skerryvore, the Bell Rock, and other great sea-lights along the north-
5 ern coast of Britain. Much of the best writing of the author of David Balfour — can any one forget the dedication of that book? — thrills and tingles with the feeling of race and native land. I have in mind at this moment The Foreigner at Home, a page or two of The Silverado
10 Squatters, and portions of the paper entitled The Manse, ending with the triumphant picture of ascent from the writer, through engineers, Picts, and what-not clans and tribes, to Probably Arboreal chattering in the top of the family tree. Less often, yet again and again, both in verse
15 and in prose, does Stevenson dwell proudly upon the exploits and the hardy lives of his forbears, and mourn the degeneracy in bodily frame and strength of their hearth-keeping descendant. His whole feeling about all this is in some enchanting lines written at Bournemouth, in a house
20 named after the chief memorial of his family : —

> " Say not of me that weakly I declined
>   The labours of my sires, and fled the sea,
>   The towers we founded and the lamps we lit,
>   To play at home with paper like a child.
25 But rather say : *In the afternoon of time*
>   *A strenuous family dusted from its hands*
>   *The sand of granite, and beholding far*
>   *Along the sounding coast its pyramids*
>   *And tall memorials catch the dying sun,*
30 *Smiled well content, and to this childish task*
>   *Around the fire addressed its evening hours.*"

It never occurred to him that he was the brightest of all the lamps they lit, but many men, even of the not inhuman,

would be content to see Skerryvore itself quenched in the
ocean, if by that extinction the light might shine again on
Vaea Mountain.

III

That Mr. Stevenson is a sworn romantic, and that he is
so much a Scot as to keep a strong flavor of the wilding, 5
in spite of each exotic graft, are truths no less conspicuous
than that he is an exquisite and a secure artist in prose
narrative, in verse, the essay, and the sketch. So perfectly,
indeed, does he write that the Philistines — and not the
mere *bourgeois* citizens of the country, but the first families 10
of Philistia — are often heard to accuse him of having
naught to say. To them, it is more than probable, he has
nothing at all to say, unless they first master certain
remarks once made by Mr. Joseph Addison on the subject
of Literary Taste. But to the minds of men who have a 15
humble and hearty admiration for good writing, Stevenson's tales of adventure gain much from his care about
form ; and his kind and sagacious thoughts gain very much
indeed from the " continual slight novelty " of his style.
This loved and lost story-teller of ours could no more con- 20
tent himself with the construction used by Dumas in his
gay and ragged volumes than with the disposition and
English of the scene in Guy Mannering which jars on him
like a false note in music or color. Yet he had read Le
Vicomte de Bragelonne five times, and hoped — let us trust 25
the hope was realized — to read it once again before he
died. And the jarring scene — which happens, by the way,
to have been that of Harry Bertram's landing at Ellan-
gowan — he respects as being in general "a model instance of
the romantic method." The Meredith jargon Mr. Stevenson 30

would no more think of putting into the mouths of his own people than he would that uttered by the purely symbolic young men and maidens whom Scott fobs off upon us as heroes and heroines. Mr. Meredith is neverthe-
5 less the breath of life to him, and Sir Walter "out and away the king of the romantics."

In these references to Stevenson's art and the frequent artlessness of Scott and Dumas, there is no slightest intention of matching him with them. He would not, if he
10 could, have written like them; he could not, if he would, have imagined and invented and swung the whole thing along as they did. They, with all their faults, are great romantics : he, with all his gifts and graces, is a little romantic ; and the many well-meaning persons who range
15 him persistently with Scott do him nothing but disservice. The appearance of Meg Merrilies to Godfrey Bertram, the abdication of Queen Mary at Lochleven, the installation of the abbot of Kennaquhair, the appeal of Jeanie Deans for Effie, a certain scene in Old Mortality, — the play and
20 stretch and headlong vigor of sheer improvisation that made all these possible, and easily possible, to Scott, are "out of the star" of the author of Kidnapped and David Balfour. Nor, in writing, do I forget Alan and Davie beside the stream, or the bewitching scenes of the wind-
25 mills in Holland, or the duel of the two brothers outside the distracted house of Durrisdeer, when all was so still that the flame of the candles went up straight and steady into the night. But Sir Walter's books seem to me like a large symphony which has many discords ; Mr. Steven-
30 son's, like a discreet yet moving theme, perfectly played on fewer instruments.

To leave the unseemly task of comparison, I am well
aware that there are those who find Mr. Stevenson's art at
fault by times within his chosen province. But The Master of Ballantrae, the chief object of their criticisms, has
been dispraised too harshly. The details, to be sure, are ill   5
blended, but each in itself is admirably worked out; and
the failure (or half failure) at last seems to have come
through a sheer lack of power to fuse the well-selected
elements of the tale. Of details and bits and episodes
there is a vast and engaging variety in the writings of this   10
author. That quaint episode, Providence and the Guitar,
which must be taken as one of the Stevensonian *cruces*,
reflects within its narrow term all the sweetness and light
of Bohemia. That fierce episode, A Story of Francis Villon,
shows forth all the bitterness and blackness which may   15
sometimes darken and make sinister the same cheerful
land. Pictures are often evoked with a few words, as
when the redcoats are seen down the valley from the high-
placed rock among the heather; or as when Jekyll discovers the unconscious transformation into Hyde by seeing   20
his hand upon the bedclothes. There has not been such a
shudder as that in our literature since Crusoe found the
footprint in the sand. Prince Otto, an *opéra bouffe* in
Dresden china, is another Stevensonian *crux*, acceptable
only to the esoteric and the inner circle; but the going of   25
night and the coming of dawn in the forest of Gerolstein
charm the eyes like the sunrise on the Bass Rock.

And so on, indefinitely, these thick-coming memories
might be set down; but it is full time for a word about
Stevenson's style, which is, in the opinion of many, his   30
chief distinction. Several London critics, in the attempt,
perhaps, to avenge certain "Bards" upon their "Reviewers,"

have spoken grudgingly of his wonderful skill, because, forsooth, he learned to write before he wrote for publication. The offense was deeper dyed because the young Scot sought aid from France, the ancient ally of Scotland, and
5 scrupled not to avow that his sojourn in Paris and the study of French writers had taught him secrets of technique. Even British critics allow a painter to study pigments before he exhibits a picture, a sculptor to model in clay before he carves the nation's heroes in marble; but, in the
10 face of repeated blows, the fine old superstition dies hard, that ill-regulated impulse is an important element in the "inspiration" of an art more subtle than either painting or sculpture. Stevenson chose to reduce this element to a minimum, and to make himself the most faithful of appren-
15 tices. He became at last the most impeccable of artists; and although the ardent study of an extraordinary variety of masters did not dull his keen, original gift, — as if, indeed, the right use of even the one talent ever failed to multiply it, — he yet keeps in his most ornate pages the
20 good tradition of the language, the classic note of the best English prose. Stevenson loves and practices the *belle phrase*, the harmonious sentence; but scarce ever does he descend to the indolent *cheville*. Never, to the best of my memory, does he make the Wegg-like change, — so often
25 made by Wegg's creator, that great, imperfect genius, — the change from rhythm to metre. In few, he nicely observes the adjective in Dryden's saying, "the *other* harmony of prose."

STUDENTS' THEMES: CRITICISM

DAILY THEMES ON VARIOUS CRITICAL SUBJECTS

I

In reading Robert Louis Stevenson's *The Merry Men,*
many passages have appealed to me, — so many that I do
not know which way to turn to make my selections of the
most fit. A beautiful description this, — real and even
pathetic: "Was the great treasure ship indeed below 5
there, with her guns and chain and treasure, as she had
sailed from Spain ; her decks a garden for the seaweed,
her cabin a breeding place for the fish, soundless but for
the dredging water, motionless but for the waving of the
tangle upon her battlements — that old, populous, sea- 10
riding castle, now a reef in Sandag bay?" Mark the last
line: "old, populous, sea-riding castle, now a reef in
Sandag bay." How well chosen is each adjective: "old,"
for she was of the mighty Armada; "populous," for
many were the Castilian feet that trampled hurriedly to 15
and fro across her timbered deck; "sea-riding castle," for
all the wealth of fair Spain was in the Armada; gold,
silver, and jewels were not spared; she was the castle of
her commander. But now, sunken, she lay like a corpse
in the bay — silent, motionless, and invisible. 20

II

The story of Jael and Sisera illustrates the immense gulf
between what was considered righteous then and what is
now. People may behave as badly nowadays, but in their
songs of triumph they omit to state the mean expedients
5 by which they conquered. Traitors, though useful, are
kept out of sight in summing up the results. Then, to
Deborah and Barak, confident, in true Hebrew style, that
the "stars in their courses fought against Sisera," Jael was
"blessed above women" for her cruelty and treachery;
10 and savage was their rejoicing at the grief of Sisera's
mother as they pictured her looking through the window
crying, "Why is his chariot so long in coming?"

At the present day woman has assumed many of man's
prerogatives, while retaining, it is said, her inborn guile;
15 but there are only isolated instances of her borrowing his
more savage grandeur, such as patriotic homicide or
diplomatic treachery. Antiquity seems to have revelled in
women like Jael, Judith, Herodias, who sharpened frank
brutality with the edge of feminine deception.

III

20   It is not so much the stately harmony of the First Book
of *Paradise Lost* which fascinates us, as the character of
Satan — great though in ruin. As a type of evil, his
character in this Book may be open to criticism, for he
possesses qualities which call forth admiration, and he
25 expresses opinions which thrill our hearts like martial
music. When he says, "What though the field be lost?
All is not lost," we feel the strength of that indomitable

will and glory in it. And again he stirs our hearts by
saying, "To be weak is miserable, Doing or suffering."
There is a fascination and power about this fallen General,
which makes us rejoice that his hosts spring up to serve
him at his call, and listen with attention to his words. 5.
Everything about him is interesting — his actions, words,
and character — and it is this which makes the First Book
of *Paradise Lost* read the most of the entire poem. Ethic-
ally it may be a mistake to have the Power of Evil such
an attractive character; for although in the other Books 10
he gradually loses every trace of majesty and becomes all
that is despicable, no one thinks of Milton's Satan but as
the colossal figure, undaunted in defeat, who hailed the
horrors of the infernal world.

IV

Why do women dislike the character of Falstaff? Well, 15
for one reason because he is fat. Thomas B. Reed once
said that no gentleman ever weighs over two hundred
pounds. If we change the word gentleman to hero, any
woman.might say the same. Nevertheless, stout men are
sometimes very popular with the opposite sex, and of this 20
Mr. Pickwick is an example. Falstaff, however, is also a
rascal. Now a gentlemanly rascal, such as Robin Hood or
Raffles, is also occasionally admired on account of some
good trait in his character, such as generosity, courteous-
ness, or daring. But to crown all, Falstaff is a coward. 25
That defect can be counterbalanced only by other extremely
prominent virtues, or excused by physical weakness. A
man who is not only fat but a rascal, and not only a fat
rascal, but a cowardly fat rascal, is a person who is de-
servedly despised by any decent, self-respecting woman. 30

V

In Thackeray, as in other writers of that time, I find a marked liking for long, involved sentences, which grow with ease into paragraphs of ten lines or more. But there is a difference between the long sentence of Thackeray and
5 that of Lamb. The latter takes apparent pleasure in using all the ordinary parenthetical marks at once, with the natural result that his work is involved and difficult to understand. The author of *Pendennis*, on the other hand, although his sentences are perhaps as long and as paren-
10 thetical, has the remarkable faculty of arranging his words and phrases in such a way that the meaning is quite evident. During all of my reading in *Pendennis*, I have not once been obliged to reread a sentence in order to understand it, but with Lamb's Essays I was constantly
15 retracing my steps to find out what the author meant. Perhaps a typical sentence taken from each will show more clearly the truth of what I have said. Thus, compare the following passage from Lamb:

" In lieu of our half-pickled Sundays, or quite fresh boiled beef
20 on Thursdays (strong as caro equina), with detestable marigolds floating in the pail to poison the broth — our scanty mutton scrags on Fridays — and rather more savory, but grudging portions of the same flesh, rotten-roasted or rare, on the Tuesdays (the only dish which excited our appetites, and disappointed our stomachs, in equal
25 proportion) — he had his hot plate of roast veal, of the more tempting griskin (exotics unknown to our palates), cooked in the paternal kitchen (a great thing), and brought him daily by his maid or aunt ! "

with this quotation from *Pendennis :*

"In the middle of the night, — as these two ladies, after reading
30 their Bibles a great deal during the evening, and after taking just a

look into Pen's room as they passed to their own, — in the middle
of the night, I say, Laura, whose head not unfrequently chose to
occupy that pillow which the night-cap of the late Pendennis had been
accustomed to press, cried out suddenly, 'Mamma, are you awake?' "

The chief things which make Thackeray's sentences so 5
easy to read are: first, that he makes his parenthetical
statements in a natural order, that is, he puts them just
where you might expect to find them ; secondly, that he
repeats a few words after a parenthesis, thus aiding the
reader to see where the main clause begins; for example, 10
his "in the middle of the night, I say" recalls the beginning of the sentence. How much better would Lamb's
sentence have been, had he inserted "in lieu of all these
things, I say" before "he had his hot plate"! There
would certainly have been an improvement in the clear- 15
ness, but perhaps the charm of Lamb's personality would
have been lost had he stuck too closely to the rules and
regulations governing other writers.

VI

Thackeray conducts the characters in *Pendennis* in a
very easy, almost lazy manner. He realizes that the 20
interests of the whole troupe must be looked after equally,
and that it is not fair to give any of the excursionists too
big a lead. So every now and then he says to Pendennis,
"You lie down and rest awhile. I'll go back and bring up
the Major, Foker, and Captain Costigan, so that you can 25
all start even again in the morning." Then, when the
party get tired, they go and sit under a tree and the
manager gives them a sermon on "How to be happy with
nothing to do," or "High life among the British aristoc-
racy." Thus they stroll happily on for about six hundred 30

and fifty miles, having a few quarrels on the way but nothing serious. Suddenly the starter yells "sprint," and they rush on the next fifty miles at full speed till the announcer calls out, "Pendennis, first! Laura, second!
5 Blanche Amory, distanced!"

VII

Roughly speaking, Ruskin uses color for two purposes,— for mere physical description, and for the further description of character. "Blue islands of Paduan hills, poised in the golden west" suggests chiefly gorgeous sunset hues ;
10 the color in this description appeals to the eye. So does the "pride of purple rocks and river pools of blue" of the Yorkshire hills. Yet in Ruskin's descriptive passages, words denoting color may suggest more; they may reveal character. "The low bronzed gleaming of sea-rusted armor
15 shot angrily under *blood-red* mantle-folds." In the "blood-red" of the mantle-folds is summed up and presented all the fearlessness, the authority, and the grimness of the "majestic" warriors of the sea. Here color suggests not merely physical aspect, but character.
20 As Ruskin uses color for two purposes, so he handles it in two ways,— through direct statement, and through the suggestion of a color by the naming of an object that possesses that color. The "white clouds of heaven" floating over English hills are directly pictured ; so, too, are the
25 "black barges" of the Thames. In the phrase, however, "the mothers and maidens, pure as her pillars of alabaster," the whiteness of purity is suggested through "pillars of alabaster." A more striking example of color-suggestion is the description of Venice, — "the city of marble, the

golden city paved with emerald, a glowing jewel set in an unsullied sea." The first method of using color is more concrete; the second allows more play to the imagination. Ruskin employs both, with the skill of a master, in his descriptions of physical aspect and character.

FORTNIGHTLY THEME: CRITICISM

KIM

For me, a lover and almost a worshiper of Rudyard Kipling, *Kim* has always held a peculiarly seductive charm. I have read reviews which criticized *Kim* viciously and pointed out its immeasurable inferiority to Kipling's
5 shorter stories. Be that as it may, I only intend to express my very humble admiration for the book. That it has faults I should never dare to deny, for every book has faults. To me, however, it has always seemed that its faults are few and that its admirable qualities are many.

10 The chief of these faults, to leave out matters of detail, is the lack of a sustained plot. Exciting at times and always lively, the plot is not steadily interesting. Kim's first journey with the lama, his life in barracks and afterwards at St. Xavier's, his later adventures with the lama
15 and Hurree Gus Chunder, the Babu, seem definitely separated from one another. The interest in the plot almost ceases at the end of each division. *Kim*, unlike some novels which are far inferior to it in other respects, has no suspended interest, gradually increasing until the climax.
20 As far as plot is concerned, then, the interest in *Kim* is not sustained.

This, however, may well be forgiven. For instead of this sort of interest, there is the much more charming interest of description and portrayal of character. For one
25 who has read the book with the slightest appreciation of

112

its beauties, the descriptive passages have great fascination. The description of the Great Road of India, for instance, can hardly be surpassed. The color, glare, and glitter of Indian life leap forth into startling distinctness. It is no mere catalogue of details that is presented there: one sees the bright sun, and feels the warm dust of the road between his toes. As the glamor of the scene overcomes him he wishes to wander with these crowded thousands and to share forever their brilliant, improvident existence.

This, however, is mere external description. So too is the description of the Himalayas, magnificent as it is. One feels that a great deal of its beauty lies in the subject. It is in another scene, almost the last in the book, that the description reaches its climax. Kim, after weeks in bed, is at last allowed to come out. The whole outdoor scene, in its sleepy quietude, is warmed and brightened by a hot, glowing sun. The almost indescribable feeling of the convalescent, which most persons have known at one time or another, infuses the whole scene. I defy anyone who has experienced it to read this passage without again feeling that delicious languor, that sense of remoteness from the surroundings, and that serene, untroubled joy in being alive. Here Kipling has done more than describe externals; he has placed the reader within the character and made him hear, see, feel, smell, and even think as a convalescent. This is more than mere literary skill; it is genius.

This description naturally leads to the consideration of character portrayal, for it is more than half a character sketch in itself. Such touches abound in *Kim*. Even the characterization of the minor actors in the book is fascinating. A sentence, a phrase, or sometimes even a word, is

enough to give us a swift view of the character. The English chaplain, unimportant as he is, belongs to us forever.
We know by heart this wrong-headed, bigoted, honest old
gentleman. The Babu, fat, fearful of pain, yet courageous
5 in the face of death, is a real person. Every little quirk
and turn of his nature is represented. We love profane, ·
wicked, lying, treacherous, and faithful Malibub Ali, faults
and all. The Maharanee, the Jat, that mysterious gentleman known as " E 23," and a score of others are not mere
10 marionettes, but real flesh and blood people who live and
breathe, and love and hate as naturally as our nearest and
dearest friends.

Even more intensely human are the major characters of
the book. If not the greatest, Kimball O'Hara is the most
15 skilfully drawn. His situation is beyond a doubt original.
An Irish lad brought up among the lowest type of Orien-
tals, he is acted upon by opposite influences. His Irish
ancestry impels him to a life of adventure for its own sake,
of violence for the joy of conflict ; his Indian environment
20 drags him to a life of narrow quiet, of deceit as a means
to an end. His Occidental birth enforces late maturity ;
his Oriental training tends toward an early manhood. One
cannot give even an outline of his character in a sentence.
Suffice it to say that he is the triumph of reconciling an
25 Irish birth with an Indian training, an hereditary tendency
toward the open fight with an environment tending toward
deceit.

However, if Kim is the best drawn character of the book,
the greatest creation of character is Tathoo Lama, benev-
30 olent, simple, kind, and good. He is a man who sees the
mote in his own eye, but disregards the beam in his
brother's eye. The dogmas of creed are nothing to him ;

the prejudices of caste trouble him but little. He spends
the declining years of his life hunting for the " River of
Healing which sprang from the Arrow of our Lord Buddha."
Tenderly he loves his " Little Friend of all the World."
Mightily he struggles to free him from his fate. Truly 5
one may say that here was a man who reached the fitting
consummation of a blameless life when, at last, freed from
the " Wheel," " he crossed his hands upon his lap and
smiled, as a man may who has won salvation for himself
and his beloved." 10

MODELS OF ARGUMENT

GOVERNMENT MANAGEMENT OF INDUS-TRIAL ENTERPRISES [1]

ARTHUR TWINING HADLEY

Introduction

By far the most important part of consumers' coöperation is exemplified in government management of industrial enterprises. This differs in two important particulars from the coöperative agencies already described. In the
5 first place the choice of managers of a government business enterprise is connected with the general political machinery of the country, and regulated by constitutional law instead of by statutes of incorporation. In the second place, these managers are likely to fall back on the taxing
10 powers of the government to make up any deficit which may arise in the operations of a public business enterprise; or in the converse case to devote any surplus above expenses to the relief of tax burdens elsewhere. A government enterprise is managed by people who
15 represent, or are supposed to represent, the consumers; but the good or bad economy of its management does not necessarily redound to the profit or loss of those who most use it.[2]

---

[1] From *Economics*, pp. 390–393. G. P. Putnam's Sons, New York, 1896.
[2] It is sometimes said that public business management is neither more nor less than *compulsory* coöperation. But it must be noted that the

It is impossible within the limits of a book like this to examine in detail the successes or failures of government management of industry in the various lines where it has been tried. But it seems both possible and desirable to group together the general causes which have given force to the demand for such management in some directions and have limited its practical usefulness in others.

In the beginning of history, the government is the power that controls the army. When tribes were in a state of warfare with one another, defense against foreign enemies was a matter of primary importance. No man could let his private convenience stand in the way of effective military operations. The discipline and subordination necessary to wage successful war were all-important; and all the powers necessary to maintain such discipline were entrusted to the leaders of the army.

Somewhat later the military authorities undertook the work of maintaining discipline in time of peace as well as of war, and of defining and enforcing the rights of members of the tribe against one another, no less than against foreign enemies. This function was not accorded to them without a struggle. The priests, under whose tutelage the religious sanction for tribal customs had grown up, tried to keep in their own hands the responsibility of upholding these customs and the physical power connected with it.

compulsion is exercised against the taxpayers in general, rather than against the consumers of goods or services provided. Where is the compulsion applied in the management of government railroad ? Not in compelling people to use the road, but in compelling taxpayers to make up any deficit which arises in its operations. Of course the government may exercise an indirect compulsion upon the users of railroads, if it prohibits the building of private lines, and thus forces people to use its services or none at all ; but this is an accidental rather than a universal feature of state railroad management.

In some races they succeeded, but among European peoples
the military authorities took the work of enforcing and
defining laws out of the hands of the priests, and made it
a function of the state as distinct from the church. As
5 security from foreign enemies increased, this law-making
power became more and more important. The government
was less exclusively identified with the army, and more
occupied with the courts, the legislatures, and the internal
police. Its judicial and legislative functions assumed a
10 prominence at least as great as its military function.

The growth of private property was also coincident with
the development of these domestic functions of government. In fact the two things reinforced one another.
The production and accumulation of capital, to which
15 private property gave so vigorous an impulse, placed the
strong men of the community in a position where they had
less to gain by war and more by peace. It put them on
the side of internal tranquillity. It thus made the government more powerful, and this in turn still further increased
20 the accumulations of capital. But along with this mutual
help, which strong domestic government and strong property right rendered one another, there was an element of
mutual antagonism. The very fulfilment of those functions
which made the accumulation of capital possible, rendered
25 it impossible for the government to do its work except at
the expense of the capitalists. It was no longer possible to
support armies by booty, or courts by fines and forfeitures.
The expense of maintaining order had to be paid by its
friends instead of its enemies. The growth of private
30 property was followed by the development of a system of
taxation, which, in theory at any rate, involved the power
to destroy such property.

The existence of such a system of taxation, with the machinery for collecting money in this way, allows the government more freedom of industrial action than any private individual can command.   It can make up a deficit by compulsory payments; and this gives it a wider range of power in deciding what services it will undertake and what prices it will charge — a power which affords almost unlimited opportunity for good or bad use, according to the degree of skill and integrity with which it is exercised.

Every extension of government activity into new fields restricts private enterprise in two ways; first by limiting the field for investment of private capital, and second, by possibly, if not probably, appropriating through taxation a part of the returns from private enterprise in all other fields.   The question whether a government should manage an industry reduces itself to this: Are the deficiencies or evils connected with private management such that it is wise to give government officials the taxing power which constitutes the distinctive feature of public industrial management?

THE FALLACY OF THE BALANCE OF TRADE[1]

DANIEL WEBSTER

Refutation

Mr. Chairman, I will now proceed to say a few words upon a topic, but for the introduction of which into this debate, I should not have given the Committee, on this occasion, the trouble of hearing me. Some days ago — I
5 believe it was when we were settling the controversy between the oil merchants and the tallow-chandlers — the *balance of trade* made its appearance in debate, and I must confess, sir, that I spoke of it, or rather spoke to it, somewhat freely and irreverently. I believe I used the hard
10 names which have been imputed to me ; and I did it simply for the purpose of laying the spectre and driving it back to its tomb. Certainly, sir, when I called the old notion on this subject nonsense, I did not suppose that I should offend any one, unless the dead should happen to
15 hear me. All the living generation, I took it for granted, would think the term very properly applied. In this, however, I was mistaken. The dead and the living rise up together to call me to account, and I must defend myself as well as I am able.

20 Let us inquire, then, sir, what is meant by an unfavorable balance of trade, and what the argument is, drawn from that source. By an unfavorable balance of trade, I

---

[1] From *Speech on the Tariff*, delivered in the House of Representatives of the United States, April 1 and 2, 1824. Webster's Works, III, 118–120. Little, Brown & Co., Boston, 1881.

understand, is meant that state of things in which impor-
tation exceeds exportation. To apply it to our own case,
if the value of goods imported exceed the value of those
exported, then the balance of trade is said to be against us,
inasmuch as we have run in debt to the amount of this   5
difference. Therefore it is said that if a nation continue
long in a commerce like this, it must be rendered absolutely bankrupt. It is in the condition of a man that buys
more than he sells ; and how can such a traffic be maintained
without ruin ? Now, sir, the whole fallacy of this argument   10
consists in supposing that, whenever the value of imports
exceeds that of exports, a debt is necessarily created to
the extent of the difference ; whereas, ordinarily, the import is no more than the result of the export, augmented
in value by the labor of transportation. The excess of im-   15
ports over exports, in truth, usually shows the gains, not
the losses, of trade ; or, in a country that not only buys
and sells goods, but employs ships in carrying goods also,
it shows the profits of commerce and the earnings of navi-
gation. Nothing is more certain than that in the usual   20
course of things, and taking a series of years together, the
value of our imports is the aggregate of our exports and
our freights. If the value of commodities imported in a
given case did not exceed the value of the outward cargo,
with which they were purchased, then it would be clear to   25
every man's common sense that the voyage had not been
profitable. If such commodities fell far short in value of
the cost of the outward cargo, then the voyage would be
a very losing one ; and yet it would present exactly that
state of things which, according to the notion of a balance   30
of trade, can alone indicate a prosperous commerce. On
the other hand, if the return cargo were found to be worth

much more than the outward cargo, while the merchant, having paid for the goods exported, and all the expenses of the voyage, finds a handsome sum yet in his hands which he calls profits, the balance of trade is still against him, and, whatever he may think of it, he is in a very bad way. Although one individual or all individuals gain, the nation loses; while all its citizens grow rich, the country grows poor. This is the doctrine of the balance of trade. Allow me, sir, to give an instance tending to show how unaccountably individuals deceive themselves and imagine themselves to be somewhat rapidly mending their condition, while they ought to be persuaded that, by that infallible standard, the balance of trade, they are on the high road to ruin. Some years ago, in better times than the present, a ship left one of the towns of New England with 70,000 specie dollars. She proceeded to Mocha, on the Red Sea, and there laid out these dollars in coffee, drugs, spices, and other articles procured in that market. With this new cargo she proceeded to Europe; two thirds of it were sold in Holland for $130,000, which the ship brought back and placed in the same bank from the vaults of which she had taken her original outfit. The other third was sent to the ports of the Mediterranean, and produced a return of $25,000 in specie and $15,000 in Italian merchandise. These sums together make $170,000 imported, which is $100,000 more than was exported, and is therefore proof of an unfavorable balance of trade, to that amount, in this adventure. We should find no great difficulty, sir, in paying off our balances if this were the nature of them all.

THE PUBLIC DUTY OF EDUCATED MEN [1]

GEORGE WILLIAM CURTIS

Persuasion

It is with diffidence that I rise to add any words of
mine to the music of these younger voices. This day,
Gentlemen of the Graduating Class, is especially yours.
It is a day of high hope and expectation; and the coun-
sels that fall from older lips should be carefully weighed, 5
lest they chill the ardor of a generous enthusiasm or stay
the all-conquering faith of youth that moves the world.
To those who, constantly and actively engaged in a thousand pursuits, are still persuaded that educated intelligence
molds states and leads mankind, no day in the year is more 10
significant, more inspiring, than this of the College Commencement. It matters not at what college it may be celebrated. It is the same at all. We stand here indeed beneath
these College walls, beautiful for situation, girt at this moment with the perfumed splendor of midsummer, and full 15
of tender memories and joyous associations to those who
hear me. But on this day, and on other days, at a hundred
other colleges, this summer sun beholds the same spectacle
of eager and earnest throngs. The faith that we hold, they
also cherish. It is the same God that is worshipped at the 20
different altars. It is the same benediction that descends
upon every reverent head and believing heart. In this

[1] From the oration delivered at the Commencement of Union College,
June 27, 1877. J. Munsell, Albany, N.Y., 1878.

annual celebration of faith in the power and the responsibility of educated men, all the colleges in the country,
in whatever state, of whatever age, of whatever religious
sympathy or direction, form but one great Union University.
5 But the interest of the day is not that of mere study,
of sound scholarship as an end, of good books for their
own sake, but of education as a power in human affairs,
of educated men as an influence in the commonwealth.
" Tell me," said an American scholar of Goethe, the many-
10 sided, " what did he ever do for the cause of man? " The
scholar, the poet, the philosopher, are men among other
men. From these unavoidable social relations spring opportunities and duties. How do they use them? How do they
discharge them? Does the scholar show in his daily walk
15 that he has studied the wisdom of ages in vain? Does the
poet sing of angelic purity and lead an unclean life? Does
the philosopher peer into other worlds, and fail to help
this world upon its way? Four years before our Civil
War, the same scholar — it was Theodore Parker — said
20 sadly: " If our educated men had done their duty, we
should not now be in the ghastly condition we bewail."
The theme of to-day seems to me to be prescribed by the
occasion. It is the festival of the departure of a body of
educated young men into the world. This company of
25 picked recruits marches out with beating drums and flying colors to join the army. We who feel that our fate
is gracious which allowed a liberal training, are here to
welcome and to advise. On your behalf, Mr. President
and Gentlemen, with your authority, and with all my
30 heart, I shall say a word to them and to you of the public
duty of educated men in America.

.   .   .   .

The first object of concerted political action is the highest welfare of the country. But the conditions of party association are such that the means are constantly and easily substituted for the end. The sophistry is subtle and seductive. Holding the ascendency of his party essen- 5 tial to the national welfare, the zealous partizan merges patriotism in party. He insists that not to sustain the party is to betray the country, and against all honest doubt and reasonable hesitation and reluctance, he vehemently urges that quibbles of conscience must be sacri- 10 ficed to the public good; that wise and practical men will not be squeamish; that every soldier in the army cannot indulge his own whims; and that if the majority may justly prevail in determining the government, it must not be questioned in the control of the party.   15

This spirit adds moral coercion to sophistry. It denounces as a traitor him who protests against party tyranny, and it makes unflinching adherence to what is called regular party action the condition of the gratification of honorable political ambition. Because a man who sympathizes with 20 the party aims refuses to vote for a thief, this spirit scorns him as a rat and a renegade. Because he holds to principle and law against party expediency and dictation, he is proclaimed to have betrayed his country, justice, and humanity. Because he tranquilly insists upon deciding for himself 25 when he must dissent from his party, he is reviled as a popinjay and a visionary fool. Seeking with honest purpose only the welfare of his country, the hot air around him hums with the cry of " the grand old party," " the traditions of the party," " loyalty to the party," " future 30 of the party," " servant of the party "; and he sees and hears the gorged and portly money-changers in the temple

usurping the very divinity of the God. Young hearts !
be not dismayed. If ever any one of you shall be the man
so denounced, do not forget that your own individual convictions are the whip of small cords which God has put
5 into your hands to expel the blasphemers.

The same party spirit naturally denies the patriotism of
its opponents. Identifying itself with the country, it regards all others as public enemies. This is substantially
revolutionary politics. It is the condition of France, where,
10 in its own words, the revolution is permanent. Instead of
regarding the other party as legitimate opponents — in the
English phrase, His Majesty's Opposition — lawfully seeking a different policy under the government, it decries that
party as a conspiracy plotting the overthrow of the gov-
15 ernment itself. History is lurid with the wasting fires of
this madness. We need not look to that of other lands.
Our own is full of it. It is painful to turn to the opening
years of the Union, and see how the great men whom we
are taught to revere, and to whose fostering care the be-
20 ginning of the republic was intrusted, fanned their hatred
and suspicion of each other. Do not trust the flattering
voices that whisper of a Golden Age behind us, and
bemoan our own as a degenerate day. The castles of
hope always shine along the horizon. Our fathers saw
25 theirs where we are standing. We behold ours where our
fathers stood. But pensive regret for the heroic past, like
eager anticipation of the future, shows only that the vision
of a loftier life forever allures the human soul. We think
our fathers to have been wiser than we, and their day
30 more enviable. But eighty years ago the Federalists ab-
horred their opponents as Jacobins, and thought Robespierre and Marat no worse than Washington's Secretary

of State. Their opponents retorted that the Federalists were plotting to establish a monarchy by force of arms. The New England pulpit anathematized Tom Jefferson as an atheist and a satyr. Jefferson denounced John Jay as a rogue, and the chief newspaper of the opposition, on the morning that Washington retired from the presidency, thanked God that the country was now rid of the man who was the source of all its misfortunes. There is no mire in which party spirit wallows to-day with which our fathers were not befouled, and how little sincere the vitu- peration was, how shallow a fury, appears when Jefferson and Adams had retired from public life. Then they corre- sponded placidly and familiarly, each at last conscious of the other's fervent patriotism; and when they died, they were lamented in common by those who in their names had flown at each other's throats, as the patriarchal Castor and Pollux of the pure age of our politics, now fixed as a constellation of hope in our heaven.

The same brutal spirit showed itself at the time of Andrew Johnson's impeachment. Impeachment is a pro- ceeding to be instituted only for great public reasons, which should, presumptively, command universal support. To prostitute the power of impeachment to a mere party purpose would readily lead to the reversal of the result of an election. But it was made a party measure. The party was to be whipped into its support; and when cer- tain senators broke the party yoke upon their necks, and voted according to their convictions, as honorable men always will, whether the party whips like it or not, one of the whippers-in exclaimed of a patriotism the struggle of obedience to which cost one senator, at least, his life, — "If there is anything worse than the treachery, it is the

cant which pretends that it is the result of conscientious
conviction; the pretense of a conscience is quite unbearable." This was the very acridity of bigotry, which in
other times and countries raised the cruel tribunal of the
5 Inquisition, and burned opponents for the glory of God.
The party madness that dictated these words, and the
sympathy that approved them, was treason not alone to
the country but to well-ordered human society. Murder
may destroy great statesmen, but corruption makes great
10 states impossible; and this was an attempt at the most
insidious corruption. The man who attempts to terrify a
senator of the United States to cast a dishonest vote, by
stigmatizing him as a hypocrite and devoting him to party
hatred, is only a more plausible rascal than his opponent
15 who gives Pat O'Flanagan a fraudulent naturalization
paper or buys his vote with a dollar or a glass of whiskey.
Whatever the offenses of the President may have been,
they were as nothing when compared with the party spirit
which declared that it was tired of the intolerable cant of
20 honesty. So the sneering cavalier was tired of the cant of
the Puritan conscience; but the conscience of which plumed
Injustice and coroneted Privilege were tired has been for
three centuries the invincible body-guard of civil and
religious liberty.

25   Gentlemen, how dire a calamity the same party spirit
was preparing for the country within a few months, we
can now perceive with amazement and with hearty thanks-
giving for a great deliverance. The ordeal of last winter
was the severest strain ever yet applied to republican
30 institutions. It was a mortal strain along the very fiber
of our system. It was not a collision of sections, nor a
conflict of principles of civilization. It was a supreme

and triumphant test of American patriotism. Greater
than the declaration of independence by colonies hopelessly alienated from the Crown and already in arms;
greater than emancipation, as a military expedient, amid
the throes of civil war, was the peaceful and reasonable 5
consent of two vast parties — in a crisis plainly foreseen
and criminally neglected — a crisis in which each party
asserted its solution to be indisputable — to devise a lawful settlement of the tremendous contest, a settlement
which, through furious storms of disappointment and 10
rage, has been religiously respected. We are told that
our politics are mean — that already, in its hundredth
year, the decadence of the American republic appears and
the hope of the world is clouded. But tell me, scholars,
in what high hour of Greece, when, as De Witt Clinton 15
declared, "the herb-woman could criticise the phraseology
of Demosthenes, and the meanest artisan could pronounce
judgment on the works of Apelles and Phidias," or at
what proud epoch of imperial Rome or millennial moment
of the fierce Italian republics, was ever so momentous a 20
party difference so wisely, so peacefully, so humanely,
composed? Had the sophistry of party prevailed, had
each side resolved that not to insist upon its own claim
at every hazard was what the mad party spirit of each
side declared it to be, a pusillanimous surrender; had the 25
spirit of Marius mastered one party and that of Sylla the
other, this waving valley of the Mohawk would not to-day
murmur with the music of industry, and these tranquil
voices of scholars blending with its happy harvest song;
it would have smoked and roared with fraternal war, and 30
this shuddering river would have run red through desolated
meadows and by burning homes.

It is because these consequences are familiar to the knowledge of educated and thoughtful men that such men are constantly to assuage this party fire and to take care that party is always subordinated to patriotism. Per-
5 fect party discipline is the most dangerous weapon of party spirit, for it is the abdication of the individual judgment: it is the application to political parties of the Jesuit principle of implicit obedience.

It is for you to help break this withering spell. It is
10 for you to assert the independence and the dignity of the individual citizen, and to prove that party was made for the voter, not the voter for party. When you are angrily told that if you erect your personal whim against the regular party behest, you make representative government
15 impossible by refusing to accept its conditions, hold fast by your own conscience and let the party go. There is not an American merchant who would send a ship to sea
. under the command of Captain Kidd, however skillful a sailor he might be. Why should he vote to send Captain
20 Kidd to the legislature or to put him in command of the ship of state because his party directs? The party which to-day nominates Captain Kidd, will to-morrow nominate Judas Iscariot; and to-morrow, as to-day, party spirit will spurn you as a traitor for refusing to sell your master.
25 "I tell you," said an ardent and well-meaning partizan, speaking of a closely contested election in another state, "I tell you it is a nasty state, and I hope we have done nasty work enough to carry it." But if your state has been carried by nasty means this year, success will require
30 nastier next year, and the nastiest means will always carry it. The party may win, but the state will have been lost, for there are successes which are failures. When a man

is sitting upon the bough of a tree and diligently sawing it off between himself and the trunk, he may succeed, but his success will break his neck.

The remedy for the constant excess of party spirit lies, and lies alone, in the courageous independence of the indi- 5 vidual citizen. The only way, for instance, to procure the party nomination of good men, is for every self-respecting voter to refuse to vote for bad men. In the mediæval theology the devils feared nothing so much as the drop of holy water and the sign of the cross, by which they 10 were exorcised. The evil spirits of party fear nothing so much as bolting and scratching. *In hoc signo vinces.* If a farmer would reap a good crop, he scratches the weeds out of his field. If we would have good men upon the ticket, we must scratch bad men off. If the scratching 15 breaks down the party, let it break; for the success of the party by such means would break down the country. The evil spirits must be taught by means that they can understand. " Them fellers " — said the captain of a canal boat of his men — " them fellers never think you mean a 20 thing until you kick 'em. They feel that, and understand."

It is especially necessary for us to perceive the vital relation of individual courage and character to the common welfare because ours is a government of public opinion, and public opinion is but the aggregate of individual 25 thought. We have the awful responsibility as a community of doing what we choose; and it is of the last importance that we choose to do what is wise and right. In the early days of the anti-slavery agitation a meeting was called at Faneuil Hall, in Boston, which a good-natured 30 mob of soldiers was hired to suppress. They took possession of the floor and danced breakdowns and shouted

choruses and refused to hear any of the orators upon the
platform. The most eloquent pleaded with them in vain.
They were urged by the memories of the Cradle of Liberty,
for the honor of Massachusetts, for their own honor as
5 Boston boys, to respect liberty of speech. But they still
laughed and sang and danced, and were proof against
every appeal. At last a man suddenly arose from among
themselves, and began to speak. Struck by his tone and
quaint appearance, and with the thought that he might
10 be one of themselves, the mob became suddenly still.
" Well, fellow-citizens," he said, "I would n't be quiet if
I did n't want to." The words were greeted with a roar
of delight from the mob, which supposed it had found its
champion, and the applause was unceasing for five minutes,
15 during which the strange orator tranquilly awaited his
chance to continue. The wish to hear more hushed the
tumult, and when the hall was still he resumed: " No, I
certainly would n't stop if I had n't a mind to; but then,
if I were you, I *would* have a mind to!" The oddity of
20 the remark and the earnestness of the tone held the crowd
silent, and the speaker continued, " not because this is
Faneuil Hall, nor for the honor of Massachusetts, nor
because you are Boston boys, but because you are men,
and because honorable and generous men always love fair
25 play." The mob was conquered. Free speech and fair
play were secured. Public opinion can do what it has
a mind to in this country. If it be debased and demoral-
ized, it is the most odious of tyrants. It is Nero and
Caligula multiplied by millions. Can there then be a
30 more stringent public duty for every man — and the
greater the intelligence the greater the duty — than to
take care, by all the influence he can command, that the

country, the majority, public opinion, shall have a mind
to do only what is just and pure, and humane?

Gentlemen, leaving this college to take your part in
the discharge of the duties of American citizenship, every
sign encourages and inspires. The year that is now end- 5
ing, the year that opens the second century of our history,
has furnished the supreme proof that in a country of rigorous party division the purest patriotism exists. That
and that only is the pledge of a prosperous future. No
mere party fervor, or party fidelity, or party discipline, 10
could fully restore a country torn and distracted by the
fierce debate of a century and the convulsions of civil
war; nothing less than a patriotism all-embracing as the
summer air could heal a wound so wide. I know — no
man better — how hard it is for earnest men to separate 15
their country from their party, or their religion from their
sect. But nevertheless the welfare of the country is dearer
than the mere victory of party, as truth is more precious
than the interest of any sect. You will hear this patriotism scorned as an impracticable theory, as the dream of a 20
cloister, as the whim of a fool. But such was the folly of
the Spartan Leonidas, staying with his three hundred the
Persian horde and teaching Greece the self-reliance that
saved her. Such was the folly of the Swiss Arnold von
Winkelried, gathering into his own breast the host of 25
Austrian spears, making his dead body the bridge of victory for his countrymen. Such was the folly of the American Nathan Hale, gladly risking the seeming disgrace of
his name, and grieving that he had but one life to give
for his country. Such are the beacon-lights of a pure pa- 30
triotism that burn forever in men's memories and answer
each other through the illuminated ages. And of the same

grandeur, in less heroic and poetic form, was the patriotism
of Sir Robert Peel in recent history. He was the leader
of a great party and the prime minister of England. The
character and necessity of party were as plain to him as
5 to any man. But when he saw that the national welfare
demanded the repeal of the corn-laws which he had always
supported, he did not quail. Amply avowing the error of
a life and the duty of avowing it—foreseeing the probable
overthrow of his party and the bitter execration that must
10 fall upon him, he tranquilly did his duty. With the eyes
of England fixed upon him in mingled amazement, admiration, and indignation, he rose in the House of Commons
to perform as great a service as any English statesman
ever performed for his country, and in closing his last
15 speech in favor of the repeal, describing the consequences
that its mere prospect had produced, he loftily exclaimed:
" Where there was dissatisfaction, I see contentment; where
there was turbulence, I see there is peace; where there
was disloyalty, I see there is loyalty. I see a disposition
20 to confide in you, and not to agitate questions that are
the foundations of your institutions." When all was over,
when he had left office, when his party was out of power,
and the fury of party execration against him was spent,
his position was greater and nobler than it had ever been.
25 Cobden said of him, " Sir Robert Peel has lost office, but
he has gained a country "; and Lord Dalling said of him,
what may truly be said of Washington: " Above all parties,
himself a party, he had trained his own mind into a dis-
interested sympathy with the intelligence of his country."
30 A public spirit so lofty is not confined to other ages
and lands. You are conscious of its stirrings in your souls.
It calls you to courageous service, and I am here to bid

you obey the call. Such patriotism may be ours. Let it be your parting vow that it shall be yours. Bolingbroke described a patriot king in England; I can imagine a patriot president in America. I can see him indeed the choice of a party, and called to administer the govern- 5 ment when sectional jealousy is fiercest and party passion most inflamed. I can imagine him seeing clearly what justice and humanity, the national law and the national welfare, require him to do, and resolved to do it. I can imagine him patiently enduring not only the mad cry of 10 party hate, the taunt of " recreant" and " traitor," of " renegade " and " coward," but what is harder to bear, the amazement, the doubt, the grief, the denunciation, of those as sincerely devoted as he to the common welfare. I can imagine him pushing firmly on, trusting the heart, 15 the intelligence, the conscience of his countrymen, healing angry wounds, correcting misunderstandings, planting justice on surer foundations, and, whether his party rise or fall, lifting his country heavenward to a more perfect union, prosperity, and peace. This is the spirit of a pa- 20 triotism that girds the commonwealth with the resistless splendor of the moral law — the invulnerable panoply of states, the celestial secret of a great nation and a happy people.

THE OPEN SHOP[1]

Lyman Abbott

Our object in this article is, first, to define the issue
joined between the " open shop " and the " closed shop " ;
and, secondly, to give our judgment on that issue and the
reasons upon which it is based.

5 An open shop is one in which union men and non-union
men may work side by side upon equal terms. A closed
shop is one from which either union men are excluded by
the employer, or non-union men are excluded by the union ;
but, ordinarily, the term is applied only to those shops
10 which are closed against non-union men by the refusal of
union men to work with them. It is in that sense we use
the phrase in this article. Are trades-unions justified in
insisting upon the closed shop — in insisting, that is, upon
the exclusion from the industry in which they are engaged
15 of all workingmen who do not belong to the union?

The arguments for the closed shop deserve careful consideration ; they may be briefly stated thus : Workingmen
have a right to choose *with* whom they shall work, as well
as *under* whom they shall work. Sometimes the industry
20 is made extra-hazardous by the employment of an incom-
petent workingman ; often it is made extra-difficult. For
this reason a fireman has a right to refuse to work with a
green locomotive engineer, or a locomotive engineer with

---

[1] From *The Outlook* (July 16, 1904), Vol. LXXVII, pp. 630 ff.

a green fireman. But a workman has a right to protect not
only his life, but also his feeling. He has the right to refuse to work in the intimacy of a common employment with
a man who is *persona non grata ;* and there is a real reason
why the non-union man is *persona non grata* to the union 5
man. Without sharing the expenses or the obligations of
the union, he gets—in improved conditions, better wages,
and shorter hours—all the benefits which the union secures
from the employer. The union man has a right to refuse
to work with a companion who takes all the advantages of 10
the union without sharing its burdens. Moreover, if the
shop is open on equal terms to both union men and non-
union men, the employer will be apt gradually to supplant
the union men with non-union men, because it is easy to
increase the hours and reduce the wages where there is no 15
union to interpose organized resistance to such industrial
injustice. Finally, the object of the union is not merely to
get larger wages, lessened hours, and better conditions.
The workingman denies the assumed right of the employer
to manage his business as he pleases. He insists that the 20
employer and employed are partners in a common enterprise, and that the employee has a right to be consulted
as to the conditions of the work, and to share in its prosperity when it is prosperous, as he is certain to share in
its adversity when it is unprosperous. The object of the 25
union is to secure a real co-operation for the workingman
with the employer, on something like equal terms. This
can be done only by "collective bargaining"; that is, by
an agreement entered into by a body of workingmen acting
together as a union, with the employer, who is generally 30
a body of capitalists acting together in a corporation.
Only thus can democratization of industry be secured and

the autocracy of industry be ended ; and this result is
indispensable in order to bring the industrial organization
of America into harmony with its political, educational,
and religious organizations.

5 These considerations seem to us to furnish very good
reasons for the organization of labor. But do they also
furnish good reasons for compelling workingmen to join
organizations of labor against their will? For the real
question at issue between the closed shop and the open
10 shop is not, Shall labor organize in order to deal on terms
of greater equality with organized capital? but, Shall the
laborer be compelled to join such organization in order to
get opportunity to labor?

This question is really two questions: Is the closed
15 shop illegal? If not illegal, is it against the public interest,
and therefore and to that extent immoral?

In a recent case in Illinois the closed shop has been
adjudged illegal. From the decision, rendered in June last,
an appeal has been taken to the Supreme Court of the
20 State, and pending that appeal the decision cannot be regarded as conclusive. In this case a draft agreement was
proposed by a trades-union, which provided that only men
of the union should be employed, and, this agreement
being rejected by the employer, a strike was declared, and
25 picketing was instituted to reinforce the strike. The
Court held not only that the picketing was unlawful
because it involved a suggestion of violence, but that the
strike was unlawful because it was an endeavor to coerce
an employer to make a contract against his will, and that
30 the contract itself would have been illegal because it would
have tended to create a monopoly. This decision does not
appear to us to accord with either fundamental principles

of justice or with the precedents set by decisions of other
courts in England and in this country. Those precedents
sustain the decision that picketing is illegal if it employs
or suggests forcible interference with the rights of free
labor ; but those precedents also affirm the right of laborers 5
to organize for the purpose of entering into collective bargaining with employers, and to refuse to enter into such a
collective bargain with the employer except on terms
acceptable to the laborers. That a strike may be so organized as to be in the nature of an illegal conspiracy against 10
persons and property we do not doubt, but a mere combination to. stop work except upon terms proposed by the
combination surely is not such a conspiracy. If it were,
there would be an end to the right of free collective bargaining ; for there can be no free bargaining if both 15
parties are not free to refuse to enter into the bargain.
Nor can an agreement by one employer to employ only
men belonging to a specified organization be said to tend
to monopoly. A monopoly is " such an exclusive privilege
to carry on a traffic, or deal in or control a given class of 20
articles, as will enable the holder to raise prices materially
above what they would be if the traffic or dealing were
free to citizens generally." An agreement by The Outlook
to buy all its paper of a particular mill does not tend to
give that mill a monopoly of paper manufacture. No more 25
does an agreement by The Outlook to get all the employees
in its composing-room from a particular labor organization
tend to give that labor organization a monopoly. Such
exclusive contracts in articles of commerce are very common. It is difficult to see why they should be illegal when 30
labor, not the product of labor, is the commodity dealt in.
Whether Judge Adams's decision is sustained by the

Supreme Court of Illinois or not, we do not believe that
the principles enunciated in that decision will be sustained
generally by the courts in this country. In a country
where labor is free, an employer has the legal right to
5 refuse to employ any union labor, and equally the legal
right to refuse to employ any non-union labor. We do not
believe that the closed shop is illegal, though, of course,
violence, threats of violence, or even remote suggestions
and intimations of violence, in order to enforce the closed
10 shop, are illegal, and ought to receive far more serious
penalty than is ordinarily inflicted.

But, if not illegal, is the closed shop against public
policy, and therefore and to that extent immoral? Our
answer to this question is in the affirmative.

15 The collective bargaining is an advantage to workingmen. It will, we believe, eventually prove an advantage
to the entire community. It tends to give the workingmen
some share in the control of the industry to which they
contribute; and some share in that control they ought to
20 possess. The organization of labor and consequent collective bargaining are a necessary consequence of the organization of capital, whose bargains are collective. The only
possible remedy for an industrial autocracy is labor organization; and industrial autocracy is unendurable in a free
25 commonwealth.

But if collective bargaining can be obtained only by
sacrificing free bargaining, the price paid would be too
great for the benefits secured. The very object of collective bargaining is to secure freedom, which is practically,
30 though not theoretically, denied if the individual workingman must make his contract single-handed with a great
collective capitalistic organization. But to deny him the

liberty to make his contract single-handed if he wishes is
not to secure him freedom of contract, but to transfer him
from one autocracy to another. And this, in fact, is what
has taken place in some trades, in which men are no longer
free, but have the question whether they shall work, when 5
they shall work, and on what terms they shall work determined for them, sometimes by a small body of men acting
in secret, sometimes by a mob of men swayed by their
passions or their prejudices. If the only remedy for the
autocracy of capital is the possibility of collective bargain- 10
ing, the only remedy for the autocracy of a labor union is
the possibility of individual bargaining.

Freedom of bargaining is not only thus essential to the
community, and especially to the workingmen; it is also
essential to the best interests of the trades-unions. The 15
trade-union, to be permanently efficient, must be an organization of free men; it must be composed of members who
believe in unionism and are loyal to it; it must be an
industrial army of volunteers, not of drafted men; it must
make its way in the labor world by persuading the laborers 20
that it is for their interest to join it and be loyal to it, not
by coercing them to join it by threats of violence on the
one hand or of starvation on the other. There is only one
organization which in a free community men may be compelled to join whether they will or not — namely, the State. 25
They are born into the State, are members of the State,
must obey the laws enacted by the State, in time of danger
must come to the defense of the State, must, if necessary,
hazard their lives for the State. This is true of no other
organism. If they are coerced into the church, as they were 30
in the Middle Ages, the same process which deprives them
of their freedom deprives the church of its spiritual vitality.

. If they are coerced into a labor organization, as some labor
leaders would have them in this twentieth century, the
same process which deprives them of their freedom deprives
the labor organizations of that spirit of brotherhood which
5 is at once the justification for its existence and the inspiration of its power. The right of labor to organize rests upon
the right of the individual to labor. Whoever denies this
right of the individual denies the foundation on which the
right of organized labor rests.

10   If any man is inclined to say that a free labor union is
the dream of an idealist, and is quite impracticable in a
world of selfish and sordid men, the answer is to be found
in the fact that some of the greatest and most successful
of the labor organizations have always adhered to the prin-
15 ciple of the open shop. We believe that all the railroad
labor organizations are free organizations. In the Pennsylvania coal-mines union and non-union miners labored together in the same mine and reaped the same benefits from
the collective bargaining carried on for them by John
20 Mitchell. In the recent anarchy in Colorado, the one
mine which went on with its work peacefully, prosper-
ously, and without disturbance, until it was closed by
military orders, was a mine which maintained the principle
of the open shop, and in which union and non-union men
25 worked peacefully together.

Our conclusion, then, is that collective bargaining in
most organized industries is for the interest of employer,
of employed, and of the general community; that this
collective bargaining will be more speedily and perma-
30 nently secured by the maintenance of free labor unions
than by swelling the ranks of labor unions through
processes of compulsion; that the closed shop is not and

ought not to be illegal; but that it is against the interests of workingmen, of labor organizations, and of the general community; and, whether closed by the employer against union men, or by organized labor against non-union men, is alike inconsistent with the fundamental principles and 5 the essential spirit of free American institutions.

RESTRICTION OF IMMIGRATION[1]

Francis Amasa Walker

When we speak of the restriction of immigration, at the
present time, we have not in mind measures undertaken
for the purpose of straining out from the vast throngs of
foreigners arriving at our ports a few hundreds, or possibly
5 thousands of persons, deaf, dumb, blind, idiotic, insane,
pauper, or criminal, who might otherwise become a hope-
less burden upon the country, perhaps even an active
source of mischief. The propriety, and even the necessity
of adopting such measures is now conceded by men of all
10 shades of opinion concerning the larger subject. There is
even noticeable a rather severe public feeling regarding
the admission of persons of any of the classes named
above; perhaps one might say, a certain resentment at the
attempt of such persons to impose themselves upon us.
15 We already have laws which cover a considerable part
of this ground; and so far as further legislation is needed,
it will only be necessary for the proper executive department of the government to call the attention of Congress
to the subject. There is a serious effort on the part of our
20 immigration officers to enforce the regulations prescribed,
though when it is said that more than five thousand
persons have passed through the gates at Ellis Island, in

[1] From *Discussions in Economics and Statistics*, Vol. II, pp. 437-449.
Henry Holt & Co., New York, 1899.

New York harbor, during the course of a single day, it will be seen that no very careful scrutiny is practicable.

It is true that in the past there has been gross and scandalous neglect of this matter on the part both of government and people, here in the United States. For nearly two generations, great numbers of persons utterly unable to earn their living, by reason of one or another form of physical or mental disability, and others who were, from widely different causes, unfit to be members of any decent community, were admitted to our ports without challenge or question. It is a matter of official record that in many cases these persons had been directly shipped to us by states or municipalities desiring to rid themselves of a burden and a nuisance; while it could reasonably be believed that the proportion of such instances was far greater than could be officially ascertained. But all this is of the past. The question of the restriction of immigration to-day does not deal with that phase of the subject. What is proposed is, not to keep out some hundreds, or possibly thousands of persons, against whom lie specific objections like those above indicated, but to exclude perhaps hundreds of thousands, the great majority of whom would be subject to no individual objections; who, on the contrary, might fairly be expected to earn their living here in this new country, at least up to the standard known to them at home, and probably much more. The question to-day is, not of preventing the wards of our almshouses, our insane asylums, and our jails from being stuffed to repletion by new arrivals from Europe; but of protecting the American rate of wages, the American standard of living, and the quality of American citizenship from degradation through the tumultuous access of vast throngs of

ignorant and brutalized peasantry from the countries of
eastern and southern Europe.

The first thing to be said respecting any serious proposition importantly to restrict immigration into the United
5 States is, that such a proposition necessarily and properly
encounters a high degree of incredulity, arising from the
traditions of our country. From the beginning, it has been
the policy of the United States, both officially and according to the prevailing sentiment of our people, to tolerate,
10 to welcome, and to encourage immigration, without quali-
fication and without discrimination. For generations, it
was the settled opinion of our people, which found no
challenge anywhere, that immigration was a source of both
strength and wealth. Not only was it thought unneces-
15 sary carefully to scrutinize foreign arrivals at our ports,
but the figures of any exceptionally large immigration
were greeted with noisy gratulation. In those days the
American people did not doubt that they derived a great
advantage from this source. It is, therefore, natural to ask,
20 Is it possible that our fathers and our grandfathers were
so far wrong in this matter? Is it not, the rather, probable that the present anxiety and apprehension on the
subject are due to transient causes or to distinctly false
opinions, prejudicing the public mind? The challenge
25 which current proposals for the restriction of immigration
thus encounter is a perfectly legitimate one, and creates
a presumption which their advocates are bound to deal
with. Is it, however, necessarily true that if our fathers
and grandfathers were right in their view of immigration
30 in their own time, those who advocate the restriction of
immigration to-day must be in the wrong? Does it not
sometimes happen, in the course of national development,

that great and permanent changes in condition require corresponding changes of opinion and of policy?

We shall best answer this question by referring to an instance in an altogether different department of public interest and activity. For nearly a hundred years after the peace of 1783 opened to settlement the lands beyond the Alleghanies, the cutting away of the primeval forest was regarded by our people not only with toleration, but with the highest approval. No physical instrument could have been chosen which was so fairly entitled to be called the emblem of American civilization as the Axe of the Pioneer. As the forests of the Ohio Valley bowed themselves before the unstaying enterprise of the adventurous settlers of that region, all good citizens rejoiced. There are few chapters of human history which recount a grander story of human achievement. Yet to-day all intelligent men admit that the cutting down of our forests, the destruction of the tree-covering of our soil, has already gone too far; and both individual States and the nation have united in efforts to undo some of the mischief which has been wrought to our agriculture and to our climate from carrying too far the work of denudation. In precisely the same way, it may be true that our fathers were right in their view of immigration; while yet the patriotic American of to-day may properly shrink in terror from the contemplation of the vast hordes of ignorant and brutalized peasantry thronging to our shores.

Before inquiring as to general changes in our national condition which may justify a change of opinion and policy in this respect, let us deal briefly, as we must, with two opinions regarding the immigration of the past, which stand in the way of any fair consideration of the subject.

These two opinions were, first, that immigration constituted a net reinforcement of our population; secondly, that, in addition to this, or irrespective of this, immigration was necessary, in order to supply the laborers who
5 should do certain kinds of work, imperatively demanded for the building up of our industrial and social structure, which natives of the soil were unwilling to undertake.

The former of these opinions was, so far as I am aware, held with absolute unanimity by our people; yet no pop-
10 ular belief was ever more unfounded. Space would not serve for the full statistical demonstration of the proposition that immigration, during the period from 1830 to 1860, instead of constituting a net reinforcement to the population, simply resulted in a replacement of native by
15 foreign elements; but I believe it would be practicable to prove this to the satisfaction of every fair-minded man. Let it suffice to state a few matters which are beyond controversy.

The population of 1790 was almost wholly a native and
20 wholly an acclimated population, and for forty years afterwards immigration remained at so low a rate as to be practically of no account; yet the people of the United States increased in numbers more rapidly than has ever elsewhere been known, in regard to any considerable popu-
25 lation, over any considerable area, through any considerable period of time. Between 1790 and 1830 the nation grew from less than four millions to nearly thirteen millions, — an increase, in fact, of two hundred and twenty-seven per cent, a rate unparalleled in history. That
30 increase was wholly out of the loins of our own people. Each decade had seen a growth of between thirty-three and thirty-eight per cent, a doubling once in twenty-two

or twenty-three years. During the thirty years which followed 1830, the conditions of life and reproduction in the United States were not less, but more favorable than in the preceding period. Important changes relating to the practice of medicine, the food and clothing of people, the general habits of living, took place, which were of a nature to increase the vitality and reproductive capability of the American people. Throughout this period, the standard of height, of weight, and of chest measurement was steadily rising, with the result that, of the men of all nationalities in the giant army formed to suppress the slaveholders' rebellion, the native American bore off the palm in respect to physical stature. The decline of this rate of increase among Americans began at the very time when foreign immigration first assumed considerable proportions; it showed itself first and in the highest degree in those regions, in those States, and in the very counties into which the foreigners most largely entered. It proceeded for a long time in such a way as absolutely to offset the foreign arrivals, so that in 1850, in spite of the incoming of two and a half millions of foreigners during thirty years, our population differed by less than ten thousand from the population which would have existed, according to the previous rate of increase, without reinforcement from abroad. These three facts, which might be shown by tables and diagrams, constitute a statistical demonstration such as is rarely attained in regard to the operation of any social or economic force.

But it may be asked, Is the proposition that the arrival of foreigners brought a check to the native increase a reasonable one? Is the cause thus suggested one which has elsewhere appeared as competent to produce such an

effect? I answer, Yes. All human history shows that the
principle of population is intensely sensitive to social and
economic changes. Let social and economic conditions
remain as they were, and population will go on increasing
5 from year to year, and from decade to decade, with a regularity little short of the marvelous. Let social and economic conditions change, and population instantly responds.
The arrival in the United States, between 1830 and 1840,
and thereafter increasingly, of large numbers of degraded
10 peasantry created for the first time in this country distinct
social classes, and produced an alteration of economic
relations which could not fail powerfully to affect population. The appearance of vast numbers of men, foreign
in birth and often in language, with a poorer standard of
15 living, with habits repellent to our native people, of an
industrial grade suited only to the lowest kind of manual
labor, was exactly such a cause as by any student of population would be expected to affect profoundly the growth
of the native population. Americans shrank alike from the
20 social contact and the economic competition thus created.
They became increasingly unwilling to bring forth sons
and daughters who should be obliged to compete in the
market for labor and in the walks of life with those whom
they did not recognize as of their own grade and condition.
25 It has been said by some that during this time habits of
luxury were entering, to reduce both the disposition and
the ability to increase among our own population. In
some small degree, in some restricted localities, this undoubtedly was the case; but prior to 1860 there was no
30 such general growth of luxury in the United States as is
competent to account for the effect seen. Indeed, I believe
this was almost wholly due to the cause which has been

indicated, — a cause recognized by every student of statistics and economics.

The second opinion regarding the immigration of the past, with which it seems well to deal before proceeding to the positive argument of the case, is that, whether desir- 5 able on other accounts or not, foreign immigration prior to 1860 was necessary in order to supply the country with a laboring class which should be able and willing to perform the lowest kind of work required in the upbuilding of our industrial and social structure, especially the mak- 10 ing of railroads and canals. The opinion which has been cited constitutes, perhaps, the best example known to me of that putting the cart before the horse which is so commonly seen in sociological inquiry. When was it that native Americans first refused to do the lowest kinds of 15 manual labor? I answer, When the foreigner came. Did the foreigner come because the native American refused longer to perform any kind of manual labor? No; the American refused because the foreigner came. Through all our early history, Americans, from Governor Winthrop, 20 through Jonathan Edwards, to Ralph Waldo Emerson, had done every sort of work which was required for the comfort of their families and for the upbuilding of the state, and had not been ashamed. They called nothing common or unclean which needed to be done for their own good or 25 for the good of all. But when the country was flooded with ignorant and unskilled foreigners, who could do nothing but the lowest kind of labor, Americans instinctively shrank from the contact and the competition thus offered to them. So long as manual labor, in whatever field, was 30 to be done by all, each in his place, there was no revolt at it; but when working on railroads and canals became the sign of a want of education and of a low social condition, our own people gave it up, and left it to those who were able to do that, and nothing better.

We have of late had a very curious demonstration of the entire fallacy of the popular mode of reasoning on this subject, due to the arrival of a still lower laboring class. Within a few years Harper's Weekly had an article in which the editor, after admitting that the Italians who have recently come in such vast numbers to our shores do not constitute a desirable element of the population, either socially or politically, yet claimed that it was a highly providential arrangement, since the Irish, who formerly did all the work of the country in the way of ditching and trenching, were now standing aside. We have only to meet the argument thus in its second generation, so to speak, to see the complete fallacy of such reasoning. Does the Italian come because the Irishman refuses to work in ditches and trenches, in gangs; or has the Irishman taken this position because the Italian has come? The latter is undoubtedly the truth; and if the administrators of Baron Hirsch's estate send to us two millions of Russian Jews, we shall soon find the Italians standing on their dignity, and deeming themselves too good to work on streets and sewers and railroads. But meanwhile, what of the republic? what of the American standard of living? what of the American rate of wages?

All that sort of reasoning about the necessity of having a mean kind of man to do a mean kind of work is greatly to be suspected. It is not possible to have a man who is too good to do any kind of work which the welfare of his family and of the community requires to be done. So long as we were left to increase out of the loins of our people

such a sentiment as that we are now commenting upon
made no appearance in American life. It is much to be
doubted whether any material growth which is to be
secured only by the degradation of our citizenship is a
national gain, even from the most materialistic point of 5
view.

Let us now inquire what are the changes in our general
conditions which seem to demand a revision of the opinion
and policy heretofore held regarding immigration. Three
of these are subjective, affecting our capability of easily 10
and safely taking care of a large and tumultuous access of
foreigners ; the fourth is objective, and concerns the character of the immigration now directed upon our shores.
Time will serve for only a rapid characterization.

First, we have the important fact of the complete ex- 15
haustion of the free public lands of the United States.
Fifty years ago, thirty years ago, vast tracts of arable land
were open to every person arriving on our shores, under
the Preemption Act, or later, the Homestead Act. A
good farm of one hundred and sixty acres could be had at 20
the minimum price of $1.25 an acre, or for merely the
fees of registration. Under these circumstances it was a
very simple matter to dispose of a large immigration. To-
day there is not a good farm within the limits of the
United States which is to be had under either of these 25
acts. The wild and tumultuous scenes which attended
the opening to settlement of the Territory of Oklahoma,
a few years ago, and, a little later, of the so-called Chero-
kee Strip, testify eloquently to the vast change in our
national conditions in this respect. This is not to say that 30
more people cannot and will not, sooner or later, with
more or less of care and pains and effort, be placed upon

the land of the United States; but it does of itself alone show how vastly the difficulty of providing for immigration has increased. The immigrant must now buy his farm from a second hand, and he must pay the price which the value of the land for agricultural purposes determines. In the case of ninety-five out of a hundred immigrants, this necessity puts an immediate occupation of the soil out of the question.

A second change in our national condition, which importantly affects our capability of taking care of large numbers of ignorant and unskilled foreigners, is the fall of agricultural prices which has gone on steadily since 1873. It is not of the slightest consequence to inquire into the causes of this fall, whether we refer it to the competition of Argentina and of India or the appreciation of gold. We are interested only in the fact. There has been a great reduction in the cost of producing crops in some favored regions where steam-ploughs and steam-reaping, steam-threshing, and steam-sacking machines can be employed; but there has been no reduction in the cost of producing crops upon the ordinary American farm at all corresponding to the reduction in the price of the produce. It is a necessary consequence of this that the ability to employ a large number of uneducated and unskilled hands in agriculture has greatly diminished.

Still a third cause which may be indicated, perhaps more important than either of those thus far mentioned, is found in the fact that we have now a labor problem. We in the United States have been wont to pride ourselves greatly upon our so easily maintaining peace and keeping the social order unimpaired. We have, partly from a reasonable patriotic pride, partly also from something like

Phariseeism, been much given to pointing at our European cousins, and boasting superiority over them in this respect. Our self-gratulation has been largely due to overlooking social differences between us and them. That boasted superiority has been owing mainly, not to our institutions, 5 but to our more favorable conditions. There is no country of Europe which has not for a long time had a labor problem; that is, which has not so largely exploited its own natural resources, and which has not a labor supply so nearly meeting the demands of the market at their fullest, 10 that hard times and periods of industrial depression have brought a serious strain through extensive non-employment of labor. From this evil condition we have, until recently, happily been free. During the last few years, however, we have ourselves come under the shadow of this evil, in spite 15 of our magnificent natural resources. We know what it is to have even intelligent and skilled labor unemployed through considerable periods of time. This change of conditions is likely to bring some abatement to our national pride. No longer is it a matter of course that every indus- 20 trious and temperate man can find work in the United States. And it is to be remembered that, of all nations, we are the one which is least qualified to deal with a labor problem. We have not the machinery, we have not the army, we have not the police, we have not the traditions 25 and instincts, for dealing with such a matter, as the great railroad and other strikes of the last few years have shown.

I have spoken of three changes in the national condition, all subjective, which greatly affect our capability of dealing with a large and tumultuous immigration. There is a 30 fourth, which is objective. It concerns the character of the foreigners now resorting to our shores. Fifty, even

thirty years ago, there was a rightful presumption regarding the average immigrant that he was among the most enterprising, thrifty, alert, adventurous, and courageous of the community from which he came. It required no small
5 energy, prudence, forethought, and pains to conduct the inquiries relating to his migration, to accumulate the necessary means, and to find his way across the Atlantic. To-day the presumption is completely reversed. So thoroughly has the continent of Europe been crossed by railways, so
10 effectively has the business of emigration there been exploited, so much have the rates of railroad fares and ocean passage been reduced, that it is now among the least thrifty and prosperous members of any European community that the emigration agent finds his best recruiting-
15 ground. The care and pains required have been reduced to a minimum; while the agent of the Red Star Line or the White Star Line is everywhere at hand, to suggest migration to those who are not getting on well at home. The intending emigrants are looked after from the moment
20 they are locked into the cars in their native villages until they stretch themselves upon the floors of the buildings on Ellis Island, in New York. Illustrations of the ease and facility with which this Pipe Line Immigration is now carried on might be given in profusion. So broad and
25 smooth is the channel, there is no reason why every foul and stagnant pool of population in Europe, which no breath of intellectual or industrial life has stirred for ages, should not be decanted upon our soil. Hard times here may momentarily check the flow; but it will not be perma-
30 nently stopped so long as *any difference of economic level* exists between our population and that of the most degraded communities abroad.

But it is not alone that the presumption regarding the immigrant of to-day is so widely different from that which existed regarding the immigrant of thirty or fifty·years ago. The immigrant of the former time came almost exclusively from western and northern Europe. We have now tapped great reservoirs of population then almost unknown to the passenger lists of our arriving vessels. Only a short time ago, the immigrants from southern Italy, Hungary, Austria, and Russia together made up hardly more than one per cent of our immigration. To-day the proportion has risen to, something like forty per cent, and threatens soon to become fifty or sixty per cent, or even more. The entrance into our political, social, and industrial life of such vast masses of peasantry, degraded below our utmost conceptions, is a matter which no intelligent patriot can look upon without the gravest apprehension and alarm. These people have no history behind them which is of a nature to give encouragement. They have none of the inherited instincts and tendencies which made it comparatively easy to deal with the immigration of the olden time. They are beaten men from beaten races ; representing the worst failures in the struggle for existence. Centuries are against them, as centuries were on the side of those who formerly came to us. They have none of the ideas and aptitudes which fit men to take up readily and easily the problem of self-care and self-government, such as belong to those who are descended from the tribes that met under the oak-trees of old Germany to make laws and choose chieftains.

Their habits of life, again, are of the most revolting kind. Read the description given by Mr. Riis of the police driving from the garbage dumps the miserable beings who try

to burrow in those depths of unutterable filth and slime
in order that they may sleep and eat there! Was it in
cement like this that the foundations of our republic were
laid? What effects must be produced upon our social
5 standards, and upon the ambitions and aspirations of our
people, by a contact so foul and loathsome? The influence
upon the American rate of wages of a competition like
this cannot fail to be injurious and even disastrous. Already it has been seriously felt in the tobacco manufacture,
10 in the clothing trade, and in many forms of mining industry; and unless this access of vast numbers of unskilled
workmen of the lowest type, in a market already fully
supplied with labor, shall be checked, it cannot fail to go
on from bad to worse, in breaking down the standard
15 which has been maintained with so much care and at so
much cost. The competition of paupers is far more telling
and more killing than the competition of pauper-made
goods. Degraded labor in the slums of foreign cities may
be prejudicial to intelligent, ambitious, self-respecting
20 labor here; but it does not threaten half so much evil as
does degraded labor in the garrets of our native cities.

Finally, the present situation is most menacing to our
peace and political safety. In all the social and industrial
disorders of this country since 1877, the foreign elements
25 have proved themselves the ready tools of demagogues in
defying the law, in destroying property, and in working
violence. A learned clergyman who mingled with the social-
istic mob which, two years ago, threatened the State
House and the governor of Massachusetts, told me that
30 during the entire disturbance he heard no word spoken
in any language which he knew, — either in English, in
German, or in French. There may be those who can

contemplate the addition to our population of vast numbers of persons having no inherited instincts of self-government and respect for law; knowing no restraint upon their own passions but the club of the policeman or the bayonet of the soldier; forming communities, by the tens of thousands, in which only foreign tongues are spoken, and into which can steal no influence from our free institutions and from popular discussion. But I confess to being far less optimistic. I have conversed with one of the highest officers of the United States army and with one of the highest officers of the civil government regarding the state of affairs which existed during the summer of 1894; and the revelations they made of facts not generally known, going to show how the ship of state grazed along its whole side upon the rocks, were enough to appall the most sanguine American, the most hearty believer in free government. Have we the right to expose the republic to any increase of the dangers from this source which now so manifestly threaten our peace and safety?

For it is never to be forgotten that self-defense is the first law of nature and of nations. If that man who careth not for his own household is worse than an infidel, the nation which permits its institutions to be endangered by any cause which can fairly be removed is guilty not less in Christian than in natural law. Charity begins at home; and while the people of the United States have gladly offered an asylum to millions upon millions of the distressed and unfortunate of other lands and climes, they have no right to carry their hospitality one step beyond the line where American institutions, the American rate of wages, the American standard of living, are brought into serious peril. All the good the United States could

do by offering indiscriminate hospitality to a few millions
more of European peasants, whose places at home will,
within another generation, be filled by others as miserable
as themselves, would not compensate for any permanent
5 injury done to our republic. Our highest duty to charity
and to humanity is to make this great experiment, here, of
free laws and educated labor, the most triumphant success
that can possibly be attained. In this way we shall do far
more for Europe than by allowing its city slums and its
10 vast stagnant reservoirs of degraded peasantry to be drained
off upon our soil. Within the decade between 1880 and
1890 five and a quarter millions of foreigners entered our
ports ! No nation in human history ever undertook to deal
with such masses of alien population. That man must be
15 a sentimentalist and an optimist beyond all bounds of
reason who believes that we can take such a load upon
the national stomach without a failure of assimilation, and
without great danger to the health and life of the nation.
For one, I believe it is time that we should take a rest,
20 and give our social, political, and industrial system some
chance to recuperate. The problems which so sternly con-
front us to-day are serious enough without being complicated and aggravated by the addition of some millions of
Hungarians, Bohemians, Poles, south Italians, and Rus-
25 sian Jews.

STUDENT'S BRIEF AND ARGUMENT

BRIEF

SHOULD A NATIONAL FOREST RESERVE BE ESTABLISHED IN THE WHITE MOUNTAINS?

INTRODUCTION

I. The question of establishing a White Mountain Reservation gains in importance from the alleged alarming destruction of forests by lumber companies.

II. The discussion of the question will be facilitated by the following explanations:

    A. A national reserve is a tract of forest land owned and managed by the national government under the most approved laws of modern forestry.

    B. The particular tract under discussion includes the Presidential Range, the Franconia Range, and other desirable tracts within forty miles of the summit of Mt. Washington.

III. It is agreed that present conditions are as favorable as they may be expected to be under private control, inasmuch as

    A. Lumber companies must cut lumber.

    B. It is but natural that they should consult none but their own interests.

IV. The conflicting arguments on the question are as follows:

    A. Those in favor of the reservation believe

        1. That the methods of the lumber companies are objectionable from the point of view of the public at large.

        2. That under government ownership and control present errors would be remedied and the condition of the forests improved.

        3. That a national reserve is the only practical solution of the problem.

        4. That the return which the forests would yield to the state under the lumber companies would be insignificant compared with the interests sacrificed.

        5. That the reservation would benefit the whole nation.

    B. Those opposed to the reservation believe

        1. That the lumber industry is conducted in a reasonably satisfactory way.

        2. That it brings a revenue which the state of New Hampshire cannot afford to lose.

        3. That sentimental reasons should not be permitted to interfere with the utilization of the forests.

V. From this conflict of opinion it appears that the points to be determined are:

    A. Are present methods of cutting lumber satisfactory from the public point of view?

    B. Would government management improve the condition of the forests?

C. Is the federal government the only power that can successfully bring about the desired improvement?

D. Is it more to the interest of New Hampshire to consider the return that these forests would yield as lumber than to consider their value as forests?

E. Would the whole nation derive benefit from a national reservation?

BRIEF PROPER

There should be a White Mountain Reserve, for

I. The methods of the lumber companies are objectionable from the point of view of the public, for

A. They increase the danger of forest fires, for

    1. They leave a dense tangle of rubbish where the forests once stood.

    2. This rubbish, in time, becomes a veritable tinderbox to kindle forest fires,[1] for

        a. One-half of the forest fires in this region originate in old cuttings.

B. They increase the danger of floods, for

    1. The forest floor has a vast influence upon the flow of brooks and streams.[2]

    2. The removal of the protecting woods leaves the forest floor open to destructive agents, for

        a. Forest fires may burn it.

---

[1] J. B. Harrison, Miscellaneous press notices issued by the New Hampshire Forestry Commission and deposited in the Harvard College Library : hereafter to be called "Miscellanies."

[2] B. E. Fernow, *Forestry Division Bulletin No. 7*, pp. 157–158.

      b. Heavy rains may wash it away.

3. The destruction of the forest floor makes the flow of streams that drain it sensitive to heavy rains and thaws,[1] for

      a. A difference of 2000 cubic feet of water per second from a square mile of territory is sufficient to cause or prevent a serious flood.[2]

      b. The difference of drainage in a deforested territory is necessarily far greater than 2000 cubic feet per second.

      c. Denuded areas in the French Alps caused a destructive flood.[2]

      d. The Bad Lands of Mississippi furnish another instance.[2]

C. They tend to diminish the water supply, for

1. The four large rivers of New England depend largely upon the floor of these forests for their water,[3] for

      a. 143 of its brooks feed the Androscoggin.[4]

      b. 148 feed the Connecticut.[4]

      c. 210 feed the Merrimac.[4]

      d. 455 feed the Saco.[4]

2. Removal of the forests has already been followed by the failing of water supply, for

---

[1] J. B. Harrison, New Hampshire Forestry Commission, Miscellanies.
[2] B. E. Fernow, *Forestry Division Bulletin No. 7*, pp. 158–160.
[3] J. B. Harrison, New Hampshire Forestry Commission, Miscellanies.
[4] Allen Chamberlain, *Forestry and Irrigation*, Vol. XI, p. 458.

        a. The flow of the Connecticut River has decreased.[1]

        b. The flow of the Contoocook has decreased.[1]

        c. Water supply failed the mills in the town of Canaan.[1]

D. They threaten the extermination of the forests, for

  1. They destroy seed trees as well as mature ones.

  2. The rubbish they leave prevents the growth of trees for a long time.

  3. Even if trees should spring up immediately, they would not be mature for from one to two centuries.[2]

  4. Destructive agents destroy the productiveness of the soil forever.

  5. The consumption of the forests is far more rapid than the production, for

        a. The lumber companies do not reforest the cleared areas.

        b. The amount of commercial forests in New England is rapidly diminishing.[3]

  6. That it will vanish altogether at the present rate needs no proof.

  7. The argument that the forests are increasing is erroneous, for

---

[1] Report of the New Hampshire Forestry Commission, 1885, pp. 16–19.

[2] J. B. Harrison, New Hampshire Forestry Commission, Miscellanies.

[3] Pamphlet of New Hampshire Land Company, published in 1880, quoted by J. B. Harrison, in N. H. Forestry Commission, Miscellanies.

        a. The alleged increase consists of infant woods not mature for at least a century to come.[1]

        b. The timber that springs up on cleared ground is of a lower grade than the original growth.[1]

E. They ruin the scenery, for

  1. They carry whole forests before them.

  2. They give the opportunity for fire and weather to make even greater defacements.

  3. They have already done great damage to the scenery, for

        a. They have defaced Mt. Washington.

        b. They have defaced Mt. Jefferson.

        c. They have defaced Franconia Notch.

        d. They have defaced Mt. Bond.

        e. They have destroyed Randolph Forest.[2]

II. Government ownership and operation would remedy these faults, for

  A. They are due to the desire of private owners for the largest possible immediate income.

  B. Government management could have no such object.

  C. Government management has already proved its efficiency, for

    1. The number and extent of government reserves have been steadily increasing.

---

[1] J. B. Harrison, New Hampshire Forestry Commission, Miscellanies.
[2] Hon. J. H. Gallinger, *Forestry and Irrigation*, Vol. XI, p. 415.

2. Government management has improved the Cascade Reserve.[1]

8. It has also improved the Olympic Reserve.[1]

III. A national reserve is the only practical solution, for

A. Private owners cannot be forced to take proper precautions.

B. The state of New Hampshire could not be expected to bear the burden of expense, for

1. All of New England except Rhode Island is as directly concerned as New Hampshire.[2]

2. New Hampshire cannot afford to undertake the enterprise alone.[2]

C. The United States is best qualified for the undertaking, for

1. She is able to buy the land.

2. She has a well equipped forestry service.

8. She has had extensive experience in the forest reserve business, for

a. There are one hundred national reserves now in operation.

IV. The return which these forests would yield to New Hampshire under the lumber companies would be insignificant compared with other interests that would be sacrificed, for

A. The revenue from the lumber companies will cease in time.

B. The present policy of these companies endangers important industries, for

---

[1] Reports of the U. S. Geological Survey, 1899–1900, Part V, pp. 151–498.

[2] Allen Chamberlain, *Forestry and Irrigation*, Vol. XI, p. 457.

1. Important industries depend upon the water supply.
2. Present methods tend to decrease the water supply.
3. The resort and tourist business stands in great peril.[1]

C. Protection of the forests by the government would insure these industries.

V. A national forest reserve in the White Mountains would benefit the whole nation,[2] for

A. The advantages of the region as a resort are sought by people from all sections.

B. The industries threatened by present methods are of interstate and hence national importance,[2] for
1. The lumber industry itself is of vital importance to the nation, for
   a. The national government's object in establishing forest reserves is to protect the lumber industry.

CONCLUSION

I. Since, therefore, the methods of the lumber companies are objectionable from the point of view of the public at large;

II. Since under government ownership and control present errors would be corrected and the condition of the forests improved;

III. Since a national reserve is the only practical solution of the problem;

[1] J. B. Harrison, New Hampshire Forestry Commission, Miscellanies.
[2] Allen Chamberlain, *Forestry and Irrigation*, Vol. XI, p. 457.

IV. Since the return which the forests would yield to the state under the lumber companies would be insignificant compared with the interests that would have to be sacrificed; and

V. Since the reservation would benefit the whole nation, —

Therefore, a national forest reserve should be established in the White Mountains.

BRIEF

INTRODUCTION

I. The question of establishing a **White Mountain Reservation** gains in importance from the alleged alarming destruction of forests by lumber companies.

Should a National Forest Reserve be Established in the White Mountains?

Forty years ago New Hampshire was sole owner of a vast tract of primeval woodland that stretched through the greater part of the counties of Carroll, Coös, and Grafton, covered the heights and valleys of the White Mountains, and contributed its part to some of the noblest natural 5 scenery in the eastern states. To-day the mountains and their forest cover are owned by private corporations, but the forest cover is but a part of its former self, and the scenery, though still beautiful, has been scarred and blemished in a thousand places by the ruthless plying of the 10 woodman's axe. The transition is alarming but not unprecedented; it is the kind of catastrophe nations have been called upon to prevent since men first knew that trees could be made into boards and boards into houses. In 1867 the New Hampshire legislature ceded the ownership of 15 these forests to the New Hampshire Land Company for the sum of $25,000. As early as 1880, citizens and state authorities began to take alarm at the speed and recklessness with which the extermination of the woods was progressing, and, in the following year, the state estab- 20 lished a forestry commission to inquire into the damage already done and its effect upon the water supply and the industries that depended upon it. The report which they returned four years later seemed to cry aloud for state intervention, but no action was taken. Valleys continued 25 to yield their precious verdure and even the difficult

II. The discussion of the question will be facilitated by
the following explanations :

A. A national reserve is a tract of forest land owned
and managed by the national government under
the most approved laws of modern forestry.

B. The particular tract under discussion includes the
Presidential Range, the Franconia Range, and
other desirable tracts within forty miles of the
summit of Mt. Washington.

III. It is agreed that present conditions are as favorable
as they may be expected to be under private
control, inasmuch as,

mountain slopes were not spared. In 1892, Mr. J. B. Harrison, secretary of the Forestry Commission, championed the cause of the mountain forests in an independent movement through numerous press articles and speeches. Many distinguished men rallied to his support, but no de- 5 cided step was taken for eleven years. In 1903 the state appropriated $5,000 to finance a "general examination of the forest lands of the White Mountain region by employés of the Bureau of Forestry in the Department of Agriculture at Washington." The upshot of the examination 10 which followed was a new and vigorous movement for a national forest reserve in the White Mountains, and a bill with this as its object was introduced in Congress in 1905.

If the pending bill should become a law, the land that was sold at such an absurdly low figure in 1867 would be 15 purchased by the national government to be held and cultivated under the most approved laws of modern forestry. That is, the parts which have been denuded would be . reforested, while the remaining parts that are now threatened with destruction would be carefully preserved, and 20 the culling system, which allows only mature trees to be cut, would be substituted for the clean-cut plan. Seedlings would be planted in place of the trees culled and a perpetual output of timber would thus be insured from this region, while the forests and the scenery, of which they 25 are such a necessary part, would be preserved. A national reserve in the White Mountains would include the Presidential Range, the Franconia Range, and other tracts within forty miles of Mt. Washington. Such is the plan of remedy for present abuses.   30

Of course, we cannot expect corporations organized for private gain to be public benefactors as well. It is no

    A. Lumber companies must cut lumber.

    B. It is but natural that they should consult none but their own interests.

IV. The conflicting arguments on the question are as follows:

    A. Those in favor of the reservation believe

        1. That the methods of the lumber companies are objectionable from the point of view of the public at large.

        2. That under government ownership and control present errors would be remedied and the condition of the forests improved.

        8. That a national reserve is the only practical solution of the problem.

        4. That the return which the forests would yield to the state under the lumber companies would be insignificant compared with the interests sacrificed.

        5. That the reservation would benefit the whole nation.

    B. Those opposed to the reservation believe

        1. That the lumber industry is conducted in a reasonably satisfactory way.

        2. That it brings a revenue which the state of New Hampshire cannot afford to lose.

        8. That sentimental reasons should not be permitted to interfere with the utilization of the forests.

V. From this conflict of opinion it appears that the points to be determined are:

    A. Are present methods of cutting lumber satisfactory from the public point of view?

more than natural that the companies that have invested money in this enterprise should consider these forests merely as the raw material of their trades, and that they should not regard the harm which may result indirectly from the removal of the trees. The present condition of the forests is as good as it can be while the land is owned by lumber companies. This is freely admitted from the beginning, and thus far the two sides of the controversy agree.

But the advocates of the present bill maintain: (1) that the methods of the lumber companies are objectionable from the point of view of the public at large; (2) that under government ownership and control, present errors would be corrected and the condition of the forests improved; (3) that a national reserve offers the only practical solution of the problem; (4) that the return which these forests would yield to the state of New Hampshire under the lumber companies would be insignificant compared with other interests which would be sacrificed, and (5) that the reservation would benefit the whole nation as well as the state of New Hampshire. Opponents of the scheme maintain: (1) that the lumber industry is conducted in a reasonably satisfactory way; (2) that it brings in a revenue which the state of New Hampshire cannot afford to lose, and (3) that sentimental reasons should not be permitted to interfere with the utilization of the forests.

This conflict of opinion brings before us the five main issues of our discussion: (1) Are the present methods of cutting lumber satisfactory from the public point of view? (2) Would government management improve the condition of the forests? (3) Is the federal government the only power which can successfully bring about the desired improvement? (4) Is it more to the interest of New Hampshire

B. Would government management improve the condition of the forests?

C. Is the federal government the only power that can successfully bring about the desired improvement?

D. Is it more to the interest of New Hampshire to consider the return that these forests would yield as lumber than to consider their value as forests?

E. Would the whole nation derive benefit from a national reservation?

BRIEF PROPER

There should be a White Mountain Reserve, for

I. The methods of the lumber companies are objectionable from the point of view of the public, for

A. They increase the danger of forest fires, for

    1. They leave a dense tangle of rubbish where the forest once stood.

    2. This rubbish, in time, becomes a veritable tinderbox to kindle forest fires,[1] for

---

[1] J. B. Harrison, Miscellaneous press notices issued by the New Hampshire Forestry Commission and deposited in the Harvard College Library: hereafter to be called "Miscellanies."

to consider the return that these forests would yield as lumber than to consider their value as forests? (5) Would the whole nation derive benefit from such a move?

How unsatisfactory the methods now employed by the · lumber companies in cutting lumber are can best be seen 5 by a consideration of the methods themselves. These companies are not in the business to protect the interests of other people, but to cut lumber in the way that is most profitable. Opportunities which I have had as an eye witness enable me to describe the methods of these lumber- 10 men and the harm which results. According to the present system of logging, an area is selected which is well covered with white pine or spruce timber. Every tree in this area that is worth cutting is cut, until often there is not a single tree left standing. Thousands of acres of 15 thickly wooded ground have thus been completely denuded of their forest cover. Instead of live trees, the lumbermen leave behind them tops and branches which have been lopped off the trunks. These cover the clearing to a depth of from three to six feet with a dense tangle of 20 rubbish. Such a mode of operating, which is followed everywhere in the White Mountains, has several serious results.

When the lumberman abandons a cleared piece of ground littered with the rubbish that he cannot use to pursue his 25 conquest yet farther up the slope, he leaves behind what nature will convert into a veritable tinderbox to kindle forest fires.[1] The thick tangle of branches and twigs dry up in the course of a couple of years, leaving a mass of

[1] J. B. Harrison, Miscellaneous press notices issued by the New Hampshire Forestry Commission and deposited in the Harvard College Library: hereafter to be called "Miscellanies."

    a. One-half of the forest fires in this
    region originate in old cuttings.

B. They increase the danger of floods, for

   1. The forest floor has a vast influence upon
     the flow of brooks and streams.[1]

   2. The removal of the protecting woods leaves the
     forest floor open to destructive agents, for

---

[1] B. E. Fernow, *Forestry Division Bulletin No. 7*, pp. 157–158.

dead wood and chips that is almost as inflammable as a
hayfield. From my own observation I believe it is safe to
say that one-half of the destructive forest fires that occur
originate in old cuttings. These fires often spread through
miles and miles of territory, but they would not constitute such a serious calamity, if the discarded trash of
the lumbermen were alone consumed. Such, however, is
not the case. The fires that are started in this way eat
deep into the loam and destroy every vestige of vegetable
matter and seeds which protect the soil and promise future
forest growth to take the place of the old.[1] They spread
often into the uncut woods and shrivel up many acres of
valuable timber before they can be checked. Thus the
devastation wrought by the lumberman with the axe is
made complete by the forest fire. Immense tracts of fire-
swept land are to-day a frequent and appalling feature of
the White Mountain landscape.

The extent of damage wrought by forest fires is not
generally appreciated for the reason that the important
function of the "forest floor" which they destroy, its vast
influence upon the flow of brooks and rivers which drain
it, is not widely understood. This floor consists of the
spongy covering which ages of forest growth and decay
have produced. Through its power to hold in reserve the
water which it absorbs from rains and snows and to release
it gradually into its natural drainage channels, it serves the
purpose of a feeding reservoir to the brooks and rivers
which drain it, regulating their flow and preventing them
from being too sensitive to heavy rains, sudden thaws, and
long droughts.[2] When the forest is removed from above

[1] J. B. Harrison, New Hampshire Forestry Commission, Miscellanies.
[2] B. E. Fernow, *Forestry Division Bulletin No. 7*, pp. 157–168.

    a. Forest fires may burn it.
    b. Heavy rains may wash it away.

3. The destruction of the forest floor makes the flow of streams that drain it sensitive to heavy rains and thaws,[1] for,

    a. A difference of 2000 cubic feet of water per second from a square mile of territory is sufficient to cause or prevent a serious flood.[2]

    b. The difference of drainage in a deforested territory is necessarily far greater than 2000 cubic feet per second.

    c. Denuded areas in the French Alps caused a destructive flood.[2]

[1] J. B. Harrison, New Hampshire Forestry Commission, Miscellanies.
[2] B. E. Fernow, *Forestry Division Bulletin No. 7*, pp. 158–159.

this natural storehouse, and fires and heavy rains come
along to destroy its filtering apparatus, the rivets that hold
it together and the canopy of brush that protects it, the
whole machinery that ages have served to perfect is shattered; its storage capacity and regulating power are forever 5
destroyed. When heavy rainstorms come, the ground is
no longer able to absorb the water fast enough. Some of
it is drained off through the ground, but the rest flows
down over the hillside to the nearest brook, gouging and
furrowing the unprotected soil in its course. The result is 10
either a freshet or a flood which does serious damage to
the surrounding country.[1] Mr. B. E. Fernow, former chief
of the Division of Forestry, speaking of this danger, says,
" A difference of 1000 to 2000 cubic feet of water per
second from a square mile of watershed may often deter- 15
mine whether a dangerous flood is to be experienced or
not. And since a square mile of moss covered forest floor
is capable of absorbing from 40,000,000 to 50,000,000
cubic feet in, say, ten minutes, — nearly all of which the
naked soil would give up some twelve to fifteen hours 20
earlier, — the surface conditions of the watershed must in
many cases be determinative in the excesses of waterflow
in rivers." [2] If this is often the case when the difference
of drainage is only 2000 cubic feet per second per square
mile, what must the danger be when the whole downpour 25
upon a given piece of deforested land for a given number
of hours is turned into a stream and its tributaries without
retardation? Denuded areas in the French Alps some
years ago were the occasion of one of the most destructive
floods in that nation's history.[2] Thousands of acres of 30

---

[1] J. B. Harrison, New Hampshire Forestry Commission, Miscellanies.
[2] B. E. Fernow, *Forestry Division Bulletin No. 7*, pp. 158–159.

d. The Bad Lands of Mississippi furnish
another instance.[1]

C. They tend to diminish the water supply, for

    1. The four large rivers of New England depend
largely upon the floor of these forests for
their water,[2] for

        a. 148 of its brooks feed the Andros-
coggin.[3]

        b. 148 feed the Connecticut.[3]

        c. 210 feed the Merrimac.[3]

[1] B. E. Fernow, *Forestry Division Bulletin No. 7*, pp. 159–160.
[2] J. B. Harrison, New Hampshire Forestry Commission, Miscellanies.
[3] Allen Chamberlain, *Forestry and Irrigation*, Vol. XI, p. 458.

fertile land were ruined by deposits of débris which the
torrents had gouged out of the unprotected slopes in their
rush toward the valleys. The Bad Lands of Mississippi
furnish an instance somewhat nearer home. The mountain
sides were ditched and gullied into hideous wastes and the 5
fertile agricultural lands below were buried as completely
as from a volcanic eruption by the débris which the torrents dragged down upon them.[1] Such are the dangers
that threaten parts of New England in the way of floods
as long as the deforestation of the watersheds of her prin- 10
cipal rivers is allowed to continue.

But there is another evil which is still more nearly
impending, and has indeed been experienced by many
New England localities. Just as the removal of the forest
floor from the mountains is likely to cause freshets and 15
floods in time of heavy rains and thaws, it is certain to
cause a diminution of the water supply of rivers in times
when there is little or no rainfall. This fact becomes more
potent when we remember that the four large rivers of
New England, the Connecticut, the Merrimac, the Andros- 20
coggin and the Saco, draw a large portion of their water
supply from the White Mountain region; that is, they
depend to a large extent upon this forest floor for their
very existence.[2] Of the 956 brooks and streams that drain
the White Mountains, 143 flow into the Androscoggin, 25
which turns mill wheels in New Hampshire and Maine;
148 flow into the Connecticut, with which the commerce
and industries of every New England state except Maine
and Rhode Island are vitally concerned; 210 feed the
Merrimac, which furnishes power to many cotton mills in 30

[1] B. E. Fernow, *Forestry Division Bulletin No. 7*, pp. 159–160.
[2] J. B. Harrison, New Hampshire Forestry Commission, Miscellanies.

d. 455 feed the Saco.[1]

2. Removal of the forests has already been followed by the failing of water supply, for

    a. The flow of the Connecticut River has decreased [2]

    b. The flow of the Contoocook has decreased.[2]

    c. Water supply failed the mills in the town of Canaan.[2]

D. They threaten the extermination of the forests, for

1. They destroy seed trees as well as mature ones.

2. The rubbish they leave prevents the growth of trees for a long time.

[1] Allen Chamberlain, *Forestry and Irrigation*, Vol. XI, p. 458.
[2] Report of the New Hampshire Forestry Commission, 1885, pp. 16–19.

New Hampshire and Massachusetts, and 455 empty into
the Saco, with which New Hampshire and Maine are
closely identified in a commercial way.[1] Every state in
New England, then, except Rhode Island, must suffer
direct commercial loss from the diminution of the water
supply from the White Mountains. And we have positive
evidence that such has already been the case. The report
of the New Hampshire Forestry Commission which was
issued in 1885 states, from the written testimony of eye
witnesses, that the volume of water in the Connecticut
River at Hanover had at that time been decreasing for
many years; that the water in the Contoocook had diminished one-third in twenty years; that in a period of sixty-
five years, during which the town of Canaan had been
denuded of its forests, its nine or more mills, formerly run
by water power, had been obliged to resort to steam; that
the Ammonoosuc at Littleton had diminished one-third
within fifty or sixty years. And thus the testimony of old
inhabitants of various parts continues for several pages.[2]
This was in 1885. The waterflow is still diminishing and
commerce and industry continue to suffer as a result.

But the direct bearing of the present system of lumbering upon the lumber industry itself is of even greater
importance. The lumber companies are exterminating the
New Hampshire forests, — the material of their own future
trade. They see immediate profit in cutting the saplings
as well as the mature trees and thus not only neglecting
to encourage, but actually preventing the reproduction of
the forests. The rubbish that they leave behind chokes

[1] Allen Chamberlain, *Forestry and Irrigation*, Vol. XI, p. 458.
[2] Report of the New Hampshire Forestry Commission, 1885, pp. 16–19;
quoted by B. E. Fernow, *Forestry Division Bulletin No. 7*, pp. 166–167.

8. Even if trees should spring up immediately, they would not be mature for from one to two centuries.[1]

4. Destructive agents destroy the productiveness of the soil forever.

5. The consumption of the forests is far more rapid than the production, for

    a. The lumber companies do not reforest the cleared areas.

[1] J. B. Harrison, New Hampshire Forestry Commission, Miscellanies.

for a long time the growth of young trees that would ordinarily spring up from scattered seed. But even such growth could be of no consequence to the present or the coming generation, since from one to two centuries would pass before the new tree could equal its fallen parent.[1] 5 The lumberman is destroying the forests for the next two generations to come; the heavy rains and forest fires follow in his trail and cancel the productive power of the· soil for the rest of eternity. Future forests may develop in the course of time in places where the rains have not 10 washed away or imbedded or forest fires burnt up the vegetation of the forest floor, but it is pretty safe to say that the slopes will always be bare of available forests where once they have been cleared, unless artificial means are soon adopted to reforest them.   15

At present, the consumption of timber by the companies is far more rapid than the production. Wooded slopes and valleys are rapidly being converted into desert wastes, and there is no thought of restocking the areas already cleared, but only of clearing the next as rapidly as possible. Nature 20 provides in the forest an interest-bearing fund of timber. If the rules of forestry are prudently observed in cutting, if the older trees only are removed and the growth of the others fostered, the principal will always remain intact and the interest will always be forthcoming.[1] But such 25 has never been the policy of the lumber companies. They are consuming both interest and principal in an alarmingly prodigal manner. Under such conditions it does not require a prophetic eye to see that New Hampshire's timber supply is doomed. Some idea of the rapid disappearance of the 30

[1] J. B. Harrison, New Hampshire Forestry Commission, Miscellanies.

b. The amount of commercial forests in New England is rapidly diminishing.[1]

6. That it will vanish altogether at the present rate needs no proof.

7. The argument that the forests are increasing is erroneous, for

a. The alleged increase consists of infant woods not mature for at least a century to come.[2]

[1] Pamphlet of New Hampshire Land Company, published in 1880, quoted by J. B. Harrison, in N. H. Forestry Commission, Miscellanies.
[2] J. B. Harrison, New Hampshire Forestry Commission, Miscellanies.

New England forests during the past century is well conveyed in a pamphlet published in 1880 by the New Hampshire Land Company, the despoilers of the vast tract of which they then seemed so proud. "Evidence accumulates on every side," it says, "of the rapid diminution of the area of forest growth, hence of the increasing value of that which remains. But a century ago and the whole face of New England was covered with forest growth, while now the New Hampshire Land Company controls the largest block of timber lands in one location in New England except in northern and eastern Maine, and the only block of any magnitude within 200 miles of Boston. It is difficult to estimate the future value of this immense area of wooded land." [1] Perhaps it would be simpler to estimate the value of what remains of this immense area of wooded land after twenty-seven years of bad husbandry. One century more and it, too, will have gone the way of all the rest of New England's primeval woods.

It has been stated that, contrary to the above facts, the forest area of New England is really increasing. Such a statement could be supported, if at all, only by taking into account the areas of cleared ground upon which infant forests have since sprung up; but two objections prevent such areas from entering into a just estimate of the present extent of forest lands. In the first place, they will not be ripe for cutting for at least a century,[2] and in the second place, in such growths of woodland, following upon the clearing of the virgin forest, the timber is of a lower grade than that which preceded it. For example, when spruce is

[1] Quoted by J. B. Harrison, in N. H. Forestry Commission, Miscellanies.
[2] J. B. Harrison, New Hampshire Forestry Commission, Miscellanies.

   b. The timber that springs up on cleared
     ground is of a lower grade than the
     original growth.[1]

E. They ruin the scenery, for

   1. They carry the whole forests before them.

   2. They give the opportunity for fire and
     weather to make even greater defacements.

   3. They have already done great damage to the
     scenery, for

     a. They have defaced Mt. Washington.
     b. They have defaced Mt. Jefferson.
     c. They have defaced Franconia Notch.
     d. They have defaced Mt. Bond.
     e. They have destroyed Randolph
      Forest.[2]

---

[1] J. B. Harrison, New Hampshire Forestry Commission, Miscellanies.
[2] Hon. J. H. Gallinger, *Forestry and Irrigation*, Vol. XI, p. 415.

cleared away, it is followed not by spruce, but by wild cherry or poplar.[1]

The question of the failing of the timber supply is a serious one which affects future generations far more than it affects us. But the one effect of the present lumbering operations in the White Mountains that is most appalling to the present generation and most apparent to the eye of every observer, is the irreparable damage they are doing the natural scenery for which the region is famous. Many a verdant valley has been turned into an ugly waste and the ambitious lumberman is pushing his conquest ever onward and upward along the mountain sides, leaving uncovered slopes for fires and rains to render even more hideous. The harm already done is colossal. Whoever has been at Fabyans and seen the devastated slope of Mt. Washington must have been distressed at the attack which the lumbermen are now making upon the very heart of the White Mountains. They have done irreparable damage to Mt. Jefferson and to the Franconia Notch. Mt. Bond has been defaced out of all resemblance to its former self, and Randolph Forest, the last primeval forest but one in the Presidential Range, has been utterly destroyed.[2] The æsthetic value of the scenery which is thus falling a prey to ruthless greed needs not to be emphasized to a beauty-loving public. It is the same scenery that inspired many of the heartfelt verses of Longfellow and Whittier and has inspired delight and wonder in millions of hearts before and since. Yet there is a more practical reason why this scenery should be preserved. The vacation seekers who flock to New Hampshire every summer, the stream of

[1] J. B. Harrison, New Hampshire Forestry Commission, Miscellanies.
[2] Hon. J. H. Gallinger, *Forestry and Irrigation*, Vol. XI, p. 415.

II. Government ownership and operation would remedy these faults, for tourists who pass through her borders year after year, are attracted there by the grandeur of the White Mountain scenery. This transient population spend much money during their stay in the state, and the revenue which the latter draws from their visits is considerable.[1] More will 5 be said of the value of this traffic to the state at another point; suffice it here to mention that the preservation of the scenery of the New Hampshire mountains is vital not only from an æsthetic but from a practical, financial point of view.[1]   10

What then, in brief, is the situation that is to be dealt with? The lumber companies now in possession of this vast tract of primeval woodland have been practicing reckless and destructive methods in the cutting of timber. By clearing the ground of all its trees and leaving only the 15 decaying branches, they have been exposing the forest floor to the destructive action of fire and weather. The sporadic changes in the flow of the rivers which are a necessary consequence of such loose methods are injurious to commerce and various industries and dangerous to agri- 20 culture. The timber industry itself will, in the end, be the chief sufferer from lack of attention to forest preservation; the woods are steadily disappearing, and no effort is being made to reforest the denuded areas. Such wholesale butchery of the forests that help to make the White 25 Mountains one of the most beautiful spots in the eastern states cannot have other than a destructive effect upon the scenery, and such an effect is clearly to be seen by every visitor to the region.

Something must be done, if the water supply, timber 30 and scenery are to be preserved in anything like their

[1] J. B. Harrison, New Hampshire Forestry Commission, Miscellanies.

A. They are due to the desire of private owners for
the largest possible immediate income.

B. Government management could have no such
object.

C. Government management has already proved its
efficiency, for

1. The number and extent of government
reserves have been steadily increasing.

pristine perfection. The faults to be overcome are trace-
able to one single cause, — the desire of the present owners
to secure the largest possible immediate income from their
investment. This being their motive, they adopt the most
effective means to gain their end, and, unfortunately, the 5
means which they employ precludes the existence of the
forests and everything that depends upon them. The question whether their *modus operandi* is defensible or inde-
fensible cannot be taken into account by those who seek
to prevent the continuation of present abuses. A remedy 10
must be found, and it seems to be the opinion of those who
care and know most about the question, that the establishment of a national forest reserve in the White Mountains
would secure the desired improvement. Two strong reasons go to recommend such a plan. First, the desire for 15
private gain would entirely disappear and with it all the
abuses that follow upon it. The forests would be preserved
and propagated, their natural output of timber would be
culled and disposed of at reasonable prices and the
whole region secured to coming generations as a rallying 20
ground for tired nature and the nucleus of many resorts.
Secondly, the plan advanced as a remedy has been duly
weighed in the balance of experience and is yet to be
found wanting. The United States government has $200,-
000,000 invested in national reserves in various parts of 25
the country west of the Mississippi, aggregating 91,000,-
000 acres in extent. The steady increase in the number
and extent of these reservations since the policy was inau-
gurated by the government, and the satisfaction with
which the plan is generally hailed in states where it is in 30
force furnish ample testimony of its effectiveness. As a
concrete instance of the satisfactory conditions which are

    2. Government management has improved the
       Cascade Reserve.[1]

    3. It has also improved the Olympic Reserve.[1]

III. A national reserve is the only practical solution, for
  A. Private owners cannot be forced to take proper
    precautions.

  B. The state of New Hampshire could not be expected
    to bear the burden of expense, for

    1. All of New England except Rhode Island is
      as directly concerned as New Hampshire.[2]

    2. New Hampshire cannot afford to undertake
      the enterprise alone.[2]

  C. The United States is best qualified for the under-
    taking, for

[1] Reports of the U. S. Geological Survey, 1899–1900, Part V, pp. 151–498.
[2] Allen Chamberlain, *Forestry and Irrigation*, Vol. XI, p. 457.

maintained in national reserves, we might mention the
Cascade Reserve in Oregon or the Olympic Reserve in
Washington, in both of which the number of forest fires
has been greatly reduced since the reserves were established, and " but little injury results from the cutting done,   5
since most of the trees cut are fully ripe, and indications
of decay are apparent." [1]

A national reserve is the only sane remedy that suggests
itself. Private owners cannot be forced to cut their timber
in accordance with the rules of forestry; the ground is   10
theirs to use or abuse as their commercial interests dictate.
The state of New Hampshire could not be expected to undertake the purchase and management of the forests as a
state reserve. It is true that New York and Pennsylvania
have both established successful state reserves, but two   15
considerations prevent such action on the part of New
Hampshire. The industrial and commercial interests of
the whole of New England are so vitally concerned in the
preservation of the White Mountain forests that it would
be unjust to ask New Hampshire alone to bear the burden   20
of expense ; [2] to ask the other states involved to help her
would be out of the question. Yet, even if she were alone
concerned, her financial status would not permit her to
make a purchase of such magnitude, or to keep up a successful reserve after purchasing.   25

Over against the incapacity of the state for such an
undertaking, the superior qualifications of the national government loom up so high that it seems superfluous to
say that the United States is alone in a position to purchase and preserve the White Mountain forests. Aside   30

[1] Reports of the U. S. Geological Survey, 1899–1900, Part V, pp. 151–498.
[2] Allen Chamberlain, *Forestry and Irrigation*, Vol. XI, p. 457.

1. She is able to buy the land.
2. She has a well equipped forestry service.

3. She has had extensive experience in the forest reserve business, for

    a. There are one hundred national reserves now in operation.

IV. The return which these forests would yield to New Hampshire under the lumber companies would be insignificant compared with other interests that would be sacrificed, for

   A. The revenue from the lumber companies will cease in time.

   B. The present policy of these companies endangers important industries, for
      1. Important industries depend upon the water supply.
      2. Present methods tend to decrease the water supply.
      3. The resort and tourist business stands in great peril.[1]

[1] J. B. Harrison, New Hampshire Forestry Commission, Miscellanies.

from her ability to buy over the land, she now maintains
a forestry service, the sole business of which is to understand and improve forest conditions throughout the country. The corps of forestry experts with which the service
is equipped have had, in the course of their labors among   5
the one hundred reserves already established, experience
wide and varied enough to qualify them for any undertaking along these lines which calls for thorough understanding and approved skill.

Considered from the point of view of the future revenue   10
to be derived by the state of New Hampshire, the question
is, whether New Hampshire can live better without the
lumber companies or without the forests. There is no
middle course. If the lumber companies stay, the forests
must eventually go. The revenue which the state now   15
draws from the lumbering industry will vanish when that
industry has exhausted its own materials. But what of
the many mills along the four large New England rivers
that draw their sustenance from the floor of the White
Mountain forests? If present indications may be taken as   20
a guide to what will happen with conditions unchanged,
the waters that have been keeping the wheels of these
mills in motion will long ago have deserted their task by
the time the last tree has fallen. These industries will
then be crippled and New Hampshire will share with the   25
other states the reduction of revenue that will follow. But
the elimination of her summer resort traffic will undoubtedly be the severest blow of all to the state of New Hampshire. It is sufficiently certain to render proof unnecessary
that her resort and tourist business depends entirely upon   30
her great central attraction, the White Mountains. This
business means an annual expenditure of about $8,000,000

C. Protection of the forests by the government would insure these industries.

V. A national forest reserve in the White Mountains would benefit the whole nation,[1] for

　A. The advantages of the region as a resort are sought by people from all sections.

　B. The industries threatened by present methods are of interstate and hence national importance,[1] for

　　1. The lumber industry itself is of vital importance to the nation, for

[1] Allen Chamberlain, *Forestry and Irrigation*, Vol. XI, p. 457.

by outsiders within the borders of the state.[1] If the scenery of the White Mountains is defaced by the removal of the forests, this immense income will certainly cease.[2] Government supervision and control of the forests, on the other hand, would prevent all of these financial calamities to the state of New Hampshire. Present conditions would even be improved in the course of time by the reforestation of the cleared areas wherever such treatment would be possible.

New Hampshire would be benefited in many ways by a national forest reserve, but the benefits that would come as a sequel to it would not be confined to New Hampshire or even to New England. The whole nation would share them.[3] People from all sections of the country seek pleasure and recuperation in this spot so richly adorned by nature. It belongs to no one section, any more than Yellowstone Park, Mammoth Cave, or Niagara can be said to belong to the localities in which they lie. They are national in interest if not in possession. So is this region national in interest; its preservation demands that it become national in possession. The industries too, which depend upon the White Mountain forests as the rim of a wheel upon the hub, are not the industries of one state, but of several.[3] Still other states look to these industries for supplies of articles which they themselves cannot produce. In other words, the industries threatened by the present methods of the lumber companies are of interstate and hence national importance. That the lumber industry falls within this category needs no proof, and this is the

---

[1] J. H. Robertson, *Forestry and Irrigation*, Vol. XI, p. 530.

[2] J. B. Harrison, New Hampshire Forestry Commission, Miscellanies.

[3] Allen Chamberlain, *Forestry and Irrigation*, Vol. XI, p. 457.

a. The national government's object in
establishing forest reserves is to
protect the lumber industry.

CONCLUSION

I. Since, therefore, the methods of the lumber companies
are objectionable from the point of view of the
public at large;

II. Since under government ownership and control present
errors would be corrected and the condition of the
forests improved;

III. Since a national reserve is the only practical solution
of the problem;

IV. Since the return which the forests would yield to the
state under the lumber companies would be insignificant compared with the interests that would have
to be sacrificed, and

V. Since the reservation would benefit the whole nation,—

Therefore, a national forest reserve should be established
in the White Mountains.

industry that stands in greatest danger. Indeed, its danger amounts to a certainty that if conditions are not bettered, the lumber supply from the White Mountain region will fail absolutely in time to come. If this is a question that does not concern the nation, its whole policy in establish- 5 ing and maintaining forest reserves in the West is founded upon a fallacy.

Then let the nation assume the burden of preserving the White Mountains in as much as possible of their pristine beauty and usefulness. Private ownership has proved a 10 failure, — a complete and lamentable failure, — from scientific, economic and æsthetic points of view. The logical remedy is a systematized reserve under government ownership and management, and the federal government is the only one that is fitted, as regards financial status, equip- 15 ment and experience, to undertake the responsibility. The economic gain which New Hampshire is drawing from the operation of the lumber companies within her borders is insignificant and doomed to vanish; the loss which she must inevitably sustain through a continuance of their 20 operations is vast and destined to increase. The whole nation must share her losses if she is permitted so ignominiously to lose; the whole nation will participate in her gains, if her wooded heights and glens are wrested from devastating hands and restored to their proper uses. The 25 White Mountain forests must be preserved. The self-seeking lumberman must cease his depredations upon the groves in which the hearts and interests of the people are so inextricably bound.

BRIEF

Should the United States Collect the Debts of San Domingo?

INTRODUCTION

I. The history of the question is as follows :

    A. The immediate cause for discussion is the submission of the San Domingo Treaty to the Senate, February 15, 1905.

    B. The origin of the discussion lies in the facts that

        1. A series of outbreaks from 1877 to 1904 impoverished the country and threw it into debt.

        2. The debts of San Domingo amount to from $24,000,000 to $30,000,000 and are steadily increasing.

            a. $4,500,000 of this is owed to the United States.

            b. About $16,000,000 is owed to European countries.

        3. San Domingo has broken her agreement with France and Belgium to pay them certain annual sums.

        4. In 1904, the United States was awarded $4,500,000, with the right to occupy certain custom-houses.

5. European creditors protested that they also had a right to have their debts paid.

6. As a result, President Roosevelt, unwilling to allow European powers to occupy custom-houses on this continent, drew up a treaty providing that the United States should collect all revenues and apply them to all debts, European and American.

7. The essential provisions of this treaty, which was drawn up at the repeated request of the San Domingo government, are as follows :

 a. The United States occupies all custom-houses, collects the revenue, allows the republic 55 per cent and applies 45 per cent *pro rata* to all the debts. .

 b. The United States has the right to fortify custom-houses, its consent is required for any change of tariff, and it will aid the home government to maintain order.

8. Since at the last session of Congress, the Senate failed to act in this treaty, the revenues have meanwhile been temporarily collected by U. S. officials.

 a. This plan was agreeable to all the parties concerned.

 b. If the treaty fails, all the money so collected will be turned back into the San Domingo treasury.

II. The advocates of the treaty contend that it should be ratified, in that

   A. The proposed plan will satisfy Europe, in that

      1. It guarantees an annual payment to all creditors.

   B. It will benefit San Domingo, in that

      1. Order will be better maintained, in that

         a. The custom-houses, which are the mainstay of revolutions, will be in our control.

   C. The plan embodied in the treaty is preferable to European intervention through the seizure of custom-houses, in that

      1. We are the natural arbiters.

      2. The latter plan involves the danger of permanent occupation of territory.

      3. The latter plan involves great possibilities of international complications.

   D. The proposed plan is preferable to an international alliance, in that

      1. Our policy is opposed to alliances.

      2. Such alliances are fruitful of great danger.

   E. The argument that the proposed action would set a dangerous precedent is not sound.

III. The negative side contends that the treaty should be defeated, in that

   A. Although the present plan may offer advantages to Europe and San Domingo,

   A'. Yet European occupation of custom-houses would be preferable, in that

      1. The proposed action is unprecedented.

      2. There is no danger of permanent occupation.

      B. Others declare that an international alliance would be preferable.

      C. The proposed plan creates a very dangerous precedent, in that

          1. We may be compelled to collect the debts of many other defaulting American states.

      D. Rather than create so dangerous a precedent, other opponents of the administration declare that we should deny Europe all right to collect debts by occupation of custom-houses.

IV. In this discussion the Monroe Doctrine is understood to embrace two principles:

      A. That no European power shall permanently hold any new territory on this continent.

      B. That no European power shall control an American state not hitherto so controlled.

  V. The following matter is excluded or admitted:

      A. Both sides agree that it is not desirable that any European power should hold new territory permanently on this continent.

      B. The question of the constitutionality of the protocol first drawn up by the administration is extraneous.

      C. The negative admits that the immediate effect of the present action will be beneficial to the San Dominicans and to the United States, in that

          1. The island will be pacified.

          2. Europe will be placated.

          3. Our own debts will be paid.

VI. The special issues then are:

      A. Is it desirable that European creditors should be denied all rights of obtaining satisfaction for their debts?

   B. Would European intervention, by way of occu-
      pation of custom-houses, be a desirable mode
      of procedure?
      1. Is there danger of permanent occupation of
         territory?
      2. Is there danger of international complica-
         tions?
   C. Would an international alliance be a desirable plan
      of action?
   D. Would the proposed action set a dangerous prece-
      dent, that is to say,
      1. Should we be compelled to perform similar
         offices for many American states?

BRIEF PROPER

The treaty should be adopted; for
I. It is not desirable that European creditors should
   be denied the right of obtaining satisfaction for
   their. debts, for
   A. Although it is argued that it is unjust to force
      payment of debts,
   A'. Yet Europe has a right to payment in San
      Domingo, for
      1. International law gives her the right, for
            a. John Bassett Moore testifies[1] that to-
               day a nation has a perfect legal
               right to enforce the contractual
               claims of its subjects.
      2. Though it be said that the claims are ex-
         travagant,

   [1] *Review of Reviews*, Vol. XXXI, p. 296.

2′. Yet there is no reason why the United States should not insist that they be submitted to arbitration.

II. It is not desirable that the European powers concerned should intervene by occupying the custom-houses, for

A. We are the natural arbiters, for

1. By adherence to the Monroe Doctrine we have for eighty years played the dominant part here.

B. Though it be said that this plan would have precedent,

B′. Yet we have never had a case just like the present one.

C. There is danger of permanent occupation of territory, for

1. Europe has a desire for territory on this continent, for

a. Only England has a coaling station on this continent.[1]

b. The action of England toward Venezuela in 1895, and of England and Germany in 1903, are such as to cause us to be suspicious of their good intentions.

c. German newspapers are continually looking for means of enhancing German interests on this continent.[1]

d. Germany is increasing her influence in Brazil.

[1] *The Outlook*, Vol. LXXIX, p. 366.

    2. Intervention in San Domingo would give her
      the means of satisfying this desire, for

        a. The European nations entering San
           Domingo would stay at least fif-
           teen years, for

           (1) The estimate of the debt is
               $20,000,000 at the lowest,
               and the highest estimate
               of the yearly amount to
               apply on it is about
               $1,500,000.

        b. The European nations will have troops
           and warships to aid them in secur-
           ing permanent possession, for

           (1) They must have means of pro-
               tecting themselves from
               insurgents.

    3. It may not be easy to eject any European
      nation if it shows a tendency to remain
      permanently, for

        a. The European nation might deny our
           charges and affirm that its debts
           were not yet paid.

        b. Force might be required.

  D. There is danger of international complications,
    for

    1. There would be half a dozen navies, armies,
      policies, — all conflicting, on one little
      island.

III. An international alliance, with one nation acting as the
    deputy for the others, would not be desirable, for

A. It would be contrary to our past policy, for

1. We have never entered foreign alliances except under conditions of extreme stress.
2. We are opposed especially to alliances governing the affairs of this continent, for
   a. The Monroe Doctrine is a reëmphasis of our policy of national aloofness, with respect to this continent alone.
   b. We have refused to allow any European nation to manage the Panama Canal with us.
3. Though it be said that of late we seem to have shown more of a tendency to take part in the world's affairs,
3'. Yet we have participated in only one alliance, — the Western movement against China in 1900.

B. The argument given above (II, A), that the United States is the natural arbiter, holds here as well.

C. If a foreign nation were named as deputy to act for the other powers in San Domingo, there would be the same danger of permanent occupation as in the case of all the nations entering the island.

D. If the United States be named the deputy, we have a situation similar to the one advocated by President Roosevelt, save that in the latter we avoid the danger of foreign complications, for
   1. President Roosevelt declared in his message of February 15, 1907, that all the powers concerned had agreed to let us act for them.

E. Such alliances are apt to lead to jealousy and complications, for

  1. Our experience in Samoa with England and Germany was such that we should shun such associations forever, for

    a. This is the testimony of J. W. Foster, in his *Century of American Diplomacy.*

IV. The precedent created by this treaty is not a dangerous one, for

  A. Although there are half a dozen American nations with large defaulted debts

  A.' Yet it is not likely that we shall be compelled to act often, for

    1. In the future we must have a state with a large defaulted debt, agreements broken, and other forcible means of collection lacking, for

      a. If the present case is to form a precedent, its general features must be repeated. .

    2. We could refuse to act unless we had debts of our own.

    3. We could refuse to act unless the country concerned were willing, as San Domingo is to-day.

    4. It is not even necessary that we act in one case precisely as in another, for

      a. J. B. Moore says [1] that we act in each case as it comes up.

----

[1] *Review of Reviews*, Vol. XXXI, p. 298.

    5. There are not likely to be many cases in the future, for

        a. Central and South America have learned that we refuse to protect them against their creditors, for

            (1) Germany and England were allowed to bombard Venezuela's ports.

            (2) Roosevelt has repeatedly made this statement.[1]

        b. Many American states are becoming more responsible.[2]

B. It is not likely that these cases which do occur would cause much hardship, for

    1. Only a few troops and a warship or so have been required in San Domingo.

CONCLUSION

The treaty should be adopted, for

I. Its plan of action is preferable to refusal to allow Europe to obtain any satisfaction.

II. It is preferable to European occupation of customhouses.

III. It is preferable to an international alliance.

IV. The proposed action will not create a dangerous precedent.

[1] Roosevelt's Message, February 16, 1905 ; Message, December 5, 1905.

[2] Roosevelt's Message, December 5, 1905.

Should the United States Collect the Debts of San Domingo?

We have doubtless all heard the story of the fair child of Venezuela who, on being asked whether she was a Daughter of the Revolution, replied scornfully that she was the daughter of a score of them. It is the impression
5 generated by just such a story, which probably prevails in the minds of most of the people both of our country and of Europe. Many of our voters are so weary of the almost incessant agitations bursting out among our Central and South American neighbors that they are apt to pass by
10 with scant attention any consideration of our policy toward them. So to-day, with many of us, there is comparative ignorance of the provisions of the San Domingo treaty submitted in February, 1905, to the United States Senate, a treaty by which the United States agrees to assume the
15 task of collecting the revenues of the turbulent island state and of applying them to its large defaulted debt. It need hardly be said that this indifference is pernicious. If those of our people who look with disfavor on the South Americans are left to have their way, they may be able to
20 pursue a course injurious through its harshness to us as well as the South Americans. On the centrary, if those who would leave our Southern neighbors strictly alone are permitted to prevail, these states may be left to the mercy of unscrupulous European powers. It behooves us,
25 therefore, to study this San Domingo case with care, in

order that we may act both to benefit ourselves and to deal justly by Europe and by San Domingo.

The conditions in San Domingo leading up to the treaty were a long series of disgraceful outbreaks, starting as early as 1871 and culminating in the years from 1899 to 1904, when six violent changes of government took place. The climax came in 1904, when a state of veritable anarchy prevailed. Naturally a country in which such conditions exist cannot hope to be prosperous enough to pay her obligations. San Domingo found her trade interfered with, her revenues squandered to meet the expenses of constantly recurring revolutions, and her custom-houses looted by insurgents in need of funds. The custom-houses indeed were the nuclei of revolutions.[1]

As a result, San Domingo was burdened with a large debt, owed partly to the United States, but very largely to Europe. The amount was $3,785,000 in 1875, on which no interest was then being paid. Since 1875 it has steadily mounted higher, until to-day it is estimated to be somewhere between $24,000,000 and $30,000,000. Of this $4,500,000 is owed to the San Domingo Improvement Company of the United States, about $3,000,000 is internal indebtedness, and the rest is owed to Europe. Of late years, the debt has been piling even higher. In 1904 the interest due from San Domingo was $1,700,000, and there was only $500,000 to apply on it. It is from these debts that the whole San Domingo discussion has arisen.

France and Belgium drew up an agreement with the little republic, calling for the payment of stated sums

[1] President Roosevelt's Messages as reported in the *Boston Herald*, February 16 and December 5, 1905; J. B. Moore, *Review of Reviews*, Vol. XXXI, p. 293.

monthly, but San Domingo soon ceased payment and violated her word. The United States submitted her claims
to joint arbitration, and on July 14, 1904, was awarded
$4,500,000 and the right to occupy certain custom-houses
5 and collect the revenues therefrom until the whole should
be paid. Immediately we proceeded to act, but were at
once met with the declarations of European creditors, who
asserted that they too deserved satisfaction. The plan
finally adopted by President Roosevelt, at the urgent and
10 repeated solicitation of the San Domingo government,
was to draw up a treaty providing that the United States
should collect the customs revenue of the island and apply
the resulting funds to the foreign and domestic debt. The
essential provisions of this treaty are as follows : (1) the
15 United States is to occupy the custom-houses of the country, collect all revenues, turn 55 per cent of the proceeds
over to the native government and apply the remaining
45 per cent *pro rata* to all the debts of San Domingo;
(2) the United States is to have the right to fortify the
20 custom-houses as far as may be deemed necessary; (3) our
consent is required for any change of tariff; and (4) we
agree to "lend our best efforts to the San Domingo government to restore its credit, preserve order, and advance its
welfare."[1] The treaty may be summed up as a debt-collect-
25 ing document. All its provisions look to the accomplishment of that end. Such, then, is the history of the question
we have under consideration.

At the last session of Congress the Senate failed to act
on this treaty. President Roosevelt, as soon as that body
30 adjourned, caused a *modus vivendi* to be drawn up by
which the revenues have in the meantime been collected

---

[1] Text of treaty in the *Boston Herald*, February 16, 1905.

by United States officials. This plan was agreeable both to Europe and to San Domingo. If the Senate, however, fails to ratify the treaty, the money so collected will be turned back into the San Domingo treasury, and the United States officials will leave the island.

Those who advocate the adoption of this treaty base their support on five general grounds:

1. The proposed plan will satisfy Europe, as it guarantees an annual payment to all creditors.

2. It will benefit San Domingo by restoring and preserving order, since the custom-houses, the mainstay of revolutions, will be under our control.

3. The plan embodied in the treaty is preferable to European intervention through the seizure of custom-houses, since there is danger of resulting permanent occupation of territory by European powers, and since we are the natural arbiters.

4. The proposed plan is preferable to an international alliance, inasmuch as an alliance is contrary to our policy and, in the present case, fraught with danger of complications.

5. It is not true that action under the present treaty would set a dangerous precedent.

The opponents of President Roosevelt, when confronted with these strong arguments, reply with counter contentions as cogent and forceful. They declare:

1. That, although the present plan may offer advantages to Europe and San Domingo, yet European occupation of custom-houses would be preferable, inasmuch as the proposed action is unprecedented, and there is no danger of permanent occupation by Europeans.

2. That an international alliance would be preferable.

3. That the proposed plan creates a very dangerous precedent, inasmuch as we may be compelled to collect the debts of many other defaulting American states.

4. That, rather than create so dangerous a precedent, 5 we should deny Europe all right to collect debts by occupation of custom-houses, especially as many of these debts are extremely fraudulent.

The bearing of the Monroe Doctrine on all these contentions and counter contentions is not at once evident to 10 the casual observer. President Roosevelt declares that devotion to the principles of that famous doctrine compelled him to act as he did. There is much confusion in the minds of many as to its definite meaning, and indeed it has been the juggler's ball of politicians so 15 long that to formulate distinct ideas concerning it is difficult.

Of course, with changing times its meaning has changed also, for no one attempts to declare it to be as immutable as the laws of the Medes and Persians. It is applied in 20 various ways to meet varying conditions. Nevertheless, I may say I believe, after a perusal of the more important works on the subject, that during the fourscore years of its existence two principles have steadily underlain it: (1) that Europe shall acquire no more territory for per- 25 manent occupation upon this continent; (2) that Europe shall affect the destinies of, that is exert influence over, no American state.[1] The motives for such action, as Lyman Abbott has well pointed out, have been either solicitude for our own welfare, or desire to protect our American

[1] A. B. Hart, *Foundations of American Foreign Policy*, chap. vii; J. W. Foster, *A Century of American Diplomacy*, chap. xii; J. A. Kasson, *The Evolution of the Constitution of the United States of America*, pp. 221 ff.

neighbors, or — and this has possibly been most frequently the case — both impulses.[1]

Both sides generally agree that it is eminently undesirable for Europe to acquire new territory here; they differ most decidedly, however, on the possibility of such a contingency resulting from European interference in this San Domingo affair. There is still other neutral ground between our opposing forces, unoccupied by the pickets of either side, and we shall profitably enhance the clearness of our argument by carefully marking it off. Besides agreeing that it is not desirable for any European power to acquire new territory on this continent where it might obtain command of the Panama Canal, both sides admit that the *immediate* effect of the present action will be beneficial both to the San Dominicans and ourselves. We shall obtain our money, San Domingo will be more pacified; both of us will gain therefrom. Finally, the clearness of our discussion will be greatly aided if all argument concerning the constitutionality of the protocol originally drawn up by President Roosevelt be rigorously excluded.

It should be clear, then, that the opponents in the present controversy clash squarely on the question of a dangerous precedent (Contentions 5 and 3, respectively); of the desirability of European occupation of custom-houses (Contentions 3 and 1); and of an international alliance (Contentions 4 and 2). The argument of the negative that Europe should obtain no satisfaction for her debts is left to be answered by the affirmative in rebuttal. The argument of the affirmative that the treaty will benefit Europe and San Domingo is partly admitted by the negative and partly answered, by some that San Domingo would pay

[1] L. Abbott, *The Outlook*, Vol. LXXIX, pp. 366, 367.

fraudulent debts and that no collection by force should be
allowed (Contention 4), by others that European intervention (Contention 1) or an international alliance (Contention 2) would be preferable and fairer to Europe.

5   Thus we see that the issues we have to weigh narrow
down considerably, and from the rather tangled mass
we find that we have the following four questions to
answer :

1. Is it desirable that European creditors should be
10 denied all right of occupying custom-houses?

2. Would European intervention by way of occupation
of custom-houses be a desirable mode of procedure?

3. Would an international alliance under the auspices
of the Hague Tribunal be a desirable plan of action?

15   4. Does the proposed plan create a dangerous precedent?

It is evident, even from a casual glance at these issues,
that we are dealing with a balanced question. Each side
would be willing to admit that there are strong arguments
backing up the claims of its adversary ; our process of
20 determining for the one or the other must depend, therefore, on the weighing carefully of the two sides. We are
dealing with various plans for solving this situation, any
one of which is exclusive of all the rest. One plan allows
no occupation of custom-houses, two plans allow Europe
25 to act, either apart from us or in an international alliance,
while the fourth plan lets the United States proceed as it
has agreed to do in the treaty. After considering these
various plans on the basis of the issues as outlined above,
I am of the opinion that the plan proposed by President
30 Roosevelt is the most desirable, and therefore I shall present the affirmative aspect of the matter in the rest of
these pages.

The first question we have to consider is whether under the circumstances there should be any action whatever. Many persons, in criticising President Roosevelt, declare that it is high time the United States took a firm stand and declared to the creditor nations of Europe that henceforth no more debts shall be collected on this continent by force. Individuals do not collect debts, it is urged; it is time nations did not. This is the now famous Drago Doctrine. Besides, it is held that many of the claims for debts in South America are fraudulent in the extreme.

Several strong objections, however, instantly arise. Indeed the argument does not agree at all with the spirit of the other plans offered by the opponents of the treaty, all of which aim at our playing a less and not a more dominant part in the matter. According to these persons, however, we should absolutely dictate to Europe and roundly assert: "You shall not collect debts on this continent by force." It is all very well to say that it would be only justice so to act, and that individuals no longer resort to violence in financial matters; it may even be said that the debts are largely fraudulent and usurious. We reply, first, that there is no reason why fraudulent claims should be paid to San Domingo. There is every reason, both of propriety and of justice, why we should protect San Domingo and insist that no debts should be paid till submitted to arbitration, either at the Hague or by arrangement between the parties concerned. Pruned thus, all claims should be paid by any self-respecting nation as well as individual. This is exactly what was done with the American claims. Are we to say that we may submit our own claims to arbitration and obtain satisfaction therefor to the exclusion of others? And yet that is precisely what this plan proposes, unless indeed the Americans, who have already been promised $4,500,000, consent to withdraw their claim.

Besides, however desirable it may be that international law should refuse to nations the right of forcible collection
5 of claims, to-day it does not do so. At present, Germany or any other nation has a perfect legal right to enforce the contractual claims of its subjects on this continent, and not with impunity may we deny it. It does not seem, then, that this plan is feasible. It would be unfair to
10 Europe and unwarranted in international law.[1]

So we come to the desirability of European intervention in San Domingo. By such intervention, I mean at present merely the occupation of custom-houses by foreign nations, and the collection of the revenues until all claims are
15 satisfied. It is understood, of course, that some arrangement would be effected with San Domingo by each of the powers concerned, whereby all the details should be arranged. This plan, declare its advocates, is the only natural one. Each nation acts independently, adjudicating
20 its own claims, providing for the collection of revenues and the payment of its own debts, dealing all through with San Domingo alone.

Inevitably there must be certain objections to such a line of action as well as to the one we have just rejected.
25 In the first place, there is no guarantee that Europe would actually submit her claims to arbitration or would cut them down to any fair extent. The opponents of President Roosevelt themselves admit that these debts are notoriously padded.[2] Granting fair dealing here, however,

[1] J. B. Moore, *Review of Reviews*, Vol. XXXI, p. 296. President Roosevelt's Message, February 16, 1905.

[2] *The Nation*, February 2, 1905.

we may well hold that on this continent the United States
is the natural arbiter of all disputes like the present one.
We are the strongest and oldest nation on this continent.
By the application of the Monroe Doctrine, now concurred
in, whether willingly or no, by the civilized world, we 5
have long played a dominant part here. It is but natural
that in this San Domingo affair we assume the accustomed rôle once more. It would mean chaos and bickering
for half a dozen nations to enter into San Domingo; if
only one nation is allowed to act, what nation is more 10
fitted for the duty than the United States?

We are told by our friends that it is unprecedented for
one nation to say to another, " No, you shall not collect
your debts in this country, but I will do it for you."
Therefore, we are informed that it is desirable for us to 15
turn to well-established lines in our conduct of this affair.
The United States, however, has never had a case presented to its notice precisely like this one. When a case
presents itself, we must needs act one way or the other,
and we have never been noted for our unwillingness to create 20
precedents. Whether the precedent so created be dangerous or not, seems so important a question that I have
reserved it for detailed treatment at the end.

We realize that if Europe is to interfere it must be by
the temporary occupation of custom-houses. As I explained 25
in the beginning, the Monroe Doctrine declares against any
increased permanent occupation of territory on this continent by Europe, and it is fair to assume, as I have before
noted, that the great majority of our people heartily con-
cur in this attitude. We should not wish to see German 30
troops in San Domingo or a French cruiser guarding a
port overlooking the way to the Panama Canal. And so

the sole question to determine here is the possibility of such temporary changing into permanent occupation, or at least generating difficulties almost as bad.

According to John Bassett Moore, Professor of Inter-
5 national Law at Columbia University and special investi-
gator of the San Domingo situation, there are at least half a dozen nations with claims against the island republic.[1] These are England, France, Belgium, Italy, Germany, and the United States. Under the plan we are now consider-
10 ing each of these nations would proceed to occupy a custom-house, protecting it by such troops and war ships as it deemed essential. Then these nations would remain, at the shortest, until all their debts were paid. Estimating these debts at the lowest amount given, perhaps
15 $20,000,000, and admitting that about $1,500,000 will flow in every year[2] (above the share of San Domingo), we come easily to the conclusion that fifteen years is the shortest time it is rational to believe that European nations would remain in San Domingo.

20 Now it will not do for anyone to affirm that fifteen years' occupation will necessarily lead to permanent occu-
pation. But the converse is just as true. When we let such nations in no one knows what the result will be. At least we may be morally certain that complications will
25 ensue. Think of it! For at least fifteen years, six nations, six navies, six different sets of troops, perhaps six different policies! Traditional chaos might well break loose.

Nor is the idea of permanent occupation a mere bugbear. We know in the first place that Europe has had always,
30 and cherishes still, a strong desire to gain a foothold here,

---

[1] *Review of Reviews*, Vol. XXXI, p. 295.
[2] This is the highest estimate made.

especially to obtain coaling stations on this continent. According to *The Outlook*, England to-day is the only European power which possesses such a coaling station. Germany has none, and the German newspapers — for example, *Die Deutsche Post* — are always looking for means of increasing her power here.[1] The gradual extension of her power in Brazil also looks to this one end. Besides, the action of England toward Venezuela in 1895 and the undue severity of England and Germany toward that republic in 1903 all tend to shake, though they may not undermine, our confidence in the statement that Europe has no desire to acquire American territory. Now if one nation should obtain a coaling station here, all nations would soon be hastening to do likewise.

Besides the motive, the means for the accomplishment of this end also exists. At least fifteen years, and perhaps twenty or even thirty, would elapse before the nations occupying custom-houses in San Domingo could, with any show of justice on our part, be asked to remove themselves. Indeed the time would much more likely be unreasonably increased if there were no one hand guiding all the affairs harmoniously. A further means would lie in the necessity of the European nations to bring troops and battle-ships to our shores in order to guard the custom-houses from the hands of the revolutionists. It would thus be far easier for them to strengthen their grip until it became a permanent lodgment.

We are told by our opponents that if such a permanent lodgment resulted or seemed likely to result, we could at once eject the offending nation. The latter nation, however, might deny our charges and, it is conceivable, might

---

[1] *The Outlook*, Vol. LXXIX, p. 867.

stir up a veritable international tempest. The force of arms, indeed, might be the ultimate resort.

Of course all these results are only possible ones. Even their possibility raises a presumption in the favor of the advocates of the treaty. There is no need of our balancing even such a possibility against the comparatively small expense connected with the absolutely definite plan embodied in the treaty. It seems, then, that this plan too is not desirable. It is not desirable that half a dozen European nations enter into San Domingo; there is too much danger of complications arising between the jealous powers involved; there is danger of permanent occupation; there is constant risk.

What then of the third plan offered for our consideration? Why not, say some of the opponents of the present treaty, proceed with the other creditor nations precisely as a number of individuals in a case of bankruptcy? Let one nation, it is urged, be created the deputy of the other members of the alliance; let it enter into San Domingo and, with the consent of all, proceed to collect the revenues.

One can readily grant that this plan presents several desirable features. It seems fair to all concerned, and yet several reasons for rejecting it must occur to us with great force. The most vital of all of these, and indeed the one which has had and will in the future have for our people the greatest strength, is that this course would constitute a proceeding directly contrary to our past policy. From the day of Washington's Farewell Address, it has been an axiom of our foreign policy that all entangling alliances should be shunned. Only under the stress of the greatest necessity have we departed from this straight line, as in crises such as that created by the Boxer massacres of 1900.

If we have not encouraged alliances of any sort, we have most certainly not tolerated alliances regulating affairs on this continent. The Monroe Doctrine, then, is a reëmphasis of this principle of national aloofness. The whole history of our State Department bears out this statement. Time [5] and again our Secretaries of State, as, for example, Fish, Frelinghuysen, and Blaine, have declared that the Panama Canal is entirely an American affair and must be managed by us alone.[1] So insistent and pervasive is this sentiment that Secretary Hay was compelled to present to [10] the Senate in 1902 a canal treaty, which robbed England of all her power over the interoceanic water way. The nation's idea is Olney's: "On this continent our fiat is law."

.If we are told that of late we seem to have broken from [15] our traditional attitude of aloofness and appear ready to enter into alliances now which we did not dream of ten years ago, I would reply, first, that while there has been much talk of alliances and Dreibunds, the past eight or nine years have actually seen only one alliance material- [20] ize, i.e. the Western Alliance against China, a movement dictated by the requirements of national honor itself. Although we sent a representative to the Moroccan conference, and expect to continue to take a large part in the affairs of the world, as for instance in the Hague [25] Tribunal, we have on the whole clung to our old plan as closely as ever, especially in the conduct of this hemisphere's affairs. The canal is ours; this continent is ours.

There are still other objections to an international alliance. The objection offered above to the intervention of [30]

[1] A. B. Hart, *Foundations of American Foreign Policy*, pp. 212, 221; J. W. Foster, *A Century of American Diplomacy*, pp. 459, 463–465.

the European creditors by occupation of custom-houses is
applicable here also. The United States, in other words,
is in this matter the natural arbiter. It would be strange
indeed if such an alliance did not name the United States
5 as its deputy to proceed to collect the revenues of San
Domingo. Such being the case, the result is little different
from the present case, for we have President Roosevelt's
word that all the creditor nations of Europe have consented
to his plan. But, on the other hand, in the *statu quo* we
10 avoid all dangers of not satisfying our allies and of becoming entangled in European quarrels. From still another
point of view it is conceivable that such an international
alliance might appoint some European nation to act, so to
speak, as its referee in bankruptcy. In such a contingency
15 we should be confronted with the possibility of uncertain
future troubles and possible permanent occupation by that
particular nation.

Finally, alliances such as those dealing with some ob-
streperous island state usually lead to unwelcome results.
20 All the nations concerned are more or less jealous of each
other, each fearing that one of the others is secretly trying to encroach on it. So unfortunate, for example, was
our experience with England and Germany in Samoa,
that John W. Foster[1] has declared that the lesson there
25 learned should make us shun all future alliances of such
a nature.

I have taken up in turn these three plans, all of which
are advocated by some class of the President's opponents.
All of them have admittedly contained certain advantages.
30 All, however, have been rejected for reasons outlined above.
The plan proposed by President Roosevelt does not seem

[1] *A Century of American Diplomacy*, chapter on Samoa.

to possess these disadvantages ; it is definite, certain ; it
aims to keep the United States in the ascendency on this
continent. It is true, however, that the proposed treaty
establishes a new precedent; never before have we collected the debts of an American state. This point is 5
seized upon with great avidity by the opponents of President Roosevelt as the greatest and, they feel, the almost
insuperable objection to his plan. Thus the last question
we have to consider here becomes whether the precedent
so created be a dangerous one. 10

.   We are told by the opponents of the treaty that at least
half a dozen South and Central American states have large
defaulted debts, and that at any time we may be called
upon to act in regard to them as we have been called upon
to act toward San Domingo. The report of the Associa- 15
tion of Foreign Bondholders [1] does indeed show that many
of these states have defaulted, and also that, in the case of
Costa Rica and Honduras especially, all efforts to induce
payment have so far proved unavailing. It is therefore
possible that in time we may here have to face a situation 20
where we should be asked by prominent European powers
to undertake the collection of claims as we once did in
San Domingo.

That we should be compelled so to act, however, by
reason of our action in San Domingo is not at all evident. 25
In the first place, in order to make a precedent the general features of the present situation must be repeated.
There must be a large defaulted debt; all efforts toward
collection must have failed; agreements such as France
and Belgium tried in San Domingo must have been broken; 30
even forcible means of collection should have been tried

[1] *New York Evening Post*, February 27, 1905.

first, as England and Germany tried them in Venezuela in 1903, i.e. by bombardment or other attack, before it is finally admitted that the collection of the revenue offers the sole avenue of escape. Even then we should not be forced
5 to act unless the country concerned is willing, as San Domingo is to-day. We could declare that, under such conditions, if the powers could not collect their debts by agreement or by bombardment, or other show of force, we would not occupy custom-houses to collect the debts, even
10 if our own citizens were involved. If our citizens were not involved, as they are to-day, we should have still another reason for declaring that we could not sacrifice our interests when we had nothing at stake. This latter stand would not be the most desirable, but it would be
15 perfectly allowable.

Moreover, as John Bassett Moore has said, the United States is not forced to act in any case precisely as it has in another. Precedent is not so binding. " We deal with each case as it comes up." [1]
20 It is not likely that in the future there will be many such cases. In the first place, South American countries have learned that the Monroe Doctrine does not protect them from the righteous indignation of European creditors. The ports of Venezuela have been bombarded by German
25 and English war-vessels ; President Roosevelt has publicly declared that he would protect no American state from just retribution. Moreover, we know that in many South American states there has been of late a decided advance toward respectability. President Roosevelt [2] himself has
30 praised a number of them for their progress ; in Chile,

[1] *Review of Reviews*, Vol. XXXI, p. 298.
[2] Message, December 5, 1905.

Peru, Mexico, and Argentina, especially, revolutions are absolutely things of the past.

Nor is it abandoning my position to say that if we do undertake the present task again in some future day, it is not one we should desire or ought to shun. No great 5 burden is ours as a result of the San Domingo affair. A battle-ship and a few troops are sufficient to preserve order ; for it is the testimony of all that the custom-houses have been the source or at least the mainstay of all the revolutions. 10

The present treaty calls, then, for the United States to do justice to Europe and to aid San Domingo to become a self-respecting neighbor. This end, sought also by most of the opponents of the treaty, will be attained better, we believe, by the present arrangement than by a method 15 which denies all recompense to debtors, or by one which lays us under the danger of permanent occupation of territory by European powers, or, finally, by one which opens up all the possibilities of complication of an international alliance. 20

The plan proposed is not ideal, and I have not presented it as such. It involves difficulties and even complications. But it seems, by all odds, the most desirable one that could be arranged under the circumstances.

. MODELS OF DESCRIPTION

A LOAMSHIRE LANDSCAPE[1]

George Eliot

The Green lay at the extremity of the village, and from
it the road branched off in two directions, one leading
farther up the hill by the church, and the other winding
gently down towards the valley. On the side of the Green
5 that led towards the church, the broken line of thatched
cottages was continued nearly to the churchyard gate ; but
on the opposite, northwestern side, there was nothing to
obstruct the view of gently-swelling meadow, and wooded
valley, and dark masses of distant hill. That rich undu-
10 lating district of Loamshire to which Hayslope belonged,
lies close to a grim outskirt of Stonyshire, overlooked by
its barren hills as a pretty blooming sister may sometimes
be seen linked in the arm of a rugged, tall, swarthy
brother; and in two or three hours' ride the traveller
15 might exchange a bleak treeless region, intersected by
lines of cold grey stone, for one where his road wound
under the shelter of woods, or up swelling hills, muffled
with hedgerows and long meadow-grass and thick corn :
and where at every turn he came upon some fine old coun-
20 try-seat nestled in the valley or crowning the slope, some
homestead with its long length of barn and its cluster of

[1] From *Adam Bede*, chap. ii.

golden ricks, some grey steeple looking out from a pretty confusion of trees and thatch and dark-red tiles. It was just such a picture as this last that Hayslope Church had made to the traveller as he began to mount the gentle slope leading to its pleasant uplands, and now from his station near the Green he had before him in one view nearly all the other typical features of this pleasant land. High up against the horizon were the huge conical masses of hill, like giant mounds intended to fortify this region of corn and grass against the keen and hungry winds of the north; not distant enough to be clothed in purple mystery, but with sombre greenish sides visibly specked with sheep, whose motion was only revealed by memory, not detected by sight; wooed from day to day by the changing hours, but responding with no change in themselves — left for ever grim and sullen after the flush of morning, the winged gleams of the April noonday, the parting crimson glory of the ripening summer sun. And directly below them the eye rested on a more advanced line of hanging woods, divided by bright patches of pasture or furrowed crops, and not yet deepened into the uniform leafy curtains of high summer, but still showing the warm tints of the young oak and the tender green of the ash and lime. Then came the valley, where the woods grew thicker, as if they had rolled down and hurried together from the patches left smooth on the slope, that they might take the better care of the tall mansion which lifted its parapets and sent its faint blue summer smoke among them. Doubtless there was a large sweep of park and a broad glassy pool in front of that mansion, but the swelling slope of meadow would not let our traveller see them from the village green. He saw instead a foreground that was just as lovely — the level sunlight lying like transparent gold among the gently-curving stems of the feathered grass and the tall red sorrel, and the white umbels of the hemlocks lining the bushy hedgerows. It was that moment in summer 5 when the sound of the scythe being whetted makes us cast more lingering looks at the flower-sprinkled tresses of the meadows.

NEW COLLEGE GARDENS [1]

Nathaniel Hawthorne

We first drew up at New College (a strange name for
such an old place, but it was new some time since the Conquest), and went through its quiet and sunny quadrangles,
and into its sunny and shadowy gardens. I am in despair
about the architecture and old edifices of these Oxford col- 5
leges, it is so impossible to express them in words. They
are themselves — as the architect left them, and as Time
has modified and improved them — the expression of an
idea which does not admit of being otherwise expressed, or
translated into anything else. Those old battlemented walls 10
around the quadrangles; many gables; the windows with
stone pavilions, so very antique, yet some of them adorned
with fresh flowers in pots, — a very sweet contrast; the
ivy mantling the gray stone; and the infinite repose, both
in sunshine and shadow, — it is as if half a dozen bygone 15
centuries had set up their rest here, and as if nothing of the
present time ever passed through the deeply recessed archway that shuts in the College from the street. Not but what
people have very free admittance; and many parties of
young men and girls and children came into the gardens 20
while we were there.

These gardens of New College are indescribably beautiful, — not gardens in an American sense, but lawns of the

[1] From *English Note Books* (Hawthorne's Works, Riverside Edition,
Vol. VIII), pp. 348–349. Houghton, Mifflin & Co., Boston, 1883.

richest green and softest velvet grass, shadowed over by
ancient trees, that have lived a quiet life here for centuries,
and have been nursed and tended with such care, and so
sheltered from rude winds, that certainly they must have
5 been the happiest of all trees. Such a sweet, quiet, sacred,
stately seclusion — so age-long as this has been, and, I hope,
will continue to be — cannot exist anywhere else. One side
of the garden wall is formed by the ancient wall of the city,
which Cromwell's artillery battered, and which still retains
10 its pristine height and strength. At intervals, there are
round towers that formed the bastions ; that is to say, on
the exterior they are round towers, but within, in the garden of the College, they are semicircular recesses, with iron
garden-seats arranged round them. The loop-holes through
15 which the archers and musketeers used to shoot still pierce
through deep recesses in the wall, which is here about six
feet thick. I wish I could put into one sentence the whole
impression of this garden, but it could not be done in many
pages.

AUTUMN IN WILTSHIRE[1]

CHARLES DICKENS

It was pretty late in the autumn of the year, when the declining sun, struggling through the mist which had obscured it all day, looked brightly down upon a little Wiltshire village, within an easy journey of the fair old town of Salisbury. 5

Like a sudden flash of memory or spirit kindling up the mind of an old man, it shed a glory upon the scene, in which its departed youth and freshness seemed to live again. The wet grass sparkled in the light; the scanty patches of verdure in the hedges — where a few green 10 twigs yet stood together bravely, resisting to the last the tyranny of nipping winds and early frosts — took heart and brightened up; the stream which had been dull and sullen all day long, broke out into a cheerful smile; the birds began to chirp and twitter on the naked boughs, as 15 though the hopeful creatures half believed that winter had gone by, and spring had come already. The vane upon the tapering spire of the old church glistened from its lofty station in sympathy with the general gladness; and from the ivy-shaded windows such gleams of light shone back 20 upon the glowing sky, that it seemed as if the quiet building were the hoarding-place of twenty summers, and all their ruddiness and warmth were stored within.

Even those tokens of the season which emphatically whispered of the coming winter, graced the landscape, and, 25

[1] From *The Life and Adventures of Martin Chuzzlewit*, chap. ii.

237

for the moment, tinged its livelier features with no oppressive air of sadness. The fallen leaves, with which the ground was strewn, gave forth a pleasant fragrance, and subduing all harsh sounds of distant feet and wheels,
5 created a repose in gentle unison with the light scattering of seed hither and thither by the distant husbandman, and with the noiseless passage of the plough as it turned up the rich brown earth, and wrought a graceful pattern in the stubbled fields. On the motionless branches of some
10 trees, autumn berries hung like clusters of coral beads, as in those fabled orchards where the fruits were jewels; others, stripped of all their garniture, stood, each the centre of its little heap of bright red leaves, watching their slow decay; others again, still wearing theirs, had
15 them all crunched and crackled up, as though they had been burnt; about the stems of some were piled, in ruddy mounds, the apples they had borne that year; while others (hardy evergreens this class) showed somewhat stern and gloomy in their vigour, as charged by nature with the
20 admonition that it is not to her more sensitive and joyous favourites she grants the longest term of life. Still athwart their darker boughs, the sunbeams struck out paths of deeper gold; and the red light, mantling in among their swarthy branches, used them as foils to set its brightness
25 off, and aid the lustre of the dying day.

A moment, and its glory was no more. The sun went down beneath the long dark lines of hill and cloud which piled up in the west an air city, wall heaped on wall, and battlement on battlement; the light was all withdrawn;
30 the shining church turned cold and dark; the stream forgot to smile; the birds were silent; and the gloom of winter dwelt on everything.

JULY DAYS[1]

Rowland E. Robinson

The woods are dense with full-grown leafage. Of all the trees, only the basswood has delayed its blossoming, to crown the height of summer and fill the sun-steeped air with a perfume that calls all the wild bees from hollow tree and scant woodside gleaning to a wealth of honey 5 gathering, and all the hive-dwellers from their board-built homes to a finer and sweeter pillage than is offered by the odorous white sea of buckwheat. Half the flowers of wood and fields are out of bloom. Herdsgrass, clover, and daisy are falling before the mower. The early grain fields have 10 already caught the color of the sun, and the tasseling corn rustles its broad leaves above the rich loam that the woodcock delights to bore.

The dwindling streams have lost their boisterous clamor of springtide and wimple with subdued voices over beds too 15 shallow to hide a minnow or his poised shadow on the sunlit shallows. The sharp eye of the angler probes the green depths of the slowly swirling pools, and discovers the secrets of the big fish which congregate therein.

The river has marked the stages of its decreasing volume 20 with many lines along its steep banks. It discloses the muskrat's doorway, to which he once dived so gracefully, but now must clumsily climb to. Rafts of driftwood bridge

---

[1] From *In New England Fields and Woods*, pp. 91–93. Houghton, Mifflin & Co., Boston, 1896.

the shallow current sunk so low that the lithe willows
bend in vain to kiss its warm bosom. This only the sway-
ing trails of water-weeds and rustling sedges toy with now;
and swift-winged swallows coyly touch. There is not depth
5 to hide the scurrying schools of minnows, the half of whom
fly into the air in a curving burst of silver shower before
the rush of a pickerel, whose green and mottled sides gleam
like a swift-shot arrow in the downright sunbeams.

The sandpiper tilts along the shelving shore. Out of an
10 embowered harbor a wood duck convoys her fleet of duck-
lings, and on the ripples of their wake the anchored argosies
of the water lilies toss and cast adrift their cargoes of perfume. Above them the green heron perches on an overhanging branch, uncouth but alert, whether sentinel or
15 scout, flapping his awkward way along the ambient bends
and reaches. With slow wing-beats he signals the coming
of some more lazily moving boat that drifts at the languid
will of the current or indolent pull of oars that grate on the
golden-meshed sand and pebbles.

20 Lazily, unexpectantly, the angler casts his line, to be
only a convenient perch for the dragonflies; for the fish,
save the affrighted minnows and the hungry pickerel, are
as lazy as he. To-day he may enjoy to the full the con-
templative man's recreation, nor have his contemplations
25 disturbed by any finny folk of the under-water world, while
dreamily he floats in sunshine and dappled shadow, so at
one with the placid waters and quiet shores that wood duck,
sandpiper, and heron scarcely note his unobtrusive presence.

THE WILLEBROEK CANAL [1]

Robert Louis Stevenson

The canal was busy enough. Every now and then we
met or overtook a long string of boats, with great green
tillers; high sterns with a window on either side of the
rudder, and perhaps a jug or a flower-pot in one of the
windows; a dingy following behind; a woman busied 5
about the day's dinner, and a handful of children. These
barges were all tied one behind the other with tow ropes,
to the number of twenty-five or thirty; and the line was
headed and kept in motion by a steamer of strange construction. It had neither paddle-wheel nor screw; but by 10
some gear not rightly comprehensible to the unmechanical
mind, it fetched up over its bow a small bright chain which
lay along the bottom of the canal, and paying it out again
over the stern, dragged itself forward, link by link, with
its whole retinue of loaded scows. Until one had found 15
out the key to the enigma, there was something solemn and
uncomfortable in the progress of one of these trains, as it
moved gently along the water with nothing to mark its
advance but an eddy alongside dying away into the wake.

Of all the creatures of commercial enterprise, a canal 20
barge is by far the most delightful to consider. It may
spread its sails, and then you see it sailing high above the
tree-tops and the wind-mill, sailing on the aqueduct, sailing

[1] From *An Inland Voyage*, pp. 8-10 (Thistle Edition). Charles
Scribner's Sons, New York, 1895.

through the green corn-lands: the most picturesque of
things amphibious. Or the horse plods along at a foot-pace
as if there were no such thing as business in the world;
and the man dreaming at the tiller sees the same spire on
5 the horizon all day long. It is a mystery how things ever
get to their destination at this rate; and to see the barges
waiting their turn at a lock, affords a fine lesson of how
easily the world may be taken. There should be many contented spirits on board, for such a life is both to travel and
10 to stay at home.

The chimney smokes for dinner as you go along; the
banks of the canal slowly unroll their scenery to contem-
plative eyes; the barge floats by great forests and through
great cities with their public buildings and their lamps at
15 night; and for the bargee, in his floating home, " travelling
abed," it is merely as if he were listening to another man's
story or turning the leaves of a picture book in which he
had no concern. He may take his afternoon walk in some
foreign country on the banks of the canal, and then come
20 home to dinner at his own fireside.

A TROPICAL RIVER[1]

Joseph Conrad

The white man, leaning with both arms over the roof of the little house in the stern of the boat, said to the steersman: "We will pass the night in Arsat's clearing. It is late."

The Malay only grunted, and went on looking fixedly at the river. The white man rested his chin on his crossed 5 arms and gazed at the wake of the boat. At the end of the straight avenue of forests cut by the intense glitter of the river, the sun appeared unclouded and dazzling, poised low over the water that shone smoothly like a band of metal. The forests, sombre and dull, stood motionless and silent 10 on each side of the broad stream. At the foot of the big, towering trees, trunkless nipa palms rose from the mud of the bank, in bunches of leaves enormous and heavy, that hung unstirring over the brown swirl of eddies. In the stillness of the air every tree, every leaf, every bough, every 15 tendril of creeper, and every petal of minute blossoms seemed to have been bewitched into an immobility perfect and final. Nothing moved on the river but the eight paddles that rose flashing regularly, dipped together with a single splash; while the steersman swept right and left with a periodic 20 and sudden flourish of his blade describing a glinting semicircle above his head. The churned-up water frothed alongside with a confused murmur. And the white man's canoe,

[1] From "The Lagoon," in *Tales of Unrest*, pp. 319–323. Charles Scribner's Sons, New York, 1898.

advancing up stream in the short-lived disturbance of its own making, seemed to enter the portals of a land from which the very memory of motion had for ever departed.

The white man, turning his back upon the setting sun, looked along the empty and broad expanse of the sea-reach. For the last three miles of its course the wandering, hesitating river, as if enticed irresistibly by the freedom of an open horizon, flows straight into the sea, flows straight to the east — to the east that harbours both light and darkness. Astern of the boat the repeated call of some bird, a cry discordant and feeble, skipped along over the smooth water and lost itself, before it could reach the other shore, in the breathless silence of the world.

The steersman dug his paddle into the stream, and held hard with stiffened arms, his body thrown forward. The water gurgled aloud ; and suddenly the long straight reach seemed to pivot on its center, the forests swung in a semicircle, and the slanting beams of sunset touched the broadside of the canoe with a fiery glow, throwing the slender and distorted shadows of its crew upon the streaked glitter of the river. The white man turned to look ahead. The course of the boat had been altered at right-angles to the stream, and the carved dragon-head of its prow was pointing now at a gap in the fringing bushes of the bank. It glided through, brushing the overhanging twigs, and disappeared from the river like some slim and amphibious creature leaving the water for its lair in the forests.

The narrow creek was like a ditch : tortuous, fabulously deep ; filled with gloom under the thin strip of pure and shining blue of the heaven. Immense trees soared up, invisible behind the festooned draperies of creepers. Here and there, near the glistening blackness of the water, a twisted root of some tall tree showed amongst the tracery of small ferns, black and dull, writhing and motionless, like an arrested snake. The short words of the paddlers reverberated loudly between the thick and sombre walls of vegetation. Darkness oozed out from between the trees, 5 through the tangled maze of the creepers, from behind the great fantastic and unstirring leaves ; the darkness, mysterious and invincible ; the darkness scented and poisonous of impenetrable forests.

The men poled in the shoaling water. The creek broad- 10 ened, opening out into a wide sweep of a stagnant lagoon. The forests receded from the marshy bank, leaving a level strip of bright green, reedy grass to frame the reflected blueness of the sky. A fleecy pink cloud drifted high above, trailing the delicate colouring of its image under 15 the floating leaves and the silvery blossoms of the lotus. A little house, perched on high piles, appeared black in the distance. Near it, two tall nibong palms, that seemed to have come out of the forests in the background, leaned slightly over the ragged roof, with a suggestion of sad 20 tenderness and care in the droop of their leafy and soaring heads.

The steersman, pointing with his paddle, said: "Arsat is there. I see his canoe fast between the piles."

SUNDAY IN CENTRAL PARK[1]

Brander Matthews

It was the last Sunday in September, and the blue sky
arched above the Park, clear, cloudless, unfathomable.
The afternoon sun was hot, and high overhead. Now and
then a wandering breeze came without warning and lingered
5 only for a moment, fluttering the broad leaves of the aquatic
plants in the fountain below the Terrace. At the Casino,
on the hill above the Mall, men and women were eating
and drinking, some of them inside the dingy and sprawling
building, and some of them outdoors at little tables set
10 in curving lines under the gayly colored awnings, which
covered the broad walk bending away from the door of the
restaurant. From the bandstand in the thick of the throng
below came the brassy staccato of a cornet, rendering " The
Last Rose of Summer." Even the Ramble was full of
15 people ; and the young couples, seeking sequestered nooks
under the russet trees, were often forced to share their
benches with strangers. Beneath the reddening maples
lonely men lounged on the grass by themselves, or sat solitary and silent in the midst of chattering family groups.

20 The crowd was cosmopolitan and unhurried. For the
most part it was good-natured and well-to-do. There was
not a beggar to be seen ; there was no appealing poverty.
Fathers of families there were in abundance, well-fed and

[1] From "A Vista in Central Park," in *Vignettes of Manhattan*, pp.
123–126. Harper & Brothers, New York, 1894.

well-clad, with their wives and with their sons' wives and
with their sons' children. Maids in black dresses and white
aprons pushed baby-carriages. Young girls in groups of
three and four giggled and gossiped. Young men in couples
leaned over the bridge of the Lake, smoking and exchang- 5
ing opinions. There was a general air of prosperity gladly
displaying itself in the sunshine ; the misery and the want
and the despair of the great city were left behind and
thrust out of mind.

Two or three yards after a portly German with a little 10
boy holding each of his hands, while a third son still younger
rode ahead astride of his father's solid cane, there came two
slim Japanese gentlemen, small and sallow, in their neatly
cut coats and trousers. A knot of laughing mulatto-girls
followed, arm in arm ; they, too, seemed ill-dressed in the 15
accepted costume of civilization, especially when contrasted
with half a dozen Italians who passed slowly, looking about
them with curious glances ; the men in worn olive velveteens
and with gold rings in their ears, the women with bright
colors in their skirts and with embroidery on their necker- 20
chiefs. Where the foot-path touched the carriage-drive
there stood a plain but comfortably plump Irishwoman,
perhaps thirty years of age ; she had a baby in her arms,
and a little girl of scant three held fast to her patched
calico dress ; with her left hand she was proffering a 25
basket containing apples, bananas, and grapes ; two other
children, both under six, played about her skirts ; and two
more, a boy and a girl, kept within sight of her — the girl,
about ten years old, having a basket of her own filled with
thin round brown cakes ; and a boy, certainly not yet thir- 30
teen, holding out a wooden box packed with rolls of loz-
enges, put up in red and yellow and green papers. Now and

again the mother or one of the children made a sale to a
pedestrian on his way to the music. The younger children
watched, with noisy glee, the light leaps of a gray squirrel
bounding along over the grass behind the path and bal-
5 ancing himself with his horizontal tail.

The broad carriage-drive was as crowded as any of the
foot-paths. Bicyclists in white sweaters and black stock-
ings toiled along in groups of three and four, bent forward
over the bars of their machines. Politicians with cigars in
10 the corners of their mouths held in impatient trotters.
Park omnibuses heavily laden with women and children
drew up for an instant before the Terrace, and then went
on again to skirt the Lake. Old-fashioned and shabby
landaus lumbered along with strangers from the hotels.
15 Now and then there came in sight a hansom cab with a
young couple framed in the front of it, or a jolting dog-
cart, on the high seat of which a British-looking young man
was driving tandem. Here and there were other private
carriages — coupés and phaëtons, for the most part, with
20 once and again a four-in-hand coach rumbling heavily on
the firmly packed road.

MULBERRY BEND [1]

BRANDER MATTHEWS

At this corner Suydam turned out of the side street, and went down a street no wider perhaps, but extending north and south in a devious and hesitating way not common in the streets of New York. The sidewalks of this sinuous street were inconveniently narrow for its crowded popula- 5 tion, and they were made still narrower by tolerated encroachments of one kind or another. Here, for instance, from the side of a small shop projected a stand on which unshelled pease wilted under the strong rays of the young June sun. There, for example, were steps down to the low 10 basement, and in a corner of the hollow at the foot of these stairs there might be a pail with dingy ice packed about a can of alleged ice-cream, or else a board bore half a dozen tough brown loaves, also proffered for sale to the chance customer. Here and there, again, the dwellers in the tall 15 tenements had brought chairs to the common door, and were seated, comfortably conversing with their neighbors, regardless of the fact that they thus blocked the sidewalk, and compelled the passer-by to go out into the street itself. 20

And the street was as densely packed as the sidewalk. In front of Suydam and De Ruyter as they picked their way along was a swarthy young fellow with his flannel

[1] From "In Search of Local Color," in *Vignettes of Manhattan*, pp. 71-73. Harper & Brothers, New York, 1894.

shirt open at the throat and rolled up on his tawny arms; he was pushing before him a hand-cart heaped with gayly colored calicoes. Other hand-carts there were, from which other men, young and old, were vending other wares —
5 fruit more often than not; fruit of a most untempting frowziness. Now and then a huge wagon came lumbering through the street, heaped high with lofty cases of furniture from a rumbling and clattering factory near the corner. And before the heavy horses of this wagon the children
10 scattered, waiting till the last moment of possible escape. There were countless children, and they were forever swarming out of the houses and up from the cellars and over the sidewalks and up and down the street. They were of all ages, from the babe in the arms of its dumpy, thick-
15 set mother to the sweet-faced and dark-eyed girl of ten or twelve really, though she might seem a precocious fourteen. They ran wild in the street; they played about the knees of their mothers, who sat gossiping in the doorways; they hung over the railing of the fire-escapes, which gridironed
20 the front of every tall house.

Everywhere had the Italians treated the balcony of the fire-escape as an out-door room added to their scant accommodation. They adorned it with flowers growing in broken wooden boxes; they used its railings to dry their parti-
25 colored flannel shirts; they sat out on it as though it were the loggia of a villa in their native land.

Everywhere, also, were noises and smells. The roar of the metropolis was here sharpened by the rattle of near machinery heard through open windows, and by the inces-
30 sant clatter and shrill cries of the multitude in the street. The rancid odor of ill-kept kitchens mingled with the miti-
. gated effluvium of decaying fruits and vegetables.

But over and beyond the noises and the smells and the bustling business of the throng, Rupert de Ruyter felt as though he were receiving an impression of life itself. It was as if he had caught a glimpse of the mighty movement of existence, incessant and inevitable. What he saw did not strike him as pitiful ; it did not weigh him down with despondency. The spectacle before him was not beautiful ; it was not even picturesque ; but never for a moment, even, did it strike him as pathetic. Interesting it was, of a certainty — unfailingly interesting.

TENNYSON [1]

Thomas Carlyle

Alfred is the son of a Lincolnshire Gentleman Farmer, I think ; indeed, you see in his verses that he is a native of " moated granges," and green, fat pastures, not of mountains and their torrents and storms. He had his
5 breeding at Cambridge, as if for the Law or Church; being master of a small annuity on his Father's decease, he preferred clubbing with his Mother and some Sisters, to live unpromoted and write Poems. In this way he lives still, now here, now there ; the family always within reach of
10 London, never in it ; he himself making rare and brief visits, lodging in some old comrade's rooms. I think he must be under forty, not much under it. One of the finest-looking men in the world. A great shock of rough dusty-dark hair ; bright-laughing hazel eyes ; massive aquiline
15 face, most massive yet most delicate ; of sallow-brown complexion, almost Indian-looking; clothes cynically loose, free-and-easy ; — smokes infinite tobacco. His voice is musical metallic, — fit for loud laughter and piercing wail, and all that may lie between ; speech and speculation free
20 and plenteous : I do not meet, in these late decades, such company over a pipe !

[1] From *The Carlyle-Emerson Correspondence*, ed. C. E. Norton, II, 66–67. Houghton, Mifflin & Co., Boston, 1892.

DANIEL WEBSTER [1]

THOMAS CARLYLE

Not many days ago I saw at breakfast the notablest of all your Notabilities, Daniel Webster. He is a magnificent specimen; you might say to all the world, This is your Yankee Englishman, such Limbs *we* make in Yankeeland! As a Logic-fencer, Advocate, or Parliamentary Hercules, one would incline to back him at first sight against all the extant world. The tanned complexion, that amorphous crag-like face; the dull black eyes under their precipice of brows, like dull anthracite furnaces, needing only to be *blown;* the mastiff-mouth, accurately closed : — I have not traced as much of *silent Berserkir-rage*, that I remember of, in any other man.

[1] From *The Carlyle-Emerson Correspondence*, ed. C. E. Norton, I, pp. 260–261. Houghton, Mifflin & Co., Boston, 1892.

THOMAS DE QUINCEY[1]

Thomas Carlyle

He was a pretty little creature, full of wire-drawn ingenuities; bankrupt enthusiasms, bankrupt pride; with the finest silver-toned low voice, and most elaborate gently-winding courtesies and ingenuities in conversation: "What
5 would n't one give to have him in a Box, and take him out to talk!" (That was *Her* criticism of him; and it was right good.) A bright, ready and melodious talker; but in the end an inconclusive and long-winded. One of the smallest man-figures I ever saw; shaped like a pair of
10 tongs; and hardly above five feet in all: when he sat, you would have taken him, by candlelight, for the beautifullest little child; blue-eyed, blonde-haired, sparkling face, — had there not been a something, too, which said, "*Eccovi, this Child has been in Hell!*"

[1] From *Reminiscences*, pp. 202–203. Charles Scribner's Sons, New York, 1881.

TWO PORTRAITS BY RAEBURN [1]

ROBERT LOUIS STEVENSON

One interesting portrait was that of Duncan of Camper-down. He stands in uniform beside a table, his feet slightly straddled with the balance of an old sailor, his hand poised upon a chart by the finger tips. The mouth is pursed, the nostril spread and drawn up, the eye-brows very highly 5 arched. The cheeks lie along the jaw in folds of iron, and have the redness that comes from much exposure to salt sea winds. From the whole figure, attitude and coun-tenance, there breathes something precise and decisive, something alert, wiry, and strong. You can understand, 10 from the look of him, that sense, not so much of humour, as of what is grimmest and driest. in pleasantry, which inspired his address before the fight at Camperdown. He had just overtaken the Dutch fleet under Admiral de Winter. "Gentlemen," says he, "you see a severe winter 15 approaching ; I have only to advise you to keep up a good fire." Somewhat of this same spirit of adamantine drollery must have supported him in the days of the mutiny at the Nore, when he lay off the Texel with his own flagship, the *Venerable*, and only one other vessel, and kept up active 20 signals, as though he had a powerful fleet in the offing, to intimidate the Dutch.

[1] From "Some Portraits by Raeburn," in *Virginibus Puerisque* (Thistle Edition), pp. 129–131. Charles Scribner's Sons, New York, 1895.

Another portrait which irresistibly attracted the eye, was the half-length of Robert M'Queen, of Braxfield, Lord Justice-Clerk. If I know gusto in painting when I see it, this canvas was painted with rare enjoyment. The tart, 5 rosy, humorous look of the man, his nose like a cudgel, his face resting squarely on the jowl, has been caught and perpetuated with something that looks like brotherly love. A peculiarly subtle expression haunts the lower part, sensual and incredulous, like that of a man tasting good Bordeaux with half a fancy it has been somewhat too long uncorked. From under the pendulous eyelids of old age, the eyes look out with a half-youthful, half-frosty twinkle. Hands, with no pretence to distinction, are folded on the judge's stomach. So sympathetically is the character conceived by the portrait painter, that it is hardly possible to avoid some movement of sympathy on the part of the spectator.

AN OLD WOMAN[1]

NATHANIEL HAWTHORNE

The happiest person whom I saw there (and, running
hastily through my experiences, I hardly recollect to have
seen a happier one in my life, if you take a careless flow
of spirits as happiness) was an old woman that lay in bed
among ten or twelve heavy-looking females, who plied 5
their knitting-work round about her. She laughed, when
we entered, and immediately began to talk to us, in a thin,
little, spirited quaver, claiming to be more than a century
old; and the governor (in whatever way he happened to be
cognizant of the fact) confirmed her age to be a hundred 10
and four. Her jauntiness and cackling merriment were
really wonderful. It was as if she had got through with
all her actual business in life two or three generations
ago, and now, freed from every responsibility for herself
or others, had only to keep up a mirthful state of mind 15
till the short time, or long time (and, happy as she was,
she appeared not to care whether it were long or short),
before Death, who had misplaced her name in his list,
might remember to take her away. She had gone quite
round the circle of human existence, and come back to the 20
play-ground again. And so she had grown to be a kind
of miraculous old pet, the plaything of people seventy or

---

[1] From "Glimpses of English Poverty" in *Our Old Home* (Hawthorne's
Works, Riverside Edition, VII), pp. 349–350. Houghton, Mifflin & Co.,
Boston, 1883.

eighty years younger than herself, who talked and laughed
with her as if she were a child, finding great delight in
her wayward and strangely playful responses, into some
of which she cunningly conveyed a gibe that caused their
5 ears to tingle a little. She had done getting out of bed in
this world, and lay there to be waited upon like a queen
or a baby.

BEATRIX ESMOND[1]

WILLIAM MAKEPEACE THACKERAY

In the hall of Walcote House . . . is a staircase that
leads from an open gallery, where are the doors of the
sleeping chambers: and from one of these, a wax candle
in her hand, and illuminating her, came Mistress Beatrix
— the light falling indeed upon the scarlet riband which ₅
she wore, and upon the most brilliant white neck in the
world.

Esmond had left a child and found a woman, grown
beyond the common height; and arrived at such a dazzling completeness of beauty, that his eyes might well show ₁₀
surprise and delight at beholding her. In hers there was
a brightness so lustrous and melting, that I have seen a
whole assembly follow her as if by an attraction irresistible:
and that night the great Duke was at the playhouse after
Ramillies, every soul turned and looked (she chanced to ₁₅
enter at the opposite side of the theatre at the same
moment) at her, and not at him. She was a brown beauty:
that is, her eyes, hair, and eyebrows and eyelashes were
dark: her hair curling with rich undulations, and waving
over her shoulders; but her complexion was as dazzling ₂₀
white as snow in sunshine: except her cheeks, which were
a bright red, and her lips, which were of a still deeper
crimson. Her mouth and chin, they said, were too large

[1] From *The History of Henry Esmond, Esq.*, Bk. II, chap. vii.

and full, and so they might be for a goddess in marble,
but not for a woman whose eyes were fire, whose look was
love, whose voice was the sweetest low song, whose shape
was perfect symmetry, health, decision, activity, whose foot
5 as it planted itself on the ground was firm but flexible,
and whose motion, whether rapid or slow, was always perfect grace — agile as a nymph, lofty as a queen — now
melting, now imperious, now sarcastic — there was no single movement of hers but was beautiful. As he thinks of
10 her, he who writes feels young again, and remembers a
paragon.

So she came holding her dress with one fair rounded
arm, and her taper before her, tripping down the stair
to greet Esmond.

DR. DOLLIVER[1]

Nathaniel Hawthorne

While the patriarch was putting on his small-clothes, he
took care to stand in the parallelogram of bright sunshine
that fell upon the uncarpeted floor. The summer warmth
was very genial to his system, and yet made him shiver;
his wintry veins rejoiced at it, though the reviving blood 5
tingled through them with a half-painful and only half-
pleasurable titillation. For the first few moments after
creeping out of bed, he kept his back to the sunny window, and seemed mysteriously shy of glancing thither-
ward; but, as the June fervor pervaded him more and 10
more thoroughly, he turned bravely about, and looked
forth at a burial-ground on the corner of which he dwelt.
There lay many an old acquaintance, who had gone to
sleep with the flavor of Dr. Dolliver's tinctures and pow-
ders upon his tongue; it was the patient's final bitter 15
taste of this world, and perhaps doomed to be a recollected
nauseousness in the next. Yesterday, in the chill of his
forlorn old age, the Doctor expected soon to stretch out
his weary bones among that quiet community, and might
scarcely have shrunk from the prospect on his own account, 20
except, indeed, that he dreamily mixed up the infirmities
of his present condition with the repose of the approach-

---

[1] From *The Dolliver Romance* (Hawthorne's Works, Riverside Edition,
XI), pp. 18–21. Houghton, Mifflin & Co., Boston, 1884.

ing one, being haunted by a notion that the damp earth, under the grass and dandelions, must needs be pernicious for his cough and his rheumatism. But, this morning, the cheerful sunbeams, or the mere taste of his grandson's cor-
5 dial that he had taken at bed time, or the fitful vigor that often sports irreverently with aged people, had caused an unfrozen drop of youthfulness, somewhere within him, to expand.

"Hem! ahem!" quoth the Doctor, hoping with one
10 effort to clear his throat of the dregs of a ten-years' cough. "Matters are not so far gone with me as I thought. I have known mighty sensible men, when only a little age-stricken or otherwise out of sorts, to die of mere faint-heartedness, a great deal sooner than they need."

15 He shook his silvery head at his own image in the look-ing glass, as if to impress the apothegm on that shadowy representative of himself; and, for his part, he determined to pluck up a spirit and live as long as he possibly could, if it were only for the sake of little Pansie, who stood as
20 close to one extremity of human life as her great-grand-father to the other. This child of three years old occupied all the unfossilized portion of good Dr. Dolliver's heart. Every other interest that he formerly had, and the entire confraternity of persons whom he once loved, had long
25 ago departed; and the poor Doctor could not follow them, because the grasp of Pansie's baby-fingers held him back.

So he crammed a great silver watch into his fob, and drew on a patch-work morning-gown of an ancient fashion.
30 Its original material was said to have been the embroidered front of his own wedding-waistcoat and the silken skirt of his wife's bridal attire, which his eldest grand-daughter had

taken from the carved chest-of-drawers, after poor Bessie,
the beloved of his youth, had been half a century in the
grave. Throughout many of the intervening years, as the
garment got ragged, the spinsters of the old man's family
had quilted their duty and affection into it in the shape of 5
patches upon patches, rose-color, crimson, blue, violet, and
green, and then (as their hopes faded, and their life kept
growing shadier, and their attire took a sombre hue) sober
gray and great fragments of funereal black, until the Doctor
could revive the memory of most things that had befallen 10
him by looking at his patchwork-gown, as it hung upon a
chair. And now it was ragged again, and all the fingers
that should have mended it were cold. It had an Eastern
fragrance, too, a smell of drugs, strong-scented herbs, and
spicy gums, gathered from the many potent infusions that 15
had from time to time been spilt over it; so that, snuffing him afar off, you might have taken Dr. Dolliver for a
mummy, and could hardly have been undeceived by his
shrunken and torpid aspect, as he crept nearer.

Wrapt in his odorous and many-colored robe, he took 20
staff in hand, and moved pretty vigorously to the head of
the staircase. As it was somewhat steep, and but dimly
lighted, he began cautiously to descend, putting his left
hand on the banister, and poking down his long stick to
assist him in making sure of the successive steps; and thus 25
he became a living illustration of the accuracy of Scripture,
where it describes the aged as being " afraid of that which
is high," — a truth that is often found to have a sadder
purport than its external one. Half-way to the bottom,
however, the Doctor heard the impatient and authorita- 30
tive tones of little Pansie, — Queen Pansie, as she might
fairly have been styled, in reference to her position in the

household, — calling amain for grand-papa and breakfast.
He was startled into such perilous activity by the summons,
that his heels slid on the stairs, the slippers were shuffled
off his feet, and he saved himself from a tumble only by
5 quickening his pace, and coming down at almost a run.

A PORTRAIT [1]

Robert Louis Stevenson

He went boldly to the door and knocked with an assured hand. On both previous occasions, he had knocked timidly and with some dread of attracting notice ; but now when he had just discarded the thought of a burglarious entry, knocking at a door seemed a mighty simple and innocent proceeding. The sound of his blows echoed through the house with thin, phantasmal reverberations, as though it were quite empty ; but these had scarcely died away before a measured tread drew near, a couple of bolts were withdrawn, and one wing was opened broadly, as though no guile or fear of guile were known to those within. A tall figure of a man, muscular and spare, but a little bent confronted Villon. The head was massive in bulk, but finely sculptured ; the nose blunt at the bottom, but refining upward to where it joined a pair of strong and honest eyebrows ; the mouth and eyes surrounded with delicate markings, and the whole face based upon a thick white beard, boldly and squarely trimmed. Seen as it was by the light of a flickering hand-lamp, it looked perhaps nobler than it had a right to do ; but it was a fine face, honourable rather than intelligent, strong, simple, and righteous.

[1] From "A Lodging for the Night," in *New Arabian Nights* (Thistle Edition), p. 303. Charles Scribner's Sons, New York, 1895.

CÀFÉ DES EXILÉS [1]

George Washington Cable

That which in 1835 — I think he said thirty-five — was
a reality in the Rue Burgundy — I think he said Burgundy
— is now but a reminiscence. Yet so vividly was its story
told me, that at this moment the old Café des Exilés appears
5 before my eye, floating in the clouds of revery, and I doubt
not I see it just as it was in the old times.

An antiquated story-and-a-half Creole cottage sitting
right down on the banquette, as do the Choctaw squaws
who sell bay and sassafras and life-everlasting, with a high,
10 close board-fence shutting out of view the diminutive garden on the southern side. An ancient willow droops over
the roof of round tiles, and partly hides the discolored
stucco, which keeps dropping off into the garden as though
the old café was stripping for the plunge into oblivion —
15 disrobing for its execution. I see, well up in the angle of
the broad side gable, shaded by its rude awning of clapboards, as the eyes of an old dame are shaded by her
wrinkled hand, the window of Pauline. Oh, for the image
of the maiden, were it but for one moment, leaning out of
20 the casement to hang her mocking-bird and looking down
into the garden, — where, above the barrier of old boards,
I see the top of the fig-tree, the pale green clump of bananas,
the tall palmetto with its jagged crown, Pauline's own two

[1] From *Old Creole Days*, pp. 85–88. Copyright, 1879, 1883, 1897, by
Charles Scribner's Sons, New York.

orange-trees holding up their hands toward the window, heavy with the promises of autumn ; the broad, crimson mass of the many-stemmed oleander, and the crisp boughs of the pomegranate loaded with freckled apples, and with here and there a lingering scarlet blossom. 5

The Café des Exilés, to use the figure, flowered, bore fruit, and dropped it long ago — or rather Time and Fate, like some uncursed Adam and Eve, came side by side and cut away its clusters, as we sever the golden burden of the banana from its stem ; then, like a banana which has borne 10 its fruit, it was razed to the ground and made way for a newer, brighter growth. I believe it would set every tooth on edge should I go by there now, — now that I have heard the story, — and see the old site covered by the "Shoo-fly Coffee-house." Pleasanter far to close my eyes and call to 15 view the unpretentious portals of the old café, with her children — for such those exiles seem to me — dragging their rocking-chairs out, and sitting in their wonted group under the long, out-reaching eaves which shaded the banquette of the Rue Burgundy. 20

It was in 1835 that the Café des Exiles was, as one might say, in full blossom. Old M. D'Hemecourt, father of Pauline and host of the café, himself a refugee from San Domingo, was the cause — at least the human cause — of its opening. As its white-curtained, glazed doors expanded, emitting a 25 little puff of his own cigarette smoke, it was like the bursting of catalpa blossoms, and the exiles came like bees, pushing into the tiny room to sip its rich variety of tropical sirups, its lemonades, its orangeades, its orgeats, its barley-waters, and its outlandish wines, while they talked of dear 30 home — that is to say, of Barbadoes, of Martinique, of San Domingo, and of Cuba.

There were Pedro and Benigno, and Fernandez and Francisco, and Benito. Benito was à tall, swarthy man, with immense gray moustachios, and hair as harsh as tropical grass and gray as ashes. When he could spare his cigarette from
5 his lips, he would tell you in a cavernous voice, and with a wrinkled smile, that he was "a t-thorty-seveng."

There was Martinez of San Domingo, yellow as a canary, always sitting with one leg curled under him, and holding the back of his head in his knitted fingers against the back
10 of his rocking-chair. Father, mother, brother, sisters, all, had been massacred in the struggle of '21 and '22; he alone was left to tell the tale, and told it often, with that strange, infantile insensibility to the solemnity of his bereavement so peculiar to Latin people.

15 But, besides these, and many who need no attention, there were two in particular, around whom all the story of the Café des Exilés, of old M. D'Hemecourt and of Pauline, turns as on a double center. First, Manuel Mazaro, whose small, restless eyes were as black and bright as those of a
20 mouse, whose light talk became his dark girlish face, and whose redundant locks curled so prettily and so wonderfully black under the fine white brim of his jaunty Panama. He hád the hands of a woman, save that the nails were stained with the smoke of cigarettes. He could play the guitar
25 delightfully, and wore his knife down behind his coat-collar.

The second was "Major" Galahad Shaughnessy. I imagine I can see him, in his white duck, brass-buttoned roundabout, with his sabreless belt peeping out beneath, all his boyishness in his sea-blue eyes, leaning lightly against
30 the door-post of the Café des Exilés as a child leans against his mother, running his fingers over a basketful of fragrant limes, and watching his chance to strike some solemn Creole under the fifth rib with a good old Irish joke.

VILLON AND HIS CREW [1]

Robert Louis Stevenson

It was late in November, 1456. The snow fell over Paris
with rigorous, relentless persistence; sometimes the wind
made a sally and scattered it in flying vortices; sometimes
there was a lull, and flake after flake descended out of the
black night air, silent, circuitous, interminable. To poor 5
people, looking up under moist eyebrows, it seemed a wonder where it all came from. Master Francis Villon had
propounded an alternative that afternoon, at a tavern window: was it only Pagan Jupiter plucking' geese upon
Olympus? or were the holy angels moulting? He was 10
only a poor Master of Arts, he went on; and as the question somewhat touched upon divinity, he durst not venture
to conclude. A silly old priest from Montargis, who was
among the company, treated the young rascal to a bottle
of wine in honour of the jest and grimaces with which it 15
was accompanied, and swore on his own white beard that
he had been just such another irreverent dog when he was
Villon's age.

The air was raw and pointed, but not far below freezing;
and the flakes were large, damp, and adhesive. The whole 20
city was sheeted up. An army might have marched from
end to end and not a footfall given the alarm. If there were
any belated birds in heaven, they saw the island like a large

[1] From "A Lodging for the Night," in *New Arabian Nights* (Thistle
Edition), pp. 287–290. Charles Scribner's Sons, New York, 1895.

white patch, and the bridges like slim white spars, on the
black ground of the river. High up overhead the snow
settled among the tracery of the cathedral towers. Many
a niche was drifted full ; many a statue wore a long white
5 bonnet on its grotesque or sainted head. The gargoyles
had been transformed into great false noses, drooping
towards the point. The crockets were like upright pillows
swollen on one side. In the intervals of the wind, there
was a dull sound of dripping about the precincts of the
10 church.

The cemetery of St. John had taken its own share of the
snow. All the graves were decently covered ; tall white
housetops stood around in grave array ; worthy burghers
were long ago in bed, be-nightcapped like their domiciles ;
15 there was no. light in all the neighborhood but a little peep
from a lamp that hung swinging in the church choir, and
tossed the shadows to and fro in time to its oscillations.
The clock was hard on ten when the patrol went by with
halberds and a lantern, beating their hands ; and they saw
20 nothing suspicious about the cemetery of St. John.

Yet there was a small house, backed up against the
cemetery wall, which was still awake, and awake to evil
purpose, in that snoring district. There was not much to
betray it from without ; only a stream of warm vapor from
25 the chimney-top, a patch where the snow melted on the
roof, and a few half-obliterated footprints at the door. But
within, behind the shuttered windows, Master Francis Villon the poet, and some of the thievish crew with whom he
consorted, were keeping the night alive and passing round
30 the bottle.

A great pile of living embers diffused a strong and ruddy
glow from the arched chimney. Before this straddled Dom

Nicolas, the Picardy monk, with his skirts picked up and
his fat legs bared to the comfortable warmth. His dilated
shadow cut the room in half ; and the firelight only escaped
on either side of his broad person, and in a little pool between his outspread feet. His face had the beery, bruised 5
appearance of the continual drinker's ; it was covered with
a network of congested veins, purple in ordinary circumstances, but now pale violet, for even with his back to the
fire the cold pinched him on the other side. His cowl had
half fallen back, and made a strange excrescence on either 10
side of his bull neck. So he straddled, grumbling, and cut
the room in half with the shadow of his portly frame.

On the right, Villon and Guy Tabary were huddled
together over a scrap of parchment ; Villon making a
ballade which he was to call the " Ballade of Roast Fish," 15
and Tabary spluttering admiration at his shoulder. The
poet was a rag of a man, dark, little, and lean, with hollow
cheeks and thin black locks. He carried his four-and-twenty
years with feverish animation. Greed had made folds about
his eyes, evil smiles had puckered his mouth. The wolf and 20
pig struggled together in his face. It was an eloquent, sharp,
ugly, earthly countenance. His hands were small and pre-
hensile, with fingers knotted like a cord ; and they were
continually flickering in front of him in violent and expressive pantomime. As for Tabary, a broad, complacent, ad- 25
miring imbecility breathed from his squash nose and slob-
bering lips : he had become a thief, just as he might have
become the most decent of burgesses, by the imperious
chance that rules the lives of human geese and human
donkeys.   30

At the monk's other hand, Montigny and Thevenin
Pensete played a game of chance. About the first there

clung some flavour of good birth and training, as about a
fallen angel ; something long, lithe, and courtly in the
person ; something aquiline and darkling in the face.
Thevenin, poor soul, was in great feather : he had done a
5 good stroke of knavery that afternoon in the Faubourg St.
Jacques, and all night he had been gaining from Montigny.
A flat smile illuminated his face ; his bald head shone rosily
in a garland of red curls ; his little protuberant stomach
shook with silent chucklings as he swept in his gains.

THE ARMY OF FRANCE [1]

Guy Wetmore Carryl

Oh, it was all very well, the wonderful French army, all very well if one could have been a marshal or a general, or even a soldier of the line in time of war. ·There was a chance for glory, bon sang! But to be a drummer —'a drummer one metre seventy in height, with flaming red hair and a 5 freckled face — a drummer who was called Little Tapin; and to have, for one's most important duty, to drum the loungers out of a public garden! No, evidently he would desert.

"But why?" said a grave voice beside him. Little Tapin 10 was greatly startled. He had not thought he was saying the words aloud. And his fear increased when, on turning to see who had spoken, he found himself looking into the eyes of one who was evidently an officer, though his uniform was unfamiliar. He was plain-shaven and very short, 15 almost as short, indeed, as Little Tapin himself, but about him there was a something of dignity and command which could not fail of its effect. He wore a great black hat like a gendarme's, but without trimming, and a blue coat with a white plastron, the tails lined with scarlet, and the sleeves 20 ending in red and white cuffs. White breeches, and knee-boots carefully polished, completed the uniform, and from over his right shoulder a broad band of crimson silk was

[1] From "Little Tapin," in *Zut*, pp. 294–303. Houghton, Mifflin & Co., Boston, 1903.

drawn tightly across his breast. A short sword hung straight at his hip, and on his left breast were three orders on red ribbons, — a great star, with an eagle in the centre, backed by a sunburst studded with brilliants ; another 5 eagle, this one of white enamel, pendant from a jeweled crown, and a smaller star of enameled white and green, similar to the large one.

Little Tapin had barely mastered these details when the other spoke again.

10 " Why art thou thinking to desert ? " he said.

" Monsieur is an officer ? " faltered the drummer, — " a general, perhaps. Pardon, but I do not know the uniform."

"A corporal, simply — a soldier of France, like thyself. 15 Be not afraid, my little one. All thou sayest shall be held in confidence. Tell me thy difficulties."

His voice was very kind, the kindest Little Tapin had heard in three long months, and suddenly the barrier of his Breton reserve gave and broke. The nervous strain 20 had been too great. He must have sympathy and advice — yes, even though it meant confiding in a stranger and the possible discovery and failure of his dearly cherished plans.

" A soldier of France ! " he exclaimed, impulsively. " Ah, monsieur, there you have all my difficulty. What a 25 thing it is to be a soldier of France ! And not even that, but a drummer, a drummer who is called Little Tapin because he is the smallest and weakest in the corps. To be taken from home, from the country he loves, from Brittany, and made to serve among men who despise him, 30 who laugh at him, who avoid him in the hours of leave, because he is not bon camarade. To wear a uniform that has been already worn. To sleep in a dormitory where there are bêtes funestes. To have no friends. To know that he is not to see Plougastel, and the sweetheart, and the Little Mother for three years. Never to fight, but, at best, to drum voyous out of a garden! That, monsieur, is what it is to be a soldier of France!" 5

There were tears in Little Tapin's eyes now, but he was more angry than sad. The silence of months was broken, and the hoarded resentment and despair of his long martyrdom, once given rein, were not to be checked a second time. He threw back his narrow shoulders defiantly, and 10 said a hideous thing:—

"Conspuez l'armée française!"

There was an instant's pause, and then the other leaned forward, and with one white-gloved hand touched Little Tapin on the eyes. 15

. . . .

Before them a great plain, sloping very gradually upward in all directions, like a vast, shallow amphitheatre, spread away in a long series of low terraces to where, in the dim distance, the peaks of a range of purple hills nicked and notched a sky of palest turquoise. From where they stood, 20 upon a slight elevation, the details of even the farthest slopes seemed singularly clean-cut and distinct,—the groups of grey willows; the poplars, standing stiffly in twos and threes; the short silver reaches of a little river, lying in the hollows where the land occasionally dipped; 25 at long intervals, a white-washed cottage, gleaming like a sail against this sea of green; even, on the most distant swell of all, a herd of ruddy cattle, moving slowly up toward the crest,—each and all of these, although in merest miniature, as clear and vivid in form and color as 30 if they had been the careful creations of a Claude Lorrain.

Directly before the knoll upon which they were stationed,
a wide road, dazzling white in the sunlight, swept in a
superb full curve from left to right, and on its further side
the ground was covered with close-cropped turf, and com-
5 pletely empty for a distance of two hundred metres.
But beyond! Beyond, every hectare of the great semicircle was occupied by dense masses of cavalry, infantry,
and artillery, regiment upon regiment, division upon division, corps upon corps, an innumerable multitude, motion-
10 less, as if carved out of many-colored marbles !

In some curious, unaccountable fashion, Little Tapin
seemed to know all these by name. There, to the left,
were the chasseurs à pied, their huge bearskins flecked·
with red and green pompons, and their white· cross-belts
15 slashed like capital X's against the blue of their tunics ;
there, beside them, the foot artillery, a long row of metal
collar plates, like dots of gold, and gold trappings against
dark blue; to the right, the Garde Royale Hollandaise, in
brilliant crimson and white ; in the centre, the infantry of
20 the Guard, with tall, straight pompons, red above white,
and square black shakos, trimmed with scarlet cord.

Close at hand, surrounding Little Tapin and his companion, were the most brilliant figures of the scene, and
these, too, he seemed to know by name. None was missing.
25 Prince Murat, in a cream-white uniform blazing with gold
embroidery, and with a scarlet ribbon across his breast ;
a group of marshals, Ney, Oudinot, Duroc, Macdonald,
Augereau, and Soult, with their yellow sashes, and cocked
hats laced with gold ; a score of generals, Larouche,
30 Durosnel, Marmont, Letort, Henrion, Chasteller, and the
rest, with white instead of gold upon their hats, — clean-
shaven, severe of brow and lip-line, they stood without

movement, their gauntleted hands upon their sword-hilts, gazing straight before them.

Little Tapin drew a deep breath.

Suddenly from somewhere came a short, sharp bugle note, and instantly the air was full of the sound of hoofs, and the ring of scabbards and stirrup-irons, and the wide white road before them alive with flying cavalry. Squadron after squadron, they thundered by : mounted chasseurs, with pendants of orange-colored cloth fluttering from their shakos, and plaits of powdered hair bobbing at their cheeks ; Polish light horse, with metal sunbursts gleaming on their square-topped helmets, and crimson and white pennons snapping in the wind at the points of their lances; Old Guard cavalry, with curving helmets like Roman legionaries ; Mamelukes, with full red trousers, white and scarlet turbans, strange standards of horsehair surmounted by the imperial eagle, brazen stirrups singularly fashioned, and horse trappings of silver with flying crimson tassels ; Horse Chasseurs of the Guard, in hussar tunics and yellow breeches, their sabretaches swinging as they rode :- and Red Lancers, in gay uniforms of green and scarlet. Like a whirlwind they went past, — each squadron, in turn, wheeling to the left, and coming to a halt in the open space beyond the road, until the last lancer swept by.

· A thick cloud of white dust, stirred into being by the flying horses, now hung between the army and the knoll, and through this one saw dimly the mounted band of the 20th Chasseurs, on gray stallions, occupying the centre of the line, and heard, what before had been drowned by the thunder of hoofs, the strains of " Partant pour la Syrie."

Slowly, slowly, the dust cloud thinned and lifted, so
slowly that it seemed as if it would never wholly clear.
But, on a sudden, a sharp puff of wind sent it whirling
off in arabesques to the left, and the whole plain lay
5 revealed.

"Bon Dieu!" said Little Tapin.

The first rank of cavalry was stationed within a metre
of the further border of the road, the line sweeping off to
the left and right until details became indistinguishable.
10 And beyond, reaching away in a solid mass, the vast host
dwindled and dwindled, back to where the ascending
slopes were broken by the distant willows and the reaches
of the silver stream. With snowy white of breeches and
plastrons, with lustre of scarlet velvet and gold lace, with
15 sparkle of helmet and cuirass, and dull black of bearskin
and smoothly groomed flanks, the army blazed and glowed
in the golden sunlight like a mosaic of a hundred thousand jewels. Silent, expectant, the legions flashed crimson,
emerald, and sapphire, rolling away in broad swells of light
20 and color, motionless save for a long, slow heave, as of the
ocean, lying, vividly iridescent, under the last rays of the
setting sun. Then, without warning, as if the touch of a
magician's wand had roused the multitude to life, a myriad
sabres swept twinkling from their scabbards, and, by tens
25 of thousands, the guns of the infantry snapped with a
sharp click to a present arms. The bugles sounded all along
the line, the tricolors dipped until their golden fringes
almost swept the ground, the troopers stood upright in
their stirrups, their heads thrown back, their bronzed faces
30 turned toward the knoll, their eyes blazing. And from the
farthest slopes inward, like thunder that growls afar, and,
coming nearer, swells into unbearable volume, a hoarse cry

ran down the massed battalions and broke in a stupendous
roar upon the shuddering air, —

"Vive l'empereur !"

.   .   .   .

Little Tapin rubbed his eyes.

"I am ill," he murmured. "I have been faint. I seemed 5
to see —"

"Thou hast seen," said the voice of his companion, very
softly, very solemnly, — "thou hast seen simply what it is
to be a soldier of France!"

CRAIGIE HOUSE[1]

SAMUEL LONGFELLOW

All visitors to Cambridge are familiar with the spacious old-fashioned house [Craigie House], painted in yellow and white, which stands far back from Brattle Street on the right, as one goes from Harvard Square to Mount Auburn.
5 A gateway in the oddly patterned fence opens through a lilac hedge into the long walk, at the end of which, up low flights of steps, the house stands on its grassy terraces. Its ample front of two stories extends, including the broad verandas, to a width of more than eighty feet. There are
10 large clumps of lilac bushes upon the greensward, and on the left an aged and lofty elm tree throws its shadows upon the house, and sighs for its companion, killed many years ago by canker worms and too vigorous pruning. An Italian balustrade along the first terrace is a late addition; but
15 the roof is crowned with a similar railing of the old days. Between the tall white pilasters which mark the width of the hallway, the front door still retains the brass knocker which announced many a visitor to the ancient hospitalities, and which even now occasionally answers to the hand of a
20 stranger, or the small boy who does not see the modern bell-knob, and whose wonder is duly roused by the cumbrous old lock, with its key that might have belonged to a

[1] From *Life of Henry Wadsworth Longfellow*, Vol. I, chap. xviii, pp. 258-259. Ticknor & Co., Boston, 1886.

Bastile. In the white-wainscoted hall is a handsome staircase, with broad, low steps, and variously twisted balusters. On the left opens the drawing-room, which, with its deep window-seats, its arched recesses, its marble mantel surmounted by a broad panel set in an architectural frame, 5 remains a fine specimen of a " colonial " interior. Opposite to this is a similar room, of much simpler, but still substantial style, — in all the later years the poet's study. Beyond is a spacious apartment now used as a library, whose windows command the garden and grounds. Above 10 are the chambers, whose broad fireplaces are framed in old-fashioned Dutch tiles.

WESTMINSTER HALL[1]

Thomas Babington Macaulay

The place was worthy of such a trial. It was the great
hall of William Rufus ; the hall which had resounded with
acclamations at the inauguration of thirty kings ; the hall
which had witnessed the just sentence of Bacon and the
5 just absolution of Somers ; the hall where the eloquence of
Strafford had for a moment awed and melted a victorious
party inflamed with just resentment ; the hall where Charles
had confronted the High Court of Justice with the placid
courage which has half redeemed his fame. Neither mili-
10 tary nor civil pomp was wanting. The avenues were lined
with grenadiers. The streets were kept clear by cavalry.
The peers, robed in gold and ermine, were marshalled by
the heralds under Garter King-at-Arms. The judges, in
their vestments of state, attended to give advice on points
15 of law. Near a hundred and seventy Lords, three-fourths
of the Upper House, as the Upper House then was, walked
in solemn order from their usual place of assembling to the
tribunal. The junior baron present led the way — Lord
Heathfield, recently ennobled for his memorable defence of
20 Gibraltar against the fleets and armies of France and Spain.
The long procession was closed by the Duke of Norfolk,
Earl Marshal of the realm, by the great dignitaries, and by
the brothers and sons of the king. Last of all came the

1 From "Warren Hastings," in *Critical and Miscellaneous Essays.*
282

Prince of Wales, conspicuous by his fine person and noble bearing. The gray old walls were hung with scarlet. The long galleries were crowded by such an audience as has rarely excited the fears or the emulation of an orator. There were gathered together, from all parts of a great, free, enlight- 5 ened, and prosperous realm, grace and female loveliness, wit and learning, the representatives of every science and of every art. There were seated around the queen the fair-haired young daughters of the house of Brunswick. There the ambassadors of great kings and commonwealths gazed 10 with admiration on a spectacle which no other country in the world could present. There Siddons, in the prime of her majestic beauty, looked with emotion on a scene surpassing all the imitations of the stage. There the historian of the Roman Empire thought of the days when Cicero 15 pleaded the cause of Sicily against Verres; and when, before a senate which had still some show of freedom, Tacitus thundered against the oppressor of Africa. There was seen, side by side, the greatest painter and the greatest scholar of the age. The spectacle had allured Reynolds 20 from that easel which has preserved to us the thoughtful foreheads of so many writers and statesmen, and the sweet smiles of so many noble matrons. It had induced Parr to suspend his labours in that dark and profound mine from which he had extracted a vast treasure of erudition — a 25 treasure too often buried in the earth, too often paraded with injudicious and inelegant ostentation; but still precious, massive, and splendid. There appeared the voluptuous charms of her to whom the heir of the throne had in secret plighted his faith. There, too, was she, the beauti- 30 ful mother of a beautiful race, the Saint Cecilia, whose delicate features, lighted up by love and music, art has

rescued from the common decay. There were the members of that brilliant society which quoted, criticised, and exchanged repartees, under the rich peacock hangings of Mrs. Montague. And there, the ladies, whose lips, more
5 persuasive than those of Fox himself, had carried the Westminster election against palace and treasury, shone round Georgiana Duchess of Devonshire.

The Sergeants made proclamation. Hastings advanced to the bar and bent his knee. The culprit was indeed not
10 unworthy of that great presence. He had ruled an extensive and populous country, had made laws and treaties, had sent forth armies, had set up and pulled down princes. And in his high place he had so borne himself, that all had feared him, that most had loved him, and that hatred
15 itself could deny him no title to glory, except virtue. He looked like a great man, and not like a bad man. A person small and emaciated, yet deriving dignity from a carriage which, while it indicated deference to the court, indicated also habitual self-possession and self-respect; a high and
20 intellectual forehead; a brow pensive, but not gloomy; a mouth of inflexible decision; a face pale and worn, but serene, on which was written, as legibly as under the great picture in the Council-chamber at Calcutta, *Mens aequa in arduis;* — such was the aspect with which the great
25 proconsul presented himself to his judges.

CUMNOR PLACE[1]

SIR WALTER SCOTT

Four apartments which occupied the western side of the old quadrangle at Cumnor Place, had been fitted up with extraordinary splendour. This had been the work of several days prior to that on which our story opened. Workmen sent from London, and not permitted to leave the premises until the work was finished, had converted the apartments in that side of the building from the dilapidated appearance of a dissolved monastic house into the semblance of a royal palace. A mystery was observed in all these arrangements: the workmen came thither and returned by night, and all measures were taken to prevent the prying curiosity of the villagers from observing or speculating upon the changes which were taking place in the mansion of their once indigent, but now wealthy, neighbour Anthony Foster. Accordingly, the secrecy desired was so far preserved that nothing got abroad but vague and uncertain reports, which were received and repeated, but without much credit being attached to them.

On the evening of which we treat, the new and highly decorated suite of rooms were for the first time illuminated, and that with a brilliancy which might have been visible half a dozen miles off, had not oaken shutters, carefully secured with bolt and padlock, and mantled with long

---

[1] From *Kenilworth*, chap. vi.

curtains of silk and velvet, deeply fringed with gold, prevented the slightest gleam of radiance from being seen without.

The principal apartments, as we have seen, were four in number, each opening into the other. Access was given to them by a large scale staircase, as they were then called, of unusual length and height, which had its landing-place at the door of an ante-chamber, shaped somewhat like a gallery. This apartment the abbot had used as an occasional council-room, but it was now beautifully wainscoted with dark foreign wood of a brown colour, and bearing a high polish, said to have been brought from the Western Indies, and to have been wrought in London with infinite difficulty, and with much damage to the tools of the workmen. The dark colour of this finishing was relieved by the number of lights in silver sconces which hung against the walls, and by six large and richly-framed pictures by the first masters of the age. A massy oaken table, placed at the lower end of the apartment, served to accommodate such as chose to play at the then fashionable game of shovel-board; and there was at the other end an elevated gallery for the musicians or minstrels, who might be summoned to increase the festivity of the evening.

From this ante-chamber opened a banqueting-room of moderate size, but brilliant enough to dazzle the eyes of the spectator with the richness of its furniture. The walls, lately so bare and ghastly, were now clothed with hangings of sky-blue velvet and silver; the chairs were of ebony, richly carved, with cushions corresponding to the hangings; and the place of the silver sconces which enlightened the ante-chamber was supplied by a huge chandelier of the same precious metal. The floor was covered with a

Spanish foot-cloth, or carpet, on which flowers and fruits
were represented in such glowing and natural colours that
you hesitated to place the foot on such exquisite workmanship. The table, of old English oak, stood ready covered
with the finest linen, and a large portable court-cupboard 5
was placed with the leaves of its embossed folding-doors
displayed, showing the shelves within, decorated with a
full display of plate and porcelain. In the midst of the
table stood a salt-cellar of Italian workmanship — a beautiful and splendid piece of plate about two feet high, moulded 10
into a representation of the giant Briareus, whose hundred
hands of silver presented. to the guest various sorts of
spices, or condiments, to season their food withal.

The third apartment was called the withdrawing-room.
It was hung with the finest tapestry, representing the fall 15
of Phaeton; for the looms of Flanders were now much
occupied on classical subjects. The principal seat of this
apartment was a chair of state, raised a step or two from
the floor, and large enough to contain two persons. It was
surmounted by a canopy, which, as well as the cushions, 20
side-curtains, and the very foot-cloth, was composed of
crimson velvet, embroidered with seed-pearl. On the top
of the canopy were two coronets, resembling those of an
earl and countess. Stools covered with velvet, and some
cushions disposed in the Moorish fashion, and ornamented 25
with Arabesque needlework, supplied the place of chairs in
this apartment, which contained musical instruments, embroidery frames, and other articles for ladies' pastime.
Besides lesser lights, the withdrawing-room was illuminated by four tall torches of virgin wax, each of which was 30
placed in the grasp of a statue, representing an armed
Moor, who held in his left arm a round buckler of silver,

highly polished, interposed betwixt his breast and the
light, which was thus brilliantly reflected as from a crystal mirror.

The sleeping-chamber belonging to this splendid suite
5 of apartments was decorated in a taste less showy, but not
less rich, than had been displayed in the others. Two
silver lamps, fed with perfumed oil, diffused at once a
delicious odour and a trembling twilight-seeming shimmer
through the quiet apartment. It was carpeted so thick
10 that the heaviest step could not have been heard; and the
bed, richly heaped with down, was spread with an ample
coverlet of silk and gold, from under which peeped forth
cambric sheets, and blankets as white as the lambs which
yielded the fleece that made them. The curtains were of
15 blue velvet, lined with crimson silk, deeply festooned with
gold, and embroidered with the loves of Cupid and Psyche.
On the toilet was a beautiful Venetian mirror, in a frame
of silver filigree, and beside it stood a gold posset-dish to
contain the night-draught. A pair of pistols and a dagger,
20 mounted with gold, were displayed near the head of the
bed, being the arms for the night, which were presented to
honoured guests, rather, it may be supposed, in the way of
ceremony than from any apprehension of danger. We must
not omit to mention, what was more to the credit of the
25 manners of the time, that in a small recess, illuminated by
a taper, were disposed two hassocks of velvet and gold,
corresponding with the bed furniture, before a desk of
carved ebony. This recess had formerly been the private
oratory of the abbot, but the crucifix was removed, and
30 instead there were placed on the desk two Books of Common Prayer, richly bound and embossed with silver. With
this enviable sleeping-apartment, which was so far removed

from every sound, save that of the wind sighing among the oaks of the park, that Morpheus might have coveted it for his own proper repose, corresponded two wardrobes, or dressing-rooms, as they are now termed, suitably furnished, and in a style of the same magnificence which we have 5 already described. It ought to be added, that a part of the building in the adjoining wing was occupied by the kitchen and its offices, and served to accommodate the personal attendants of the great and wealthy nobleman for whose use these magnificent preparations had been made. 10

THE WHEAT PIT [1]

FRANK NORRIS

It was a vast enclosure, lighted on either side by great windows of coloured glass, the roof supported by thin iron pillars elaborately decorated. To the left were the bulletin blackboards, and beyond these, in the northwest angle of 5 the floor, a great railed-in space where the Western Union Telegraph was installed. To the right, on the other side of the room, a row of tables, laden with neatly arranged paper bags half full of samples of grains, stretched along the east wall from the doorway of the public room at one 10 end to the telephone room at the other.

The centre of the floor was occupied by the pits. To the left and to the front of Landry the provision pit, to the right the corn pit, while further on at the north extremity of the floor, and nearly under the visitors' gal- 15 lery, much larger than the other two, and flanked by the wicket of the official recorder, was the wheat pit itself.

Directly opposite the visitors' gallery, high upon the south wall, a great dial was affixed, and on the dial a mark- ing hand that indicated the current price of wheat, fluc- 20 tuating with the changes made in the Pit. Just now it stood at ninety-three and three-eighths, the closing quota- tion of the preceding day.

As yet all the pits were empty. It was some fifteen minutes after nine. Landry checked his hat and coat at

[1] From *The Pit*, pp. 91 ff. Doubleday, Page & Co., New York, 1903. Copyright, 1903, by Doubleday, Page & Co.

the coat-room near the north entrance, and slipped into an old tennis jacket of striped blue flannel. Then, hatless, his hands in his pockets, he leisurely crossed the floor, and sat down in one of the chairs that were ranged in files upon the floor in front of the telegraph enclosure. He scrutinised again the despatches and orders that he held in his hands; then, having fixed them in his memory, tore them into very small bits, looking vaguely about the room, developing his plan of campaign for the morning.

. . . .

Meanwhile the floor was beginning to fill up. Over in the railed-in space, where the hundreds of telegraph instruments were in place, the operators were arriving in twos and threes. They hung their hats and ulsters upon the ·pegs in the wall back of them, and in linen coats, or in their shirt-sleeves, went to their seats, or, sitting upon their tables, called back and forth to each other, joshing, cracking jokes. Some few addressed themselves directly to work, and here and there the intermittent clicking of a key began, like a diligent cricket busking himself in advance of its mates.

From the corridors on the ground floor up through the south doors came the pit traders in increasing groups. The noise of footsteps began to echo from the high vaulting of the roof. A messenger boy crossed the floor chanting an unintelligible name.

The groups of traders gradually converged upon the corn and wheat pits, and on the steps of the latter, their arms crossed upon their knees, two men, one wearing a silk skull cap all awry, conversed earnestly in low tones.

. . . .

But by now it was near to half-past nine. From the Western Union desks the clicking of the throng of instruments rose into the air in an incessant staccato stridulation. The messenger boys ran back and forth at top speed, dodg-
5 ing in and out among the knots of clerks and traders, colliding with one another, and without interruption intoning the names of those for whom they had despatches. The throng of traders concentrated upon the pits, and at every moment the deep-toned hum of the murmur of many voices
10 swelled like the rising of a tide.

.   .   .   .

The official reporter climbed to his perch in the little cage on the edge of the Pit, shutting the door after him. By now the chanting of the messenger boys was an uninterrupted chorus. From all sides of the building, and in.
15 every direction, they crossed and recrossed each other, always running, their hands full of yellow envelopes. From the telephone alcoves came the prolonged, musical rasp of the call bells. In the Western Union booths the keys of the multitude of instruments raged incessantly.
20 Bare-headed young men hurried up to one another, conferred an instant comparing despatches, then separated, darting away at top speed. Men called to each other halfway across the building. Over by the bulletin boards clerks and agents made careful memoranda of primary
25 receipts, and noted down the amount of wheat on passage, the exports and the imports.

And all these sounds, the chatter of the telegraph, the intoning of the messenger boys, the shouts and cries of clerks and traders, the shuffle and trampling of hundreds of
30 feet, the whirring of telephone signals rose into the troubled air, and mingled overhead to form a vast note, prolonged,

sustained, that reverberated from vault to vault of the airy
roof, and issued from every doorway, every opened window in one long roll of interrupted thunder. In the
Wheat Pit the bids, no longer obedient of restraint, began
one by one to burst out, like the first isolated shots of a 5
skirmish line.

.   .   .   .

Then suddenly, cutting squarely athwart the vague
crescendo of the floor, came the single incisive stroke of a
great gong. Instantly a tumult was unchained. Arms '
were flung upward in strenuous gestures, and from above 10
the crowding heads in the Wheat Pit a multitude of hands,
eager, the fingers extended, leaped into the air. All articulate expression was lost in the single explosion of sound
as the traders surged downwards to the centre of the Pit,
grabbing each other, struggling towards each other, tramp- 15
ing, stamping, charging through with might and main.
Promptly the hand on the great dial above the clock
stirred and trembled, and as though driven by the tempest
breath of the Pit moved upward through the degrees of
its circle. It paused, wavered, stopped at length, and on 20
the instant the hundreds of telegraph keys scattered
throughout the building began clicking off the news to
the whole country, from the Atlantic to the Pacific
and from Mackinac to Mexico, that the Chicago market
had made a slight advance and that May wheat, which had 25
closed the day before at ninety-three and three-eighths,
had opened that morning at ninety-four and a half.

.   .   .   .

By degrees the clamour died away, ceased, began again
irregularly, then abruptly stilled. Here and there a bid

was called, an offer made, like the intermittent crack of
small arms after the stopping of the cannonade.

"'Sell five May at one-eighth."

"'Sell twenty at one-quarter."

5   "'Give one-eighth for May."

For an instant the shoutings were renewed. Then suddenly the gong struck. The traders began slowly to leave
the Pit. One of the floor officers, an old fellow in uniform
and vizored cap, appeared, gently shouldering towards the
10 door the groups wherein the bidding and offering were
still languidly going on. His voice full of remonstration,
he repeated continually: "Time's up, gentlemen. Go on
now and get your lunch. Lunch time now. Go on now,
or I'll have to report you. Time's up."

15 The tide set toward the doorways. In the gallery the
few visitors rose, putting on coats and wraps. Over by
the check counter, to the right of the south entrance to
the floor, a throng of brokers and traders jostled each
other, reaching over one another's shoulders for hats and
20 ulsters. In steadily increasing numbers they poured out
of the north and south entrances, on their way to turn in
their trading cards to the offices.

Little by little the floor emptied. The provision and
grain pits were deserted, and as the clamour of the place
25 lapsed away the telegraph instruments began to make
themselves heard once more, together with the chanting of
the messenger boys.

Swept clean in the morning, the floor itself, seen now
through the thinning groups, was littered from end to
30 end with scattered grain — oats, wheat, corn, and barley,
with wisps of hay, peanut shells, apple parings, and orange
peel, with torn newspapers, odds and ends of memoranda,

crushed paper darts, and above all with a countless multitude of yellow telegraph forms, thousands upon thousands, crumpled and muddied under the trampling of innumerable feet. It was the débris of the battle-field, the abandoned impedimenta and broken weapons of contending armies, the detritus of conflict, torn, broken, and rent, that at the end of each day's combat encumbered the field.

At last even the click of the last of telegraph keys died down. Shouldering themselves into their overcoats, the operators departed, calling back and forth to one another, making "dates," and cracking jokes. Washerwomen appeared with steaming pails ; porters pushing great brooms before them began gathering the refuse of the floor into heaps.

＊　＊　＊　＊　＊　＊　＊　＊　＊　＊　＊　＊

A cat, grey and striped, and wearing a dog collar of nickel and red leather, issued from the coat-room and picked her way across the floor. Evidently she was in a mood of the most ingratiating friendliness, and as one after another of the departing traders spoke to her, raised her tail in the air and arched her back against the legs of the empty chairs. The janitor put in an appearance, lowering the tall colored windows with a long rod. A noise of hammering and the scrape of saws began to issue from a corner where a couple of carpenters tinkered about one of the sample tables.

Then at last even the settlement clerks took themselves off. At once there was a great silence, broken only by the harsh rasp of the carpenters' saws and the voice of the janitor exchanging jokes with the washerwomen. The sound of footsteps in distant quarters re-echoed as if in a church.

The washerwomen invaded the floor, spreading soapy and steaming water before them. Over by the sample tables a negro porter in shirt-sleeves swept entire bushels of spilled wheat, crushed, broken, and sodden, into his dust pans.

5 The day's campaign was over. It was past two o'clock. On the great dial against the eastern wall the indicator stood — sentinel fashion — at ninety-three. Not till the following morning would the whirlpool, the great central force that spun the Niagara of wheat in its grip, thunder 10 and bellow again.

Later on even the washerwomen, even the porter and janitor, departed. An unbroken silence, the peacefulness of an untroubled calm, settled over the place. The rays of the afternoon sun flooded through the west windows in 15 long parallel shafts full of floating golden motes. There was no sound; nothing stirred. The floor of the Board of Trade was deserted. Alone, on the edge of the abandoned Wheat Pit, in a spot where the sunlight fell warmest — an atom of life, lost in the immensity of the empty floor — 20 the grey cat made her toilet, diligently licking the fur on the inside of her thigh, one leg, as if dislocated, thrust into the air above her head.

TREASURE ISLAND [1]

ROBERT LOUIS STEVENSON

The appearance of the island when I came on deck next morning was altogether changed. Although the breeze had now utterly ceased, we had made a great deal of way during the night, and were now lying becalmed about half a mile to the south-east of the low eastern coast. Grey- 5 coloured woods covered a large part of the surface. This even tint was indeed broken up by streaks of yellow sand-break in the lower lands, and by many tall trees of the pine family, out-topping the others — some singly, some in clumps ; but the general colouring was uniform and sad. 10 The hills ran up clear above the vegetation in spires of naked rock. All were strangely shaped, and the Spy-glass, which was by three or four hundred feet the tallest on the island, was likewise the strangest in configuration, running up sheer from almost every side, and then suddenly cut off 15 at the top like a pedestal to put a statue on.

The *Hispaniola* was rolling scuppers under in the ocean swell. The booms were tearing at the blocks, the rudder was banging to and fro, and the whole ship creaking, groaning, and jumping like a manufactory. I had to cling tight 20 to the backstay, and the world turned giddily before my eyes ; for though I was a good enough sailor when there was way on, this standing still and being rolled about

[1] From *Treasure Island* (Thistle Edition), pp. 97–98. Charles Scribner's Sons, New York, 1895.

like a bottle was a thing I never learned to stand without a qualm or so, above all in the morning, on an empty stomach.

Perhaps it was this — perhaps it was the look of the
5 island, with its grey, melancholy woods, and wild stone spires, and the surf that we could both see and hear foaming and thundering on the steep beach — at least, although the sun shone bright and hot, and the shore birds were fishing and crying all around us, and you would have
10 thought any one would have been glad to get to land after being so long at sea, my heart sank, as the saying is, into my boots; and from that first look onward, I hated the very thought of Treasure Island.

THE PRISON DOOR [1]

NATHANIEL HAWTHORNE

A throng of bearded men, in sad-colored garments, and gray, steeple-crowned hats, intermixed with women, some wearing hoods and others bareheaded, was assembled in front of a wooden edifice, the door of which was heavily timbered with oak, and studded with iron spikes. 5

The founders of a new colony, whatever Utopia of human virtue and happiness they might originally project, have invariably recognized it among their earliest practical necessities to allot a portion of the virgin soil as a cemetery, and another portion as the site of a prison. In accord- 10 ance with this rule, it may safely be assumed that the forefathers of Boston had built the first prison-house somewhere in the vicinity of Cornhill, almost as seasonably as they marked out the first burial-ground, on Isaac Johnson's lot, and round about his grave, which subsequently became the 15 nucleus of all the congregated sepulchres in the old churchyard of King's Chapel. Certain it is, that, some fifteen or twenty years after the settlement of the town, the wooden jail was already marked with weather-stains and other indications of age, which gave a yet darker aspect to its beetle- 20 browed and gloomy front. The rust on the ponderous iron-work of its oaken door looked more antique than anything else in the New World. Like all that pertains to crime, it seemed never to have known a youthful era. Before this

[1] From *The Scarlet Letter*, Chapter 1.

ugly edifice, and between it and the wheel-track of the
street, was a grass-plot, much overgrown with burdock,
pigweed, apple-peru, and such unsightly vegetation, which
evidently found something congenial in the soil that had
5 so early borne the black flower of civilized society, a prison.
But, on one side of the portal, and rooted almost at the
threshold, was a wild rose-bush, covered, in this month of
June, with its delicate gems, which might be imagined to
offer their fragrance and fragile beauty to the prisoner as
10 he went in, and to the condemned criminal as he came
forth to his doom, in token that the deep heart of Nature
could pity and be kind to him.

This rose-bush, by a strange chance, has been kept alive
in history ; but whether it had merely survived out of the
15 stern old wilderness, so long after the fall of the gigantic pines and oaks that originally overshadowed it, — or
whether, as there is fair authority for believing, it had
sprung up under the footsteps of the sainted Ann Hutch-
inson, as she entered the prison-door, — we shall not take
20 upon us to determine. Finding it so directly on the threshold of our narrative, which is now about to issue from that
inauspicious portal, we could hardly do otherwise than
pluck one of its flowers, and present it to the reader. It
may serve, let us hope, to symbolize some sweet moral blos-
25 som, that may be found along the track, or relieve the
darkening close of a tale of human frailty and sorrow.

IN THE FOREST[1]

NATHANIEL HAWTHORNE

Thus conversing, they entered sufficiently deep into the
wood to secure themselves from the observation of any
casual passenger along the forest track. Here they sat
down on a luxuriant heap of moss ; which, at some epoch
of the preceding century, had been a gigantic pine, with 5
its roots and trunk in the darksome shade, and its head
aloft in the upper atmosphere. It was a little dell where
they had seated themselves, with a leaf-strewn bank rising
gently on either side, and a brook flowing through the
midst, over a bed of fallen and drowned leaves. The trees 10
impending over it had flung down great branches, from
time to time, which choked up the current and compelled
it to form eddies and black depths at some points ; while,
in its swifter and livelier passages, there appeared a channel-
way of pebbles, and brown sparkling sand. Letting the 15
eyes follow along the course of the stream, they could
catch the reflected light from its water, at some short distance within the forest, but soon lost all traces of it amid
the bewilderment of tree-trunks and underbrush, and here
and there a huge rock covered over with gray lichens. All 20
these giant trees and bowlders of granite seemed intent on
making a mystery of the course of this small brook ; fearing
perhaps, that, with its never-ceasing loquacity, it should

[1] From *The Scarlet Letter* (Hawthorne's Works, Riverside Edition),
V, 223-224. Houghton, Mifflin & Co., Boston, 1883.

whisper tales out of the heart of the old forest whence it
flowed, or mirror its revelations on the smooth surface of
a pool. Continually, indeed, as it stole onward, the streamlet kept up a babble, kind, quiet, soothing, but melancholy,
5 like the voice of a young child that was spending its infancy
without playfulness, and knew not how to be merry among
sad acquaintances and events of sombre hue.

CHRISTMAS EVE[1]

WASHINGTON IRVING

As we approached the house, we heard the sound. of music, and now and then a burst of laughter, from one end of the building. This, Bracebridge said, must proceed from the servants' hall, where a great deal of revelry was permitted, and even encouraged by the squire, throughout 5 the twelve days of Christmas, provided every thing was done conformably to ancient usage. Here were kept up the old games of hoodman blind, shoe the wild mare, hot cockles, steal the white loaf, bob apple, and snap dragon: the Yule log and Christmas candle were regularly burnt, 10 and the mistletoe, with its white berries, hung up, to the imminent peril of all the pretty housemaids.[2]

So intent were the servants upon their sports that we had to ring repeatedly before we could make ourselves heard. On our arrival being announced, the squire came 15 out to receive us, accompanied by his two other sons; one a young officer in the army, home on leave of absence; the other an Oxonian, just from the university. The squire was a fine healthy-looking old gentleman, with silver hair curling lightly round an open florid countenance; in which 20

[1] From "Christmas Eve" in *The Sketch-Book* (Author's Revised Edition), pp. 244-248. G. P. Putnam's Sons, New York, 1861.

[2] The mistletoe is still hung up in farmhouses and kitchens at Christmas; and the young men have the privilege of kissing the girls under it, plucking each time a berry from the bush. When the berries are all plucked, the privilege ceases.

the physiognomist, with the advantage, like myself, of a
previous hint or two, might discover a singular mixture
of whim and benevolence.

The family meeting was warm and affectionate: as the
5 evening was far advanced, the squire would not permit us
to change our travelling dresses, but ushered us at once
to the company, which was assembled in a large old-
fashioned hall. It was composed of different branches of
a numerous family connection, where there were the usual
10 proportion of old uncles and aunts, comfortable married
dames, superannuated spinsters, blooming country cousins,
half-fledged striplings, and bright-eyed boarding-school hoy-
dens. They were variously occupied; some at a round game
of cards; others conversing around the fireplace; at one
15 end of the hall was a group of the young folks, some nearly
grown up, others of a more tender and budding age, fully
engrossed by a merry game; and a profusion of wooden
horses, penny trumpets, and tattered dolls, about the floor,
showed traces of a troop of little fairy beings, who, having
20 frolicked through a happy day, had been carried off to
slumber through a peaceful night.

While the mutual greetings were going on between
young Bracebridge and his relatives, I had time to scan
the apartment. I have called it a hall, for so it had cer-
25 tainly been in old times, and the squire had evidently endeavored to restore it to something of its primitive state.
Over the heavy projecting fireplace was suspended a picture of a warrior in armor, standing by a white horse, and
on the opposite wall hung a helmet, buckler, and lance.
30 At one end an enormous pair of antlers were inserted in
the wall, the branches serving as hooks on which to suspend hats, whips, and spurs; and in the corners of the

apartment were fowling-pieces, fishing rods, and other sporting implements. The furniture was of the cumbrous workmanship of former days, though some articles of modern convenience had been added, and the oaken floor had been carpeted; so that the whole presented an odd 5 mixture of parlor and hall.

The grate had been removed from the wide overwhelming fireplace, to make way for a fire of wood, in the midst of which was an enormous log glowing and blazing, and sending forth a vast volume of light and heat: this I 10 understood was the Yule clog, which the squire was particular in having brought in and illumined on a Christmas eve, according to ancient custom.[1]

It was really delightful to see the old squire seated in his hereditary elbow chair, by the hospitable fireside of his 15

[1] The *Yule clog* is a great log of wood, sometimes the root of a tree, brought into the house with great ceremony, on Christmas eve, laid in the fireplace, and lighted with the brand of last year's clog. While it lasted, there was great drinking, singing, and telling of tales. Sometimes it was accompanied by Christmas candles; but in the cottages the only light was from the ruddy blaze of the great wood fire. The Yule clog was to burn all night; if it went out, it was considered a sign of ill-luck.

Herrick mentions it in one of his songs : —

> Come, bring with a noise,
> My merrie, merrie boyes,
> The Christmas log to the firing ;
> While my good dame, she
> Bids ye all be free,
> And drink to your hearts desiring.

The Yule clog is still burnt in many farmhouses and kitchens in England, particularly in the north, and there are several superstitions connected with it among the peasantry. If a squinting person come to the house while it is burning, or a person barefooted, it is considered an ill omen. The brand remaining from the Yule clog is carefully put away to light the next year's Christmas fire.

ancestors, and looking around him like the sun of a system, beaming warmth and gladness to every heart. Even the very dog that lay stretched at his feet, as he lazily shifted his position and yawned, would look fondly up in

5 his master's face, wag his tail against the floor, and stretch himself again to sleep, confident of kindness and protection. There is an emanation from the heart in genuine hospitality which cannot be described, but is immediately felt, and puts the stranger at once at his ease. I had not

10 been-seated many minutes by the comfortable hearth of the worthy old cavalier, before I found myself as much at home as if I had been one of the family.

NOON IN THE PLAZA [1]

· FRANK NORRIS

It was high noon, and the rays of the sun, that hung
poised directly overhead in an intolerable white glory, fell
straight as plummets upon the roofs and streets of Guad-
alajara. The adobe walls and sparse brick sidewalks of
the drowsing town radiated the heat in an oily, quivering 5
shimmer. The leaves of the eucalyptus trees around the
Plaza drooped motionless, limp and relaxed under the
scorching, searching blaze. The shadows of these trees
had shrunk to their smallest circumference, contracting
close about the trunks. The shade had dwindled to the 10
breadth of a mere line. The sun was everywhere. The
heat exhaling from brick and plaster and metal met
the heat that steadily descended blanketwise and smother-
ing, from the pale, scorched sky. Only the lizards — they
lived in chinks of the crumbling adobe and in interstices 15
of the sidewalk — remained without, motionless, as if
stuffed, their eyes closed to mere slits, basking, stupefied
with heat. At long intervals the prolonged drone of an
insect developed out of the silence, vibrated a moment in
a soothing, somnolent, long note, then trailed slowly into 20
the quiet again. Somewhere in the interior of one of the
'dobe houses a guitar snored and hummed sleepily. On
the roof of the hotel a group of pigeons cooed incessantly

[1] From *The Octopus*, chap. vi, pp. 212–213. Doubleday, Page & Co.,
New York, 1901. Copyright, 1901, by Doubleday, Page & Co.

with subdued, liquid murmurs, very plaintive ; a cat, perfectly white, with a pink nose and thin, pink lips, dozed
complacently on a fence rail, full in the sun. In a corner
of the Plaza three hens wallowed in the baking hot dust,
5 their wings fluttering, clucking comfortably.

A COLD DAY[1]

Leigh Hunt

Now the moment people wake in the morning they perceive the coldness with their faces, though· they are warm
with their bodies, and exclaim "Here's a day!" and pity
the poor little sweep, and the boy with the water-cresses.
How anybody can go to a cold ditch, and gather·water-   5
cresses, seems marvellous. Perhaps we hear great lumps in
the street of something falling ; and, looking through the
window, perceive the roofs of the neighbouring houses thick
with snow. The breath is visible, issuing from the mouth
as we lie. Now we hate getting up, and hate shaving, and   10
hate the empty grate in one's bed-room ; and water freezes
in ewers, and you may set the towel upright on its own
hardness, and the window-panes are frost-whitened, or it is
foggy, and the sun sends a dull, brazen beam into one's
room ; or, if it is fine, the windows outside are stuck with   15
icicles ; or a detestable thaw has begun, and they drip ; but,
at all events, it is horribly cold, and delicate shavers fidget
about their chambers, looking distressed, and cherish their
hard-hearted enemy, the razor, in their bosoms, to warm him
a little, and coax him into a consideration of their chins.   20
Savage is a cut, and makes them think destiny really too hard.

Now breakfast is fine ; and the fire seems to laugh at us
as we enter the breakfast-room, and say, "Ha ! ha ! here's

[1] From "A 'Now.' Descriptive of a Cold Day," in *Essays by Leigh
Hunt* (Camelot Edition), pp. 63–66. Walter Scott, London.

a better room than the bed-chamber ! " and we always poke
it before we do anything else ; and people grow selfish
about seats near it; and little boys think their elders
tyrannical for saying, " Oh, *you* don't want the fire ; your
5 blood is young." And truly that is not the way of stating
the case, albeit young blood is warmer than old. Now the
butter is too hard to spread ; and the rolls and toast are at
their maximum ; and the former look glorious as they issue
smoking out of the flannel in which they come from the
10 baker's ; and people who come with single knocks at the
door are pitied ; and the voices of boys are loud in the street,
sliding or throwing snow-balls ; and the dustman's bell
sounds cold ; and we wonder how anybody can go about
selling fish, especially with that hoarse voice ; and school-
15 boys hate their slates, and blow their fingers, and detest
infinitely the no-fire school ; and the parish-beadle's nose is
redder than ever.

Now sounds in general are dull, and smoke out of chimneys looks warm and rich, and birds are pitied, hopping
20 about for crumbs, and the trees look wiry and cheerless,
albeit they are still beautiful to imaginative eyes, especially
the evergreens, and the birch with boughs like dishevelled
hair. Now mud in roads is stiff, and the kennel ices over,
and boys make illegal slides in the pathways, and ashes are
25 strewed before doors ; or you crunch the snow as you tread,
or kick mud-flakes before you, or are horribly muddy in
cities. But if it is a hard frost, all the world is buttoned up
and great-coated, except ostentatious elderly gentlemen, and
pretended beggars with naked feet ; and the delicious sound
30 of " All hot " is heard from roasted apple and potato stalls,
the vendor himself being cold, in spite of his " hot " and
stamping up and down to warm his feet ; and the little boys

are astonished to think how he can eat bread and cold meat
for his dinner, instead of the smoking apples.

Now skaters are on the alert ; the cutlers' shop-windows
abound with their swift shoes; and as you approach the
scene of action (pond or canal) you hear the dull grinding   5
noise of the skates to and fro, and see tumbles, and Banbury
cake-men and blackguard boys playing " hockey," and ladies
standing shivering on the banks, admiring everybody but
their brother, especially the gentleman who is cutting figures
of eight, who, for his part, is admiring his own figure.   10
Beginners affect to laugh at their tumbles, but are terribly
angry, and long to thump the by-standers. On thawing
days, idlers persist to the last in skating or sliding amidst
the slush and bending ice, making the Humane-Society-man
ferocious. He feels as if he could give them the deaths   15
from which it is his business to save them. When you have
done skating you come away, feeling at once warm and
numb in the feet, from the tight effect of the skates ; and
you carry them with an ostentatious air of indifference, as
if you had done wonders; whereas you have fairly had   20
three slips, and can barely achieve the inside edge.

Now riders look sharp, and horses seem brittle in the
legs, and old gentlemen feel so ; and coachmen, cabmen,
and others stand swinging their arms across at their sides
to warm themselves; and blacksmiths' shops look pleasant,   25
and potato shops detestable; the fishmongers' still more
so. We wonder how he can live in that plash of wet and
cold fish without even a window. Now clerks in offices
envy the one next the fire-place; and men from behind
counters hardly think themselves repaid by being called   30
out to speak to, a countess in her chariot ; and the wheezy
and effeminate pastry-cook, hatless and aproned, and with

his hand in his breeches-pockets (as the graphic Cruikshank
noticeth in his almanack) stands outside his door, chilling
his household warmth with attending to the ice which is
brought him, and seeing it unloaded into his cellar like
5 coals. Comfortable look the Miss Joneses, coming this way
with their muffs and furs; and the baker pities the maid-
servant cleaning the steps, who, for her part, says she is
not cold, which he finds it difficult to believe.

Now dinner rejoiceth the gatherers together, and cold
10 meat is despised, and the gout defieth the morrow, thinking
it but reasonable on such a day to inflame itself with
" t' other bottle"; and the sofa is wheeled round to the fire
after dinner, and people proceed to burn their legs in their
boots, and little boys their faces ; and young ladies are
15 tormented between the cold and their complexions, and
their fingers freeze at the pianoforte, but they must not say
so, because it will vex their poor, comfortable grand-aunt,
who is sitting with her knees in the fire, and who is so
anxious that they should not be spoilt.

20 . Now the muffin-bell soundeth sweetly in the streets,
reminding us, not of the man, but his muffins, and of twilight, and evening, and curtains, and the fireside. Now
play-goers get cold feet, and invalids stop up every crevice
in their rooms, and make themselves worse ; and the streets
25 are comparatively silent ; and the wind rises and falls in
moanings ; and the fire burns blue and crackles ; and an
easy-chair with your feet by it on a stool, the lamp or
candles a little behind you, and an interesting book just
opened where you left off, is a bit of heaven upon earth.
30 People in cottages crowd close into the chimney, and tell
stories of ghosts and murders, the blue flame affording
something like evidence of the facts.

"The owl, with all her feathers, is a-cold," or you think
her so. The whole country feels like a petrifaction of slate
and stillness, cut across by the wind; and nobody in the
mail-coach is warm but the horses, who steam pitifully
when they stop. The " oldest man " makes a point of never 5
having " seen such weather." People have a painful doubt
whether they have any chins or not; ears ache with the
wind; and the waggoner, setting his teeth together, goes
puckering up his cheeks, and thinking the time will never
arrive when he shall get to the Five Bells. 10

At night, people become sleepy with the fireside, and
long to go to bed, yet fear it on account of the different
temperature of the bed-room; which is furthermore apt to
wake them up. Warming-pans and hot-water bottles are in
request; and naughty boys eschew their night-shirts, and 15
go to bed in their socks.

" Yes," quoth a little boy, to whom we read this passage,
" and make their younger brother go to bed first."

A STABLE-YARD ON A RAINY DAY[1]

Washington Irving

It was a rainy Sunday in the gloomy month of November.
I had been detained, in the course of a journey, by a slight
indisposition, from which I was recovering; but was still
feverish, and obliged to keep within doors all day, in an inn
5 of the small town of Derby. A wet Sunday in a country
inn! — whoever has had the luck to experience one can
alone judge of my situation. The rain pattered against the
casements; the bells tolled for church with a melancholy
sound. I went to the windows in quest of something to
10 amuse the eye; but it seemed as if I had been placed completely out of the reach of all amusement. The windows
of my bedroom looked out among tiled roofs and stacks
of chimneys, while those of my sitting-room commanded
a full view of the stable-yard. I know of nothing more
15 calculated to make a man sick of this world than a stable-
yard on a rainy day. The place was littered with wet
straw that had been kicked about by travellers and stable-
boys. In one corner was a stagnant pool of water, surrounding an island of muck; there were several half-
20 drowned fowls crowded together under a cart, among
which was a miserable, crest-fallen cock, drenched out of
all life and spirit; his drooping tail matted, as it were,
into a single feather, along which the water trickled from

1 From "The Stout Gentleman" in *Bracebridge Hall* (Author's Revised Edition), pp. 75-76. G. P. Putnam's Sons, New York, 1861.

314

his back ; near the cart was a half-dozing cow, chewing the
cud, and standing patiently to be rained on, with wreaths
of vapor rising from her reeking hide ; a wall-eyed horse,
tired of the loneliness of the stable, was poking his spectral
head·out of a window, with the rain dripping on it from 5
the eaves ; an unhappy cur, chained to a dog-house hard
by, uttered something every now and then, between a bark
and a yelp; a drab of a kitchen wench tramped backwards
and forwards through the yard in pattens, looking as sulky
as the weather itself ; everything in short was comfortless 10
and forlorn, excepting a crew of hardened ducks, assembled
like boon companions round a puddle, and making a riot-
ous noise over their liquor.

THE HOUSE OF USHER [1]

EDGAR ALLAN POE

During the whole of a dull, dark, and soundless day in
the autumn of the year, when the clouds hung oppressively
low in the heavens, I had been passing alone, on horseback,
through a singularly dreary tract of country ; and at length
5 found myself, as the shades of the evening drew on, within
view of the melancholy House of Usher. I know not how
it was — but, with the first glimpse of the building, a sense
of insufferable gloom pervaded my spirit. I say insufferable ; for the feeling was unrelieved by any of that half-
10 pleasurable, because poetic, sentiment with which the mind
usually receives even the sternest natural images of the
desolate or terrible. I looked upon the scene before me —
upon the mere house, and the simple landscape features of
the domain, upon the bleak walls, upon the vacant eye-like
15 windows, upon a few rank sedges, and upon a few white
trunks of decayed trees — with an utter depression of soul
which I can compare to no earthly sensation more properly
than to the after-dream of the reveller upon opium : the
bitter lapse into every-day life, the hideous dropping off of
20 the veil. There was an iciness, a sinking, a sickening of
the heart, an unredeemed dreariness of thought which no
goading of the imagination could torture into aught of the
sublime. What was it — I paused to think — what was it

[1] From "The Fall of the House of Usher," in Poe's *Works*, ed. Stedman
and Woodberry, I, 131 ff. Stone & Kimball, Chicago, 1894.

that so unnerved me in the contemplation of the House of
Usher? It was a mystery all insoluble; nor could I grapple
with the shadowy fancies that crowded upon me as I pon-
dered. I was forced to fall back upon the unsatisfactory
conclusion, that while, beyond doubt, there *are* combina- 5
tions of very simple natural objects which have the power
of thus affecting us, still the analysis of this power lies
among considerations beyond our depth. It was possible,
I reflected, that a mere different arrangement of the particulars of the scene, of the details of the picture, would be 10
sufficient to modify, or perhaps to annihilate, its capacity
for sorrowful impression; and acting upon this idea, I reined
my horse to the precipitous brink of a black and lurid tarn
that lay in unruffled lustre by the dwelling, and gazed down
— but with a shudder even more thrilling than before — 15
upon the remodelled and inverted images of the gray sedge,
and the ghastly tree-stems, and the vacant and eye-like
windows.

.   .   .   .

I have said that the sole effect of my somewhat childish
experiment, that of looking down within the tarn, had been 20
to deepen the first singular impression. There can be no
doubt that the consciousness of the rapid increase of my
superstition — for why should I not so term it? — served
mainly to accelerate the increase itself. Such, I have long
known, is the paradoxical law of all sentiments having terror 25
as a basis. And it might have been for this reason only,
that, when I again uplifted my eyes to the house itself,
from its image in the pool, there grew in my mind a strange
fancy — a fancy so ridiculous, indeed, that I but mentioned
it to show the vivid force of the sensations which oppressed 30
me. I had so worked upon my imagination as really to

believe that about the whole mansion and domain there hung an atmosphere peculiar to themselves and their immediate vicinity : an atmosphere which had no affinity with the air of heaven, but which had reeked up from the
5 decayed trees, and the gray wall, and the silent tarn : a pestilent and mystic vapor, dull, sluggish, faintly discernible, and leaden-hued.

Shaking off from my spirit what *must* have been a dream, I scanned more narrowly the real aspect of the building.
10 Its principal feature seemed to be that of an excessive antiquity. The discoloration of ages had been great. Minute fungi overspread the whole exterior, hanging in a fine tangled web-work from the eaves. Yet all this was apart from any extraordinary dilapidation. No portion of the masonry had
15 fallen ; and there appeared to be a wild inconsistency between its still perfect adaptation of parts and the crumbling condition of the individual stones. In this there was much that reminded me of the specious totality of old wood-work which has rotted for long years in some neglected vault,
20 with no disturbance from the breath of the external air. Beyond this indication of extensive decay, however, the fabric gave little token of instability. Perhaps the eye of a scrutinizing observer might have discovered a barely perceptible fissure, which, extending from the roof of the
25 building in front, made its way down the wall in a zigzag direction, until it became lost in the sullen waters of the tarn.

Noticing these things, I rode over a short causeway to the house. A servant in waiting took my horse, and I
30 entered the Gothic archway of the hall. A valet, of stealthy step, thence conducted me, in silence, through many dark and intricate passages in my progress to the studio of his

master. Much that I encountered on the way contributed,
I know not how, to heighten the vague sentiments of which
I have already spoken. While the objects around me —
while the carvings of the ceilings, the sombre tapestries of
the walls, the ebon blackness of the floors, and the phantas- 5
magoric armorial trophies which rattled as I strode, were
but matters to which, or to such as which, I had been
accustomed from my infancy — while I hesitated not to
acknowledge how familiar was all this — I still wondered
to find how unfamiliar were the fancies which ordinary 10
images were stirring up. On one of the staircases, I met
the physician of the family. His countenance, I thought,
wore a mingled expression of low cunning and perplexity.
He accosted me with trepidation and passed on. The valet
now threw open a door and ushered me into the presence 15
of his master.

The room in which I found myself was very large and
lofty. The windows were long, narrow, and pointed, and
at so vast a distance from the black oaken floor as to be
altogether inaccessible from within. Feeble gleams of 20
encrimsoned light made their way through the trellised
panes, and served to render sufficiently distinct the more
prominent objects around ; the eye, however, struggled in
vain to reach the remoter angles of the chamber, or the
recesses of the vaulted and fretted ceiling. Dark draperies 25
hung upon the walls. The general furniture was profuse,
comfortless, antique, and tattered. Many books and musical instruments lay scattered about, but failed to give any
vitality to the scene. I felt that I breathed an atmosphere
of sorrow. An air of stern, deep, and irredeemable gloom 30
hung over and pervaded all.

A POINT OF VIEW[1]

ROBERT LOUIS STEVENSON

I have named, among many rivers that make music in
my memory, that dirty Water of Leith. Often and often I
desire to look upon it again; and the choice of a point of
view is easy to me. It should be at a certain water-door,
5 embowered in shrubbery. The river is there dammed back
for the service of the flour-mill just below, so that it lies
deep and darkling, and the sand slopes into brown obscurity
with a glint of gold; and it has but newly been recruited
by the borrowings of the snuff-mill just above, and these,
10 tumbling·merrily in, shake the pool to its black heart, fill
it with drowsy eddies, and set the curded froth of many
other mills solemnly steering to and fro upon the surface.
Or so it was when I was young; for change, and the
masons, and the pruning-knife, have been busy; and if I
15 could hope to repeat a cherished experience, it must be on
many and impossible conditions. I must choose, as well
as the point of view, a certain moment in my growth, so
that the scale may be exaggerated, and the trees on the
steep opposite side may seem to climb to heaven, and the
20 sand by the water-door, where I am standing, seem as low
as Styx. And I must choose the season also, so that the
valley may be brimmed like a cup with sunshine and the
songs of birds; — and the year of grace, so that when I
turn to leave the riverside I may find the old manse and
25 its inhabitants unchanged.

[1] From "The Manse," in *Memories and Portraits* (Thistle Edition),
pp. 241–242. Charles Scribner's Sons, New York, 1895.

THE DOMAIN OF ARNHEIM[1]

EDGAR ALLAN POE

The usual approach to Arnheim was by the river. The
visitor left the city in the early morning. During the
forenoon he passed between shores of a tranquil and
domestic beauty, on which grazed innumerable sheep,
their white fleeces spotting the vivid green of rolling   5
meadows. By degrees the idea of cultivation subsided
into that of merely pastoral care. This slowly became
merged in a sense of retirement — this again in a consciousness of solitude. As the evening approached, the
channel grew more narrow; the banks more and more   10
precipitous; and these latter were clothed in richer, more
profuse, and more sombre foliage. The water increased in
transparency. The stream took a thousand turns, so that
at no moment could its gleaming surface be seen for a
greater distance than a furlong. At every instant the ves-   15
sel seemed imprisoned within an enchanted circle, having
insuperable and impenetrable walls of foliage, a roof of
ultra-marine satin, and *no* floor — the keel balancing itself
with an admirable nicety on that of a phantom bark which,
by some accident having been turned upside down, floated   20
in constant company with the substantial one, for the purpose of sustaining it. The channel now became a *gorge* —
although the term is somewhat inapplicable, and I employ

---

[1] From "The Domain of Arnheim," in *Poe's Works*, ed. Stedman and
Woodberry, II, 106–112. Stone & Kimball, Chicago, 1894.

it merely because the language has no word which better represents the most striking, not the most distinctive, feature of the scene. The character of gorge was maintained only in the height and parallelism of the shores ; it
5 was lost altogether in their other traits. The walls of the ravine (through which the clear water still tranquilly flowed) arose to an elevation of a hundred and occasionally of a hundred and fifty feet, and inclined so much toward each other as, in a great measure, to shut out the light of
10 day ; while the long plume-like moss, which depended densely from the intertwining shrubberies overhead, gave the whole chasm an air of funereal gloom. The windings became more frequent and intricate, and seemed often as if returning in upon themselves, so that the voyager had
15 long lost all idea of direction. He was, moreover, enwrapt in an exquisite sense of the strange. The thought of nature still remained, but her character seemed to have undergone modification ; there was a weird symmetry, a thrilling uniformity, a wizard propriety in these her works. Not a dead
20 branch — not a withered leaf — not a stray pebble — not a patch of the brown earth was anywhere visible. The crystal water welled up against the clean granite, or the unblemished moss, with a sharpness of outline that delighted while it bewildered the eye.
25 Having threaded the mazes of this channel for some hours, the gloom deepening every moment, a sharp and unexpected turn of the vessel brought it suddenly, as if dropped from heaven, into a circular basin of very considerable extent when compared with the width of the gorge.
30 It was about two hundred yards in diameter, and girt in at all points but one — that immediately fronting the vessel as it entered — by hills equal in general height to the

walls of the chasm, although of a thoroughly different character. Their sides sloped from the water's edge at an angle of some forty-five degrees, and they were clothed from base to summit — not a perceptible point escaping — in a drapery of the most gorgeous flower-blossoms ; scarcely 5 a green leaf being visible among the sea of odorous and fluctuating color. This basin was of great depth, but so transparent was the water that the bottom, which seemed to consist of a thick mass of small round alabaster pebbles, was distinctly visible by glimpses : that is to say, when- 10 ever the eye could permit itself *not* to see, far down in the inverted heaven, the duplicate blooming of the hills. On these latter there were no trees, nor even shrubs of any size. The impressions wrought on the observer were those of richness, warmth, color, quietude, uniformity, softness, 15 delicacy, daintiness, voluptuousness, and a miraculous extremeness of culture that suggested dreams of a new race of fairies, laborious, tasteful, magnificent, and fastidious; but as the eye traced upward the myriad-tinted slope, from its sharp junction with the water to its vague termina- 20 tion amid the folds of overhanging cloud, it became, indeed, difficult not to fancy a panoramic cataract of rubies, sapphires, opals and golden onyxes, rolling silently out of the sky.

The visitor, shooting suddenly into this bay from out the gloom of the ravine, is delighted but astounded by the 25 full orb of the declining sun, which he had supposed to be already far below the horizon, but which now confronts him, and forms the sole termination of an otherwise limitless vista seen through another chasm-like rift in the hills.

But here the voyager quits the vessel which has borne 30 him so far, and descends into a light canoe of ivory, stained with arabesque devices in vivid scarlet, both within and

without. The poop and beak of this boat rise high above
the water, with sharp points, so that the general form is
that of an irregular crescent. It lies on the surface of the
bay with the proud grace of a swan. On its ermined floor
5 reposes a single feathery paddle of satin-wood; but no
oarsman or attendant is to be seen. The guest is bidden to
be of good cheer — that the fates will take care of him.
The larger vessel disappears, and he is left alone in the
canoe, which lies apparently motionless in the middle of
10 the lake. While he considers what course to pursue, however, he becomes aware of a gentle movement in the fairy
bark. It slowly swings itself around until its prow points
toward the sun. It advances with a gentle but gradually
accelerated velocity, while the slight ripples it creates seem
15 to break about the ivory sides in divinest melody — seem
to offer the only possible explanation of the soothing yet
melancholy music for whose unseen origin the bewildered
voyager looks around him in vain.

The canoe steadily proceeds, and the rocky gate of the
20 vista is approached, so that its depths can be more distinctly seen. To the right arises a chain of lofty hills
rudely and luxuriantly wooded. It is observed, however,
that the trait of exquisite *cleanness* where the bank dips
into the water, still prevails. There is not one token of the
25 usual river débris. To the left the character of the scene is
softer and more obviously artificial. Here the bank slopes
upward from the stream in a very gentle ascent, forming a
broad sward of grass of a texture resembling nothing so
much as velvet, and of a brilliancy of green which would
30 bear comparison with the tint of the purest emerald. This
plateau varies in width from ten to three hundred yards;
reaching from the river-bank to a wall, fifty feet high,

which extends, in an infinity of curves, but following the
general direction of the river, until lost in the distance to
the westward. This wall is of one continuous rock, and
has been formed by cutting perpendicularly the once rugged
precipice of the stream's southern bank ; but no trace of 5
the labor has been suffered to remain. The chiselled stone ‑
has the hue of ages, and is profusely overhung and overspread with the ivy, the coral honeysuckle, the eglantine,
and the clematis. The uniformity of the top and bottom
lines of the wall is fully relieved by occasional trees of 10
gigantic height, growing singly or in small groups, both
along the plateau and in the domain behind the wall, but
in close proximity to it ; so that frequent limbs (of the
black walnut especially) reach over and dip their pendent
extremities into the water. Farther back within the domain 15
the vision is impeded by an impenetrable screen of foliage.

These things are observed during the canoe's gradual
approach to what I have called the gate of the vista. On
drawing nearer to this, however, its chasm-like appearance
vanishes ; a new outlet from the bay is discovered to the 20
left — in which direction the wall is also seen to sweep,
still following the general course of the stream. Down
this new opening the eye cannot penetrate very far ; for
the stream, accompanied by the wall, still bends to the
left, until both are swallowed up by the leaves. 25

The boat, nevertheless, glides magically into the winding channel ; and here the shore opposite the wall is found
to resemble that opposite the wall in the straight vista.
Lofty hills, rising occasionally into mountains, and covered
with vegetation in wild luxuriance, still shut in the scene. 30

Floating gently outward, but with a velocity slightly
augmented, the voyager, after many short turns, finds his

progress apparently barred by a gigantic gate or rather door of burnished gold, elaborately carved and fretted, and reflecting the direct rays of the now fast-sinking sun with an effulgence that seems to wreathe the whole sur-
5 rounding forest in flames. This gate is inserted in the lofty wall; which here appears to cross the river at right angles. In a few moments, however, it is seen that the main body of the water still sweeps in a gentle and extensive curve to the left, the wall following it as before, while a stream
10 of considerable volume, diverging from the principal one, makes its way, with a slight ripple, under the door, and is thus hidden from sight. The canoe falls into the lesser channel and approaches the gate. Its ponderous wings are slowly and musically expanded. The boat glides between
15 them, and commences a rapid descent into a vast amphitheatre entirely begirt with purple mountains, whose bases are laved by a gleaming river throughout the full extent of their circuit. Meantime the whole Paradise of Arnheim bursts upon the view. There is a gush of entrancing
20 melody; there is an oppressive sense of strange sweet odor; there is a dreamlike intermingling to the eye of tall slender Eastern trees — bosky shrubberies — flocks of golden and crimson birds — lily-fringed lakes — meadows of violets, tulips, poppies, hyacinths, and tuberoses — long
25 intertangled lines of silver streamlets — and, upspringing confusedly from amid all, a mass of semi-Gothic, semi-Saracenic architecture, sustaining itself as if by miracle in mid-air; glittering in the red sunlight with a hundred oriels, minarets, and pinnacles; and seeming the phantom
30 handiwork, conjointly, of the Sylphs, of the Fairies, of the Genii, and of the Gnomes.

AUTUMN ON CAPE COD[1]

Henry David Thoreau

Before sunset, having already seen the mackerel fleet returning into the Bay, we left the seashore on the north of Provincetown, and made our way across the desert to the eastern extremity of the town. From the first high sand-hill, covered with beach-grass and bushes to its top, on the edge of the desert, we overlooked the shrubby hill and swamp country which surrounds Provincetown on the north, and protects it, in some measure, from the invading sand. Notwithstanding the universal barrenness, and the contiguity of the desert, I never saw an autumnal landscape so beautifully painted as this was. It was like the richest rug imaginable spread over an uneven surface ; no damask nor velvet, nor Tyrian dye of stuffs, nor the work of any loom, could ever match it. There was the incredibly bright red of the Huckleberry, and the reddish brown of the Bayberry, mingled with the bright and living green of small Pitch-Pines, and also the duller green of the Bayberry, Boxberry, and Plum, the yellowish green of the Shrub-Oaks, and the various golden and yellow and fawn-colored tints of the Birch and Maple and Aspen, — each making its own figure, and, in the midst, the few yellow sand-slides on the sides of the hills looked like the white floor seen through rents in the rug. Coming from the country as I

---

[1] From *Cape Cod* (Riverside Edition), pp. 232–234. Houghton, Mifflin & Co., Boston, 1894.

did, and many autumnal woods as I had seen, this was
perhaps the most novel and remarkable sight that I saw on
the Cape. Probably the brightness of the tints was en-
hanced by contrast with the sand which surrounded this
5 tract. This was a part of the furniture of Cape Cod. We
had for days walked up the long and bleak piazza which
runs along her Atlantic side, then over the sanded floor of
her halls, and now we were being introduced into her
boudoir. The hundred white sails crowding round Long
10 Point into Provincetown Harbor, seen over the painted
hills in front, looked like toy ships upon a mantel-piece.

The peculiarity of this autumnal landscape consisted in
the lowness and thickness of the shrubbery, no less than in
the brightness of the tints. It was like a thick stuff of
15 worsted or a fleece, and looked as if a giant could take it
up by the hem, or rather the tasseled fringe which trailed
out on the sand, and shake it, though it needed not to be
shaken. But no doubt the dust would fly in that case, for
not a little has accumulated underneath it. Was it not such
20 an autumnal landscape as this which suggested our high-
colored rugs and carpets? Hereafter when I look on a
richer rug than usual, and study its figures, I shall think,
there are the huckleberry hills, and there the denser swamps
of boxberry and blueberry; there the shrub-oak patches
25 and the bayberries, there the maples and the birches and
the pines.

THE COLOR OF WALDEN POND [1]

HENRY DAVID THOREAU

All our Concord waters have two colors at least: one
when viewed at a distance, and another, more proper, close
at hand. The first depends more on the light, and follows
the sky. In clear weather, in summer, they appear blue at
a little distance, especially if agitated, and at a great dis- 5
tance all appear alike. In stormy weather they are sometimes of a dark slate color. The sea, however, is said to be
blue one day and green another without any perceptible
change in the atmosphere. I have seen our river, when,
the landscape being covered with snow, both water and ice 10
were almost as green as grass. Some consider blue " to be
the color of pure water, whether liquid or solid." But,
looking directly down into our waters from a boat, they
are seen to be of very different colors. Walden is blue at
one time and green at another, even from the same point 15
of view. Lying between the earth and the heavens, it par-
takes of the color of both. Viewed from a hill-top it reflects
the color of the sky; but near at hand it is of a yellowish
tint next the shore where you can see the sand, then a light
green, which gradually deepens to a uniform dark green in 20
the body of the pond. In some lights, viewed even from a
hill-top, it is of a vivid green next the shore. Some have
referred this to the reflection of the verdure; but it is
equally green there against the rail-road sand-bank, and in
the spring, before the leaves are expanded, and it may be 25

[1] From *Walden* (Riverside Edition), pp. 275-278. Houghton, Mifflin &
Co., Boston, 1894.

simply the result of the prevailing blue mixed with the yellow of the sand. Such is the color of its iris. This is that portion, also, where in the spring, the ice being warmed by the heat of the sun reflected from the bottom, and also

5 transmitted through the earth, melts first and forms a narrow canal about the still frozen middle. Like the rest of our waters, when much agitated, in clear weather, so that the surface of the waves may reflect the sky at the right angle, or because there is more light mixed with it, it appears

10 at a little distance of a darker blue than the sky itself ; and at such a time, being on its surface, and looking with divided vision, so as to see the reflection, I have discerned a matchless and indescribable light blue, such as watered or changeable silks and sword blades suggest, more cerulean

15 than the sky itself, alternating with the original dark green on the opposite sides of the waves, which last appeared but muddy in comparison. It is a vitreous greenish blue, as I remember it, like those patches of the winter sky seen through cloud vistas in the west before sundown. Yet a

20 single glass of its water held up to the light is as colorless as an equal quantity of air. It is well known that a large plate of glass will have a green tint, owing, as the makers say, to its "body," but a small piece of the same will be colorless. How large a body of Walden water would be

25 required to reflect a green tint I have never proved. The water of our river is black or a very dark brown to one looking directly down on it, and, like that of most ponds, imparts to the body of one bathing in it a yellowish tinge ; but this water is of such crystalline purity that the body of

30 the bather appears of an alabaster whiteness, still more unnatural, which, as the limbs are magnified and distorted withal, produces a monstrous effect, making fit studies for a Michael Angelo.

A STUDY OF LIGHT ON THE CAMPAGNA[1]

John Ruskin

It had been wild weather when I left Rome, and all across the Campagna the clouds were sweeping in sulphurous blue, with a clap of thunder or two, and breaking gleams of sun along the Claudian aqueduct, lighting up the infinity of its arches like the bridge of chaos. But as I climbed the long slope of the Alban Mount, the storm swept finally to the north, and the noble outlines of the domes of Albano, and graceful darkness of its ilex grove, rose against pure streaks of alternate blue and amber; the upper sky gradually flushing through the last fragments of rain-cloud in deep palpitating azure, half ether and half dew. The noon-day sun came slanting down the rocky slopes of La Riccia, and its masses of entangled and tall foliage, whose autumnal tints were mixed with the wet verdure of a thousand evergreens, were penetrated with it as with rain. I cannot call it color, it was conflagration. Purple, and crimson and scarlet, like the curtains of God's tabernacle, the rejoicing trees sank into the valley in showers of light, every separate leaf quivering with buoyant and burning life; each, as it turned to reflect or to transmit the sunbeam, first a torch and then an emerald. Far up into the recesses of the valley, the green vistas arched like the hollows of mighty waves of some crystalline sea, with the arbutus flowers dashed along their flanks

[1] From *Modern Painters*, Vol. I, Part II, sect. 2, chap. ii.

for foam, and silver flakes of orange spray tossed into the
air around them, breaking over the grey walls of rock into
a thousand separate stars, fading and kindling alternately
as the weak wind lifted and let them fall. Every glade of
5 grass burned like the golden floor of heaven, opening in
sudden gleams as the foliage broke and closed above it, as
sheet-lightning opens in a cloud at sunset; the motionless
masses of dark rock — dark though flushed with scarlet
lichen, — casting their quiet shadows across its restless
10 radiance, the fountain underneath them filling its marble
hollow with blue mist and fitful sound, and over all — the
multitudinous bars of amber and rose, the sacred clouds
that have no darkness, and only exist to illume, were seen
in fathomless intervals between the solemn and orbed
15 repose of the stone pines, passing to lose themselves in
the last, white, blinding lustre of the measureless line
where the Campagna melted into the blaze of the sea.

THE CLAMOR OF BIRDS [1]

John Burroughs

To strong, susceptible characters the music of nature is
not confined to sweet sounds. The defiant scream of
the hawk circling aloft, the wild whinney of the loon, the
whooping of the crane, the booming of the bittern, the vul-
pine bark of the eagle, the loud trumpeting of the migra- 5
tory geese sounding down out of the midnight sky ; or by
the sea-shore, the coast of New Jersey or Long Island, the
wild crooning of the flocks of gulls, repeated, continued
by the hour, swirling sharp and shrill, rising and falling
like the wind in a storm, as they circle above the beach, 10
or dip to the dash of the waves — are much more welcome
in certain moods than any and all mere bird-melodies, in
keeping as they are with the shaggy and untamed features
of ocean and woods, and suggesting something like the
Richard Wagner music in the ornithological orchestra. 15

[1] From *Birds and Poets*, p. 12. Houghton, Mifflin & Co., Boston, 1878.

THE NOISE OF LONDON [1]

William Dean Howells

One hears a good deal of the greater quiet of London after New York. I think that what you notice is a difference in the quality of the noise in London. What is with us mainly a harsh, metallic shriek, a grind of trolley wheels
5 upon trolley tracks, and a wild battering of their polygonized circles upon the rails, is in London the dull, tormented roar of the omnibuses and the incessant cloop-cloop of the cab-horses' hoofs. Between the two sorts of noise there is little choice for one who abhors both. The real difference is that
10 in many neighborhoods you can more or less get away from the specialized noises in London, but you never can do this in New York. You hear people saying that in these refuges the London noise is mellowed to a soft pour of sound, like the steady fall of a cataract, which effectively is silence;
15 but that is not accurate. The noise is broken and crushed in a huge rumble without a specialized sound, except when, after midnight, the headlong clatter of a cab-horse distinguishes itself from the prevailing bulk. But the New York noise is never broken and crushed into a rumble; it bristles
20 with specific accents, night and day, which agonizingly assort themselves one from another, and there is no nook or corner where you can be safe from them, as you can measurably be in London.

[1] From *London Films*, pp. 52–53. Harper & Brothers, New York, 1905.

THE FARMYARD [1]

George Eliot

Plenty of life there ! though this is the drowsiest time
of the year, just before hay-harvest ; and it is the drowsiest
time of the day too, for it is close upon three by the sun,
and it is half-past three by Mrs. Poyser's handsome eight-
day clock. But there is always a stronger sense of life 5
when the sun is brilliant after rain ; and now he is pouring
down his beams, and making sparkles among the wet straw,
and lighting up every patch of vivid green moss on the
red tiles of the cow-shed, and turning even the muddy
water that is hurrying along the channel to the drain into 10
a mirror for the yellow-billed ducks, who are seizing the
opportunity of getting a drink with as much body in it as
possible. There is quite a concert of noises : the great
bulldog, chained against the stables, is thrown into furious
exasperation by the unwary approach of a cock too near 15
the mouth of his kennel, and sends forth a thundering
bark, which is answered by two fox-hounds shut up in the
opposite cow-house ; the old topknotted hens, scratching
with their chicks among the straw, set up a sympathetic
croaking as the discomfited cock joins them ; a sow with 20
her brood, all very muddy as to the legs, and curled as to
the tail, throws in some deep staccato notes ; our friends
the calves are bleating from the home croft ; and, under all,
a fine ear discerns the continuous hum of human voices.

[1] From *Adam Bede*, chap. vi.

THE VOICE OF THE PACIFIC [1]

Robert Louis Stevenson

The one common note of all this country is the haunting presence of the ocean. A great faint sound of breakers follows you high up into the inland cañons ; the roar of water dwells in the clean, empty rooms of Monterey as in
5 a shell upon the chimney; go where you will, you have but to pause and listen to hear the voice of the Pacific. You pass out of the town to the southwest, and mount the hill among pine woods. Glade, thicket, and grove surround you. You follow winding sandy tracks that lead
10 nowhither. You see a deer; a multitude of quail arises. But the sound of the sea still follows you as you advance, like that of wind among the trees, only harsher and stranger to the ear; and when at length you gain the summit, out breaks on every hand and with freshened
15 vigour, that same unending, distant, whispering rumble of the ocean ; for now you are on the top of Monterey peninsula, and the noise no longer only mounts to you from behind along the beach towards Santa Cruz, but from your right also, round by Chinatown and Pinos lighthouse, and
20 from down before you to the mouth of the Carmello river. The whole woodland is begirt with thundering surges. The silence that immediately surrounds you where you stand is not so much broken as it is haunted by this distant,

[1] From "The Old Pacific Capital" in *Across the Plains* (Thistle Edition), p. 151. Charles Scribner's Sons, New York, 1895.

circling rumour. It sets your senses upon edge ; you
strain your attention ; you are clearly and unusually conscious of small sounds near at hand ; you walk listening
like an Indian hunter ; and that voice of the Pacific is a
sort of disquieting company to you in your walk.

APRIL ODORS[1]

JOHN BURROUGHS

Then its odors! I am thrilled by its fresh and indescribable odors — the perfume of the bursting sod, of the quickened roots and rootlets, of the mould under the leaves, of the fresh furrows. No other month has odors like it. The
5 west wind the other day came fraught with a perfume that was to the sense of smell what a wild and delicate strain of music is to the ear. It was almost transcendental. I walked across the hill with my nose in the air taking it in. It lasted for two days. I imagined it came from the willows of a
10 distant swamp, whose catkins were affording the bees their first pollen, — or did it come from much farther — from beyond the horizon, the accumulated breath of innumerable farms and budding forests? The main characteristic of these April odors is their uncloying freshness. They are
15 not sweet, they are oftener bitter, they are penetrating and lyrical. I know well the odors of May and June, of the world of meadows and orchards bursting into bloom, but they are not so ineffable and immaterial and so stimulating to the sense as the incense of April.

[1] From *Birds and Poets*, pp. 110–111. Houghton, Mifflin & Co., Boston, 1878.

THE RIDE OF LITTLE TOOMAI[1]

RUDYARD KIPLING

The elephant turned without a sound, took three strides
back to the boy in the moonlight, put down his trunk, swung
him up to his neck, and almost before Little Toomai had
settled his knees slipped into the forest.

There was one blast of furious trumpeting from the lines,   5
and then the silence shut down on everything, and Kala
Nag began to move. Sometimes a tuft of high grass washed
along his sides as a wave washes along the sides of a ship,
and sometimes a cluster of wild-pepper vines would scrape
along his back, or a bamboo would creak where his shoulder 10
touched it ; but between those times he moved absolutely
without any sound, drifting through the thick Garo forest
as though it had been smoke. He was going up-hill, but
though Little Toomai watched the stars in the rifts of the
trees, he could not tell in what direction.   15

Then Kala Nag reached the crest of the ascent and stopped
for a minute, and Little Toomai could see the tops of the
trees lying all speckled and furry under the moonlight for
miles and miles, and the blue-white mist over the river in
the hollow. Toomai leaned forward and looked, and he   20
felt that the forest was awake below him — awake and
alive and crowded. A big brown fruit-eating bat brushed

---

[1] From "Toomai of the Elephants," in *The Second Jungle Book*
(Outward Bound Edition), pp. 80–82. Charles Scribner's Sons, New
York, 1897.

past his ear; a porcupine's quills rattled in the thicket; and in the darkness between the tree-stems he heard a hog-bear digging hard in the moist, warm earth, and snuffing as it digged.

5 Then the branches closed over his head again, and Kala Nag began to go down into the valley — not quietly this time, but as a runaway gun goes down a steep bank — in one rush. The huge limbs moved as steadily as pistons, eight feet to each stride, and the wrinkled skin of the elbow-
10 points rustled. The undergrowth on either side of him ripped with a noise like torn canvas, and the saplings that he heaved away right and left with his shoulders sprang back again, and banged him on the flank, and great trails of creepers, all matted together, hung from his tusks as he
15 threw his head from side to side and plowed out his path-way. Then Little Toomai laid himself down close to the great neck, lest a swinging bough should sweep him to the ground, and he wished that he were back in the lines again.

SWIMMING THE WHIRLPOOL[1]

HENRY MILNER RIDEOUT

He was off, running to the beach, and along it northward, to make his start as far as possible above the line where the whirlpool might appear. Ripping off his clothes, he ran naked down to the water's edge, doused the oil over his body, and rubbed hastily till the great white muscles glistened in the sun. He felt hollow from lack of food and sleep; the water stretched hopelessly far to the mainland; but the excitement as he ran splashing out, and the cold shock of the plunge, set his heart thumping stoutly. His first thought was one of despair, " It's too cold." But he shut his mind to that, and clove his way ahead through the bright green water, swimming with a powerful side stroke. That lowness of vision over a flat surface which is peculiar to swimming made colors and lines abnormally distinct. With his cheek gouging through the water, he could see the ruddy cliffs retreating behind him, the greenness and the black shadows of little trees that clung in crevices, the pink curve of the beach, the shining, shifting lines of the water, his own legs, distorted by refraction till they looked ridiculously pale and green and thin, kicking away like alien marine things in pursuit of his body and of the big, glistening deltoid that capped his shoulder, strongly contracting and relaxing. Ahead, as he shot his

---

[1] From " Blue Peter," in *Beached Keels*, pp. 92–98. Houghton, Mifflin & Co., Boston, 1906.

arm forward, appeared his first distance mark, a white can-
buoy two thirds of the way across the channel; beyond that,
a broad eddy of the tide, a slightly raised surface, smooth
and yellowish-white, like a sheet of ice, where hundreds
5 of white gulls wheeled or floated in search of breakfast;
and beyond these again, the wharves and meagre shipping
of the town, — the square-rigged shapely tangle of his own
ship, the Elizabeth Fanning.

The numbness began to leave him, though an ice-cold
10 ring circled his neck where wind and water met. Like all
swimmers, he grew confused in his sense of time, and had
strange thoughts. Halfway to the can-buoy now ; no longer
slack water ; must hurry. A half-eaten apple came bobbing
peacefully toward him on the young flood. He wondered
15 who had eaten it, and whether it were sweet or sour. But
where the devil had all his Latin gone to? Her father had
said "enaviganda." Did that mean it could be swum
through, or it couldn't? He suffered a morbid worry over
the meaning of this word, as if it contained the secret of his
20 present fate. The thing had been done — that fellow in '56.
At all events, he shifted his stroke again, and swam on
tediously.

Of a sudden he noticed that the apple was bearing
rapidly down, — was alongside, on a little raised rim of
25 water like a moving flaw in glass. Next instant he had
spun about and was facing seaward. Something below
twirled his legs violently.

"Hello!" he sputtered aloud. "Good Lord!" he
thought. "This is bad. I must get out of this."
30 But the running ocean was stronger. The water hissed,
curved on a slant, boiled upward, regurgitated in patches
white as with melting snow-flakes. A submarine force,

gigantic and appalling, spun him round and round and
whirled him downward. He wrestled frantically. His
head sank inside a wide cylinder of smooth green glass,
laced about spirally with running silver threads. His ears,
long deafened by the noise of swimming, were filled with 5
a strange roar. "Whirlpool! It's all up. I'll see where
it goes to, anyway," he thought insanely, and strained for
a last breath as he shot under. In a green light he was
slatted about dreadfully, spinning upright, then horizontal,
his useless arms and legs flying wide and shaken. A giant 10
weight, a personal, hateful weight, began pressing on his
back, pressing him slowly down into the dark. Acute
worry seized him because this thing was unfair — would
not give him a chance to get just one more breath — was
squeezing him down into a funnel, and he did not think 15
the bore at the end was big enough to let him through.
"Why," he thought, "why, this is It! This is dying.
What they call Death! — I'm very sorry for them all up
there." And then he thought, as suddenly, "Hold on! I
can't yet, because before this sort of thing I'm due to 20
come back to the island, — I've drunk from her spring —
Helen — that was the agreement — " But still he was
pressed downward, and the pain grew heavy and dull. No
one would ever tell her of the cold, the dark, the loneliness.
It was all years ago, anyway, and very deep.   25

Slowly he was rising. "Where next?" he thought
cynically. Perhaps it was over now, and this was just the
fellow's soul going up, up. "No, by golly, there's too
much pain about it. It's lighter — The sun — It's me,
and I'm out — Air!"   30

He struck out in leaden imitation of swimming, just to
take it up where he had left off; then stopped; then

began again. He was more interested in a pale thing that accompanied him, large and speckled, like a potato, but twitching round the edges, round the nostrils. "Why, it's my nose, and I've got one eye shut. How silly!" The
5 humor of this woke him up, and now he really swam. "I've wasted a lot of time down there," he mourned.

Something large, white, and round came rushing at him through the water. The can-buoy, — the tide was carrying him past, he mustn't lose that. He lashed out for it
10 blindly, and managed to be flung against the slope. Though it dipped, swayed, and rolled, he slowly climbed up, over barnacles and painted sheet-iron, to where he could grasp the iron ring at the top. It must have been for a long time that he clung there. The tiny knives of
15 the barnacles had sliced his legs, and blood ran in slow, red streams through the hair on his shins. "It's all up," he reflected, watching the tide race by. "I've come through the upper tip-edge of the whirlpools, off there. Just a baby one that got me; but it's done the trick.
20 This is a mighty poor exhibition. What will Peter say, and Helen?" The only answer was despair; he grew colder and weaker, his aching fingers loosened, time dragged on, and he longed to go to sleep.

THE TIME OF NEW TALK[1]

Rudyard Kipling

In an Indian Jungle the seasons slide one into the other almost without division. There seem to be only two — the wet and the dry; but if you look closely below the torrents of rain and the clouds of char and dust you will find all four going round in their regular ring. Spring is 5 the most wonderful, because she has not to cover a clean, bare field with new leaves and flowers, but to drive before her and to put away the hanging-on, over-surviving raffle of half-green things which the gentle winter has suffered to live, and to make the partly-dressed stale earth feel new 10 and young once more. And this she does so well that there is no spring in the world like the Jungle spring.

There is one day when all things are tired, and the very smells, as they drift on the heavy air, are old and used. One cannot explain this, but it feels so. Then there is 15 another day — to the eye nothing whatever has changed — when all the smells are new and delightful, and the whiskers of the Jungle People quiver to their roots, and the winter hair comes away from their sides in long, draggled locks. Then, perhaps, a little rain falls, and all 20 the trees and the bushes and the bamboos and the mosses and the juicy-leaved plants wake with a noise of growing that you can almost hear, and under this noise runs, day

---

[1] From "The Spring Running," in *The Jungle Book* (Outward Bound Edition), pp. 266–267. Charles Scribner's Sons, New York, 1897.

and night, a deep hum. *That* is the noise of the spring —
a vibrating boom which is neither bees, nor falling water,
nor the wind in tree-tops, but the purring of the warm,
happy world.

5   Up to this year Mowgli had always delighted in the
turn of the seasons. It was he who generally saw the first
Eye-of-the-Spring deep down among the grasses, and the
first bank of spring clouds, which are like nothing else in
the Jungle. His voice could be heard in all sorts of wet,
10 star-lighted, blossoming places, helping the big frogs through
their choruses, or mocking the little up-side-down owls
that hoot through the white nights. Like all his people,
spring was the season he chose for his flittings — moving,
for the mere joy of rushing through the warm air, thirty,
15 forty, or fifty miles between twilight and the morning star,
and coming back panting and laughing and wreathed with
strange flowers. The Four did not follow him on these
wild ringings of the Jungle, but went off to sing songs
with other wolves. The Jungle People are very busy in
20 the spring, and Mowgli could hear them grunting and
screaming and whistling according to their kind. Their
voices then are different from their voices at other times
of the year, and that is one of the reasons why spring in
the Jungle is called the Time of New Talk.

THE JUNGLE AT NIGHT[1]

RUDYARD KIPLING

It was a perfect white night, as they call it. All green
things seemed to have made a month's growth since the
morning. The branch that was yellow-leaved the day
before dripped sap when Mowgli broke it. The mosses
curled deep and warm over his feet, the young grass had 5
no cutting edges, and all the voices of the Jungle boomed
like one deep harp-string touched by the moon — the Moon
of New Talk, who splashed her light full on rock and pool,
slipped it between trunk and creeper, and sifted it through
a million leaves. Forgetting his unhappiness, Mowgli sang 10
aloud with pure delight as he settled into his stride. It
was more like flying than anything else, for he had chosen
the long downward slope that leads to the Northern
Marshes through the heart of the main Jungle, where the
springy ground deadened the fall of his feet. A man- 15
taught man would have picked his way with many stumbles
through the cheating moonlight, but Mowgli's muscles,
trained by years of experience, bore him up as though he
were a feather. When a rotten log or a hidden stone turned
under his foot he saved himself, never checking his pace, 20
without effort and without thought. When he tired of
ground-going he threw up his hands monkey-fashion to the
nearest creeper, and seemed to float rather than to climb

[1] From "The Spring Running," in *The Jungle Book* (Outward Bound
Edition), pp. 272–274. Charles Scribner's Sons, New York, 1897.

up into the thin branches, whence he would follow a tree-road till his mood changed, and he shot downward in a long, leafy curve to the levels again. There were still, hot hollows surrounded by wet rocks where he could hardly
5 breathe for the heavy scents of the night flowers and the bloom along the creeper buds ; dark avenues where the moonlight lay in belts as regular as checkered marbles in a church aisle ; thickets where the wet young growth stood breast-high about him and threw its arms round his waist;
10 and hilltops crowned with broken rock, where he leaped from stone to stone above the lairs of the frightened little foxes. He would hear, very faint and far off, the *chug-drug* of a boar sharpening his tusks on a bole ; and would come across the great gray brute all alone, scribing and
15 rending the bark of a tall tree, his mouth dripping with foam, and his eyes blazing like fire. Or he would turn aside to the sound of clashing horns and hissing grunts, and dash past a couple of furious sambhur, staggering to and fro with lowered heads, striped with blood that showed
20 black in the moonlight. Or at some rushing ford he would hear Jacala the Crocodile bellowing like a bull, or disturb a twined knot of the Poison People, but before they could strike he would be away and across the glistening shingle, deep in the Jungle again.

25   So he ran, sometimes shouting, sometimes singing to himself, the happiest thing in all the Jungle that night, till the smell of the flowers warned him that he was near the marshes, and those lay far beyond his furthest hunting-grounds.

A NIGHT AMONG THE PINES[1]

ROBERT LOUIS STEVENSON

From *Bleymard* after dinner, although it was already late, I set out to scale a portion of the *Lozère*. An ill-marked stony drove-road guided me forward; and I met nearly half a dozen bullock-carts descending from the woods, each laden with a whole pine-tree for the winter's 5 firing. At the top of the woods, which do not climb very high upon this cold ridge, I struck leftward by a path among the pines, until I hit on a dell of green turf, where a streamlet made a little spout over some stones to serve me for a water-tap. "In a more sacred or sequestered 10 bower — nor nymph nor faunus haunted." The trees were not old, but they grew thickly round the glade: there was no outlook, except north-eastward upon distant hill-tops, or straight upward to the sky; and the encampment felt secure and private like a room. By the time I had made 15 my arrangements and fed *Modestine*, the day was already beginning to decline. I buckled myself to the knees into my sack and made a hearty meal; and as soon as the sun went down, I pulled my cap over my eyes and fell asleep.

Night is a dead monotonous period under a roof; but in 20 the open world it passes lightly, with its stars and dews and perfumes, and the hours are marked by changes in the face of Nature. What seems a kind of temporal death to

[1] From *Travels with a Donkey* (Thistle Edition), pp. 219–224. Charles Scribner's Sons, New York, 1896.

people choked between walls and curtains, is only a light and living slumber to the man who sleeps afield. All night long he can hear Nature breathing deeply and freely; even as she takes her rest she turns and smiles; and there is one
5 stirring hour unknown to those who dwell in houses, when a wakeful influence goes abroad over the sleeping hemisphere, and all the outdoor world are on their feet. It is then that the cock first crows, not this time to announce the dawn, but like a cheerful watchman speeding the
10 course of night. Cattle awake on the meadows; sheep break their fast on dewy hillsides, and change to a new lair among the ferns; and houseless men, who have lain · down with the fowls, open their dim eyes and behold the beauty of the night.
15 At what inaudible summons, at what gentle touch of Nature, are all these sleepers thus recalled in the same hour to life? Do the stars rain down an influence, or do we share some thrill of mother earth below our resting bodies? Even shepherds and old country-folk, who are
20 the deepest read in these arcana, have not a guess as to the means or purpose of this nightly resurrection. Towards two in the morning they declare the thing takes place; and neither know nor inquire further. And at least it is a pleasant incident. We are disturbed in our slumber only,
25 like the luxurious *Montaigne*, "that we may the better and more sensibly relish it." We have a moment to look upon the stars, and there is a special pleasure for some minds in the reflection that we share the impulse with all out-door creatures in our neighbourhood, that we have
30 escaped out of the *Bastille* of civilisation, and are become, for the time being, a mere kindly animal and a sheep of Nature's flock.

When that hour came to me among the pines, I awakened
thirsty. My tin was standing by me half full of water. I
emptied it at a draught; and feeling broad awake after this
internal cold aspersion, sat upright to make a cigarette.
The stars were clear, coloured, and jewel-like, but not
frosty. A faint silvery vapour stood for the Milky Way.
All around me the black fir-points stood upright and stock-
still. By the whiteness of the pack-saddle, I could see
Modestine walking round and round at the length of her
tether; I could hear her steadily munching at the sward;
but there was not another sound, save the indescribable
quiet talk of the runnel over the stones. I lay lazily
smoking and studying the colour of the sky, as we call
the void of space, from where it showed a reddish gray
behind the pines to where it showed a glossy blue-black
between the stars. As if to be more like a pedlar, I wear
a silver ring. This I could see faintly shining as I raised
or lowered the cigarette; and at each whiff the inside of
my hand was illuminated, and became for a second the
highest light in the landscape.

A faint wind, more like a moving coolness than a stream
of air, passed down the glade from time to time; so that
even in my great chamber the air was being renewed all
night long. I thought with horror of the inn at *Chasseradès*
and the congregated nightcaps; with horror of the nocturnal prowesses of clerks and students, of hot theatres and
pass-keys and close rooms. I have not often enjoyed a
more serene possession of myself, nor felt more independent of material aids. The outer world, from which we
cower into our houses, seemed after all a gentle habitable
place; and night after night a man's bed, it seemed, was
laid and waiting for him in the fields, where God keeps an

open house. I thought I· had re-discovered one of those
truths which are revealed to savages and hid from political
economists: at the least, I had discovered a new pleasure
for myself. And yet even while I was exulting in my
5 solitude I became aware of a strange lack. I wished a
companion to lie near me in the starlight, silent and not
moving, but ever within touch. For there is a fellowship
more quiet even than solitude, and which, rightly understood, is solitude made perfect. And to live out of doors
10 with the woman a man loves is of all lives the most complete and free.

As I thus lay, between content and longing, a faint noise
stole towards me through the pines. I thought, at first, it
was the crowing of cocks or the barking of dogs at some
15 very distant farm; but steadily and gradually it took articulate shape in my ears, until I became aware that a passenger was going by upon the highroad in the valley, and
singing loudly as he went. There was more of good-will
than grace in his performance; but he trolled with ample
20 lungs; and the sound of his voice took hold upon the hillside and set the air shaking in the leafy glens. I have
heard people passing by night in sleeping cities; some of
them sang; one, I remember, played loudly on the bag-
pipes. I have heard the rattle of a cart or carriage spring
25 up suddenly after hours of stillness, and pass, for some
minutes, within the range of my hearing as I lay abed.
There is a romance about all who are abroad in the black
hours, and with something of a thrill we try to guess their
business. But here the romance was double: first, this
30 glad passenger, lit internally with wine, who sent up his
voice in music through the night; and then I, on the other
hand, buckled into my sack, and smoking alone in the

pine-woods between four and five thousand feet towards the stars.

When I awoke again (*Sunday, 29th September*), many of the stars had disappeared; only the stronger companions of the night still burned visibly overhead; and away towards the east I saw a faint haze of light upon the horizon, such as had been the Milky Way when I was last awake. Day was at hand. I lit my lantern, and by its glowworm light put on my boots and gaiters; then I broke up some bread for *Modestine*, filled my can at the water-tap, and lit my spirit-lamp to boil myself some chocolate. The blue darkness lay long in the glade where I had so sweetly slumbered; but soon there was a broad streak of orange melting into gold along the mountain-tops of *Vivarais*. A solemn glee possessed my mind at this gradual and lovely coming in of day. I heard the runnel with delight; I looked round me for something beautiful and unexpected; but the still black pine-trees, the hollow glade, the munching ass, remained unchanged in figure. Nothing had altered but the light, and that, indeed, shed over all a spirit of life and of breathing peace, and moved me to a strange exhilaration.

I drank my water chocolate, which was hot if it was not rich, and strolled here and there, and up and down about the glade. While I was thus delaying, a gush of steady wind, as long as a heavy sigh, poured direct out of the quarter of the morning. It was cold, and set me sneezing. The trees near at hand tossed their black plumes in its passage; and I could see the thin distant spires of pine along the edge of the hill rock slightly to and fro against the golden east. Ten minutes after, the sunlight spread at a gallop along the hillside, scattering shadows and sparkles, and the day had come completely.

I hastened to prepare my pack, and tackle the steep
ascent that lay before me; but I had something on my
mind. It was only a fancy; yet a fancy will sometimes be
importunate. I had been most hospitably received and
5 punctually served in my green caravanserai. The room
was airy, the water excellent, and the dawn had called me
to a moment. I say nothing of the tapestries or the inimi-
table ceiling, nor yet of the view which I commanded from
the windows; but I felt I was in some one's debt for all
10 this liberal entertainment. And so it pleased me, in a half-
laughing way, to leave pieces of money on the turf as I
went along, until I had left enough for my night's lodging.
I trust they did not fall to some rich and churlish drover.

STUDENTS' THEMES : DESCRIPTION

I

Chill sunlight fell softly over the broad country-side. A road bordered by stone walls wound between bare orchards and level fields. Colder and more piercing grew the wind; everything was still. On the slope of a hill near the road, an old colored man was slowly gathering dead branches 5 from the fruit trees into a huge pile ready for burning.

II

Brisk winds had swept bare the deserted street. A dark tracery of leafless branches arched over it. Long rows of brilliant arc lights, glittering like violet fire-flies in the cold, extended in gently converging lines toward a sky 10 still faintly colored by the light of a vanished sun.

III

"Rockland! Rockland!" the watchman thundered in my ears. I awoke with a start. Rubbing the sleep from my eyes, I rolled out of the bunk, scrambled into my clothes as quickly as possible, and went up on deck. A 15 chilling breeze struck my cheek as I stepped out that made me draw my overcoat more tightly about me. The sun had not yet risen: in the east streaks of red were just beginning to tinge the sky and the water. On the left the outlines of Owl's Head with its twinkling light were just visible; on the right a few islands extended their rocky backs indistinctly into the darkness. Occasionally the lanterns of a fishing-boat came into view, or a lone sea-gull fluttered past. Then the lights of Rockland gradually drew nearer, the steamer puffed on and reached the now active pier, just as the first rays of the sun glistened over the sea and made myriad tints and hues upon the dew-drenched decks.

IV

A dry little lady, enveloped in that indefinable atmosphere which goes with a life isolated from humanity, entered the car with a light but firm step. She was just about to sit down when the car started. The result was that a big, rough-looking workman found the little lady in his lap. On subsiding into her proper place, she coughed a shocked little cough and rustled slightly, like a dry leaf.

V

A pale, fat little woman opened a door in the row of dark houses that all looked alike, and called something in a merry, inarticulate voice that suggested false teeth. Thereupon a fat white dog rose slowly from the sidewalk. He took a step or two forward, and then stood perfectly still, with his head and his stub of a tail dejected, as if he were loath to leave the warm sun that sank into his back. As the old lady kept on calling, the dog shoved himself painfully along until he reached the steps, then he waited a long time, with his front paws on the first step, wiggling heavily. When I last saw him, he was dragging his hind feet slowly, reluctantly, from the second to the third step.

VI

The narrow trail, making its laborious ascent up the steep slope of the mountain, stretched white in the moonlight. Here and there a projecting rock or loose boulder left deep splashes of shadow that lay on its surface like puddles of ink. Two riders, each leading an extra mount 5 loaded with camp-bed, cooking utensils, and food and provender, came creeping up from the valley. They stopped on the flat "saddle," where the narrow scar in the sagebrush started downward, and stood out sharply against the sky. The horses drew deep, sighing breaths and shook 10 themselves; the moisture from their warm bodies steamed up in clouds. Quickly they raised their nervous heads, shot forward their alert ears, and gazed intently off into space as, from somewhere in the lonely waste below, there came faintly the sharp, quick bark and wavering falsetto 15 cry of a solitary coyote.

One of the night riders was an old man whose long white beard contrasted queerly with his saddle-colored face and keen eyes. He had filled and lighted an ancient pipe which he had fished from somewhere in his weather-stained 20 canvas jacket, and was leaning back in his saddle, fanning himself gently with his faded sombrero and sending up luxurious clouds from the rank tobacco. His young companion, one leg thrown over the saddle horn, was slowly rolling a cigarette as he stared down at the ghostly valley. 25 After a while, the patriarch cleared his throat. " I guess," said the old man, " if we want to make that blamed waterhole to-night, we 'd better be hittin' the trail." And silently the little cavalcade moved on.

VII

The storm, though still roaring in fiercely from the sea, had abated, and in the east behind the masts of the wrecked steamer the cold dawn was dimly breaking. On the beach the little crowd of rescuers was huddling in the lee of a
5 fire that flapped in the wind. Nothing more could be done for the boat; they could only sit and wait till the waves brought the dead ashore, and then carry them to the little lighthouse. Suddenly from up the beach a watcher called. "The seventeenth," said one, and they hurried to the spot
10 just as the breakers swept far up on the sand a body — a woman's. The little band crowded around; somebody held up a lantern. There was a minute of hushed silence, not impassive but involuntary, broken at length by a wondering voice, "Ain't she beautiful!" The spell broke, and
15 with unusual care the rough fishermen laid the body on the little cart, stopping to look once again before it was wheeled off.

VIII

Doctor, as we called him, was our principal. An M.D., an A.M., a principal of a school, and bald-headed at that,
20 suggests something very dignified and stately. Doctor did not fit the suggestion. He was a short, perfectly proportioned, trim little gentleman, with a moustache that made him look fierce or paternal according to whether he was teaching Latin or patting some prospective pupil on the
25 head, and a forehead which, by pursuing his hair half over his head, had gained a breadth not intended by nature but equally useful in both the above cases as conveying an impression of deep learning. He was always dressed in

the latest style of neckwear, and his socks were a perpetual wonder to the class; some bold spirit in past ages had
ventured to call him a sport (not in his presence, of course)
and to apply to him the mysterious term "nifty," which
appellation clung to him even till our time. But while it 5
grew old, he kept perpetually youthful, always with the
same exact crease in his exact little trousers, always with
some fresh design around his neck or ankle. Nevertheless,
his forehead spoke true: he was a scholar.

A STUDY OF DAWN

The church bell tolled four. Just one bright star was set in the square blackness of my window. Everything else was darkness. Half wondering if all the familiar objects in my room might not have disappeared, I stretched
5 out my hand, and felt the wall cold and smooth at my side. An invisible clock ticked insistently in the stillness, which was relieved only by a sharp rattle of the wind at the curtain.

A streak of gray was crossing a corner of the black
10 square, the star had sunk farther into the darkness, and I could see the movement of the curtain tassel swinging in the breeze. The dim light crept around the corner and across the window-sill, showing the bureau, table, and chairs as queer-shaped monsters looming up in the darkness.

15 As the ray grew bolder it reached the middle of the room, disclosed the curving gilt lines decorating the edge of a picture-frame, and brought out a flash of light in the brass at the foot of the bed. The corners of the pictures began to appear, then the eyes of my grandmother smiled
20 at me from the gray light. One by one I could distinguish the pictures of my friends. Something black and mis-shapen crouched in one corner. I named over to myself all the objects in the room which might answer to its description, but I could not account for it. Finally, deciding
25 that the dog must have found his way upstairs, I leaned on my elbow to whisper hoarsely, "Rex." The mass did

not move, and I bent closer to find a piece of paper sticking out of my waste-basket. As I did so I noticed that the carpet had changed from a neutral gray to an indistinctly beflowered buff-color.

A faint streak of pink again called my attention to the window. The square was no longer black, the star had gone, and the limbs of a distant pine had taken its place. The breeze brought with it the clank of cans, and the heavy step of the milkman. In the distance an early car hummed and bumped along the rails. A factory whistle shrieked through the stillness, and, as if in answer to its summons, a squad of laborers clumped heavily past the house.

A moment later a single sunbeam danced through the curtains. All the room flashed into its familiar day-time aspect, the clock whirred out a furious alarm, and with the click of the lamp-lighter's pole, the last vestige of night was gone.

A DESERTED SAW-MILL

Half a day's journey westward from the little Vermont
village of Stratton the mountain road tops the ridge of the
Green Mountain chain and begins its tortuous descent into
the valley of the Battenkill. Here, at an elevation of some
5 three thousand feet above the sea, stood a deserted saw-mill,
far gone in decay. A sturdy second growth of birch and
pine had closed in upon it since it made its last deep inroad
into the surrounding forest, and even the bright summer sunlight which filtered through the branches of the trees could
10 not dispel the air of utter loneliness that hung about it.

In the full flush of its youth the mill had laid bare the
ridges and the valley slopes, and every giant of the forest
round about had felt the keen edge of its might. But
when its work was done, it slept; and while it lay thus
15 dormant the great creative forces of the Earth repaired
the damage, and the forest grew again. The birch shot
up between the rotting floor planks and the green tops
of elm and maple met above its sagging roof in derisive
silence at the puny deeds of man. A sparkling mountain
20 rivulet swirled by a few yards distant, and mocked the
mill before it ducked beneath the road. A pair of lapwings
built their nest beneath the eaves, and a family of hedge-
hogs had found a permanent residence beneath its floors.
The huge saw-dust heap behind the ruin was colored a
25 deep brown by the storms of many winters, and yellow
butterflies hovered above the flowering fireweed which
grew rank around the edges of the pile. Within, a wild

grape vine had wound its tendrils round the rusted cranks and levers; great spiders spun down from the bending rafters, or lurked in corner cobwebs for stray wasps or flies, and bits of broken window glass reflected the glint of sunlight through the leaves of silver birches. 5

It was as though the gods, offended by the havoc man had wrought, had granted to the woodland full revenge, and as though the forest, with its slow but sure advance on its enemy, was wreaking vengeance and in time would leave no trace whatever of the mill. All human life seemed 10 out of place ; for here elemental forces were surely in control (which know neither forgiveness nor forgetfulness, but which act by rigid law), and every living thing, from the gray green lichens which clung to the mouldy shingles, to the hedgehog which gnawed at the foundation logs, 15 spelt destruction for that trifling handiwork of man.

IN THE MISSION ROOM

It was a dark, rainy night. The ill-lighted North-End street was so dim that men peered uncertainly into each other's faces. One side of the street would have been called residential in some parts of the city, but here people never
5 reside; they huddle, large foreign families, in tall, narrow tenements. The other side of the street was almost one continuous saloon, alternating with dingy tailor shops and second-hand furniture stores with signs, "Dining-room chairs like new at only fifty cents each."

10 In the basement of one block, with saloons left, right, and opposite, a long, low mission room was lighted but little better than the street outside, by two green bracket-lamps with wicks so poor that the light flickered. The plastering on the walls had crumbled and left gray holes,
15 and the ceiling was veined and wrinkled into ridges and hubbles.

A spectacled old maid sleepily pressed the keys of a small organ which a red-headed boy was pumping. Evidently the *forte* stops were out of order, for in spite of
20 the efforts of the panting boy the organ squeaked faintly, while one bass note kept up a constant groan. Half a roomful of people were singing spiritedly, if not consistently, "Darkness without but light within," then "There'll be no dark valley," and "Let the blessed sunshine in."

25 There were perhaps fifty poor wretches present, half-fed, hollow-chested men, who coughed, some of them, until

their bony frames fairly shook. Many of them in a drunken
stupor had dropped in because it was drier and warmer
than the side-walk. One great bloated-faced fellow dozed
contentedly with his frowzy head in a hard-bottomed
chair and his feet, barely covered by a pair of cast-off
slippers, braced up against the wall. Another old fellow
had not taken off his hat, a battered rim of felt with a hole
where the crown used to be. As he sang fervently and
nodded when the words pleased him, a long gray tuft of
hair which stuck up through the hole nodded in time with
the music. At the end of each stanza, he shouted "Halle-
lujah!" and so missed the beginning of the next. His
voice shook and quavered above all the rest.

The women were almost all bare-headed, though some
of them wore bedraggled hats, — plumed wrecks with
feathers that had lost their curl and hung limply at just
the wrong angle. Those who did not wear elegantly
shabby wraps, had scant shawls pinned around scrawny
shoulders. Their faces showed signs of want and struggle
rather than of dissipation. One sad-eyed little foreigner,
with a straight, hard mouth, told of her struggles in
America. She had not found it a land "with milk and
honey blest," but longed for sunny Italy. When she sat
down, an old Irishwoman unfastened her big warm cape
and threw it around the shivering little Italian.

Then an old man, so tall that his knees almost met under
his chin when he sat in the low wooden chair, jumped
to his feet, with a vapid smile on his pumpkin-shaped
face. His watery blue eyes squinted when he laughed
until they almost disappeared under his bulging forehead. He began with the story of the Charge of the Light
Brigade, in which he insisted that he had taken part, then

he led us back to his mother's knee: " Noo, lads, I 'll sing ye a song me mither sang to me on her knee.' He refused to sing it until he had a Bible in his hand. Then he began, " Holy B-o-o-k, Precious B-o-o-k," drawling out the " oo," 5 and accompanying it with lively gestures. First he pointed stiffly at the ceiling, then he beat the air. This performance ended the meeting and all filed out into the dark night, leaving the red-faced fat man sleeping audibly, with a smile on his face, more childlike than maudlin. The meeting 10 had done him good.

MODELS OF NARRATION

THE BATTLE OF KILLIECRANKIE[1]

THOMAS BABINGTON MACAULAY

Early in the morning of Saturday the twenty-seventh of July, Dundee arrived at Blair Castle. There he learned that Mackay's troops were already in the ravine of Killie-crankie. It was necessary to come to a prompt decision. A council of war was held. The Saxon officers were gen- 5 erally against hazarding a battle. The Celtic chiefs were of a different opinion. Glengarry and Lochiel were now both of a mind. "Fight, my Lord," said Lochiel with his usual energy: "fight immediately: fight, if you have only one to three. Our men are in heart. Their only fear is 10 that the enemy should escape. Give them their way; and be assured that they will either perish or gain a complete victory. But if you restrain them, if you force them to remain on the defensive, I answer for nothing. If we do not fight, we had better break up and retire to our 15 mountains."

Dundee's countenance brightened. "You hear, gentle-men," he said to his Lowland officers, "you hear the opinion of one who understands Highland war better than any of us." No voice was raised on the other side. It was 20

[1] From *The History of England from the Accession of James the Second*, III, 357–363. Longmans, London, 1863.

determined to fight ; and the confederated clans in high
spirits set forward to encounter the enemy.

The enemy meanwhile had made his way up the pass.
The ascent had been long and toilsome : for even the foot
5 had to climb by twos and threes ; and the baggage horses,
twelve hundred in number, could mount only one at a
time. No wheeled carriage had ever been tugged up that
arduous path. The head of the column had emerged and
was on the table land, while the rearguard was still in the
10 plain below. At length the passage was effected ; and the
troops found themselves in a valley of no great extent.
Their right was flanked by a rising ground, their left by
the Garry. Wearied with the morning's work, they threw
themselves on the grass to take some rest and refreshment.
15 Early in the afternoon, they were roused by an alarm
that the Highlanders were approaching. Regiment after
regiment started up and got into order. In a little while the
summit of an ascent which was about a musket shot before
them was covered with bonnets and plaids. Dundee rode
20 forward for the purpose of surveying the force with which
he was to contend, and then drew up his own men with
as much skill as their peculiar character permitted him to
exert. It was desirable to keep the clans distinct. Each
tribe, large or small, formed a column separated from the
25 next column by a wide interval. One of these battalions
might contain seven hundred men, while another consisted
of only a hundred and twenty. Lochiel had represented
that it was impossible to mix men of different tribes without destroying all that constituted the peculiar strength
30 of a Highland army.

On the right, close to the Garry, were the Macleans.
Nearest to them were Cannon and his Irish foot. Next

stood the Macdonalds of Clanronald, commanded by the guardian of their young prince. On their left were other bands of Macdonalds. At the head of one large battalion towered the stately form of Glengarry, who bore in his hand the royal standard of King James the Seventh. Still further to the left were the cavalry, a small squadron, consisting of some Jacobite gentlemen who had fled from the Lowlands to the mountains, and of about forty of Dundee's old troopers. The horses had been ill fed and ill tended among the Grampians, and looked miserably lean and feeble. Beyond them was Lochiel with his Camerons. On the extreme left, the men of Sky were marshalled by Macdonald of Sleat.

In the Highlands, as in all countries where war has not become a science, men thought it the most important duty of a commander to set an example of personal courage and of bodily exertion. Lochiel was especially renowned for his physical prowess. His clansmen looked big with pride when they related how he had himself broken hostile ranks and hewn down tall warriors. He probably owed quite as much of his influence to these achievements as to the high qualities which, if fortune had placed him in the English Parliament or at the French court, would have made him one of the foremost men of his age. He had the sense, however, to perceive how erroneous was the notion which his countrymen had formed. He knew that to give and to take blows was not the business of a general. He knew with how much difficulty Dundee had been able to keep together, during a few days, an army composed of several clans; and he knew that what Dundee had effected with difficulty Cannon would not be able to effect at all. The life on which so much depended must

not be sacrificed to a barbarous prejudice. Lochiel therefore adjured Dundee not to run into any unnecessary
danger. "Your Lordship's business," he said, "is to over-
look every thing, and to issue your commands. Our busi-
5 ness is to execute those commands bravely and promptly."
Dundee answered with calm magnanimity that there was
much weight in what his friend Sir Ewan had urged, but that
no general could effect any thing great without possessing
the confidence of his men. "I must establish my character
10 for courage. Your people expect to see their leaders in
the thickest of the battle; and to-day they shall see me
there. I promise you, on my honour, that in future fights
I will take more care of myself."

Meanwhile a fire of musketry was kept up on both sides,
15 but more skilfully and more steadily by the regular soldiers than by the mountaineers. The space between the
armies was one cloud of smoke. Not a few Highlanders
dropped; and the clans grew impatient. The sun, however, was low in the west before Dundee gave the order
20 to prepare for action. His men raised a great shout. The
enemy, probably exhausted by the toil of the day, returned
a feeble and wavering cheer. "We shall do it now," said
Lochiel: "that is not the cry of men who are going to
win." He had walked through all his ranks, had addressed
25 a few words to every Cameron, and had taken from every
Cameron a promise to conquer or die.

It was past seven o'clock. Dundee gave the word. The
Highlanders dropped their plaids. The few who were so
luxurious as to wear rude socks of untanned hide spurned
30 them away. It was long remembered in Lochaber that
Lochiel took off what probably was the only pair of shoes
in his clan, and charged barefoot at the head of his men.

The whole line advanced firing. The enemy returned the fire and did much execution. When only a small space was left between the armies, the Highlanders suddenly flung away their firelocks, drew their broadswords, and rushed forward with a fearful yell. The Lowlanders prepared to receive the shock; but this was then a long and awkward process; and the soldiers were still fumbling with the muzzles of their guns and the handles of their bayonets when the whole flood of Macleans, Macdonalds, and Camerons came down. In two minutes the battle was lost and won. The ranks of Balfour's regiment broke. He was cloven down while struggling in the press. Ramsay's men turned their backs and dropped their arms. Mackay's own foot were swept away by the furious onset of the Camerons. His brother and nephew exerted themselves in vain to rally the men. The former was laid dead on the ground by a stroke from a claymore. The latter, with eight wounds on his body, made his way through the tumult and carnage to his uncle's side. Even in that extremity Mackay retained all his self-possession. He had still one hope. A charge of horse might recover the day; for of horse the bravest Highlanders were supposed to stand in awe. But he called on the horse in vain. Belhaven indeed behaved like a gallant gentleman; but his troopers, appalled by the rout of the infantry, galloped off in disorder: Annandale's men followed: all was over; and the mingled torrent of red-coats and tartans went raving down the valley to the gorge of Killiecrankie.

Mackay, accompanied by one trusty servant, spurred bravely through the thickest of the claymores and targets, and reached a point from which he had a view of the field. His whole army had disappeared, with the exception of

some Borderers whom Leven had kept together, and of the
English regiment, which had poured a murderous fire into
the Celtic ranks, and which still kept unbroken order. All
the men that could be collected were only a few hundreds.
5 The general made haste to lead them across the Garry, and,
having put that river between them and the enemy, paused
for a moment to meditate on his situation.

He could hardly understand how the conquerors could
be so unwise as to allow him even that moment for delibera-
10 tion. They might with ease have killed or taken all who
were with him before the night closed in. But the energy
of the Celtic warriors had spent itself in one furious rush
and one short struggle. The pass was choked by the twelve
hundred beasts of burden which carried the provisions and
15 baggage of the vanquished army. Such a booty was irresistibly tempting to men who were impelled to war quite
as much by the desire of rapine as by the desire of glory.
It is probable that few even of the chiefs were disposed to
leave so rich a prize for the sake of King James. Dundee
20 himself might at that moment have been unable to persuade
his followers to quit the heaps of spoil, and to complete the
great work of the day; and Dundee was no more.

At the beginning of the action he had taken his place in
front of his little band of cavalry. He bade them follow
25 him, and rode forward. But it seemed to be decreed that,·
on that day, the Lowland Scotch should in both armies
appear to disadvantage. The horse hesitated. Dundee
turned around, stood up in his stirrups, and, waving his
hat, invited them to come on. As he lifted his arm, his
30 cuirass rose, and exposed the lower part of his left side.
A musket ball struck him : his horse sprang forward and
plunged into a cloud of smoke and dust, which hid from

both armies the fall of the victorious general. A person named Johnstone was near him, and caught him as he sank down from the saddle. " How goes the day ? " said Dundee. " Well for King James," answered Johnstone: " but I am sorry for Your Lordship." " If it is well for him," answered the dying man, " it matters the less for me." He never spoke again: but when, half an hour later, Lord Dunfermline and some other friends came to the spot, they thought they could still discern some faint remains of life. The body, wrapped in two plaids, was carried to the Castle of Blair.

HOW I CAUGHT SALMON IN THE CLACKAMAS[1]

RUDYARD KIPLING

Imagine a stream seventy yards broad divided by a
pebbly island, running over seductive riffles, and swirling
into deep, quiet pools where the good salmon goes to
smoke his pipe after meals. Set such a stream amid fields
5 of breast-high crops surrounded by hills of pines, throw in
where you please quiet water, log-fenced meadows, and a
hundred-foot bluff just to keep the scenery from growing
too monotonous, and you will get some faint notion of the
Clackamas.

10 Portland had no rod. He held the gaff and the whisky.
California sniffed upstream and downstream across the
racing water, chose his ground, and let the gaudy spoon
drop in the tail of a riffle. I was getting my rod together
when I heard the joyous shriek of the reel and the yells of
15 California, and three feet of living silver leaped into the
air far across the water. The forces were engaged. The
salmon tore upstream, the tense line cutting the water
like a tide-rip behind him, and the light bamboo bowed to
breaking. What happened after I cannot tell. California
20 swore and prayed, and Portland shouted advice, and I did
all three for what appeared to be half a day, but was in
reality a little over a quarter of an hour, and sullenly our

[1] From *From Sea to Sea* (Kipling's Works, Outward Bound Edition),
XVI, Part II, 106-111. Charles Scribner's Sons, New York, 1899.

fish came home with spurts of temper, dashes head-on, and
sarabands in the air ; but home to the bank came he, and
the remorseless reel gathered up the thread of his life inch
by inch. We landed him in a little bay, and the spring-
weight checked at eleven and a half pounds. Eleven and 5
one-half pounds of fighting salmon ! We danced a war-
dance on the pebbles, and California caught me round the
waist in a hug that went near to breaking my ribs while he
shouted : " Partner ! Partner ! This *is* glory ! Now you
catch your fish ! Twenty-four years I 've waited for this ! " 10

I went into that icy-cold river and made my cast just
above a weir, and all but foul-hooked a blue and black water-
snake with a coral mouth who coiled herself on a stone and
hissed maledictions. The next cast— ah, the pride of it,
the regal splendour of it ! the thrill that ran down from 15
finger-tip to toe ! The water boiled. He broke for the fly
and got it ! There remained enough sense in me to give
him all he wanted when he jumped not once but twenty
times before the upstream flight that ran my line out to
the last half-dozen turns, and I saw the nickeled reel-bar 20
glitter under the thinning green coils. My thumb was
burned deep when I strove to stopper the line, but I did
not feel it till later, for my soul was out in the dancing
water praying for him to turn ere he took my tackle away.
The prayer was heard. As I bowed back, the butt of the 25
rod on my left hip-bone and the top joint dipping like unto
a weeping-willow, he turned, and I accepted each inch of
slack that I could by any means get in as a favour from on
High. There be several sorts of success in this world that
taste well in the moment of enjoyment, but I question 30
whether the stealthy theft of line from an able-bodied
salmon who knows exactly what you are doing and why

you are doing it is not sweeter than any other victory within human scope. Like California's fish, he ran at me head-on and leaped against the line, but the Lord gave me two hundred and fifty pairs of fingers in that hour. The banks and
5 the pine trees danced dizzily round me, but I only reeled — reeled as for life — reeled for hours, and at the end of the reeling continued to give him the butt while he sulked in a pool. California was farther up the reach, and with the corner of my eye I could see him casting with long
10 casts and much skill. Then he struck, and my fish broke for the weir in the same instant, and down the reach we came, California and I; reel answering reel even as the morning stars sung together.

The first wild enthusiasm of capture had died away. We
15 were both at work now in deadly earnest to prevent the lines fouling, to stall off a downstream rush for deep water just above the weir, and at the same time to get the fish into the shallow bay downstream that gave the best practicable landing. Portland bade us both be of good heart, and
20 volunteered to take the rod from my hands. I would rather have died among the pebbles than surrender my right to play and land my first salmon, weight unknown, on an eight-ounce rod. I heard California, at my ear it seemed, gasping : " He 's a fighter from Fightersville sure ! " as his fish
25 made a fresh break across the stream. I saw Portland fall off a log-fence, break the overhanging bank, and clatter down to the pebbles, all sand and landing-net, and I dropped on a log to rest for a moment. As I drew breath the weary hands slackened their hold, and I forgot to give him the
30 butt. A wild scutter in the water, a plunge and a break for the headwaters of the Clackamas was my reward, and the hot toil of reeling in with one eye under the water and

the other on the top joint of the rod was renewed. Worst
of all, I was blocking California's path to the little landing-
bay aforesaid, and he had to halt and tire his prize where
he was. "The Father of all Salmon!" he shouted. "For
the love of Heaven, get your *trout* to bank, Johnny Bull!" 5
But I could no more. Even the insult failed to move me.
The rest of the game was with the salmon. He suffered
himself to be drawn, skipping with pretended delight at
getting to the haven where I would fain have him. Yet
no sooner did he feel shoal water under his ponderous belly 10
than he backed like a torpedo-boat, and the snarl of the
reel told me that my labour was in vain. A dozen times at
least this happened ere the line hinted he had given up that
battle and would be towed in. He was towed. The landing-net was useless for one of his size, and I would not have 15
him gaffed. I stepped into the shallows and heaved him
out with a respectful hand under the gill, for which kindness he battered me about the legs with his tail, and I felt
the strength of him and was proud. California had taken
my place in the shallows, his fish hard held. I was up the 20
bank lying full length on the sweet-scented grass, and gasping in company with my first salmon caught, played and
landed on an eight-ounce rod. My hands were cut and
bleeding. I was dripping with sweat, spangled like harle-
quin with scales, wet from the waist down, nose-peeled by 25
the sun, but utterly, supremely, and consummately happy.
He, the beauty, the darling, the daisy, my Salmon Bahadur,
weighed twelve pounds, and I had been seven-and-thirty
minutes bringing him to bank! He had been lightly hooked
on the angle of the right jaw, and the hook had not wearied 30
him. That hour I sat among princes and crowned heads —
greater than them all.

AN ELK HUNT[1]

THEODORE ROOSEVELT

One day Merrifield and I went out together and had a
rather exciting chase after some bull elk. The previous
evening, toward sunset, I had seen three bulls trotting off
across an open glade toward a great stretch of forest and
5 broken ground, up near the foot of the rocky peaks. Next
morning early we started off to hunt through this country.
The walking was hard work, especially up and down the
steep cliffs, covered with slippery pine needles; or among
the windfalls, where the rows of dead trees lay piled up
10 across one another in the wildest confusion. We saw nothing until we came to a large patch of burnt ground, where
we at once found the soft, black soil marked up by elk
hoofs; nor had we penetrated into it more than a few hundred yards before we came to tracks made but a few minutes
15 before, and almost instantly afterward saw three bull elk,
probably those I had seen on the preceding day. We had
been running briskly up-hill through the soft, heavy loam,
in which our feet made no noise but slipped and sank deeply;
as a consequence, I was all out of breath and my hand so
20 unsteady that I missed my first shot. Elk, however, do not
vanish with the instantaneous rapidity of frightened deer,
and these three trotted off in a direction quartering to us.
I doubt if I ever went through more violent exertion than

[1] From *Hunting Trips of a Ranchman* (Medora Edition), pp. 286-289.
G. P. Putnam's Sons, New York, 1885.

in the next ten minutes. We raced after them at full speed,
opening fire; I wounded all three, but none of the wounds
were immediately disabling. They trotted on and we panted
afterwards, slipping on the wet earth, pitching headlong
over charred stumps, leaping on dead logs that broke 5
beneath our weight, more than once measuring our full
length on the ground, halting and firing whenever we got
a chance. At last one bull fell; we passed him by after
the others which were still running up-hill. The sweat
streamed into my eyes and made furrows in the sooty mud 10
that covered my face, from having fallen full length down
on the burnt earth; I sobbed for breath as I toiled at a
shambling trot after them, as nearly done out as could well
be. At this moment they turned down-hill. It was a great
relief; a man who is too done up to go a step up-hill can 15
still run fast enough down; with a last spurt I closed in
near enough to fire again; one elk fell; the other went
off at a walk. We passed the second elk and I kept on
alone after the third, not able to go at more than a slow
trot myself, and too much winded to dare risk a shot at any 20
distance. He got out of the burnt patch, going into some
thick timber in a deep ravine; I closed pretty well, and
rushed after him into a thicket of young evergreens. Hardly
was I in when there was a scramble and bounce among them
and I caught a glimpse of a yellow body moving out to one 25
side; I ran out toward the edge and fired through the twigs
at the moving beast. Down it went, but when I ran up, to
my disgust I found that I had jumped and killed, in my
haste, a black-tail deer, which must have been already roused
by the passage of the wounded elk. I at once took up the 30
trail of the latter again, but after a little while the blood
grew less, and ceased, and I lost the track; nor could I

find it, hunt as hard as I might. The poor beast could not have gone five hundred yards; yet we never found the carcass.

Then I walked slowly back past the deer I had slain by so curious a mischance, to the elk. The first one shot down was already dead. The second was only wounded, though it could not rise. When it saw us coming it sought to hide from us by laying its neck flat on the ground, but when we came up close it raised its head and looked proudly at us, the heavy mane bristling up on the neck, while its eyes glared and its teeth grated together. I felt really sorry to kill it. Though these were both well-grown elks, their antlers, of ten points, were small, twisted, and ill-shaped; in fact hardly worth preserving, except to call to mind a chase in which during a few minutes I did as much downright hard work as it has often fallen to my lot to do. The burnt earth had blackened our faces and hands till we looked like negroes.

CHASING A LOON [1]

HENRY DAVID THOREAU

In the fall the loon (Colymbus glacialis) came, as usual,
to moult and bathe in the pond, making the woods ring
with his wild laughter before I had risen. At rumor of
his arrival all the Milldam sportsmen are on the alert, in
gigs and on foot, two by two and three by three, with 5
patent rifles and conical balls and spy-glasses. They come
rustling through the woods like autumn leaves, at least
ten men to one loon. Some station themselves on this side
of the pond, some on that, for the poor bird cannot be
omnipresent; if he dive here he must come up there. But 10
now the kind October wind rises, rustling the leaves and
rippling the surface of the water, so that no loon can be
heard or seen, though his foes sweep the pond with spy-
glasses, and make the woods resound with their discharges.
The waves generously rise and dash angrily, taking sides 15
with all waterfowl, and our sportsmen must beat a retreat
to town and shop and unfinished jobs. But they were too
often successful. When I went to get a pail of water
early in the morning I frequently saw this stately bird
sailing out of my cove within a few rods. If I endeavored 20
to overtake him in a boat, in order to see how he would
manœuvre, he would dive and be completely lost, so that
I did not discover him again, sometimes, till the latter

[1] From *Walden* (Riverside Edition), pp. 363–368. Houghton, Mifflin
& Co., Boston, 1894.

part of the day. But I was more than a match for him on
the surface. He commonly went off in a rain.

As I was paddling along the north shore one very calm
October afternoon, for such days especially they settle on
5 to the lakes, like the milkweed down, having looked in
vain over the pond for a loon, suddenly one, sailing out
from the shore toward the middle a few rods in front of
me, set up his wild laugh and betrayed himself. I pursued
with a paddle and he dived, but when he came up I was
10 nearer than before. He dived again, but I miscalculated
the direction he would take, and we were fifty rods apart
when he came to the surface this time, for I had helped to
widen the interval; and again he laughed long and loud,
and with more reason than before. He manœuvred so cun-
15 ningly that I could not get within half a dozen rods of
him. Each time, when he came to the surface, turning his
head this way and that, he coolly surveyed the water and
the land, and apparently chose his course so that he might
come up where there was the widest expanse of water and
20 at the greatest distance from the boat. It was surprising
how quickly he made up his mind and put his resolve into
execution. He led me at once to the widest part of the
pond, and could not be driven from it. While he was
thinking one thing in his brain, I was endeavoring to
25 divine his thought in mine. It was a pretty game, played
on the smooth surface of the pond, a man against a loon.
Suddenly your adversary's checker disappears beneath the
board, and the problem is to place yours nearest to where
his will appear again. Sometimes he would come up unex-
30 pectedly on the opposite side of me, having apparently
passed directly under the boat. So long-winded was he and
so unweariable, that when he had swum farthest he would

immediately plunge again, nevertheless ; and then no wit
could divine where in the deep pond, beneath the smooth
surface, he might be speeding his way like a fish, for he had
time and ability to visit the bottom of the pond in its deepest part. It is said that loons have been caught in the New 5
York lakes eighty feet beneath the surface, with hooks set
for trout, — though Walden is deeper than that. How surprised must the fishes be to see this ungainly visitor from
another sphere speeding his way amid their schools ! Yet
he appeared to know his course as surely under water as 10
on the surface, and swam much faster there. Once or
twice I saw a ripple where he approached the surface, just
put his head out to reconnoitre, and instantly dived again.
I found that it was as well for me to rest on my oars and
wait his reappearing as to endeavor to calculate where he 15
would rise ; for again and again, when I was straining my
eyes over the surface one way, I would suddenly be startled
by his unearthly laugh behind me. But why, after displaying so much cunning, did he invariably betray himself the
moment he came up by that loud laugh? Did not his 20
white breast enough betray him? He was indeed a silly
loon, I thought. I could commonly hear the plash of the
water when he came up, and so also detected him. But
after an hour he seemed as fresh as ever, dived as willingly,
and swam yet farther than at first. It was surprising to 25
see how serenely he sailed off with unruffled breast when
he came to the surface, doing all the work with his webbed
feet beneath. His usual note was this demoniac laughter,
yet somewhat like that of a water-fowl; but occasionally,
when he had balked me most successfully and come up 30
a long way off, he uttered a long-drawn unearthly howl,
probably more like that of a wolf than any bird ; as when

a beast puts his muzzle to the ground and deliberately
howls. This was his looning, — perhaps the wildest sound
that is ever heard here, making the woods ring far and
wide. I concluded that he laughed in derision of my
5 efforts, confident of his own resources. Though the sky
was by this time overcast, the pond was so smooth that I
could see where he broke the surface when I did not hear
him. His white breast, the stillness of the air, and the
smoothness of the water were all against him. At length,
10 having come up fifty rods off, he uttered one of those prolonged howls, as if calling on the god of loons to aid him,
and immediately there came a wind from the east and
rippled the surface, and filled the whole air with misty
rain, and I was impressed as if it were the prayer of the
15 loon answered, and his god was angry with me.; and so I
left him disappearing far away on the tumultuous surface.

THE BATTLE OF THE ANTS[1]

HENRY DAVID THOREAU .

One day when I went out to my wood-pile, or rather my pile of stumps, I observed two large ants, the one red, the other much larger, nearly half an inch long, and black, fiercely contending with one another. Having once got hold they never let go, but struggled and wrestled and 5 rolled on the chips incessantly. Looking farther, I was surprised to find that the chips were covered with such combatants, that it was not a *duellum*, but a *bellum*, a war between two races of ants, the red always pitted against the black, and frequently two red ones to one black. The 10 legions of these Myrmidons covered all the hills and vales in my wood-yard, and the ground was already strewn with the dead and dying, both red and black. It was the only battle which I have ever witnessed, the only battlefield I ever trod while the battle was raging; internecine war; 15 the red republicans on the one hand, and the black imperialists on the other. On every side they were engaged in deadly combat, yet without any noise that I could hear, and human soldiers never fought so resolutely. I watched a couple that were fast locked in each other's embraces, in 20 a little sunny valley amid the chips, now at noon-day prepared to fight till the sun went down, or life went out. The smaller red champion had fastened himself like a vice

---

[1] From *Walden* (Riverside Edition), pp. 355–360. Houghton, Mifflin & Co., Boston, 1894.

to his adversary's front, and through all the tumblings on
that field never for an instant ceased to gnaw at one of his
feelers near the root, having already caused the other to
go by the board; while the stronger black one dashed him
5 from side to side, and, as I saw on looking nearer, had
already divested him of several of his members. They
fought with more pertinacity than bull-dogs. Neither
manifested the least disposition to retreat. It was evident
that their battle-cry was Conquer or Die. In the mean
10 while there came along a single red ant on the hill-side of
this valley, evidently full of excitement, who either had
despatched his foe, or had not yet taken part in the battle;
probably the latter, for he had lost none of his limbs ;
whose mother had charged him to return with his shield
15 or upon it. Or perchance he was some Achilles, who had
nourished his wrath apart, and had now come to avenge or
rescue his Patroclus. He saw this unequal combat from
afar, — for the blacks were nearly twice the size of the
reds, — he drew near with rapid pace till he stood on his
20 guard within half an inch of the combatants ; then, watching his opportunity, he sprang upon the black warrior, and
commenced his operations near the root of his right fore-
leg, leaving the foe to select among his own members ; and
so there were three united for life, as if a new kind of
25 attraction had been invented which put all other locks and
cements to shame. I should not have wondered by this
time to find that they had their respective musical bands
stationed on some eminent chip, and playing their national
airs the while, to excite the slow and cheer the dying com-
30 batants. I was myself excited somewhat even as if they
had been men. The more you think of it, the less the difference. And certainly there is not the fight recorded in

Concord history, at least, if in the history of America, that will bear a moment's comparison with this, whether for the numbers engaged in it, or for the patriotism and heroism displayed. For numbers and for carnage it was an Austerlitz or Dresden. Concord Fight! Two killed 5 on the patriots' side, and Luther Blanchard wounded! Why here every ant was a Buttrick, — "Fire! for God's sake, fire!" — and thousands shared the fate of Davis and Hosmer. There was not one hireling there. I have no doubt that it was a principle they fought for, as much as 10 our ancestors, and not to avoid a three-penny tax on their tea; and the results of this battle will be as important and memorable to those whom it concerns as those of the battle of Bunker Hill, at least.

I took up the chip on which the three I have particularly 15 described were struggling, carried it into my house, and placed it under a tumbler on my window-sill, in order to see the issue. Holding a microscope to the first-mentioned red ant, I saw that, though he was assiduously gnawing at the near fore-leg of his enemy, having severed his remain- 20 ing feeler, his own breast was all torn away, exposing what vitals he had there to the jaws of the black warrior, whose breast-plate was apparently too thick for him to pierce; and the dark carbuncles of the sufferer's eyes shone with ferocity such as war only could excite. They struggled 25 half an hour longer under the tumbler, and when I looked again the black soldier had severed the heads of his foes from their bodies, and the still living heads were hanging on either side of him like ghastly trophies at his saddle-bow, still apparently as firmly fastened as ever, and he 30 was endeavoring with feeble struggles, being without feelers and with only the remnant of a leg, and I know

not how many other wounds, to divest himself of them ;
which at length, after half an hour more, he accomplished.
I raised the glass, and he went off over the window-sill in
that crippled state. Whether he finally survived that com-
5 bat, and spent the remainder of his days in some Hôtel des
Invalides, I do not know; but I thought that his industry
would not be worth much thereafter. I never learned
which party was victorious, nor the cause of the war; but
I felt for the rest of that day as if I had had my feelings
10 excited and harrowed by witnessing the struggle, the
ferocity and carnage, of a human battle before my door.

THE STORY OF MUHAMMAD DIN[1]

RUDYARD KIPLING

Who is the happy man? He that sees in his own house at home little children crowned with dust, leaping and falling and crying. — *Munichandra*, translated by Professor Peterson.

The polo-ball was an old one, scarred, chipped, and dinted. It stood on the mantelpiece among the pipe-stems 5 which Imam Din, *khitmatgar*, was cleaning for me.

"Does the Heaven-born want this ball?" said Imam Din deferentially.

The Heaven-born set no particular store by it; but of what use was a polo-ball to a *khitmatgar?* 10

"By Your Honour's favour, I have a little son. He has seen this ball, and desires it to play with. I do not want it for myself."

No one would for an instant accuse portly old Imam Din of wanting to play with polo-balls. He carried out the 15 battered thing into the verandah; and there followed a hurricane of joyful squeaks, a patter of small feet, and the *thud-thud-thud* of the ball rolling along the ground. Evidently the little son had been waiting outside the door to secure his treasure. But how had he managed to see that 20 polo-ball?

Next day, coming back from office half an hour earlier than usual, I was aware of a small figure in the dining-room — a tiny, plump figure in a ridiculously inadequate shirt

[1] From *Plain Tales from the Hills* (Outward Bound Edition), pp. 307–312. Charles Scribner's Sons, New York, 1897.

389

which came, perhaps, half-way down the tubby stomach.
It wandered round the room, thumb in mouth, crooning to
itself as it took stock of the pictures. Undoubtedly this
was the "little son."

5   He had no business in my room, of course; but was so
deeply absorbed in his discoveries that he never noticed me
in the doorway. I stepped into the room and startled him
nearly into a fit. He sat down on the ground with a gasp.
His eyes opened, and his mouth followed suit. I knew
10 what was coming, and fled, followed by a long, dry howl
which reached the servants' quarters far more quickly than
any command of mine had ever done. In ten seconds Imam
Din was in the dining-room. Then despairing sobs arose,
and I returned to find Imam Din admonishing the small
15 sinner, who was using most of his shirt as a handkerchief.

"This boy," said Imam Din judicially, "is a *budmash* —
a big *budmash*. He will, without doubt, go to the *jail-khana*
for his behaviour." Renewed yells from the penitent, and
an elaborate apology to myself from Imam Din.

20   "Tell the baby," said I, "that the Sahib is not angry,
and take him away." Imam Din conveyed my forgiveness
to the offender, who had now gathered all his shirt around
his neck, stringwise, and the yell subsided into a sob. The
two set off for the door. "His name," said Imam Din, as
25 though the name were part of the crime, "is Muhammad
Din, and he is a *budmash*." Freed from present danger,
Muhammad Din turned round in his father's arms, and
said gravely, "It is true that my name is Muhammad Din,
Tahib, but I am not a *budmash*. I am a *man!*"

30   From that day dated my acquaintance with Muhammad
Din. Never again did he come into my dining-room, but
on the neutral ground of the garden, we greeted each other

with much state, though our conversation was confined to
" *Talaam*, Tahib" from his side, and "*Salaam*, Muhammad
Din" from mine. Daily on my return from office, the little
white shirt and the fat little body used to rise from the
shade of the creeper-covered trellis where they had been
hid ; and daily I checked my horse here, that my salutation
might not be slurred over or given unseemly.

Muhammad Din never had any companions. He used to
trot about the compound, in and out of the castor-oil bushes,
on mysterious errands of his own. One day I stumbled
upon some of his handiwork far down the grounds. He had
half buried the polo-ball in the dust, and stuck six shrivelled
old marigold flowers in a circle round it. Outside that
circle again was a rude square, traced out in bits of red
brick alternating with fragments of broken china ; the
whole bounded by a little bank of dust. The water-man
from the well-curb put in a plea for the small architect,
saying that it was only the play of a baby and did not
much disfigure my garden.

Heaven knows that I had no intention of touching the
child's work then or later ; but, that evening, a stroll
through the garden brought me unawares full on it ; so
that I trampled, before I knew, marigold-heads, dust-bank,
and fragments of broken soap-dish into confusion past all
hope of mending. Next morning, I came upon Muhammad
Din crying softly to himself over the ruin I had wrought.
Some one had cruelly told him that the Sahib was very
angry with him for spoiling the garden, and had scattered
his rubbish, using bad language the while. Muhammad
Din laboured for an hour at effacing every trace of the
dust-bank and pottery fragments, and it was with a tearful
and apologetic face that he said, " *Talaam*, Tahib," when I
came home from office. A hasty inquiry resulted in Imam

Din informing Muhammad Din that, by my singular favour, he was permitted to disport himself as much as he pleased. Whereat the child took heart and fell to tracing the ground-plan of an edifice which was to eclipse the marigold-polo-
5 ball creation.

For some months the chubby little eccentricity revolved in his humble orbit among the castor-oil bushes and in the dust ; always fashioning magnificent palaces from stale flowers thrown away by the bearer, smooth water-worn peb-
10 bles, bits of broken glass, and feathers pulled, I fancy, from my fowls — always alone, and always crooning to himself.

A gaily-spotted sea-shell was dropped one day close to the last of his little buildings ; and I looked that Muhammad Din should build something more than ordinarily splendid
15 on the strength of it. Nor was I disappointed. He meditated for the better part of an hour, and his crooning rose to a jubilant song. Then he began tracing in the dust. It would certainly be a wondrous palace, this one, for it was two yards long and a yard broad in ground-plan. But
20 the palace was never completed.

Next day there was no Muhammad Din at the head of the carriage-drive, and no " *Talaam*, Tahib " to welcome my return. I had grown accustomed to the greeting, and its omission troubled me. Next day Imam Din told me
25 that the child was suffering slightly from fever and needed quinine. He got the medicine, and an English Doctor.

" They have no stamina, these brats," said the Doctor, as he left Imam Din's quarters.

A week later, though I would have given much to have
30 avoided it, I met on the road to the Mussulman burying-ground Imam Din, accompanied by one other friend, carrying in his arms, wrapped in a white cloth, all that was left of little Muhammad Din.

THE BENNETS[1]

JANE AUSTEN

I

It is a truth universally acknowledged, that a single man in possession of a good fortune must be in want of a wife.

However little known the feelings or views of such a man may be on his first entering a neighbourhood, this truth is so well fixed in the minds of the surrounding families, that he is considered as the rightful property of some one or other of their daughters.

"My dear Mr. Bennet," said his lady to him one day, "have you heard that Netherfield Park is let at last?"

Mr. Bennet replied that he had not.

"But it is," returned she; "for Mrs. Long has just been here, and she told me all about it."

Mr. Bennet made no answer.

"Do not you want to know who has taken it?" cried his wife impatiently.

"*You* want to tell me, and I have no objection to hearing it."

This was invitation enough.

"Why, my dear, you must know, Mrs. Long says that Netherfield is taken by a young man of large fortune from the north of England; that he came down on Monday

---

[1] From *Pride and Prejudice*, Chapters I and II.

in a chaise and four to see the place, and was so much
delighted with it, that he agreed with Mr. Morris immediately; that he is to take possession before Michaelmas,
and some of his servants are to be in the house by the end
5 of next week."

"What is his name?"

"Bingley."

"Is he married or single?"

"Oh! single, my dear, to be sure! A single man of
10 large fortune; four or five thousand a-year. What a fine
thing for our girls!"

"How so? how can it affect them?"

"My dear Mr. Bennet," replied his wife, "how can you
be so tiresome! you must know that I am thinking of his
15 marrying one of them."

"Is that his design in settling here?"

"Design! nonsense, how can you talk so! But it is
very likely that he *may* fall in love with one of them, and
therefore you must visit him as soon as he comes."

20 "I see no occasion for that. You and the girls may go,
or you may send them by themselves, which perhaps will
be still better, for as you are as handsome as any of them,
Mr. Bingley might like you the best of the party."

"My dear, you flatter me. I certainly *have* had my share
25 of beauty, but I do not pretend to be anything extraordinary now. When a woman has five grown-up daughters,
she ought to give over thinking of her own beauty."

"In such cases, a woman has not often much beauty to
think of."

30 "But, my dear, you must indeed go and see Mr. Bingley
when he comes into the neighbourhood."

"It is more than I engage for, I assure you."

"But consider your daughters. Only think what an establishment it would be for one of them. Sir William and Lady Lucas are determined to go, merely on that account, for in general, you know, they visit no new-comers. Indeed you must go, for it will be impossible for *us* to visit him if you do not."

"You are over-scrupulous, surely. I dare say Mr. Bingley will be very glad to see you; and I will send a few lines by you to assure him of my hearty consent to his marrying whichever he chuses of the girls; though I must throw in a good word for my little Lizzy."

"I desire you will do no such thing. Lizzy is not a bit better than the others; and I am sure she is not half so handsome as Jane, nor half so good-humoured as Lydia. But you are always giving *her* the preference."

"They have none of them much to recommend them," replied he; "they are all silly and ignorant, like other girls; but Lizzie has something more of quickness than her sisters."

"Mr. Bennet, how can you abuse your own children in such a way! You take delight in vexing me. You have no compassion on my poor nerves."

"You mistake me, my dear. I have a high respect for your nerves. They are my old friends. I have heard you mention them with consideration these twenty years at least."

"Ah! you do not know what I suffer."

"But I hope you will get over it, and live to see many young men of four thousand a-year come into the neighbourhood."

"It will be no use to us, if twenty such should come, since you will not visit them."

"Depend upon it, my dear, that when there are twenty, I will visit them all."

Mr. Bennet was so odd a mixture of quick parts, sarcastic humour, reserve, and caprice, that the experience of 5 three-and-twenty years had been insufficient to make his wife understand his character. *Her* mind was less difficult to develope. She was a woman of mean understanding, little information, and uncertain temper. When she was discontented, she fancied herself nervous. The business of 10 her life was to get her daughters married; its solace was visiting and news.

II

Mr. Bennet was among the earliest of those who waited on Mr. Bingley. He had always intended to visit him, though to the last always assuring his wife that he should 15 not go ; and till the evening after the visit was paid she had no knowledge of it. It was then disclosed in the following manner : —

Observing his second daughter employed in trimming a hat, he suddenly addressed her with,

20 "I hope Mr. Bingley will like it, Lizzy."

"We are not in a way to know *what* Mr. Bingley likes," said her mother resentfully, "since we are not to visit."

"But you forget, mamma," said Elizabeth, "that we shall meet him at the assemblies, and that Mrs. Long has 25 promised to introduce him."

"I do not believe Mrs. Long will do any such thing. She has two nieces of her own. She is a selfish, hypocritical woman, and I have no opinion of her."

"No more have I," said Mr. Bennet; "and I am glad 30 to find that you do not depend on her serving you."

Mrs. Bennet deigned not to make any reply, but, unable to contain herself, began scolding one of her daughters.

"Don't keep coughing so, Kitty, for Heaven's sake! Have a little compassion on my nerves. You tear them to pieces." 5

"Kitty has no discretion in her coughs," said her father; "she times them ill."

"I do not cough for my own amusement," replied Kitty fretfully. "When is your next ball to be, Lizzy?"

"To-morrow fortnight." 10

"Aye, so it is," cried her mother, "and Mrs. Long does not come back till the day before; so it will be impossible for her to introduce him, for she will not know him herself."

"Then, my dear, you may have the advantage of your friend, and introduce Mr. Bingley to *her*." 15

"Impossible, Mr. Bennet, impossible, when I am not acquainted with him myself; how can you be so teazing?"

"I honour your circumspection. A fortnight's acquaintance is certainly very little. One cannot know what a man really is by the end of a fortnight. But if *we* do not 20 venture somebody else will; and after all, Mrs. Long and her nieces must stand their chance; and, therefore, as she will think it an act of kindness, if you decline the office, I will take it on myself."

The girls stared at their father. Mrs. Bennet said only, 25 "Nonsense, nonsense!"

"What can be the meaning of that emphatic exclamation?" cried he. "Do you consider the forms of introduction, and the stress that is laid on them, as nonsense? I cannot quite agree with you *there*. What say you, Mary? 30 for you are a young lady of deep reflection, I know, and read great books and make extracts."

Mary wished to say something very sensible, but knew not how.

"While Mary is adjusting her ideas," he continued, "let us return to Mr. Bingley."

5 "I am sick of Mr. Bingley," cried his wife.

"I am sorry to hear *that;* but why did not you tell me so before? If I had known as much this morning I certainly would not have called upon him, It is very unlucky; but as I have actually paid the visit, we cannot escape the 10 acquaintance now."

The astonishment of the ladies was just what he wished; that of Mrs. Bennet perhaps surpassing the rest; though, when the first tumult of joy was over, she began to declare that it was what she had expected all the while.

15 "How good it was in you, my dear Mr. Bennet! But I knew I should persuade you at last. I was sure you loved your girls too well to neglect such an acquaintance. Well, how pleased I am! and it is such a good joke, too, that you should have gone this morning and never said a word 20 about it till now."

"Now, Kitty, you may cough as much as you chuse," said Mr. Bennet; and, as he spoke, he left the room, fatigued with the raptures of his wife.

"What an excellent father you have, girls!" said she, 25 when the door was shut. "I do not know how you will ever make him amends for his kindness; or me either, for that matter. At our time of life it is not so pleasant, I can tell you, to be making new acquaintance every day; but for your sakes, we would do anything. Lydia, my love, 30 though you *are* the youngest, I dare say Mr. Bingley will dance with you at the next ball."

"Oh!" said Lydia stoutly, "I am not afraid; for though I *am* the youngest, I 'm the tallest."

The rest of the evening was spent in conjecturing how soon he would return Mr. Bennet's visit, and determining when they should ask him to dinner.

5

THE KING OF BOYVILLE[1]

WILLIAM ALLEN WHITE

Boys who are born in a small town are born free and
equal. In the big city it may be different; there are
doubtless good little boys who disdain bad little boys, and
poor little boys who are never to be noticed under any
5 circumstances. But in a small town, every boy, good or
bad, rich or poor, stands among boys on his own merits.
The son of the banker who owns a turning-pole in the
back yard, does homage to the baker's boy who can sit on
the bar and drop and catch by his legs; while the good
10 little boy, who is kept in wide collars and cuffs by a mistaken mother, gazes through the white paling of his father's
fence at the troop headed for the swimming hole, and pays
all the reverence which his dwarfed nature can muster to
the sign of the two fingers. In the social order of boys
15 who live in country towns, a boy is measured by what he
can do, and not by what his father is. And so, Winfield
Hancock Pennington, whose boy name was Piggy Pennington, was the King of Boyville. For Piggy could walk
on his hands, curling one foot gracefully over his back,
20 and pointing the other straight in the air; he could hang
by his heels on a flying trapeze; he could chin a pole so
many times that no one could count the number; he
could turn a somersault in the air from the level ground,

---

[1] From *The Real Issue.* Way & Williams, Chicago, 1897. (The copyright is now owned by Messrs. McClure, Phillips & Co.)

both backwards and forwards; he could "tread" water and
"lay" his hair; he could hit any marble in any ring from
"taws" and "knucks down,"—and better than all, he could
cut his initials in the ice on skates, and whirl around and
around so many times that he looked like an animated shadow, 5
when he would dart away up the stream, his red "comfort" flapping behind him like a laugh of defiance. In the
story books such a boy would be the son of a widowed
mother, and turn out very good or very bad, but Piggy
was not a story book boy, and his father kept a grocery 10
store, from which Piggy used to steal so many dates that
the boys said his father must have cut up the almanac to
supply him. As he never gave the goodies to the other
boys, but kept them for his own use, his name of " Piggy "
was his by all the rights of Boyville. 15

There was one thing Piggy Pennington could not do,
and it was the one of all things he most wished he could
do : he could not under any circumstances say three con-
secutive and coherent words to any girl under fifteen and
over nine. He was invited with nearly all of the boys of 20
his age in town, to children's parties. And while any
other boy, whose only accomplishment was turning a cart
wheel, or skinning the cat backwards, or, at most, hanging
by one leg and turning a handspring, could boldly ask a
girl if he could see her home, Piggy had to get his hat 25
and sneak out of the house when the company broke up.
He would comfort himself by walking along on the opposite side of the street from some couple, while he talked in
monosyllables about a joke which he and the boy knew,
but which was always a secret to the girl. Even after 30
school Piggy could not join the select coterie of boys who
followed the girls down through town to the postoffice.

He could not tease the girls about absent boys at such times
and make up rhymes like

> " First the cat and then her tail ;
> Jimmie Sears and Maggie Hale,"

5 and shout them out for the crowd to hear. Instead of
joining this courtly troupe Piggy Pennington went off
with the boys who really did n't care for such things, and
fought, or played " tracks up," or wrestled his way leisurely home in time to get in his " night wood." But his
10 heart was not in these pastimes ; it was with a red shawl
of a peculiar shade, that was wending its way to the postoffice and back to a home in one of the few two-story
houses in the little town. Time and again had Piggy
tried to make some sign to let his feelings be known, but
15 every time he had failed. Lying in wait for her at corners,
and suddenly breaking upon her with a glory of backward
and forward somersaults did not convey the state of his
heart. Hanging by his heels from an apple tree limb over
the sidewalk in front of her, unexpectedly, did not tell the
20 tender tale for which his lips could find no words. And
the nearest he could come to an expression of the longing
in his breast, was to cut her initials in the ice beside his
own when she came weaving and wobbling past on some
other boy's arm. But she would not look at the initials,
25 and the chirography of his skates was so indistinct that it
required a key ; and everything put together, poor Piggy
was no nearer a declaration at the end of the winter than
he had been at the beginning of autumn. So only one
heart beat with but a single thought, and the other took
30 motto candy and valentines and red apples and picture
cards and other tokens of esteem from other boys, and

beat on with any number of thoughts, entirely immaterial to the uses of this narrative. But Piggy Pennington did not take to the enchantment of corn silk cigarettes and rattan and grape vine cigars ; he tried to sing, and wailed dismal ballads about the "Gypsy's Warning," and "The Child in the Grave With Its Mother," and "She's a Daisy, She's a Darling, She's a Dumpling, She's a Lamb," whenever he was in hearing distance of his Heart's Desire, in the hope of conveying to her some hint of the state of his affections ; but it was useless. Even when he tried to whistle plaintively as he passed her house in the gloaming, his notes brought forth no responsive echo.

One morning in the late spring, he spent half an hour before breakfast among his mother's roses, which were just in first bloom. He had taken out there all the wire from an old broom, and all his kite string. His mother had to call three times before he would leave his work. The youngster was the first to leave the table, and by eight o'clock he was at his task again. Before the first school bell had rung, Piggy Pennington was bound for the school-house with a strange looking parcel under his arm. He tried to put his coat over it, but it stuck out and the newspaper that was wrapped around it, bulged into so many corners, that it looked like a home-tied bundle of laundry.

"What you got ?" asked the freckle-faced boy, who was learning at Piggy's feet how to do the "muscle grind" on the turning-pole.

But Piggy Pennington was the King of Boyville, and he had a right to look straight ahead of him, as if he did not hear the question, and say :

"Lookie here, Mealy, I wish you would go and tell Abe I want him to hurry up, for I want to see him."

"Abe" was Piggy's nearest friend. His other name was Carpenter. Piggy only wished to be rid of the freckle-faced boy. But the freckle-faced boy was not used to royalty and its ways, so he pushed his inquiry.

5 "Say, Piggy, have you got your red ball-pants in that bundle?"

There was no reply. The freckle-faced boy grew tired of tattooing with a stick, as they walked beside a paling fence, so he began touching every tree on the other side 10 of the path with his fingers. They had gone a block when the freckle-faced boy could stand it no longer and said:

"Say, Piggy, you need n't be so smart about your old bundle; now honest, Piggy, what have you got in that 15 bundle?"

"Aw — soft soap, take a bite — good fer yer appetite," said the King, as he faced about and drew up his left cheek and lower eye-lid pugnaciously. The freckle-faced boy saw he would have to fight if he stayed, so he turned 20 to go, and said, as though nothing had happened, "Where do you suppose old Abe is, anyhow?"

Just before school was called Piggy Pennington was playing "scrub" with all his might, and a little girl — his Heart's Desire — was taking out of her desk a wreath of 25 roses, tied to a shaky wire frame. There was a crowd of girls around her admiring it, and speculating about the possible author of the gift; but to these she did not show the patent medicine card, on which was scrawled, over the druggist's advertisement: "Yours truly, W. H. P."

30 When the last bell rang, Piggy Pennington was the last boy in, and he did not look toward the desk, where he had put the flowers, until after the singing.

Then he stole a sidewise glance that way, and his Heart's Desire was deep in her geography. It was an age before she filed past him with the "B" class in geography, and took a seat directly in front of him, where he could look at her all the time, unobserved by her. Once she squirmed in her place and looked toward him, but Piggy Pennington was head over heels in the "Iser rolling rapidly." When their eyes did at last meet, just as Piggy, leading the marching around the room, was at the door to go out for recess, the thrill amounted to a shock that sent him whirling in a pin wheel of handsprings toward the ball ground, shouting "scrub — first bat, first bat, first bat," from sheer, bubbling joy. Piggy made four tallies that recess, and the other boys could n't have put him out, if they had used a hand-grenade or a Babcock fire extinguisher.

He received four distinct shots that day from the eyes of his Heart's Desire, and the last one sent him home on the run, tripping up every primary urchin whom he found tagging along by the way, and whooping at the top of his voice. When his friends met in his barn, some fifteen minutes later, Piggy tried to turn a double somersault from his spring board, to the admiration of the crowd, and was only calmed by falling with his full weight on his head and shoulders at the edge of the hay, with the life nearly jolted out of his little body.

The next morning, Piggie Pennington astonished his friends by bringing a big armful of red and yellow and pink and white roses to school.

He had never done this before, and when he had run the gauntlet of the big boys, who were not afraid to steal them from him, he made straight for his schoolroom, and

stood holding them in his hands while the girls gathered
about him teasing for the beauties. It was nearly time
for the last bell to ring, and Piggy knew that his Heart's
Desire would be in the room by the time he got there.
5 He was not mistaken. But Heart's Desire did not clamor
with the other girls for one of the roses. Piggy stood off
their pleadings as long as he could with "Naw," "Why
naw, of course I won't," "Naw, what I want to give you
one for," and "Go way from here I tell you," and still
10 Heart's Desire did not ask for her flowers. There were
but a few moments left before school would be called to
order, and in desperation Piggy gave one rose away. It
was not a very pretty rose, but he hoped she would see
that the others were to be given away, and ask for one.
15 But she — his Heart's Desire — stood near a window,
talking to the freckle-faced boy. Then Piggy gave away
one rose after another. As the last bell began to ring he
gave them to the boys, as the girls were all supplied. And
still she came not. There was one rose left, the most
20 beautiful of all. She went to her desk, and as the teacher
came in, bell in hand, Piggy surprised himself, the teacher,
and the school by laying the beautiful flower without a word
on the teacher's desk. That day was a dark day. When
a new boy, who did n't belong to the school, came up at re-
25 cess to play, Piggy shuffled over to him and asked gruffly:
"What's your name?"
"Puddin' 'n' tame, ast me agin an' I'll tell you the
same," said the new boy, and then there was a fight. It
did n't soothe Piggy's feelings one bit that he whipped the
30 new boy, for the new boy was smaller than Piggy. And
he dared not turn his flushed face towards his Heart's
Desire. It was almost four o'clock when Piggy Pennington

walked to the master's desk to get him to work out a problem, and as he passed the desk of Heart's Desire he dropped
a note in her lap. It read :

" Are you mad ? "

But he dared not look for the answer, as they marched   5
out that night, so he contented himself with punching the
boy ahead of him with a pin, and stepping on his heels,
when they were in the back part of the room, where the
teacher would not see him. The King of Boyville walked
home alone that evening. The courtiers saw plainly that 10
his majesty was troubled.

So his lonely way was strewn with broken stick-horses,
which he took from the little boys, and was marked by trees
adorned with the string, which he took from other youngsters, who ran across his pathway playing horse. In his 15
barn he sat listlessly on a nail keg, while Abe and the
freckle-faced boy did their deeds of daring, on the rings
and the trapeze. Only when the new boy came in, did
Piggy arouse himself to mount the flying bar, and, swinging in it to the very rafters, drop and hang by his knees, 20
and again drop from his knees, catching his ankle in the
angle of the rope where it meets the swinging bar. That
was to awe the new boy.

After this feat the King was quiet.

At dusk, when the evening chores were done, Piggy 25
Pennington walked past the home of his Heart's Desire
and howled out a doleful ballad which began :

> " You ask what makes this darkey wee-eep,
>   Why he like others am not gay."

But a man on the sidewalk passing said, " Well, son, 30
that's pretty good, but would n't you just as lief sing as

to make that noise?" So the King went to bed with a
heavy heart.

He took that heart to school with him, the next morning,
and dragged it over the school ground, playing crack the
5 whip and "stink-base." But when he saw Heart's Desire
wearing in her hair one of the white roses from his mother's
garden — the Penningtons had the only white roses in the
little town — he knew it was from the wreath which he
had given her, and so light was his boyish heart, that it was
10 with an effort that he kept it out of his throat. There were
smiles and smiles that day. During the singing they began,
and every time she came past him from a class, and every
time he could pry his eyes behind her geography, or her
grammar, a flood of gladness swept over his soul. That
15 night Piggy Pennington followed the girls from the school-
house to the postoffice, and in a burst of enthusiasm, he
walked on his hands in front of the crowd, for nearly half
a block. When his Heart's Desire said :

"Oh, ain't you afraid you'll hurt yourself, doing that?"
20 Piggy pretended not to hear her, and said to the boys:

"Aw, that ain't nothin'; come down to my barn, an'
I'll do somepin that'll make yer head swim."

He was too exuberant to contain himself, and when he
left the girls he started to run after a stray chicken, that
25 happened along, and ran till he was out of breath. He did
not mean to run in the direction his Heart's Desire had
taken, but he turned a corner, and came up with her
suddenly.

Her eyes beamed upon him, and he could not run away
30 as he wished. She made room for him on the sidewalk, and
he could do nothing but walk beside her. For a block they
were so embarrassed that neither spoke.

It was Piggy who broke the silence. His words came from his heart. He had not yet learned to speak otherwise.

" Where 's your rose ? " he asked, not seeing it.

" What rose ? " said the girl, as though she had never in her short life heard of such an absurd thing as a rose. 5

" Oh, you know," returned the boy, stepping irregularly, to make the tips of his toes come on the cracks of the sidewalk. There was another pause, during which Piggy picked up a pebble, and threw it at a bird in a tree. His heart was sinking rapidly. 10

" Oh, that rose ? " said his Heart's Desire, turning full upon him with the enchantment of her childish eyes. " Why, here it is in my grammar. I 'm taking it to keep with the others. Why ? "

" Oh, nuthin' much," replied the boy. " I bet you can't 15 do this," he added, as he glowed up into her eyes from an impulsive handspring.

And thus the King of Boyville first set his light, little foot upon the soil of an unknown country.

A WINTER COURTSHIP[1]

Sarah Orne Jewett

The passenger and mail transportation between the
towns of North Kilby and Sanscrit Pond was carried on
by Mr. Jefferson Briley, whose two-seated covered wagon
was usually much too large for the demands of business.
5 Both the Sanscrit Pond and North Kilby people were
stayers-at-home, and Mr. Briley often made his seven-mile
journey in entire solitude, except for the limp leather mail-
bag, which he held firmly to the floor of the carriage with
his heavily shod left foot. The mail-bag had almost a per-
10 sonality to him, born of long association. Mr. Briley was
a meek and timid-looking body, but he held a warlike soul,
and encouraged his fancies by reading awful tales of blood-
shed and lawlessness in the far West. Mindful of stage
robberies and train thieves, and of express messengers who
15 died at their posts, he was prepared for anything; and
although he had trusted to his own strength and bravery
these many years, he carried a heavy pistol under his front-
seat cushion for better defense. This awful weapon was
familiar to all his regular passengers, and was usually
20 shown to strangers by the time two of the seven miles of
Mr. Briley's route had been passed. The pistol was not
loaded. Nobody (at least not Mr. Briley himself) doubted
that the mere sight of such a weapon would turn the boldest
adventurer aside.

[1] From *Strangers and Wayfarers*, pp. 1–17. Houghton, Mifflin & Co.,
Boston, 1890.

Protected by such a man and such a piece of armament,
one gray Friday morning in the edge of winter, Mrs. Fanny
Tobin was traveling from Sanscrit Pond to North Kilby.
She was an elderly and feeble-looking woman, but with a
shrewd twinkle in her eyes, and she felt very anxious about   5
her numerous pieces of baggage and her own personal
safety. She was enveloped in many shawls and smaller
wrappings, but they were not securely fastened, and kept
getting undone and flying loose, so that the bitter December cold seemed to be picking a lock now and then, and 10
creeping in to steal away the little warmth she had. Mr.
Briley was cold, too, and could only cheer himself by re-
membering the valor of those pony-express drivers of the
pre-railroad days, who had to cross the Rocky Mountains
on the great California route. He spoke at length of their 15
perils to the suffering passenger, who felt none the warmer,
and at last gave a groan of weariness.

"How fur did you say 't was now?"

"I do' know 's I said, Mis' Tobin," answered the driver,
with a frosty laugh. "You see them big pines, and the side 20
of a barn just this way, with them yellow circus bills?
That's my three-mile mark."

"Be we got four more to make? Oh, my laws!" mourned
Mrs. Tobin. "Urge the beast, can't ye, Jeff'son? I ain't
used to bein' out in such bleak weather. Seems if I couldn't 25
git my breath. I'm all pinched up and wigglin' with
shivers now. 'T ain't no use lettin' the hoss go step-a-ty-
step this fashion."

"Landy me!" exclaimed the affronted driver. "I don't
see why folks expects me to race with the cars. Everybody 30
that gits in wants me to run the hoss to death on the road.
I make a good everage o' time, and that's all I can do. Ef
you was to go back an' forth every day but Sabbath fur

eighteen years, *you* 'd want to ease it all you could, and let
those thrash the spokes out o' their wheels that wanted to.
North Kilby, Mondays, Wednesdays, and Fridays; Sanscrit
Pond, Tuesdays, Thu'sdays, an' Saturdays. Me an' the
5 beast's done it eighteen years together, and the creatur'
warn't, so to say, young when we begun it, nor I neither.
I re'lly did n't know's she'd hold out till this time. There,
git up, will ye, old mar' !'" as the beast of burden stopped
short in the road.

10   There was a story that Jefferson gave this faithful
creature a rest three times a mile, and took four hours for
the journey by himself, and longer whenever he had a
passenger. But in pleasant weather the road was delightful, and full of people who drove their own conveyances,
15 and liked to stop and talk. There were not many farms,
and the third growth of white pines made a pleasant shade,
though Jefferson liked to say that when he began to carry
the mail his way lay through an open country of stumps
and sparse underbrush, where the white pines nowadays
20 completely arched the road.

They had passed the barn with circus posters, and felt
colder than ever when they caught sight of the weather-
beaten acrobats in their tights.

"My gorry!" exclaimed Widow Tobin, "them pore
25 creatur's looks as cheerless as little birch-trees in snow-
time. I hope they dresses 'em warmer this time o' year.
Now, there ! look at that one jumpin' through the little
hoop, will ye?"

"He could n't git himself through there with two pairs
30 o' pants on," answered Mr. Briley. "I expect they must
have to keep limber as eels. I used to think, when I was
a boy, that 't was the only thing I could ever be reconciled
to do for a livin'. I set out to run away an' follow a rovin'

showman once, but mother needed me to home. There warn't nobody but me an' the little gals."

"You ain't the only one that's be'n disapp'inted o' their heart's desire," said Mrs. Tobin sadly. "'T warn't so that I could be spared from home to learn the dressmaker's trade."

"'T would a come handy later on, I declare," answered the sympathetic driver, "bein' 's you went an' had such a passel o' gals to clothe an' feed. There, them that's livin' is all well off now, but it must ha' been some inconvenient for ye when they was small."

"Yes, Mr. Briley, but then I've had my mercies, too," said the widow somewhat grudgingly. "I take it master hard now, though, havin' to give up my own home and live round from place to place, if they be my own child'en. There was Ad'line and Susan Ellen fussin' an' bickerin' yesterday about who'd got to have me next; and, Lord be thanked, they both wanted me right off, but I hated to hear 'em talkin' of it over. I'd rather live to home, and do for myself."

"I've got consider'ble used to boardin'," said Jefferson, "sence ma'am died, but it made me ache 'long at the fust on 't, I tell ye. Bein' on the road 's I be, I could n't do no ways at keepin' house. I should want to keep right there and see to things."

"Course you would," replied Mrs. Tobin, with a sudden inspiration of opportunity which sent a welcome glow all over her. "Course you would, Jeff'son," — she leaned toward the front seat; "that is to say, onless you had jest the right one to do it for ye."

And Jefferson felt a strange glow also, and a sense of unexpected interest and enjoyment.

"See here, Sister Tobin," he exclaimed with enthusiasm. "Why can't ye take the trouble to shift seats, and come front here long o' me? We could put one buff'lo top o' the other, — they're both wearin' thin, — and set close, and
5 I do' know but we sh'd be more protected ag'inst the weather."

"Well, I could n't be no colder if I was froze to death," answered the widow, with an amiable simper. "Don't ye let me delay you, nor put you out, Mr. Briley. I don't
10 know 's I 'd set forth to-day if I 'd known 't was so cold; but I had all my bundles done up, and I ain't one that puts my hand to the plough an' looks back, 'cordin' to Scriptur'."

"You would n't want me to ride all them seven miles
15 alone?" asked the gallant Briley sentimentally, as he lifted her down, and helped her up again to the front seat. She was a few years older than he, but they had been schoolmates, and Mrs. Tobin's youthful freshness was suddenly revived to his mind's eye. She had a little farm;
20 there was nobody left at home now but herself, and so she had broken up housekeeping for the winter. Jefferson himself had savings of no mean amount.

They tucked themselves in, and felt better for the change, but there was a sudden awkwardness between
25 them; they had not had time to prepare for an unexpected crisis.

"They say Elder Bickers, over to East Sanscrit, 's been and got married again to a gal that 's four year younger than his oldest daughter," proclaimed Mrs. Tobin presently.
30 "Seems to me 't was fool's business."

"I view it so," said the stage-driver. "There 's goin' to be a mild open winter for that fam'ly."

"What a joker you be for a man that's had so much responsibility!" smiled Mrs. Tobin, after they had done laughing. "Ain't you never 'fraid, carryin' mail matter and such valuable stuff, that you'll be set on an' robbed, 'specially by night?"

Jefferson braced his feet against the dasher under the worn buffalo skin. "It is kind o' scary, or would be for some folks, but I'd like to see anybody get the better o' me. I go armed, and I don't care who knows it. Some o' them drover men that comes from Canady looks as if they didn't care what they did, but I look 'em right in the eye every time."

"Men folks is brave by natur'," said the widow admiringly. "You know how Tobin would let his fist right out at anybody that ondertook to sass him. Town-meetin' days. if he got disappointed about the way things went, he'd lay 'em out in win'rows; and ef he hadn't been a church-member he'd been a real fightin' character. I was always 'fraid to have him roused, for all he was so willin' and meechin' to home, and set round clever as anybody. My Susan Ellen used to boss him same's the kitten, when she was four year old."

"I've got a kind of a sideways cant to my nose, that Tobin give me when we was to school. I don't know's you ever noticed it," said Mr. Briley. "We was scufflin', as lads will. I never bore him no kind of a grudge. I pitied ye, when he was taken away. I re'lly did, now, Fanny. I liked Tobin first-rate, and I liked you. I used to say you was the han'somest girl to school."

"Lemme see your nose. 'T is all straight, for what I know," said the widow gently, as with a trace of coyness she gave a hasty glance. "I don't know but what 't is warped a little, but nothin' to speak of. You've got real nice features, like your marm's folks."

It was becoming a sentimental occasion, and Jefferson
Briley felt that he was in for something more than he
had bargained. He hurried the faltering sorrel horse,
and began to talk of the weather. It certainly did look
5 like snow, and he was tired of bumping over the frozen
road.

"I should n't wonder if I hired a hand here another year,
and went off out West myself to see the country."

"Why, how you talk!" answered the widow.

10 "Yes 'm," pursued Jefferson. "'T is tamer here than I
like, and I was tellin' 'em yesterday I 've got to know this
road most too well. I 'd like to go an' ride in the mountains
with some o' them great clipper coaches, where the driver
don't know one minute but he 'll be shot dead the next.
15 They carry an awful sight o' gold down from the mines,
I expect."

"I should be scairt to death," said Mrs. Tobin. "What
creatur's men folks be to like such things! Well, I do
declare."

20 "Yes," explained the mild little man. "There 's sights
of desp'radoes makes a han'some livin' out o' followin'
them coaches, an' stoppin' an' robbin' 'em clean to the
bone. Your money *or* your life!" and he flourished his
stub of a whip over the sorrel mare.

25 "Landy me! you make me run all of a cold creep. Do
tell somethin' heartenin', this cold day. I shall dream bad
dreams all night."

"They put on black crape over their heads," said the
driver mysteriously. "Nobody knows who most on 'em be,
30 and like as not some o' them fellows come o' good families.
They 've got so they stop the cars, and go right through
'em bold as brass. I could make your hair stand on end,
Mis' Tobin, — I could *so*!"

"I hope none on 'em 'll git round our way, I 'm sure," said Fanny Tobin. "I don't want to see none on 'em in their crape bunnits comin' after me."

"I ain't goin' to let nobody touch a hair o' your head," and Mr. Briley moved a little nearer, and tucked in the buffaloes again.

"I feel considerable warm to what I did," observed the widow by way of reward.

"There, I used to have my fears," Mr. Briley resumed, with an inward feeling that he never would get to North Kilby depot a single man. "But you see I had n't nobody but myself to think of. I 've got cousins, as you know, but nothin' nearer, and what I 've laid up would soon be parted out; and — well, I suppose some folks would think o' me if anything was to happen."

Mrs. Tobin was holding her cloud over her face, — the wind was sharp on that bit of open road, — but she gave an encouraging sound, between a groan and a chirp.

"'T would n't be like nothin' to me not to see you drivin' by," she said, after a minute. "I should n't know the days o' the week. I says to Susan Ellen last week I was sure 't was Friday, and she said no, 't was Thursday; but next minute you druv by and headin' toward North Kilby, so we found I was right."

"I 've got to be a featur' of the landscape," said Mr. Briley plaintively. "This kind o' weather the old mare and me, we wish we was done with it, and could settle down kind o' comfortable. I 've been lookin' this good while, as I drove the road, and I 've picked me out a piece o' land two or three times. But I can't abide the thought o' buildin', — 't would plague me to death; and both Sister Peak to North Kilby and Mis' Deacon Ash to the

Pond, they vie with one another to do well by me, fear I 'll
like the other stoppin'-place best."

"*I* should n't covet livin' long o' neither one o' them
women," responded the passenger with some spirit. "I see
5 some o' Mis' Peak's cookin' to a farmers' supper once, when
I was visitin' Susan Ellen's folks, an' I says 'Deliver me
from sech pale-complected baked beans as them!' and she
gave a kind of a quack. She was settin' jest at my left hand,
and could n't help hearin' of me. I would n't have spoken
10 if I had known, but she need n't have let on they was hers
an' make everything unpleasant. 'I guess them beans
taste just as well as other folks',' says she, and she would n't
never speak to me afterward."

"Do' know 's I blame her," ventured Mr. Briley.
15 "Women folks is dreadful pudjicky about their cookin'.
I 've always heard you was one o' the best cooks, Mis' Tobin.
I know them doughnuts an' things you 've give me in times
past, when I was drivin' by. Wish I had some on 'em now. I
never let on, but Mis' Ash's cookin' 's the best by a long
20 chalk. Mis' Peak 's handy about some things, and looks
after mendin' of me up."

"It does seem as if a man o' your years and your quiet
make ought to have a home you could call your own,"
suggested the passenger. "I kind of hate to think o' your
25 bangein' here and boardin' there, and one old woman
mendin', and the other settin' ye down to meals that
like 's not don't agree with ye."

"Lor', now, Mis' Tobin, le's not fuss round no longer,"
said Mr. Briley impatiently. "You know you covet me
30 same 's I do you."

"I don't nuther. Don't you go an' say fo'lish things
you can't stand to."

"I 've been tryin' to git a chance to put in a word with you ever sence — Well, I expected you 'd want to get your feelin's kind o' calloused after losin' Tobin."

"There 's nobody can fill his place," said the widow.

"I do' know but I can fight for ye town-meetin' days, 5 on a pinch," urged Jefferson boldly.

"I never see the beat o' you men fur conceit," and Mrs. Tobin laughed. "I ain't goin' to bother with ye, gone half the time as you be, an' carryin' on with your Mis' Peaks and Mis' Ashes. I dare say you 've promised your- 10 self to both on 'em twenty times."

"I hope to gracious if I ever breathed a word to none on 'em!" protested the lover. "'T ain't for lack o' opportunities set afore me, nuther;" and then Mr. Briley craftily kept silence, as if he had made a fair proposal, and expected 15 a definite reply.

The lady of his choice was, as she might have expressed it, much beat about. As she soberly thought, she was getting along in years, and must put up with Jefferson all the rest of the time. It was not likely she would ever have the 20 chance of choosing again, though she was one who liked variety.

Jefferson was n't much to look at, but he was pleasant and appeared boyish and young-feeling. "I do' know 's I should do better," she said unconsciously and half aloud. 25 "Well, yes, Jefferson, seein' it 's you. But we 're both on us kind of old to change our situation." Fanny Tobin gave a gentle sigh.

"Hooray!" said Jefferson. "I was scairt you meant to keep me sufferin' here a half an hour. I declare, I 'm more 30 pleased than I calc'lated on. An' I expected till lately to die a single man!"

"'T would re'lly have been a shame; 't ain't natur'," said Mrs. Tobin, with confidence. "I don't see how you held out so long with bein' solitary."

"I'll hire a hand to drive for me, and we'll have a
5 good comfortable winter, me an' you an' the old sorrel. I've been promisin' of her a rest this good while."

"Better keep her a steppin'," urged thrifty Mrs. Fanny. "She'll stiffen up master, an' disapp'int ye, come spring."

"You'll have me, now, won't ye, sartin?" pleaded
10 Jefferson, to make sure. "You ain't one o' them that plays with a man's feelin's. Say right out you'll have me."

"I s'pose I shall have to," said Mrs. Tobin somewhat mournfully. "I feel for Mis' Peak an' Mis' Ash, pore creatur's. I expect they'll be hardshipped. They've
15 always been hard-worked, an' may have kind o' looked forward to a little ease. But one o' 'em would be left lamentin', anyhow," and she gave a girlish laugh. An air of victory animated the frame of Mrs. Tobin. She felt but twenty-five years of age. In that moment she made plans
20 for cutting her Briley's hair, and make him look smartened-up and ambitious. Then she wished that she knew for certain how much money he had in the bank; not that it would make any difference now. "He needn't bluster none before me," she thought gaily. "He's harmless as a fly." ·
25 "Who'd have thought we'd done such a piece of engineerin', when we started out?" inquired the dear one of Mr. Briley's heart, as he tenderly helped her to alight at Susan Ellen's door.

"Both on us, jest the least grain," answered the lover.
30 "Gimme a good smack, now, you clever creatur';" and so they parted. Mr. Briley had been taken on the road in spite of his pistol.

THE THREE STRANGERS[1]

Thomas Hardy

Among the few features of agricultural England which retain an appearance but little modified by the lapse of centuries, may be reckoned the high, grassy and furzy downs, coombs, or ewe-leases, as they are indifferently called, that fill a large area of certain counties in the south 5 and south-west. If any mark of human occupation is met with hereon, it usually takes the form of the solitary cottage of some shepherd.

Fifty years ago such a lonely cottage stood on such a down, and may possibly be standing there now. In spite 10 of its loneliness, however, the spot, by actual measurement, was not more than five miles from a county-town. Yet that affected it little. Five miles of irregular upland, during the long inimical seasons, with their sleets, snows, rains, and mists, afford withdrawing space enough to 15 isolate a Timon or a Nebuchadnezzar; much less, in fair weather, to please that less repellent tribe, the poets, philosophers, artists, and others who 'conceive and meditate of pleasant things.'

Some old earthen camp or barrow, some clump of trees, 20 at least some starved fragment of ancient hedge is usually taken advantage of in the erection of these forlorn dwellings. But, in the present case, such a kind of shelter had been disregarded. Higher Crowstairs, as the house was

[1] From *Wessex Tales*, pp. 33–61. Harper & Brothers, 1896.

called, stood quite detached and undefended. The only
reason for its precise situation seemed to be the crossing
of two footpaths at right angles hard by, which may have
crossed there and thus for a good five hundred years.
5 Hence the house was exposed to the elements on all sides.
But, though the wind up here blew unmistakably when it
did blow, and the rain hit hard whenever it fell, the various weathers of the winter season were not quite so formidable on the coomb as they were imagined to be by
10 dwellers on low ground. The raw rimes were not so pernicious as in the hollows, and the frosts were scarcely so
severe. When the shepherd and his family who tenanted
the house were pitied for their sufferings from the exposure, they said that upon the whole they were less inconven-
15 ienced by 'wuzzes and flames' (hoarses and phlegms) than
when they had lived by the stream of a snug neighbouring
valley.

The night of March 28, 182–, was precisely one of the
nights that were wont to call forth these expressions of
20 commiseration. The level rainstorm smote walls, slopes,
and hedges like the clothyard shafts of Senlac and Crecy.
Such sheep and outdoor animals as had no shelter stood
with their buttocks to the winds; while the tails of little
birds trying to roost on some scraggy thorn were blown
25 inside-out like umbrellas. The gable-end of the cottage
was stained with wet, and the eavesdroppings flapped
against the wall. Yet never was commiseration for the
shepherd more misplaced. For that cheerful rustic was
entertaining a large party in glorification of the christen-
30 ing of his second girl.

The guests had arrived before the rain began to fall,
and they were all now assembled in the chief or living

room of the dwelling. A glance into the apartment at eight o'clock on this eventful evening would have resulted in the opinion that it was as cosy and comfortable a nook as could be wished for in boisterous weather. The calling of its inhabitant was proclaimed by a number of highly- 5 polished sheep-crooks without stems that were hung ornamentally over the fireplace, the curl of each shining crook varying from the antiquated type engraved in the patriarchal pictures of old family Bibles to the most approved fashion of the last local sheep-fair. The room was lighted 10 by half-a-dozen candles, having wicks only a trifle smaller than the grease which enveloped them, in candlesticks that were never used but at high-days, holy-days, and family feasts. The lights were scattered about the room, two of them standing on the chimney-piece. This position of 15 candles was in itself significant. Candles on the chimney-piece always meant a party.

On the hearth, in front of a back-brand to give substance, blazed a fire of thorns, that crackled 'like the laughter of the fool.' 20

Nineteen persons were gathered here. Of these, five women, wearing gowns of various bright hues, sat in chairs along the wall ; girls shy and not shy filled the window-bench ; four men, including Charley Jake the hedge-carpenter, Elijah New the parish-clerk, and John Pitcher, a 25 neighbouring dairyman, the shepherd's father-in-law, lolled in the settle ; a young man and maid, who were blushing over tentative *pourparlers* on a life-companionship, sat beneath the corner-cupboard ; and an elderly engaged man of fifty or upward moved restlessly about from spots where 30 his betrothed was not to the spot where she was. Enjoyment was pretty general, and so much the more prevailed

in being unhampered by conventional restrictions. Absolute confidence in each other's good opinion begat perfect
ease, while the finishing stroke of manner, amounting to a
truly princely serenity, was lent to the majority by the
5 absence of any expression or trait denoting that they
wished to get on in the world, enlarge their minds, or do
any eclipsing thing whatever — which nowadays so generally nips the bloom and *bonhomie* of all except the two
extremes of the social scale.

10   Shepherd Fennel had married well, his wife being a
dairyman's daughter from a vale at a distance, who brought
fifty guineas in her pocket — and kept them there, till
they should be required for ministering to the needs of a
coming family. This frugal woman had been somewhat
15 exercised as to the character that should be given to the
gathering. A sit-still party had its advantages; but an
undisturbed position of ease in chairs and settles was apt
to lead on the men to such an unconscionable deal of toping
that they would sometimes fairly drink the house dry. A
20 dancing-party was the alternative; but this, while avoiding
the foregoing objection on the score of good drink, had a
counterbalancing disadvantage in the matter of good vic-
tuals, the ravenous appetites engendered by the exercise
causing immense havoc in the buttery. Shepherdess Fennel
25 fell back upon the intermediate plan of mingling short
dances with short periods of talk and singing, so as to
hinder any ungovernable rage in either. But this scheme
was entirely confined to her own gentle mind: the shepherd himself was in the mood to exhibit the most reckless
30 phases of hospitality.

The fiddler was a boy of those parts, about twelve years
of age, who had a wonderful dexterity in jigs and reels,

though his fingers were so small and short as to necessitate
a constant shifting for the high notes, from which he
scrambled back to the first position with sounds not of
unmixed purity of tone. At seven the shrill tweedle-dee
of this youngster had begun, accompanied by a booming 5
ground-bass from Elijah New, the parish-clerk, who had
thoughtfully brought with him his favourite musical instrument, the serpent. Dancing was instantaneous, Mrs. Fennel privately enjoining the players on no account to let
the dance exceed the length of a quarter of an hour.   10

But Elijah and the boy, in the excitement of their position, quite forgot the injunction. Moreover, Oliver Giles,
a man of seventeen, one of the dancers, who was enam-
oured of his partner, a fair girl of thirty-three rolling years,
had recklessly handed a new crown-piece to the musicians, 15
as a bribe to keep going as long as they had muscle and
wind. Mrs. Fennel, seeing the steam begin to generate on
the countenances of her guests, crossed over and touched
the fiddler's elbow and put her hand on the serpent's
mouth. But they took no notice, and fearing she might 20
lose her character of genial hostess if she were to interfere
too markedly, she retired and sat down helpless. And so
the dance whizzed on with cumulative fury, the performers
moving in their planet-like courses, direct and retrograde,
from apogee to perigee, till the hand of the well-kicked 25
clock at the bottom of the room had travelled over the
circumference of an hour.

While these cheerful events were in course of enactment
within Fennel's pastoral dwelling, an incident having considerable bearing on the party had occurred in the gloomy 30
night without. Mrs. Fennel's concern about the growing
fierceness of the dance corresponded in point of time with

the ascent of a human figure to the solitary hill of Higher
Crowstairs from the direction of the distant town. This
personage strode on through the rain without a pause,
following the little-worn path which, further on in its
5 course, skirted the shepherd's cottage.

It was nearly the time of full moon, and on this account,
though the sky was lined with a uniform sheet of dripping
cloud, ordinary objects out of doors were readily visible.
The sad wan light revealed the lonely pedestrian to be a
10 man of supple frame; his gait suggested that he had somewhat passed the period of perfect and instinctive agility,
though not so far as to be otherwise than rapid of motion
when occasion required. At a rough guess, he might have
been about forty years of age. He appeared tall, but a
15 recruiting sergeant, or other person accustomed to the
judging of men's heights by the eye, would have discerned
that this was chiefly owing to his gauntness, and that he
was not more than five-feet-eight or nine.

Notwithstanding the regularity of his tread, there was
20 caution in it, as in that of one who mentally feels his way;
and despite the fact that it was not a black coat nor a
dark garment of any sort that he wore, there was something about him which suggested that he naturally belonged to the black-coated tribes of men. His clothes were
25 of fustian, and his boots hobnailed, yet in his progress he
showed not the mud-accustomed bearing of hobnailed and
fustianed peasantry.

By the time that he had arrived abreast of the shepherd's
premises the rain came down, or rather came along, with
30 yet more determined violence. The outskirts of the little
settlement partially broke the force of wind and rain, and
this induced him to stand still. The most salient of the

shepherd's domestic erections was an empty sty at the forward corner of his hedgeless garden, for in these latitudes
the principle of masking the homelier features of your
establishment by a conventional frontage was unknown.
The traveller's eye was attracted to this small building by ₅
the pallid shine of the wet slates that covered it. He
turned aside, and, finding it empty, stood under the pent-
roof for shelter.

While he stood, the boom of the serpent within the
adjacent house, and the lesser strains of the fiddler, reached ₁₀
the spot as an accompaniment to the surging hiss of the
flying rain on the sod, its louder beating on the cabbage-
leaves of the garden, on the eight or ten beehives just discernible by the path, and its dripping from the eaves into
a row of buckets and pans that had been placed under the ₁₅
walls of the cottage. For at Higher Crowstairs, as at all
such elevated domiciles, the grand difficulty of housekeeping was an insufficiency of water; and a casual rainfall
was utilized by turning out, as catchers, every utensil that
the house contained. Some queer stories might be told of ₂₀
the contrivances for economy in suds and dish-waters that
are absolutely necessitated in upland habitations during
the droughts of summer. But at this season there were no
such exigencies; a mere acceptance of what the skies be-
stowed was sufficient for an abundant store.   ₂₅

At last the notes of the serpent ceased and the house
was silent. This cessation of activity aroused the solitary
pedestrian from the reverie into which he had lapsed, and,
emerging from the shed, with an apparently new intention,
he walked up the path to the house-door. Arrived here, ₃₀
his first act was to kneel down on a large stone beside the
row of vessels, and to drink a copious draught from one of

them. Having quenched his thirst he rose and lifted his
hand to knock, but paused with his eye upon the panel.
Since the dark surface of the wood revealed absolutely
nothing, it was evident that he must be mentally looking
through the door, as if he wished to.measure thereby all
the possibilities that a house of this sort might include,
and how they might bear upon the question of his entry.

In his indecision he turned and surveyed the scene
around. Not a soul was anywhere visible. The garden-
path stretched downward from his feet, gleaming like the
track of a snail; the roof of the little well (mostly dry),
the well-cover, the top rail of the garden-gate, were var-
nished with the same dull liquid glaze; while, far away
in the vale, a faint whiteness of more than usual extent
showed that the rivers were high in the meads. Beyond
all this winked a few bleared lamplights through the beating drops — lights that denoted the situation of the county-
town from which he had appeared to come. The absence
of all notes of life in that direction seemed to clinch his
intentions, and he knocked at the door.

Within, a desultory chat had taken the place of movement and musical sound. The hedge-carpenter was suggesting a song to the company, which nobody just then
was inclined to undertake, so that the knock afforded a
not unwelcome diversion.

'Walk in!' said the shepherd promptly.

The latch clicked upward, and out of the night our
pedestrian appeared upon the door-mat. The shepherd
arose, snuffed two of the nearest candles, and turned to
look at him.

Their light disclosed that the stranger was dark in complexion and not unprepossessing as to feature. His hat,

which for a moment he did not remove, hung low over
his eyes, without concealing that they were large, open,
and determined, moving with a flash rather than a glance
round the room. He seemed pleased with his survey, and,
baring his shaggy head, said, in a rich deep voice, 'The
rain is so heavy, friends, that I ask leave to come in and
rest awhile.'

'To be sure, stranger,' said the shepherd. 'And faith,
you 've been lucky in choosing your time, for we are having a bit of a fling for a glad cause — though, to be sure,
a man could hardly wish that glad cause to happen more
than once a year.'

'Nor less,' spoke up a woman. 'For 't is best to get
your family over and done with, as soon as you can, so
as to be all the earlier out of the fag o 't.'

'And what may be this glad cause?' asked the stranger.

'A birth and christening,' said the shepherd.

The stranger hoped his host might not be made unhappy
either by too many or too few of such episodes, and being
invited by a gesture to a pull at the mug, he readily acqui-
esced. His manner, which, before entering, had been so dubi-
ous, was now altogether that of a careless and candid man.

'Late to be traipsing athwart this coomb — hey?' said
the engaged man of fifty.

'Late it is, master, as you say. — I 'll take a seat in the
chimney-corner, if you have nothing to urge against it,
ma'am; for I am a little moist on the side that was next
the rain.'

Mrs. Shepherd Fennel assented, and made room for the
self-invited comer, who, having got completely inside the
chimney-corner, stretched out his legs and his arms with
the expansiveness of a person quite at home.

'Yes, I am rather cracked in the vamp,' he said freely, seeing that the eyes of the shepherd's wife fell upon his boots, 'and I am not well fitted either. I have had some rough times lately, and have been forced to pick up what 5 I can get in the way of wearing, but I must find a suit better fit for working-days when I reach home.'

'One of hereabouts?' she inquired.

'Not quite that — further up the country.'

'I thought so. And so be I; and by your tongue you 10 come from my neighbourhood.'

'But you would hardly have heard of me,' he said quickly. 'My time would be long before yours, ma'am, you see.'

This testimony to the youthfulness of his hostess had 15 the effect of stopping her cross-examination.

. 'There is only one thing more wanted to make me happy,' continued the new-comer. 'And that is a little baccy, which I am sorry to say I am out of.'

'I'll fill your pipe,' said the shepherd.

20 'I must ask you to lend me a pipe likewise.'

'A smoker, and no pipe about 'ee?'

'I have dropped it somewhere on the road.'

The shepherd filled and handed him a new clay pipe, saying, as he did so, 'Hand me your baccy-box — I'll fill 25 that too, now I am about it.'

The man went through the movement of searching his pockets.

'Lost that too?' said his entertainer, with some surprise.

'I am afraid so,' said the man with some confusion.

30 'Give it to me in a screw of paper.' Lighting his pipe at the candle with a suction that drew the whole flame into the bowl, he resettled himself in the corner and bent his

looks upon the faint steam from his damp legs, as if he wished to say no more.

Meanwhile the general body of guests had been taking little notice of this visitor by reason of an absorbing discussion in which they were engaged with the band about 5
a tune for the next dance. The matter being settled, they were about to stand up when an interruption came in the shape of another knock at the door.

At sound of the same the man in the chimney-corner took up the poker and began stirring the brands as if do- 10
ing it thoroughly were the one aim of his existence; and a second time the shepherd said, ' Walk in ! ' In a moment another man stood upon the straw-woven door-mat. He too was a stranger.

This individual was one of a type radically different 15
from the first. There was more of the commonplace in his manner, and a certain jovial cosmopolitanism sat upon his features. He was several years older than the first arrival, his hair being slightly frosted, his eyebrows bristly, and his whiskers cut back from his cheeks. His face was 20
rather full and flabby, and yet it was not altogether a face without power. A few grog-blossoms marked the neighbourhood of his nose. He flung back his long drab greatcoat, revealing that beneath it he wore a suit of cinder-gray shade throughout, large heavy seals, of some metal or othei 25
that would take a polish, dangling from his fob as his only personal ornament. Shaking the water-drops from his low-crowned glazed hat, he said, ' I must ask for a few minutes' shelter, comrades, or I shall be wetted to my skin before I get to Casterbridge.' 30

' Make yourself at home, master,' said the shepherd, perhaps a trifle less heartily than on the first occasion.

Not that Fennel had the least tinge of niggardliness in his composition; but the room was far from large, spare chairs were not numerous, and damp companions were not altogether desirable at close quarters for the women
5 and girls in their bright-coloured gowns.

However, the second comer, after taking off his great-coat, and hanging his hat on a nail in one of the ceiling-beams as if he had been specially invited to put it there, advanced and sat down at the table. This had been pushed
10 so closely into the chimney-corner, to give all available room to the dancers, that its inner edge grazed the elbow of the man who had ensconced himself by the fire; and thus the two strangers were brought into close companionship. They nodded to each other by way of breaking the
15 ice of unacquaintance, and the first stranger handed his neighbour the family mug — a huge vessel of brown ware, having its upper edge worn away like a threshold by the rub of whole generations of thirsty lips that had gone the way of all flesh, and bearing the following inscription
20 burnt upon its rotund side in yellow letters: —

THERE IS NO FUN
UNTILL i CUM.

The other man, nothing loth, raised the mug to his lips, and drank on, and on, and on — till a curious blueness
25 overspread the countenance of the shepherd's wife, who had regarded with no little surprise the first stranger's free offer to the second of what did not belong to him to dispense.

'I knew it!' said the toper to the shepherd with much
30 satisfaction. 'When I walked up your garden before coming in, and saw the hives all of a row, I said to myself,

"Where there's bees there's honey, and where there's honey there's mead." But mead of such a truly comfortable sort as this I really did n't expect to meet in my older days.' He took yet another pull at the mug, till it assumed an ominous elevation. 5

'Glad you enjoy it!' said the shepherd warmly.

'It is goodish mead,' assented Mrs. Fennel, with an absence of enthusiasm which seemed to say that it was possible to buy praise for one's cellar at too heavy a price. 'It is trouble enough to make — and really I hardly think 10 we shall make any more. For honey sells well, and we ourselves can make shift with a drop o' small mead and metheglin for common use from the comb-washings.'

'O, but you'll never have the heart!' reproachfully cried the stranger in cinder-gray, after taking up the mug 15 a third time and setting it down empty. 'I love mead, when 't is old like this, as I love to go to church o' Sundays, or to relieve the needy any day of the week.'

'Ha, ha, ha!' said the man in the chimney-corner, who, in spite of the taciturnity induced by the pipe of tobacco, 20 could not or would not refrain from this slight testimony to his comrade's humour.

Now the old mead of those days, brewed of the purest first-year or maiden honey, four pounds to the gallon — with its due complement of white of eggs, cinnamon, gin- 25 ger, cloves, mace, rosemary, yeast, and processes of working, bottling, and cellaring — tasted remarkably strong; but it did not taste so strong as it actually was. Hence, presently, the stranger in cinder-gray at the table, moved by its creeping influence, unbuttoned his waistcoat, threw 30 himself back in his chair, spread his legs, and made his presence felt in various ways.

'Well, well, as I say,' he resumed, 'I am going to Caster-bridge, and to Casterbridge I must go. I should have been almost there by this time; but the rain drove me into your dwelling, and I 'm not sorry for it.'

5 'You don't live in Casterbridge?' said the shepherd.

'Not as yet; though I shortly mean to move there.'

'Going to set up in trade, perhaps?'

'No, no,' said the shepherd's wife. 'It is easy to see that the gentleman is rich, and don't want to work at 10 anything.'

The cinder-gray stranger paused, as if to consider whether he would accept that definition of himself. He presently rejected it by answering, 'Rich is not quite the word for me, dame. I do work, and I must work. And even if I 15 only get to Casterbridge by midnight I must begin work there at eight to-morrow morning. Yes, het or wet, blow or snow, famine or sword, my day's work to-morrow must be done.'

'Poor man! Then, in spite o' seeming, you be worse off 20 than we?' replied the shepherd's wife.

''T is the nature of my trade, men and maidens. 'T is the nature of my trade more than my poverty. . . . But really and truly I must up and off, or I shan't get a lodging in the town.' However, the speaker did not move, and 25 directly added, 'There's time for one more draught of friendship before I go; and I 'd perform it at once if the mug were not dry.'

'Here's a mug o' small,' said Mrs. Fennel. 'Small, we call it, though to be sure 't is only the first wash o' the 30 combs.'

'No,' said the stranger disdainfully. 'I won't spoil your first kindness by partaking o' your second.'

'Certainly not,' broke in Fennel. 'We don't increase and multiply every day, and I 'll fill the mug again.' He went away to the dark place under the stairs where the barrel stood. The shepherdess followed him.

'Why should you do this?' she said reproachfully, as 5 soon as they were alone. 'He 's emptied it once, though it held enough for ten people; and now he 's not contented wi' the small, but must needs call for more o' the strong ! And a stranger unbeknown to any of us. For my part, I don't like the look o' the man at all.' 10

'But he 's in the house, my honey; and 't is a wet night, and a christening. Daze it, what 's a cup of mead more or less? There 'll be plenty more next bee-burning.'

'Very well — this time, then,' she answered, looking wistfully at the barrel. 'But what is the man's calling, 15 and where is he one of, that he should come in and join us like this?'

'I don't know. I 'll ask him again.'

The catastrophe of having the mug drained dry at one pull by the stranger in cinder-gray was effectually guarded 20 against this time by Mrs. Fennel. She poured out his allowance in a small cup, keeping the large one at a discreet distance from him. When he had tossed off his portion the shepherd renewed his inquiry about the stranger's occupation. 25

The latter did not immediately reply, and the man in the chimney-corner, with sudden demonstrativeness, said, 'Anybody may know my trade — I 'm a wheelwright.'

'A very good trade for these parts,' said the shepherd. 30

'And anybody may know mine — if they 've the sense to find it out,' said the stranger in cinder-gray.

'You may generally tell what a man is by his claws,' observed the hedge-carpenter, looking at his own hands. 'My fingers be as full of thorns as an old pin-cushion is of pins.'

5 The hands of the man in the chimney-corner instinctively sought the shade, and he gazed into the fire as he resumed his pipe. The man at the table took up the hedge-carpenter's remark, and added smartly, 'True; but the oddity of my trade is that, instead of setting a mark upon me, it sets
10 a mark upon my customers.'

No observation being offered by anybody in elucidation of this enigma, the shepherd's wife once more called for a song. The same obstacles presented themselves as at the former time — one had no voice, another had forgotten the
15 first verse. The stranger at the table, whose soul had now risen to a good working temperature, relieved the difficulty by exclaiming that, to start the company, he would sing himself. Thrusting one thumb into the arm-hole of his waistcoat, he waved the other hand in the air, and, with
20 an extemporizing gaze at the shining sheep-crooks above the mantelpiece, began : —

'O my trade it is the rarest one,
　　　　Simple shepherds all —
　　My trade is a sight to see ;
25　　For my customers I tie, and take them up on high,
　　And waft 'em to a far countree !'

The room was silent when he had finished the verse — with one exception, that of the man in the chimney-corner, who, at the singer's word, 'Chorus!' joined him in a deep bass
30 voice of musical relish —

'And waft 'em to a far countree !'

Oliver Giles, John Pitcher the dairyman, the parish-clerk, the engaged man of fifty, the row of young women against the wall, seemed lost in thought not of the gayest kind. The shepherd looked meditatively on the ground, the shepherdess gazed keenly at the singer, and with some suspicion; she was doubting whether this stranger were merely singing an old song from recollection, or was composing one there and then for the occasion. All were as perplexed at the obscure revelation as the guests at Belshazzar's Feast, except the man in the chimney-corner, who quietly said, 'Second verse, stranger,' and smoked on.

The singer thoroughly moistened himself from his lips inwards, and went on with the next stanza as requested: —

> ' My tools are but common ones,
> Simple shepherds all —
> My tools are no sight to see:
> A little hempen string, and a post whereon to swing,
> Are implements enough for me ! '

Shepherd Fennel glanced round. There was no longer any doubt that the stranger was answering his question rhythmically. The guests one and all started back with suppressed exclamations. The young woman engaged to the man of fifty fainted half-way, and would have proceeded, but finding him wanting in alacrity for catching her she sat down trembling.

' O, he 's the ——— !' whispered the people in the background, mentioning the name of an ominous public officer. 'He 's come to do it! 'T is to be at Casterbridge jail tomorrow — the man for sheep-stealing — the poor clockmaker we heard of, who used to live away at Shottsford and had no work to do — Timothy Summers, whose family were

a-starving, and so he went out of Shottsford by the high-road, and took a sheep in open daylight, defying the farmer and the farmer's wife and the farmer's lad, and every man jack among 'em. He' (and they nodded towards the
5 stranger of the deadly trade) ' is come from up the country to do it because there 's not enough to do in his own county-town, and he 's got the place here now our own county man 's dead; he 's going to live in the same cottage under the prison wall.'

10 The stranger in cinder-gray took no notice of this whispered string of observations, but again wetted his lips. Seeing that his friend in the chimney-corner was the only one who reciprocated his joviality in any way, he held out his cup towards that appreciative comrade, who also held
15 out his own. They clinked together, the eyes of the rest of the room hanging upon the singer's actions. He parted his lips for the third verse; but at that moment another knock was audible upon the door. This time the knock was faint and hesitating.

20 The company seemed scared; the shepherd looked with consternation towards the entrance, and it was with some effort that he resisted his alarmed wife's deprecatory glance, and uttered for the third time the welcoming words, ' Walk in ! '

25 The door was gently opened, and another man stood upon the mat. He, like those who had preceded him, was a stranger. This time it was a short, small personage, of fair complexion, and dressed in a decent suit of dark clothes.

' Can you tell me the way to ——? ' he began: when,
30 gazing round the room to observe the nature of the company amongst whom he had fallen, his eyes lighted on the stranger in cinder-gray. It was just at the instant when the

latter, who had thrown his mind into his song with such a will that he scarcely heeded the interruption, silenced all whispers and inquiries by bursting into his third verse: —

> 'To-morrow is my working day,
>> Simple shepherds all —
>> To-morrow is a working day for me:
> For the farmer's sheep is slain, and the lad who did it ta'en,
>> And on his soul may God ha' merc-y!'

The stranger in the chimney-corner, waving cups with the singer so heartily that his mead splashed over on the hearth, repeated in his bass voice as before: —

> 'And on his soul may God ha' merc-y!'

All this time the third stranger had been standing in the doorway. Finding now that he did not come forward or go on speaking, the guests particularly regarded him. They noticed to their surprise that he stood before them the picture of abject terror — his knees trembling, his hand shaking so violently that the door-latch by which he supported himself rattled audibly: his white lips were parted, and his eyes fixed on the merry officer of justice in the middle of the room. A moment more and he had turned, closed the door, and fled.

'What a man can it be?' said the shepherd.

The rest, between the awfulness of their late discovery and the odd conduct of this third visitor, looked as if they knew not what to think, and said nothing. Instinctively they withdrew further and further from the grim gentleman in their midst, whom some of them seemed to take for the Prince of Darkness himself, till they formed a remote circle, an empty space of floor being left between them and him —

> '. . . circulus, cujus centrum diabolus.'

The room was so silent—though there were more than twenty people in it—that nothing could be heard but the patter of the rain against the window-shutters, accompanied by the occasional hiss of a stray drop that fell down the chimney into the fire, and the steady puffing of the man in the corner, who had now resumed his pipe of long clay.

The stillness was unexpectedly broken. The distant sound of a gun reverberated through the air—apparently from the direction of the county-town.

'Be jiggered!' cried the stranger who had sung the song, jumping up.

'What does that mean?' asked several.

'A prisoner escaped from the jail—that's what it means.'

All listened. The sound was repeated, and none of them spoke but the man in the chimney-corner, who said quietly, 'I've often been told that in this county they fire a gun, at such times; but I never heard it till now.'

'I wonder if it is *my* man?' murmured the personage in cinder-gray.

'Surely it is!' said the shepherd involuntarily. 'And surely we've zeed him! That little man who looked in at the door by now, and quivered like a leaf when he zeed ye and heard your song!'

'His teeth chattered, and the breath went out of his body,' said the dairyman.

'And his heart seemed to sink within him like a stone,' said Oliver Giles.

'And he bolted as if he'd been shot at,' said the hedge-carpenter.

'True—his teeth chattered, and his heart seemed to sink; and he bolted as if he'd been shot at,' slowly summed up the man in the chimney-corner.

'I did n't notice it,' remarked the hangman.

'We were all a-wondering what made him run off in such a fright,' faltered one of the women against the wall, 'and now 't is explained!'

The firing of the alarm-gun went on at intervals, low and sullenly, and their suspicions became a certainty. The sinister gentleman in cinder-gray roused himself. 'Is there a constable here?' he asked, in thick tones. 'If so, let him step forward.'

The engaged man of fifty stepped quavering out from the wall, his betrothed beginning to sob on the back of the chair.

'You are a sworn constable?'

'I be, sir.'

'Then pursue the criminal at once, with assistance, and bring him back here. He can't have gone far.'

'I will, sir, I will — when I 've got my staff. I 'll go home and get it, and come sharp here, and start in a body.'

'Staff! — never mind your staff; the man 'll be gone!'

'But I can't do nothing without my staff — can I, William, and John, and Charles Jake? No; for there 's the king's royal crown a painted on en in yaller and gold, and the lion and the unicorn, so as when I raise en up and hit my prisoner, 't is made a lawful blow thereby. I would n't 'tempt to take up a man without my staff — no, not I. If I had n't the law to gie me courage, why, instead o' my taking up him he might take up me!'

'Now, I 'm a king's man myself, and can give you authority enough for this,' said the formidable officer in gray. 'Now then, all of ye, be ready. Have ye any lanterns?'

'Yes — have ye any lanterns ? — I demand it ! ' said the constable.

'And the rest of you able-bodied ——'

'Able-bodied men — yes — the rest of ye !' said the
5 constable.

'Have you some good stout staves and pitchforks ——'

'Staves and pitchforks — in the name o' the law ! And take 'em in yer hands and go in quest, and do as we in authority tell ye !'

10 Thus aroused, the men prepared to give chase. The evidence was, indeed, though circumstantial, so convincing, that but little argument was needed to show the shepherd's guests that after what they had seen it would look very much like connivance if they did not instantly pursue the
15 unhappy third stranger, who could not as yet have gone more than a few hundred yards over such uneven country.

A shepherd is always well provided with lanterns ; and, lighting these hastily, and with hurdle-staves in their hands, they poured out of the door, taking a direction along the
20 crest of the hill, away from the town, the rain having fortunately a little abated.

Disturbed by the noise, or possibly by unpleasant dreams of her baptism, the child who had been christened began to cry heart-brokenly in the room overhead. These notes
25 of grief came down through the chinks of the floor to the ears of the women below, who jumped up one by one, and seemed glad of the excuse to ascend and comfort the baby, for the incidents of the last half-hour greatly oppressed them. Thus in the space of two or three minutes the room
30 on the ground-floor was deserted quite.

But it was not for long. Hardly had the sound of foot-steps died away when a man returned round the corner of the house from the direction the pursuers had taken. Peeping in at the door, and seeing nobody there, he entered leisurely. It was the stranger of the chimney-corner, who had gone out with the rest. The motive of his return was shown by his helping himself to a cut piece of skimmer- 5 cake that lay on a ledge beside where he had sat, and which he had apparently forgotten to take with him. He also poured out half a cup more mead from the quantity that remained, ravenously eating and drinking these as he stood. He had not finished when another figure came in just as 10 quietly — his friend in cinder-gray.

'O — you here?' said the latter, smiling. 'I thought you had gone to help in the capture.' And this speaker also revealed the object of his return by looking solicitously round for the fascinating mug of old mead. 15

'And I thought you had gone,' said the other, continuing his skimmer-cake with some effort.

'Well, on second thoughts, I felt there were enough without me,' said the first confidentially, 'and such a night as it is, too. Besides, 't is the business o' the Government 20 to take care of its criminals — not mine.'

'True; so it is. And I felt as you did, that there were enough without me.'

'I don't want to break my limbs running over the humps and hollows of this wild country.' 25

'Nor I neither, between you and me.'

'These shepherd-people are used to it — simple-minded souls, you know, stirred up to anything in a moment. They 'll have him ready for me before the morning, and no trouble to me at all.' 30

'They 'll have him, and we shall have saved ourselves all labour in the matter.'

'True, true. Well, my way is to Casterbridge; and 't is
as much as my legs will do to take me that far. Going the
same way?'

'No, I am sorry to say! I have to get home over there'
5 (he nodded indefinitely to the right), 'and I feel as you do,
that it is quite enough for my legs to do before bedtime.'

The other had by this time finished the mead in the mug,
after which, shaking hands heartily at the door, and wish-
ing each other well, they went their several ways.

10   In the meantime the company of pursuers had reached
the end of the hog's-back elevation which dominated this
part of the down. They had decided on no particular plan
of action; and, finding that the man of the baleful trade
was no longer in their company; they seemed quite unable
15 to form any such plan now. They descended in all directions down the hill, and straightway several of the party
fell into the snare set by Nature for all misguided midnight
ramblers over this part of the cretaceous formation. The
'lanchets,' or flint slopes, which belted the escarpment at
20 intervals of a dozen yards, took the less cautious ones unawares, and losing their footing on the rubbly steep they
slid sharply downwards, the lanterns rolling from their
hands to the bottom, and there lying on their sides till the
horn was scorched through.

25   When they had again gathered themselves together,
the shepherd, as the man who knew the country best, took
the lead, and guided them round these treacherous inclines.
The lanterns, which seemed rather to dazzle their eyes and
warn the fugitive than to assist them in the exploration,
30 were extinguished, due silence was observed; and in this
more rational order they plunged into the vale. It was a
grassy, briery, moist defile, affording some shelter to any

person who had sought it; but the party perambulated it
in vain, and ascended on the other side. Here they wandered apart, and after an interval closed together again to
report progress. At the second time of closing in they
found themselves near a lonely ash, the single tree on this 5
part of the coomb, probably sown there by a passing bird
some fifty years before. And here, standing a little to one
side of the trunk, as motionless as the trunk itself, appeared
the man they were in quest of, his outline being well defined against the sky beyond. The band noiselessly drew 10
up and faced him.

'Your money or your life!' said the constable sternly to
the still figure.

'No, no,' whispered John Pitcher. ''T is n't our side
ought to say that. That's the doctrine of vagabonds like 15
him, and we be on the side of the law.'

'Well, well,' replied the constable impatiently; 'I must
say something, must n't I? and if you had all the weight
o' this undertaking upon your mind, perhaps you'd say
the wrong thing too!— Prisoner at the bar, surrender, in 20
the name of the Father— the Crown, I mane!'

The man under the tree seemed now to notice them for
the first time, and, giving them no opportunity whatever
for exhibiting their courage, he strolled slowly towards
them. He was, indeed, the little man, the third stranger; 25
but his trepidation had in a great measure gone.

'Well, travellers,' he said, 'did I hear ye speak to me?'

'You did: you've got to come and be our prisoner at
once!' said the constable. 'We arrest 'ee on the charge
of not biding in Casterbridge jail in a decent proper man- 30
ner to be hung to-morrow morning. Neighbours, do your
duty, and seize the culpet!'

On hearing the charge, the man seemed enlightened, and, saying not another word, resigned himself with preternatural civility to the search-party, who, with their staves in their hands, surrounded him on all sides, and marched him
5 back towards the shepherd's cottage.

It was eleven o'clock by the time they arrived. The light shining from the open door, a sound of men's voices within, proclaimed to them as they approached the house that some new events had arisen in their absence.
10 On entering they discovered the shepherd's living room to be invaded by two officers from Casterbridge jail, and a well-known magistrate who lived at the nearest country-seat, intelligence of the escape having become generally circulated.

15 'Gentlemen,' said the constable, 'I have brought back your man — not without risk and danger; but every one must do his duty! He is inside this circle of able-bodied persons, who have lent me useful aid, considering their ignorance of Crown work. Men, bring forward your
20 prisoner!' And the third stranger was led to the light.

'Who is this?' said one of the officials.

'The man,' said the constable.

'Certainly not,' said the turnkey; and the first corroborated his statement.

25 'But how can it be otherwise?' asked the constable. 'Or why was he so terrified at sight o' the singing instrument of the law who sat there?' Here he related the strange behaviour of the third stranger on entering the house during the hangman's song.

30 'Can't understand it,' said the officer coolly. 'All I know is that it is not the condemned man. He's quite a different character from this one; a gauntish fellow,

with dark hair and eyes, rather good-looking, and with a
musical bass voice that if you heard it once you'd never
mistake as long as you lived.'

'Why, souls —'t was the man in the chimney-corner!'

'Hey — what?' said the magistrate, coming forward
after inquiring particulars from the shepherd in the background. 'Have n't you got the man after all?'

'Well, sir,' said the constable, 'he's the man we were
in search of, that's true; and yet he's not the man we were
in search of. For the man we were in search of was not
the man we wanted, sir, if you understand my every-day
way; for 't was the man in the chimney-corner!'

'A pretty kettle of fish altogether!' said the magistrate.
'You had better start-for the other man at once.'

The prisoner now spoke for the first time. The mention
of the man in the chimney-corner seemed to have moved
him as nothing else could do. 'Sir,' he said, stepping forward to the magistrate, 'take no more trouble about me.
The time is come when I may as well speak. I have done
nothing; my crime is that the condemned man is my
brother. Early this afternoon I left home at Shottsford to
tramp it all the way to Casterbridge jail to bid him farewell.
I was benighted, and called here to rest and ask the way.
When I opened the door I saw before me the very man, my
brother, that I thought to see in the condemned cell at
Casterbridge. He was in this chimney-corner; and jammed
close to him, so that he could not have got out if he had
tried, was the executioner who'd come to take his life,
singing a song about it and not knowing that it was his
victim who was close by, joining in to save appearances.
My brother looked a glance of agony at me, and I knew
he meant, "Don't reveal what you see; my life depends

on it." I was so terror-struck that I could hardly stand, and, not knowing what I did, I turned and hurried away.'

The narrator's manner and tone had the stamp of truth, and his story made a great impression on all around. 'And 5 do you know where your brother is at the present time?' asked the magistrate.

'I do not. I have never seen him since I closed this door.'

'I can testify to that, for we've been between ye ever 10 since,' said the constable.

'Where does he think to fly to? — what is his occupation?'

'He's a watch-and-clock-maker, sir.'

''A said 'a was a wheelwright — a wicked rogue,' said 15 the constable.

'The wheels of clocks and watches he meant, no doubt,' said Shepherd Fennel. 'I thought his hands were palish for's trade.'

'Well, it appears to me that nothing can be gained by 20 retaining this poor man in custody,' said the magistrate; 'your business lies with the other, unquestionably.'

And so the little man was released off-hand; but he looked nothing the less sad on that account, it being beyond the power of magistrate or constable to raze out the 25 written troubles in his brain, for they concerned another whom he regarded with more solicitude than himself. When this was done, and the man had gone his way, the night was found to be so far advanced that it was deemed useless to renew the search before the next morning.

30 Next day, accordingly, the quest for the clever sheepstealer became general and keen, to all appearance at least. But the intended punishment was cruelly disproportioned

to the transgression, and the sympathy of a great many
country-folk in that district was strongly on the side of
the fugitive. Moreover, his marvellous coolness and daring in hob-and-nobbing with the hangman, under the unprecedented circumstances of the shepherd's party, won 5
their admiration. So that it may be questioned if all those
who ostensibly made themselves so busy in exploring woods
and fields and lanes were quite so thorough when it came
to the private examination of their own lofts and outhouses.
Stories were afloat of a mysterious figure being occasionally 10
seen in some old overgrown trackway or other, remote from
turnpike roads; but when a search was instituted in any
of these suspected quarters nobody was found. Thus the
days and weeks passed without tidings.

In brief, the bass-voiced man of the chimney-corner was 15
never recaptured. Some said that he went across the sea,
others that he did not, but buried himself in the depths of
a populous city. At any rate, the gentleman in cinder-gray
never did his morning's work at Casterbridge, nor met
anywhere at all, for business purposes, the genial comrade 20
with whom he had passed an hour of relaxation in the
lonely house on the coomb.

The grass has long been green on the graves of Shepherd
Fennel and his frugal wife; the guests who made up the
christening party have mainly followed their entertainers 25
to the tomb; the baby in whose honour they all had met
is a matron in the sere and yellow leaf. But the arrival of
the three strangers at the shepherd's that night, and the
details connected therewith, is a story as well known as
ever in the country about Higher Crowstairs. 30

TANGLED TRAPS

" Time for you get up. I been down lake; got big trout t'rough de ice."

Sandy was lying rolled up in his blankets in the little trapper's lean-to. It was a bitter cold Sunday morning,
5 and Sandy had no mind to get up.

" I 'm all busted up. Hurt my ankle yesterday coming home. You get breakfast, Jose."

The twinkle in Sandy's eyes made Jose suspicious, but he said nothing and got the breakfast. When it was ready
10 he called, and Sandy, forgetting all about his ankle, jumped out of bed, doused his head with water from the lake, and soon had a large pile of bones stacked by his plate to testify to the size of his appetite.

When breakfast was over, Sandy left Jose to wash the
15 dishes, and picking up his axe, began chopping wood for the next week's fire. This was a duty in which both men usually took a part, but to-day, when the dishes were done, Jose instead of picking up his axe, sat down by the fire and filled his pipe. He did not like the tricks that
20 Sandy was always playing on him. Besides, they did not appear like tricks to him : his mind was too machine-like to get pleasure from anything out of his daily routine. The affair of the morning nettled him so that he did not realize that Sandy was chopping all the wood. All day

450

he sat glumly smoking his pipe, puffing the smoke out in little angry clouds; nor could Sandy with his greasy pack of cards coax him out of this mood.

Next morning the men started out on their trap-lines to meet again only in the middle of the week, for they had arranged their traps in a great circle that took a week to work over. Just before starting, Sandy had borrowed Jose's tobacco and had forgotten to return it. Jose did not notice his loss until he made his noon halt; the discovery set him thinking again about Sandy's tricks. All the rest of the day his anger kept growing. Why was Sandy always shirking his part of the work? Why was he keeping those beaver skins cached in the woods instead of bringing them to camp? Of course they were safe where Jose had accidentally found them, but it was not the custom to cache skins in the woods and not say anything about them in camp.

In his lone camp that night the loss of his accustomed smoke again turned his thoughts to Sandy. The beaver skins again troubled him, for beaver skins were getting valuable. He began to recall all Sandy's actions before they had set out that morning. Why had Sandy taken a fresh box of cartridges? He had said he had seen bear signs, but usually a full magazine in their rifles was all the men carried, for they used traps and shot only for bait. For an hour or more he sat brooding, an angry flush spreading over his face. He saw it all now. Sandy was going to shoot a bear, and *he* was the bear. It was getting towards spring; he had been allowed to work all winter, and was now to be killed and his furs taken to some distant post. Well, two could play at the bear game, and now was the time for him to act.

All the rest of the night Jose swung along the back
trail through the moon-lit woods, and just before dawn
broke he stuck his snow-shoes into the drift by the lean-to.
He stopped only for a meal and then, with a heavy pack,
5 started off again on his trap-line. The going was easier
now that it was fully light, and at noon he was back at
his last night's camp. Here again he stopped for a meal
and then, heedless of his traps, pushed straight on to the
mid-week camp where he was to meet Sandy in the even-
10 ing of the next day. Here he camped for the night, worn
out by his long tramp. Still he did not sleep well, and
with the first glimmer of light he was up and cooking his
breakfast. When this was over, he again shouldered his
pack and started off on the trail.

15   He walked until he came in sight of two great boulders,
between which the trail ran as if in a narrow gorge. Here
he made a detour and came up to the trail again just below
the rocks. Next he slipped off his snow-shoes and, using
one as a shovel, dug a pit in the trail through the soft
20 snow. Then he opened the pack and drew out a great
steel bear trap. It took him several minutes to open its
great jaws, but with the aid of the trap-wrench he finally
managed to set it, placed it in the hole, chained it to a sap-
ling, and covered the whole with snow. Then, smoothing
25 out the snow with a pine bough so that everything looked
as before, he backed away behind a thick clump of bushes
to wait.

He did not have to wait long, for not many of the traps
on Sandy's line had been touched and, in consequence, his
30 work had been light. Soon Jose heard his loud voice
singing in the distance and then saw his tall figure come
swinging down the hillside. Jose waited no longer, but

slipped off through the bushes and back down the trail. A loud yell brought him to a standstill and then two shots rang out in rapid succession. Jose waited for one more shot and then started back to the trap on the run. As he came in sight of the man on the ground, he uttered a cry 5 of surprise and, dashing up, snatched the rifle from Sandy's unsuspecting hands. Then he threw it into the bushes, stepped back, and began to laugh. He laughed till the noise rang out through the woods and returned again more devilish than it began. The echo silenced him, but he 10 broke out again tauntingly.

"You catch bear? Ha! I catch him one too. *Sacré diable*, you steal my fur? You kill me? Run off? Ha ha! I find you out! I make it the first one, yes? Go on, cuss all you want. I help you. No, I go camp now; come 15 again to-night, to-morrow, see how long you live. I hope you live long time. Those skin you hide in de woods help you keep warm, hey? You got him in your pack? Like hell. You got nothing in your pack but a knife to stick in me, yes?" The wounded man raised himself and threw 20 the offending knife into the bushes.

"There, now do you believe me?" he said. "I have nothing now that can harm you. Look in the pack and see."

Jose stepped forward and kicked the pack to a safe dis- 25 tance. Something in Sandy's frank eyes seemed to tell him that perhaps he had made a mistake, but he was not convinced.

"I open it for make you one damn liar," he said. Slowly he began to untie the wet knots. One came undone and 30 he turned to leer at Sandy. He did not know why he was undoing the bundle; he was sure that he should not find

the skins, but something in those eyes told him that he
must go on. He untied another knot and now he had only
to unroll the covering. Here he stopped to fill and light
his pipe.

5   " You steal my tobacco; now I have all yours."

" Open the pack."

Jose could not endure the look in Sandy's eyes, so he
unrolled the cover and there lay the soft brown furs. He
began to feel now that he had made a mistake, but his
10 slow moving mind was not satisfied.

" You bring him into camp, then kill me with all
those cartridges you take to kill the bear. You damn
fine liar."

" You will find the bear skin back on the trail, Jose."
15 The steady eyes were getting more troublesome to Jose
now. He could not look at them squarely. For a few
moments he stood hesitating, and then the eyes conquered.
With a cry he sprang forward, trap-wrench in hand.

" I fix you up all right in one small jiffy. I make one
20 damn' poor mistake. You be all right pretty soon." The
wrench slipped in his feverish haste, but he soon had the
great saw-toothed jaws apart and was at work trying to
staunch the flow of blood that was spurting out from the
shattered ankle. A thong from a snow-shoe twisted about
25 the knee with a stick soon reduced the flow and then the
work began in real earnest. Two poles with a blanket tied
across served as an Indian drag, and with Sandy on this and
Jose pulling him they at last got into camp. Here Jose
made his companion as comfortable as he could and then
30 started for the main camp to get the toboggan with which
to carry Sandy to a doctor. Sandy was constantly growing
weaker, for he had lost much blood and the pain from his
foot was severe.

All that night Jose ran on through the silent woods, making good time while the moon still shone, but blundering and stumbling along after it had gone down. His face and clothes were torn by the bushes and his body was covered with welts and bruises from falls, but he pressed 5 doggedly on until after sunrise he reached the main camp. He was nearly spent now, but he hardly stopped. Snatching a few pieces of dried meat for nourishment, he started back again, hauling the toboggan.

Again came the blind onward rush of the night before, 10 only now he had the light to help him, but even this had some disadvantages. On every side he saw some sign of Sandy's work to remind him of his own treachery. Here was a trap set on a stump with its little box of splinters driven into the decaying wood, and there was a dead-fall 15 made in Sandy's peculiar fashion. At each new sign he pulled the toboggan thong more tightly, and the snow-shoes crunched faster.

Still, it was nearly midnight when Jose reached the camp where Sandy lay. As he came up, he noticed that 20 the fire sent out only a dull glow. He hastened on, calling, but there was no answer. As he went into the shack, he threw a few sticks on the smoldering embers and by their light he saw Sandy stretched out on the blanket. As the fire blazed higher, Jose's trained eyes read what had 25 happened. The rumpled blankets told how the man had writhed in his pain until the thong had loosened and the blood had begun to flow again. At first it had been unnoticed, but a bloody stick still held in the man's cold hand told how he had tried to tighten the thong. He had 30 been overcome in the very act and had sunk back on the blankets to die, while his blood had oozed out into a little red puddle and had now frozen.

The horror of the sight first dazed Jose, and then the terror of remorse began to eat its way into his numbed brain. Slowly he sank down on the ground beside his dead companion. Outside, the fire began to burn low. 5 A wind from the south stirred the boughs of the pines overhead. Away in the distance a little hoot-owl sent out its dismal cry. The fire slumped down to a bed of coals and then all was still.

THE QUEST OF THE BACILLUS

I

"And ever since then I've been as hungry as the dickens."

They were sitting in the dim light of red-shaded candles: the speaker, an alert young fellow, and the other his uncle, a middle-aged gentleman with the weary look which tells of dyspepsia. As the young man spoke he gave his whole attention to the oysters before him, but Rufus Prescott put down his fork and adjusted the red candle-shade abstractedly.

"Harriet must have stayed to dinner at the Peabodys'," he remarked. "But tell me some more about your typhoid fever. Sickness that makes you hungry must be a blessed sort to have! Were you very sick?"

"No; typhoid in North Carolina just means lying in bed for three or four weeks and having to take sloppy drinks. Nurse reads to you, or fans you, or does anything you want. It amounts to a big holiday. To be sure they souse ice water all over you, but you get used to that in time."

"You seem to have found typhoid fever rather a pleasant summer diversion," said Rufus Prescott, watching the boy's soup disappear.

"So it is, in North Carolina, — with a pretty nurse. But really, Uncle, everybody has typhoid down South in summer. Why, in July the purest brooks from the mountains and the artesian wells are full of fever germs. But everybody has it light down there; and it's considered poor taste to die of it."

"And isn't the getting over it rather tiresome?" asked the uncle with a show of interest, for he liked to hear the lad rattle on.

"No; that's the best part of it, 'cause you're so hungry. I used to sit up in bed and check off in the cook-book the things I wanted. Besides the appetite part, after you've had typhoid fever you're almost sure not to catch anything else. I haven't been sick a day since I came North."

"There seems to be no end to the advantages furnished by the sickness!"

"My curly hair is another thing. I could run on like this all the evening though, except"—looking at his watch—"I've got to meet a fellow down at Forty-second Street by quarter of eight, so I'm afraid I'll have to cut the rest of your excellent repast which you yourself don't seem to appreciate. Good night, Uncle; better go South and have typhoid yourself. It's the great panacea for all human ills."

When the young fellow had gone Rufus Prescott touched the bell. "James," he said, "you need not serve any more of the dinner; but send my coffee to the library."

As he sat in the library, puffing thoughtfully at his long cigar, he considered the lad's last sentence: "Better go South and have typhoid yourself, Uncle." Suddenly he smiled. What if there should be something in it after all? What if he should lay off from his business next summer, go South, and get a mild case of typhoid? What if he could get back his appetite? Wouldn't it be worth lying in bed a month or so to feel the old boyhood relish for his food once more? "If I find that boy's chatter to-night is true, I'll go to North Carolina next summer," he said aloud.

And reaching up to the bookcase, he took down the volume of the Encyclopedia labelled "Targets–Unicorn."

Two hours later, when his wife got home, she found him drawn up close under the reading lamp with several big volumes lying open around. He said nothing, for he was wondering how he could best broach his project to her.

"Why, Rufus," she said, glancing at the four cigar ends in his ash tray; "you know what the doctor said about your smoking too much."

"Well really, Harriet, I did n't realize how many cigars I was smoking," he replied, trying to smile ingratiatingly, "I've been so absorbed. You see, I've got an idea." He was almost boyish now in his eagerness to tell her. "I'm going South to catch typhoid fever and get an appetite."

"You're going crazy, Rufus Prescott! Tell me what on earth you mean."

"Now don't get excited, Harriet. I mean just what I say. To-night Harry was in for dinner and he told me all about his being sick last summer: what an easy time he had of it, how little danger there is down South, what a fine appetite he's had ever since, and how he feels better than he ever did before."

"Oh! I see; and so you want to go and do likewise. What a joker you are, Rufus. I suppose you got out all these books, and have been thinking this up all the evening."

"It's no joke, I assure you."

"Nonsense, Rufus! Why, even if I were n't here to prevent you, you can't catch typhoid whenever you want. It's caused by tenements with poor plumbing."

"No; Harry said that down South in summer all the water was simply reeking with typhoid germs. What he

says about drinking water being the infecting agent is correct. I have been reading about the disease in this excellent article in the Encyclopedia. Just listen to one or two of these sentences. 'The cause of typhoid is largely
5 due to infected water.' Here's another: 'The patient's health is apt to be much better after than before the attack.'"

"Now, Rufus, do you really expect me to take this as a serious scheme?"

10 "Yes; I've been thinking the plan out pretty carefully the last two hours. My idea is to arrange my affairs next June so that I can get away for a couple of months and then to go down with a trained nurse to some small Carolina town, and hire a cottage. The doctors down there
15 understand the treatment of the disease perfectly."

"Well, for sheer, downright absurdity, Rufus Prescott, you do certainly excel any one I ever had the pleasure of knowing. What's to become of me during all that time, I'd like to know?"

20 "Why, you'll go along too, and help take care of me."

"But I don't want to catch the fever, drinking infected water."

"My dear Harriet, I am surprised. The water that you drink will be boiled and will in that way be perfectly
25 sterilized. I think I'll go to bed now and answer your other questions to-morrow. If I'm alive next summer, and have no better appetite than I have now, I'm going to put this scheme through."

"The whole thing is simply arrant nonsense, and if I
30 can prevent it, you never shall go, never!"

II

"Well, here we are," said Rufus Prescott to his wife, as he settled back in his comfortable Pullman chair and watched the Jersey City freight yards skim backwards past the car window. "When I proposed this last December you didn't think I was in earnest, did you? And I'll 5 admit that a June day like this almost makes me wish I were back on the ferryboat. Did you get the nurse all right?"

"Yes, she's in the second car back, I think. She's not good-looking, but she seemed kind."   10

"Sounds as though you were talking about a dog," grumbled he. "If you don't care to talk I think I'll read until we get to Philadelphia." And he pulled out of his suit case an enormous volume entitled *Enteric Fevers and Their Treatment.* "I got it this morning," he con- 15 fessed. "Whole first half of the book is on typhoid. Please remember, my dear, that it is typhoid and *not* typhus fever which I am to have; there is a world of difference between the two." And he settled himself back to read.

At Philadelphia he laid down the book. "Seems a pity 20 we have to waste time stopping here," he remarked; "I'm going out to get a time-table."

When he returned he found his wife deep in the typhoid section. "Oh, Rufus," she exclaimed, "according to this book, typhoid is one of the most dangerous diseases 25 that exists. It is full of all sorts of the most fearful complications."

"There, Harriet; I thought I advised you not to read that book. I knew just how it would be if you did read it. You don't seem to realize that I have verified Harry's 30

statements about the danger of the disease. I have been corresponding with the town to which we are going and I find that the proportion of deaths is less than two per cent of the number of cases. I have also found out that
5 they have an excellent doctor in Spartaca."

"And shall you begin drinking infected water just as soon as you get to Spartaca?" ventured his wife.

"No; I shall go to the hotel first and shall look around for a suitable cottage. Then I shall send samples of
10 the drinking water from the various rentable houses to Charleston to be analyzed. When we find a house that has infected water we shall promptly take it; and then for a period of martyrdom for me, with a rich reward beyond. And," he added, "we are not to mention our
15 scheme to any one down there; they would think we were demented."

All that night they sped southward through Washington, Baltimore, and on into Virginia. The next noon they reached Charleston; there changed to an accommodation
20 train, and began to approach their final destination. When only about ten minutes from Spartaca Rufus appeared to be ill at ease.

"I'm afraid the climate down here may ruin my constitution," he murmured. "I've half a mind to let the ex-
25 periment slide, and go right back North."

"Well, let's go back then; it isn't too late yet."

"No," he returned savagely, "I'm no coward. I'll see the thing through. But Harriet," he went on more softly, "if I should happen to be among the two per cent, you'll
30 find all my affairs up North arranged."

"Nonsense, Rufus; don't look on the dark — "

"Spartaca," called the brakeman.

They did nothing that evening about a house but went straight to the hotel. The next day Rufus Prescott set out house-hunting, while his wife tried to find a cool spot on the hotel piazza.

At noon Rufus came back, hot but triumphant. "I 've found three houses," he managed to puff out to his wife, "and one of them is a beauty. I got drinking water from each house by telling the agents there was no chance of my taking the house without first determining the purity of the drinking water by analysis. The agent of that best house was most reluctant to have the water-supply examined; I guess that 's the place for us. We 'll go up and see the house this evening."

After supper they sauntered up to look over the best cottage of the three. It stood a little outside the town, on a small hill, and was surrounded by great pines.

"What a view !" exclaimed Mrs. Prescott.

"Yes; and what a piazza to see it from," echoed her husband. "I can sit out here in the evening and smo— Oh, no, I can't; not many evenings. I forgot."

"What are the upstairs rooms like? I don't feel like climbing the stairs."

"Very convenient," replied Rufus. "There 's a large sunny one for me at the front of the house, with a small adjacent one which the nurse can have. Over the dining room is one that would suit you perfectly."

The next day they spent quietly, waiting to hear from the Charleston chemist, and the day after that they received his telegram. Rufus tore it open and read it aloud to his wife: "Water pure, except number three which contains typhoid germs."

"Ah, I told you that was the place for us," Rufus said; "we'll move in to-morrow. I've got my eye on a black boy, Sam, to work for us. He says he's used to cooking; and besides, the nurse'll have to do most of that."

So the next day they moved in, and that evening sat out on their piazza in the gathering dusk. Rufus Prescott was pulling quickly at his cigar. "I shall have to quit soon, and I might as well have a few last good smokes," he remarked. Far away they could hear the monotonous song of two whip-poor-wills calling and answering one another. Inside there was the murmur of the nurse's voice as she talked with Sam. Rufus and his wife felt the charm of the misty southern moonlight which stole down through the branches of the great pines, and they sat a long time without speaking; he thinking hard, and she wondering what he was thinking about.

Finally he spoke: "Well, I don't suppose there's any use putting it off."

Then he raised his voice. "Sam, you inside there?"

A husky voice came back: "Yes, suh."

"Well, just bring me out a pitcher of ice water and a glass, Sam."

"Yes, suh; 'll you have the boiled water, suh?"

"No, that's too tasteless; bring it just as it comes from the faucet."

"All right, suh."

When the pitcher with its cool clink of ice had been brought, and Sam had gone back, Rufus Prescott filled his glass and raised it. "Here's to you, Harriet, and to my future rejuvenated self." With that he thoughtfully emptied the glass.

"Mercy, Rufus; you don't need to be so solemn about it. I feel as if you were drinking the hemlock."

"Very good water, very good indeed!" said he, totally disregarding his wife's remarks; "and now I think I'll go to bed so as to be as fit as possible when I come down with the fever."

The next day was very hot and oppressive; the thermometer registered 88°. At breakfast Rufus remarked, "I've been glancing over my book, and I find that backache, headache, and general lassitude are the most marked of the early symptoms. The fever comes on very slowly, I believe, but still I do feel an unaccountable indolence this morning."

That day, however, he went off on horseback, and came home with a large appetite — for him. After supper he again took a large dose of water. "I guess this is the most heroic water cure ever attempted, Harriet," he remarked.

The next day he felt particularly brisk and the programme of the previous day was repeated. And so a week passed and each day Rufus Prescott had more appetite and felt more alert.

"Had it occurred to you that I am eating more than I usually do?" he asked his wife one day.

"Almost twice as much, I should say," replied she; "if you keep this up you won't have to have fever."

"I must double the water dose," was his reply.

And so the second and third weeks went by, with Rufus in better spirits every day. On the last evening of their third week they were again sitting quietly on the piazza, and again the whip-poor-wills were reiterating their duet of endless complaint. They had been reading in the typhoid book until it became too dark.

The peace of the twilight was suddenly broken by Rufus jumping to his feet. "We're going back to-morrow to God's country!" he burst out. "I'm not going to tempt Providence by fishing for this accursed fever another 5 day!"

Then, snatching the carafe of ice water, he pitched it out of sight into the underbrush, and sent *Enteric Fevers and Their Treatment* whirling after it.

"Sam," he called, "go down to-night to the station and 10 engage three berths on to-morrow's Northern Limited." And then, catching a queer look in his wife's eye, he added, "You see, it's better to get them ahead and make sure of them, my dear."

III

It is a sultry day and the sun is beating down on a 15 Carolina hillside with such heat that a little lizard has come out to bask in the warmth. Motionless, he stretches himself across a curious object, — a book lying in a clump of ferns, twisted out of shape and with its leaves swollen and stained by rain and mud.

20 There are still some words which have not been washed out: "The cause of typhoid fever is largely due to infected water, but even infected water may have no effect on a person in sound physical condition. The earliest symptoms are — " But here the lizard's tail curls across 25 the page and hides the rest of the sentence.

NOTES

The following notes are not intended to be exhaustive or restrictive. Consequently teachers are at liberty to use their own methods of analysis and to invent various constructive exercises. Many, however, may wish to see a few comments which have been useful in class-room practice. Students particularly should find these notes suggestive in a detailed study of the specimens.

EXPOSITION

Taxation and Government (p. 3). This is an example of the simplest kind of exposition, i.e. definition. Unity is obtained by various means. The point of view which unifies the treatment of the subject is that of a writer who endeavors to interpret a complex subject in terms of concrete and daily experience. He shows how taxes affect the individual citizen. Notice how the two divisions of the subject — taxation and government — are treated, first individually, then in their inter-relations. A detailed plan will reveal the excellence of the structure. To secure the first element of Coherence — order — the writer proceeds from the treatment of taxes, by an inevitable transition, to the treatment of government (p. 5. ll. 9–20); then, by uniting both subjects in a single definition (p. 6, ll. 14–15), he amplifies their relations. Various technical devices to secure Coherence are "transition paragraphs" (p. 5, l. 9; p. 6, l. 7), skillful transitions from paragraph to paragraph, and transitions from sentence to sentence. A valuable exercise is to underline all words and phrases which serve as connectives. Emphasis is attained in the beginning of the article by stating in an interesting way the necessity of understanding the puzzling subject of taxation, and in the ending by a hypothetical case which explains the matter poignantly. Note how excellent the proportion is. Observe the various methods of obtaining Emphasis in paragraphs and in sentences (p. 3, par. 1; p. 4, ll. 5–12). This extract illustrates various devices especially valuable in analytic writing: the skillful definition of terms, often by stating the meaning of each before giving it a technical name; and the use of concrete and homely illustration (p. 3, ll. 3–5, 16–20; p. 4, ll. 13 ff.).

The Popular Ballad (p. 10). This is an example of definition. The effectiveness of this selection consists largely in the thoroughness with which the mind is cleared of modern notions about individual composition. Here, as often, explanation consists in clearing away misconceptions. As the discussion proceeds, the conditions, all the time really becoming more unfamiliar, are made, by the cumulative effect of the explanation, to seem more and more natural. Let the student discover the means by which Unity, Coherence, and Emphasis are secured. Note the use of parallel structure to secure Coherence in sentences.

A Gentleman (p. 16). This is an example of definition. It is now two centuries or more since it was the fashion in literature to portray a whole class of people under the guise of a typical individual. In such portrayal the task, which Cardinal Newman has here effectively accomplished, is to select traits which are of general significance and to combine them so that the result will not affront us by seeming to be a prodigy constructed for didactic purposes. Note the repetition of the pronoun, and balance the consequent gain in Coherence against the danger of a monotonous type of sentence. The balanced constructions (p. 16, ll. 17–20; p. 17, ll. 15–17) are effective. A study of the abstract and of the Latin words will enlarge the student's vocabulary.

An Indian House (p. 19). This is an exposition of a process, — how to make something. The structure of this selection has been analyzed in the Introduction (pp. xv, xvi). The conclusion is not strictly a summary, but it leaves the reader with an impression of the complete house and its inhabitants. Note the careful use of authorities: credit should always be given to authorities cited. The tendency to use the imperative monotonously, common to students in writing an exposition of a process, may be avoided as well when the tense is present or future as when it is past, by variety in sentence structure.

Self-Cultivation in English (p. 23). This is an exposition of a process, — how to do something. This selection is particularly valuable for its subject-matter — directions for enlarging the vocabulary — and for its practice of the principles it preaches. It will repay careful analysis for the means by which Unity, Coherence, and Emphasis are obtained in the whole composition and in the paragraphs. The announcement of procedure and the summary have been mentioned in the Introduction (pp. xix, xx). The illustrations and figures of speech are particularly effective, because they deal with familiar things. Note the figures of the glove (p. 24, ll. 23–27) and of the bad cook (p. 30, ll. 22–24). The quotations from Ben Jonson, Henry Ward Beecher, Thomas Jefferson, etc., add to clearness and to force, and contribute liveliness to the style.

Preparation for War (p. 33). The title given to this selection is not as exact as it should be. What would be a better title? The selection illustrates well the very serviceable method in analytic writing of mentioning the larger phases of the subject first, and then resolving each phase into its subordinate points for more specific treatment. It is profitable to study the Coherence of sentences and use of the topic sentence in the paragraphs. Wherein is the concluding paragraph excellent?

Life in the Wilderness (p. 39). The effectiveness of this exposition of a condition of civilization is due largely to the use of concrete detail. What is the order of treatment of the topics, and is it a good one for this subject? What is the purpose of the conclusion, and how does it differ from other conclusions which have been mentioned? (See Introduction, p. xx.)

The Uniformity of American Life (p. 44). This selection shows how descriptive elements contribute to the clearness of an exposition. Where are they to be found, and what is their force? Do any paragraphs seem at first ill-proportioned? Study the paragraphs on pp. 46, 47. Does not the importance of New Orleans and San Francisco call for this amount of space? Note the admirable structure of the paragraph from the foot of p. 44 to p. 46. The treatment proceeds from the familiar (America) to the less familiar (England) and to the unfamiliar (Italy) and then back again. This method of proceeding from the known to the unknown is useful in securing clearness in analytic writing. Are there any examples of parallel structure? What is their function? Note the announcement of procedure. Compare it with that in *Self-Cultivation in English.*

Coral and Coral Reefs (p. 52). Study this selection for the characteristics of good exposition: plan, method of procedure, definitions, point of view, illustrations, transitions, and summaries.

Æs Triplex (p. 59). The title of this selection is found in the following lines in Horace (Odes, Book I, Ode 3):

> Illi robur et aes triplex
> Circa pectus erat, qui fragilem truci
> Commisit pelago ratem
> Primus.

" Æs Triplex " is thus the symbol of indomitable courage. This exposition deals with abstract and eternal facts, — with man's attitude toward life and death. The definite thesis is " that we do not love life, in the sense that we are greatly preoccupied about its conservation ; that we do not, properly speaking, love life at all, but living " (p. 63). A subject which thus baldly stated would seem abstract and forbidding can be treated with extraordinary concreteness, humor, and charm. It is not formal exposition but personal exposition in which the point of view, necessary in the other cases as a means to an end, becomes here of chief importance. This essay is based on the character of the writer, and it has pathetic and heroic significance when viewed in the light of his fight for health. The consequent "happy valiancy of style" is revealed by the quaint mixture of solemnity and fun, the beauty of single phrases, the trenchant concreteness of the images, and the buoyancy and rhythm of the sentences.

68 21 Permanent Possibility of Sensation: a phrase of John Stuart Mill. See *Examination of Sir Wm. Hamilton's Philosophy*, Vol. I, chap. xi.

John Gilley (p. 73). This selection illustrates the use of the narrative element in biography; incidents are recounted that show character. What are the characteristics of this narrative style? Note the restrained eloquence of the final paragraph. Contrast the force and pregnancy of the ending with the ordinary perfunctory eulogy. This is the best kind of subject for students who are writing biography. It is well to take men who are not famous, but who ought to be.

Sir William Temple (p. 79). This selection illustrates the use of the analytic element in biography; one trait of character is explained, illustrated, and amplified. Study how Unity may be attained in analysis of character. Note how not only Unity but Coherence is attained by holding the point of view long enough to write a paragraph. How is this illustrated in the structure of sentences? Compare the method with that in *A Gentleman* (p. 16), and with that in *Westminster Hall* (p. 282).

A Poor Relation (p. 83). This is an example of the descriptive element in biography; it so deals with a man's appearance that he can be visualized. What is the point of view assumed in this particular selection, and what is the consequent gain in force? Note how suspense, held to the very end, secures Emphasis. The selection is only one paragraph in a long essay. If it were to be regarded as a complete whole composition, where should it be divided into paragraphs?

83 16 Tower: the significance of this remark is due to the fact that the Mint was in the Tower of London.

84 10 Grotiuses: Hugo Grotius (1583–1645) was a Dutch jurist, theologian, and poet, founder of the science of international law. His chief work was *De Jure Belli et Pacis* (1625).

Frank Dickson (p. 86). This is an example of the descriptive element in biography; it shows not only a man's characteristics, but how those characteristics affect his appearance and manner. Note the variety of vivid phrases emphasizing the trait of humor.

86 18 Annandale Rabelais: Annandale was the village in Scotland where Dickson lived. François Rabelais (1495–1553) was a French humorist, author of the novels *Pantagruel* (1533) and *Gargantua* (1535).

87 5 Gargantuisms: a word which Carlyle coined from *Gargantua*. See preceding note.

Sir **Walter Scott** (p. 92). This selection is an example of appreciative criticism. It analyzes the quality of romance which made Scott "the king of the romantics." Note the hearty enjoyment and the thorough manliness of the criticism. The article shows that first rate criticism is entirely worthy of the highest powers of a robust and original writer. When students' criticisms of books are perfunctory, much profit will result from the study of a critical opinion written with virility and gusto. Note the use of epigram and paradox. To understand this criticism completely, students should read the passages referred to.

95 8 Sir Arthur Wardour: see *The Antiquary*, chap. vii.

95 14 Rob Roy: see *Rob Roy*, chap. xxiii.

95 21 Colonel Mannering: See *Guy Mannering*, chap. xlix.

96 16 Clerk of Copmanhurst: Friar Tuck in *Ivanhoe.* — **Mr. Pleydell**: a character in *Guy Mannering*.

Robert Louis Stevenson (p. 97). This is an example of appreciative criticism which shows the relation between a man's life and his work. Its notable traits are sympathetic knowledge, real emotion, and charm of style. Study the variety and flexibility of sentence structure. Notice the easy command of allusion as contrasted with the heavy references common in many articles.

98 5 historian of Wessex: Thomas Hardy.

98 7 a strong young Occidental: Rudyard Kipling.

98 32 Esperance and set on: the motto of Harry Hotspur at the battle of Shrewsbury in *Henry the Fourth, Part I*.

99 12 A Christmas Sermon or Pulvis et Umbra: both in *Across the Plains*.

99 14 a great novelist: George Eliot.

99 20–23 These lines occur in *Andrea del Sarto*, by Robert Browning.

100 9 The Foreigner at Home: in *Memories and Portraits*.

100 10 The Manse: in *Memories and Portraits*.

100 13 Probably Arboreal: suggested by the following sentence in Darwin's definition of the ancestor of man, in *The Descent of Man*, Part II, chap. xxi. "Man is descended from a hairy quadruped, furnished with a tail and pointed ears, probably arboreal in its habits, and an inhabitant of the Old World."

100 20 memorial: Skerryvore.

101 3 Vaea Mountain: the place of Stevenson's burial in the Samoan Islands.

101 23 scene in Guy Mannering which jars on him: the scene is in *Guy Mannering*, chap. xli. For a discussion of this scene, see " A Gossip on Romance " in *Memories and Portraits*.

102 16 the appearance of Meg Merrilies: see *Guy Mannering*, chap. viii, toward the end.

102 17 abdication of Queen Mary: see *The Abbot*, chap. xxii. — the installation of the abbot: see *The Abbot*, chaps. xiii, xiv.

102 18 the appeal of Jeanie Deans: see *Heart of Midlothian*, chap. xxxvi.

102 19 a certain scene: see *Old Mortality*, chap. xlii.

102 23 Alan and Davie: see *Kidnapped*, chap. xx.

102 24 windmills in Holland: see *David Balfour*, chap. xxx.

102 25 duel: see *The Master of Ballantrae*, chap. iv.

103 11 Providence and the Guitar: see *New Arabian Nights.*

103 14 A Story of Francis Villon: see " A Lodging for the Night " in *New Arabian Nights.*

103 18 redcoats: see *Kidnapped*, chap. xx.

103 20 Hyde: see *Dr. Jekyll and Mr. Hyde.*

103 26 Forest of Gerolstein: see *Prince Otto*, Bk. III, chap. i.

103 27 Bass Rock: see *David Balfour*, chap. xiv.

104 24 Wegg: a character in Dickens's *Our Mutual Friend.*

ARGUMENT

Government Management of Industrial Enterprises (p. 116). This selection is simply the introduction to an argument. The student should reduce it to "brief form," after searching for the constituent elements of every introduction to a brief, i.e. what is significant in the history and the definition of the question, what matter is admitted by both sides, and what are the special issues upon which the decision of the question depends. A preliminary study of the introductions of the briefs by students (pp. 161, 204) will be of material aid.

The Fallacy of the Balance of Trade (p. 120). This selection is simply an example of the handling of refutation in an argument. Study the way in which the fallacious argument of the other side is first expounded and then refuted.

The Public Duty of Educated Men (p. 123). This selection illustrates Persuasion. It should be studied as an example of how the writer of argument can appeal to the higher motives and emotions of his audience. The following eight suggestions for Persuasion are given by Professor Baker:[1]

" 1. Ascertain the habits of mind of your proposed audience.

2. Determine the special interests and the idiosyncrasies of your audience.

3. Connect lower with higher motives.

[1] G. P. Baker and H. B. Huntington, *The Principles of Argumentation* (revised edition), p. 331.

4. Remember that the larger the audience the higher the motives to which appeal may be made.

' 5. Startling an audience may rout indifference or effectively emphasize.

6. Let the nature of your task determine the order of your persuasion.

7. Unify the persuasion for some definite purpose.

8. Be flexible; adapt the work to unexpected exigencies.''

How far are these eight methods illustrated in this speech? Note the use of forcible illustrations, figures, and anecdotes. The four paragraphs on p. 125, beginning l. 16, and on pp. 126, 127, and 128, first define the conditions of party spirit and then hold up the definitions to the scorn of all righteous citizens. What is the method of the conclusion, and why is it appropriate here?

125 32 **Money-changers**: see the *Gospel according to St. John, II, 13–17.*

126 31 **Jacobins**: a society of violent revolutionists organized during the French Revolution, who took their name from their place of meeting, — the Jacobin convent. Robespierre and Marat were leaders in the Reign of Terror.

128 28 **The ordeal of last winter**: the presidential election of 1876, contested by Hayes and Tilden and decided in favor of Hayes by a Commission created by Congress.

The Open Shop (p. 136). This selection is a complete argument. The absence of references, which good argument ordinarily possesses, is due to the fact that this appeared as an editorial for popular reading. The proper way of recording references by means of exponents and footnotes appears in the "Students' Briefs and Arguments," pp. 161 ff., 204 ff. The convincingness of this article is due to the combination of reasoning and evidence. The student should study the elements of which this argument is composed, their relation to each other, the proportion of parts, and the rhetorical structure.

Restriction of Immigration (p. 144). This selection is a complete argument. The absence of references, which good argument ordinarily possesses, is due to the fact, not only that this appeared as a magazine article for general reading, but that it was the work of an acknowledged authority on the subject. This argument is particularly firm and orderly. It will be a valuable exercise to draw a trial brief from it. The suggestions for study, in the previous note, will be helpful here. Is this article convincing, and why?

Students' Briefs and Arguments (pp. 161, 204). The arrangement of the two briefs and arguments by students calls for a word of explanation. The brief is first printed in its entirety, for the writer first constructed his case by means of this outline. The brief on the White Mountain question is printed parallel with the argument in order that the student may see the relations between the two. Argument presents many new problems in the application of the principles of composition. Let the student study Unity, Coherence, and Emphasis in this kind of writing. In regard to Unity, argumentative writing has many traps to catch the digressor, such as ambiguity in defining terms, ignoring the question, arguing beside the point, etc. It is because argument presents so many dangers that the student needs, not only to define his terms, but to limit himself to those definitions; and that he needs, not only to determine precisely the special issues, but to concentrate his argument upon them.

DESCRIPTION

In description, which is a record of sense impressions, the choice of material is quite as important as the technique. That material which gives opportunity for minute observation can be most effectively depicted. It is not limited, as many students would limit it, to melodramatic subjects, such as turbulent thunderstorms or exaggerated sunsets, but it includes a wide range of familiar subjects of everyday life. In technique, too, description is not usually limited to the expression of a single element, such as color, sound, point of view, but it includes nearly all the elements in combination. Consequently, skill in writing description is attained most easily by a study of the separate elements. The models of Description are so well sub-divided to show varieties of material and various technical elements that the chief purpose of each extract may be seen by reference to the table of contents. The following notes, then, will not deal with every selection. It will be profitable for the student to study in all the models the use of the following aids to Description : point of view, dominant tone, fundamental image, choice of salient details, reiteration, color, form, light, weather, motion, sound, odor, touch, taste, concrete vocabulary, figures of speech, description by effect.

A Loamshire Landscape (p. 232). Is the point of view here stationary or moving ? How is it managed ? How is Coherence obtained in dealing with this particular kind of material ?

Autumn in Wiltshire (p. 237). What is the dominant tone and how is it expressed ? How does this article illustrate the principle of Mass in Description ?

July Days (p. 239). What is the effect produced by the adjectives and the verbs? Analyze the dominant tone. What are the faults of Coherence in paragraphs? Compare with the paragraphs of *Villon and his Crew* (p. 269).

A Tropical River (p. 243). Note how Unity and Mass are obtained by the beginning and the ending. The vocabulary will well repay careful study. A good exercise would be to read the description of darkness on pp. 244 (l. 28) and 245, and then to write a description of darkness, known by personal experience.

Cities (pp. 246–251). Notice how in **Sunday in Central Park** (p. 246) and in **Mulberry Bend** (p. 249) the salient details have been chosen which most forcibly suggest the whole scene. Discuss these articles as examples of "local color." What other aids to Description are here used?

People (pp. 252–279). The first few selections are still life; the last few are groups and moving figures, or descriptions in the service of Narration. Note the skill with which Carlyle emphasizes great size in **Daniel Webster** (p. 253), and delicacy in **Thomas de Quincey** (p. 254).

253 11 Berserkir: the Berserkirs were furious Scandinavian warriors.

254 6 Her: Mrs. Carlyle

Two Portraits by Raeburn (p. 255). These portraits not only give details of appearance, but subtly suggest character. Examine the admirable phrasing.

255 1 Duncan: Adam Duncan, first Viscount Camperdown (1731–1804). A British admiral who gained the victory of Camperdown over the Dutch fleet, October 11, 1797. For an entertaining account of his character and his battles, see Stevenson's essay "The English Admirals" in *Virginibus Puerisque.*

256 2 Robert M'Queen: a brutal Scotch judge (1722–1799). He is the original of the hanging judge in *Weir of Hermiston.*

An Old Woman (p. 257). Note the superb phrasing, as in ll. 11, 22, and on p. 258, ll. 3–7. This description deals not so much with physical appearances as with a state of mind.

Beatrix Esmond (p. 259). Beatrix Esmond coming down the stairs is a famous scene in Thackeray's writings which one always remembers. What makes it memorable is not only the picturesque situation, which caught Du Maurier's eye, but also the fine rhythm of certain phrases, — notably on p. 260.

Dr. Dolliver (p. 261). Note in this selection the repetition for effect of traits of extreme age. This repetition produces both Unity and Emphasis.

A Portrait (p. 265). This is an illustration of Description in the service of Narration. The man who appears at the door in answer to Villon's knock is pictured chronologically. When the door is first opened, Villon sees only the man's physical stature. Then, as he looks more closely, the details of the head, face, etc., follow. The total impression is summed up in the last sentence. Meanwhile the story is moving, for it is necessary that the door should open and that Villon should be admitted by this man.

Villon and His Crew (p. 269). Study this selection as an illustration of Coherence in the service of Description. There are few better examples of the firmness with which different phases of the subject are handled in separate paragraphs, each excellently massed and each making as firm an effect of Unity as can be found in analytic writing, and of the way in which these paragraphs succeed each other with excellent transitions. **Villon**: the French vagabond and poet (1431–1484). For an analysis of his character, see Stevenson's essay in *Familiar Studies of Men and Books*.

The Army of France (p. 273). Study the treatment of color and motion in this selection and the sentence structure on p. 278.

Exteriors and Interiors. In **Craigie House** (p. 280) the Coherence is secured by introducing details in the order a visitor would naturally observe them. **Westminster Hall** (p. 282) is a good example of Coherence at all points. A favorite method of Macaulay is to announce a subject by a forward-looking statement. Examples of this are on p. 282, ll. 9–10, and on p. 283, ll. 19–20. A notable device is the use of parallel structure in sentences on p. 283. An effect of sublimity is gained here, not by details of personal appearance, but by the citation of titles, names, and qualities, phrased in Latin diction. In **The Wheat Pit** (p. 290) what peculiarities are to be noted in the structure? Notice, for instance, the crescendo to the climax and the diminuendo to the end. This is a very good example of sympathetic observation of details.

Dominant Tone (pp. 297–319). For a discussion of dominant tone see Introduction, p. xxiii. After the student has studied the means by which dominant tone is secured, he should write compositions illustrating different kinds of dominant tone. In **A Cold Day** (p. 309) the style is informal. Many of the sentences have not the strict Unity which rhetoricians require. The charm and the vividness of this essay is due largely to the rapid combinations, in single sentences, of unlike things. This method gives a lively impression of the omnipresence of cold.

Point of View (pp. 320–326). For a discussion of point of view see the Introduction, pp. xxi–xxiii.

Sound (pp. 333–337). The selections which illustrate sound should be studied particularly for their examples of onomatopoetic words.

Elements in Combination. These selections appeal to the various sensations. A good exercise is to write a short composition on the use of any one of the sensations appealed to, or on the use of any one of the aids to Description in any of the selections.

The Ride of Little Toomai (p. 339). This selection is a description of motion by effect. Contrast the slow motion suggested by "the high grass washed along his sides" (p. 339, ll. 7, 8) with the rapid motion suggested by " the undergrowth on either side of him ripped with a noise like torn canvas " (p. 340, ll. 10, 11).

Swimming the Whirlpool (p. 341). Note the ingenious point of view and study the ways in which it is held.

The Time of New Talk (p. 345). A good exercise in rhythm is to translate the second paragraph into blank verse, keeping the original phrasing as much as possible.

The Jungle at Night (p. 347). Let the student examine the way in which moonlight is vividly described, and write a description of a moonlight night which he can study at first hand.

A Night among the Pines (p. 349). The student can add to his vocabulary by noting the use of figures of speech and the choice of words. What is notable in the handling of the point of view both in place and in time ?

NARRATION

The Battle of Killiecrankie (p. 367). This selection is a good example of the method by which events of history are made to be as vivid as scenes in a novel. This result is obtained by the use of conversation, concrete detail, and lively action. Analyze the Coherence and the Mass of the paragraphs and of the sentences.

How I Caught Salmon in the Clackamas (p. 374). This selection is an example of simple incident, the kind of narration which most students are best able to write. It handles a single event, and its descriptive introduction is simply to give the setting first, because the scene remains unchanged. When once the movement starts, it is so rapid and so engrossing that there is room for nothing but the business at hand. Study the choice of verbs and note the echoes of Biblical phrasing.

An Elk Hunt (p. 378). In this narrative of simple adventure the scene changes with the progress of the hunters and hence description of landscape is brought in bit by bit. It is a good example of the treatment of physical sensation. The narration begins *in medias res* and continues with unbated swiftness. Study the choice of verbs.

The Battle of the Ants (p. 385). This selection is an illustration of how a narrative which deals with such minute things as the miniature war of ants may be quite as exciting as an account of the wars of nations. Compare with *The Battle of Killiecrankie* (p. 367).

The Story of Muhammad Din (p. 389). Let the student analyze the selection to see how unity of effect is produced. What are the advantages of the beginning and of the ending ? The rapidity with which sympathy for Muhammad Din is aroused, short as is the reader's acquaintance with him, leads to genuine sorrow at his death. Note the "local color."

The Bennets (p. 393). See the Introduction for a discussion of dialogue (pp. xxviii, xxix). The few antiquated expressions in this selection are due to the fact that the novel from which these chapters are taken was written in 1796.

The King of Boyville (p. 400). In what ways are Unity and Coherence secured in this story? Compare the beginning of this story with that of *How I Caught Salmon in the Clackamas* (p. 374) and with that of *An Elk Hunt* (p. 378). What are the merits of each? Study the movement and the climax of the narrative, its concreteness, and its truth to life. Is the dialogue natural, and why?

A Winter Courtship (p. 410). The plot of this story is discussed in the Introduction (p. xxvi). Apply to the dialogue these tests: (1) Does it reveal character? (2) Does it explain the situation? (3) Does it help the story move? (4) Is it natural? After reading this story, practise writing dialect. Study the way in which Emphasis is given to the narrative. Is this a story of action or of character?

The Three Strangers (p. 421). Both the plot and the characters should be examined in more detail than was possible in the Introduction (pp. xxvi and xxviii). Discuss the proportion of this story. Why is the introduction so long, and what is its purpose? This story gives opportunity for the study of background, or setting, in its relation to the action. Note that in this case there are two backgrounds, — that of the rainy night outside the house, and that of the dancing-party within. What is the relation of each to the total effect? Point out examples of Description in the service of Narration. Study this story in the light of Poe's and of Stevenson's statements on p. xxvii of the Introduction.

CPSIA information can be obtained
at www.ICGtesting.com
Printed in the USA
BVOW06*1914120417
481111BV00006B/15/P